NEW DIRECTIONS IN ANTHROPOLOGY AND ENVIRONMENT

NEW DIRECTIONS IN ANTHROPOLOGY AND ENVIRONMENT

Intersections

Carole L. Crumley, Editor
with
A. Elizabeth van Deventer
and Joseph J. Fletcher

ALTAMIRA PRESS
A Division of
ROWMAN & LITTLEFIELD PUBLISHERS, INC.
Walnut Creek • Lanham • New York • Oxford

ALTAMIRA PRESS
A Division of Rowman & Littlefield Publishers, Inc.
1630 North Main Street, #367
Walnut Creek, CA 94596
www.altamirapress.com

Rowman & Littlefield Publishers, Inc.
4720 Boston Way
Lanham, Maryland 20706

12 Hid's Copse Road
Cumnor Hill, Oxford OX2 9JJ, England

British Library Cataloguing in Publication Information Available

Library of Congress Cataloging-in-Publication Data

New directions in anthropology and environment : intersections.
    p.   cm.
  Includes bibliographical references and index.
  ISBN 0-7425-0264-3 (cloth : alk. paper)—ISBN 0-7425-0265-1 (pbk. : alk. paper)
    1. Human ecology. 2. Anthropology. 3. Human ecology—Cross-cultural studies. I.
Crumley, Carole L.

GF50 .N48 2000
304.2—dc21

00-059406

Contents

Introduction

Carole L. Crumley

The Anthropology and Environment Section of the American Anthropological Association (AAA) came into being in 1996, at an interesting and crucial time. The largest El Niño in recent history, far away from its South Pacific origin, was pounding the California coast. Pfisteria, the aggressive "cell from hell" that releases a water-soluble neurotoxin, was killing fish and sickening people along the U.S. East Coast from Maryland to the Gulf of Mexico. In Austria, intensive lobbying of the government by seed companies succeeded in placing a ban on the sale of heirloom varieties; similar legislation was to be introduced in the European Parliament. Those who first became members of the new section saw in these and other events new roles for anthropology and anthropologists.

A&E members represent every area of anthropology: sociocultural, historical, and biological anthropology; archaeology; linguistics. Many have training in other areas such as the earth sciences, policy, journalism, medicine, or law. They work in educational institutions and museums; for the federal, state, or international government; with international organizations; and in the corporate sector. Most express a personal concern about environmental issues, and many are active in environmental causes.

We are all aware of the sharp upturn in environmental bad news. In fact, many of us have painful firsthand information about conditions where we live or where we do research. These personal experiences impart a sense of passion and urgency to our scholarship. Nonetheless, we realize that our theories, concepts, and methods must be flexible tools that we share, revise, or discard as we learn more.

The work can begin anywhere—at any time or place or with any subject—but will eventually embrace perennial issues of context, knowledge, and power.

Some of us study contemporary or historic conditions, teasing out dynamic relationships among key factors; others remind us to scrutinize our own personal and academic biases as we examine others' perceptions. What joins us together is a willingness to de-emphasize scholarly divisions and collaborate *as anthropologists* to share with other scholars and offer the public our understandings of the complex dialectic between human activity and the planet we all call home.

While factors unrelated to human activity have for centuries been known to effect environmental change, it is only in recent decades that the public, primarily through the work of anthropologists, has been made aware of the inverse: that both intentionally and unintentionally, our species has been modifying its surroundings for several million years. Our insistence that the human species is not invariably *Homo devastans* nor are all indigenous peoples Ecologically Noble (Balee 1998: 16) is equally important. Although we have been less successful in erasing these misconceptions, we have gone far in unraveling how and why certain individuals and organizations cling to these dark or idealized images of our species.

Anthropology is poised to transcend such reductionism and frame practical and ethical guidelines for our species' future on the planet. As enduring architects of a bridge between the sciences and the humanities, anthropologists integrate diverse forms of knowledge about the world. However, inasmuch as scholarly activity is itself cultural, we must also critically examine how such knowledge is obtained. The A&E Section, by adopting an inclusive definition of the term *environment,* encourages exploration of the complex relations among physical/biotic, built, and cognitive environments.

Anthropology's persistent claim that *both* the physical *and* the mental world matter, however difficult at times that assertion has been to maintain, confers on anthropologists a certain authority: we understand the critical importance of *holism,* the assumption that the physical world and human societies are always inextricably linked. By the end of the twentieth century the industrial world had begun to awaken from a lovely dream in which technology, ingenuity, and sheer force of will could overcome the forces of nature. That was not the dream of the world's traditional peoples; ecologically, theirs has too often been a nightmare from which they could not wake, in which the economic, social, and spiritual fabric of their lives is permanently altered by the lovely dreamers.

The A&E Section seeks to coordinate a discipline-wide collaborative effort that would renew anthropology's commitment to holism, to reach beyond our own field to incorporate scholarly research and practitioners from other disciplines; join forces with indigenous peoples to explain the utility of traditional environmental knowledge; search history for successful and unsuccessful lessons in environmental management; and make our findings understandable to local, regional, and global policy makers and to the communities their decisions affect.

As professionals who are broadly knowledgeable about complicated inter-relations among humans, and between humans and their environment(s), it is appropriate that we help frame ethical guidelines, facilitate interaction, and offer examples for the conduct of research on problems that require for their solution a combination of scientific information, cultural knowledge, and egalitarian principles. Anthropologists have the knowledge to increase schol-arly, public, and governmental understanding of the complex and fragile rela-tion between our species and its biotic and built environments. The diversity of practice and the wealth of expertise within anthropology are both advanta-geous and necessary if complex environmental issues on every scale are to be addressed, their historical interconnectivity demonstrated, and equitable fu-ture courses charted. Anthropologists must enter current debates over envi-ronmental issues by as many avenues as possible, on our own behalf as well as that of those whose lives and circumstances we study.

At the 1996 AAA Annual Meeting our inaugural session, entitled "Human Dimensions of Environmental Change: Anthropology Engages the Issues," filled the room and spilled into the corridor. In the session, which was dis-cussed by Laura Nader and David Maybury-Lewis, papers by Tsing, Kempton, Fowler and Hardesty, Dove, Leatherman and Thomas, Johnston, Brosius, In-gerson, and McCay were given. This book has chapters by those authors, who are joined by Maffi, Sponsel, Winthrop, and Poncelet.

The book is intended as a reader for university courses that take as their subject contemporary environmental issues. It is divided for convenience into three parts. *Defining Environment and Interpreting Nature* offers brief histori-cal sketches of how several fields of anthropology have approached the study of the environment, then explores new questions, issues, and approaches. *Be-liefs, Values, and Environmental Justice* examines ethical and spiritual dimen-sions of the environment. *Application and Engagement* offers four examples of policy arenas in which anthropologists have become involved. Each chapter is followed by suggestions for further reading.

For classroom use, the chapters may be read in the order of the book or grouped to focus on particular issues. For example, the intersection of envi-ronmental history, historical ecology, political ecology, and political econ-omy could be explored by asking students to respond to issues raised in pa-pers by Tsing, Fowler and Hardesty, Leatherman and Thomas, Winthrop, and Ingerson. Dove, Tsing, Maffi, and Brosius treat issues on several scales and transcend disciplinary and spatial boundaries; more explicitly, McCay, Ingerson, and Poncelet could be grouped to explore issues of spatial scale as they relate to management. Students could be asked to contrast each of the book's contributors in their approach to the development of environmental knowledge. Sponsel, Kempton, Winthrop, and Maffi could be read together to explore the link between spirituality and landscapes. The unabashedly ac-tivist stance of Johnston on environmental justice could be paired for con-trast with Poncelet's more cautious examination of partnerships, or Tsing,

Brosius, and Poncelet could be contrasted in regard to their treatment of environmental alliances. In very different ways, all the contributors raise important questions about the professional, political, and sentimental involvement of anthropologists.

To explore the coevolution of humans and the environment, this volume might be paired with a treatment of the effects of environmental change on humans from the perspective of the earth sciences (Gunn 1994) or with a volume documenting the long history of human–environment interaction (Crumley 1994; Redman 1999). Several papers in this volume could be paired with books that focus on the role of history and deepen ethnographic practice, such as Lansing's treatment of Balinese temple-based water management (1991), Balee's (1998) edited volume, or Nazarea's exploration of cultural memory and biodiversity (1998).

The intersection of issues raised in this volume mirrors the synergy of the A&E Section's inaugural session, the environment of civility and potential for collaboration of which was widely felt to have been long overdue. This has been borne out through fascinating threads posted to our listserv (to subscribe, write to LISTSERV@LISTSERV.UGA.EDU and in the text of your message write SUBSCRIBE EANTH-L).

The A&E Section's cooperative endeavor owes a great deal to several individuals who led by example. Jonathan Haas and Jane Buikstra were instrumental in convening the Anthropology and Environment Task Force in 1991, which, through Emilio Moran's quiet persistence, became a AAA Section in 1996 (Moran was also A&E's first president).

The task force undertook a number of activities. Among them were assessing the level of support and interest in starting a section within the AAA, building up a database of environmental anthropologists, and providing support for efforts to create a National Institute for the Environment. This latter effort has recently resulted in a major increase in funding to the National Science Foundation for support of the environmental programmatic goals of the Committee for the National Institute for the Environment (now the National Council for Science and the Environment). A measure of the groundswell of support for the A&E is that it surpassed within months the required number of members to be a section.

Two task force colleagues, whom we have now lost, supplied consistent encouragement and firm conviction that such an endeavor could succeed in a divisive intellectual climate. Roy A. (Skip) Rappaport demonstrated theoretical flexibility, political savvy, and unflagging collegiality; Robert McCormick (Bob) Netting's gentle spirit and penetrating intellect were a welcome antidote to sometimes acrimonious debate in the discipline. It is to their memory this book is dedicated.

Carole L. Crumley
A&E President (1997–99)
Chapel Hill, N.C.
April 2000

References

Balée, William, ed. 1998. *Advances in Historical Ecology.* New York: Columbia University Press.

Crumley, Carole L., ed. 1994. *Historical Ecology: Cultural Knowledge and Changing Landscapes.* Santa Fe, N. Mex.: School of American Research Press.

Gunn, Joel, ed. 1994. *Global Climate–Human Life: Physical Contexts of Historic Landscapes. Human Ecology,* Special issue 22(1).

Lansing, J. Stephen. 1991. *Priests and Programmers: Technologies of Power in the Engineered Landscape of Bali.* Princeton: Princeton University Press.

Nazarea, Virginia D. 1998. *Cultural Memory and Biodiversity.* Tucson: University of Arizona Press.

Netting, Robert McCormick. 1981. *Balancing on an Alp: Ecological Change and Continuity in a Swiss Mountain Community.* Cambridge: Cambridge University Press.

———. 1993. *Smallholders, Householders: Farm Families and the Ecology of Intensive, Sustainable Agriculture.* Stanford, Calif.: Stanford University Press.

Rappaport, Roy A. 1999. *Ritual and Religion in the Making of Humanity.* Cambridge: Cambridge University Press.

———. 2000. *Pigs for the Ancestors: Ritual in the Ecology of a New Guinea People* (second edition; first published in 1968). Prospect Heights, Ill.: Waveland Press.

Redman, Charles L. 1999. *Human Impact on Ancient Environments.* Tucson: University of Arizona Press.

1

Defining Environment
and Interpreting Nature

1

Nature in the Making

Anna Lowenhaupt Tsing

The first principle of the UN's Rio Declaration on Environment and Development of 1992, recognizing, as it says, "the integral and interdependent nature of the Earth, our home," proclaims: "Human beings are at the center of concerns for sustainable development. They are entitled to a healthy and productive life in harmony with nature" (Johnson 1993: 118). Behind this cool sentence, one can feel the heat of intense negotiations. Who will be at the center, humans or nature? Environmentalism, it appears, has triumphed in the forum of nations, but no conservation biologist or ecosystems modeler can easily dismantle the great machinery of development, and "sustainable development" is the form of environmentalism that will be offered on the negotiating table. On that environmentalist table squabbling too are social justice struggles, human rights and indigenous rights campaigns, declarations of eco-imperialism and North–South inequality—as well as dreams of harmony, human and natural. Isn't there a human entitlement? Is there room for harmony as well as productiveness? One can hear the hot, discrepant voices wrestling through the calm proclamation. Indeed, one might argue that this kind of cool statement, with its hot underbelly, is the way most discussion of the environment works at this turn of the century. On the one hand, environmentalist rhetoric is widely used and accepted. On the other, no one agrees about what this rhetoric should do for humans and nature, and the struggle is on to bend environmental rhetoric to particular, contradictory purposes—Wise Use or preservation; privatization, national heritage, or tribal autonomy; international restructuring or democratic internationalism; and much more.

This is not just a matter of confusing but inconsequential rhetoric. Natural and social landscapes are made and remade in relation to varied environmental projects. I use the term *projects* to mean organized packages of ideas and practices that assume an at least tentative stability through their social enactment, whether as custom, convention, trend, clubbish or professional training, institutional mandate, or government policy. A project is an institutionalized discourse with social and material effects. Each environmental project propels us into a transformed natural and social world through the way it combines environmentally significant ideas, policies, and practices. Debates about the meaning and purposes of sustainable development are significant because they could shift the project's definition and organization as well as the way it reshapes local places. For scholars, then, excitement turns from the task of establishing the importance of the environment in human affairs to the question of how the environment is constituted in these landscape-making projects. What counts as "the environment" in any given political negotiation, corporate strategy, research initiative, livelihood trajectory, or policy program? How are new "environments" created within these projects? At the juncture of environmental history, science studies, political ecology, and cultural anthropology, new interdisciplinary scholarship is emerging to address these questions. Environmental history is the most developed of these fields, carrying as it does the torch of a critical environmental studies, reflexive about both scientific and social changes. Science studies introduces the provocative spark of a new attentiveness to theory and methods, new eyes to consider the status of facts and things. Political ecology offers the sober excitement of policy-oriented politics, radical critique honed to influence both technical policy and public opinion.

Drawing from these fields as well as from contemporary disciplinary concerns, cultural anthropologists of the environment are perhaps most committed to newness, since many practitioners imagine the field beginning anew on the other side of a fifteen-year gap across which lies an earlier "ecological anthropology." Simplifications of the past can provide inspiration for consolidating recent insights; in this spirit, it has been said that earlier ecological anthropologists, excited by the tools of cybernetics and ecosystems theory, were interested in systems without enough attention to histories, meanings, social movements, or the formation of knowledge. A closer look reveals that the continuities between old and new are as visible as the discontinuities, and most every "new" move has its historical precedent.[1] Yet there is some usefulness in imagining newness, to draw into focus the distinctive features of a contemporary cluster of scholarship. One might say that the new scholarship arising at the juncture of these fields reformulates the classic question of environmental studies, that is, how is society shaped by the environment, to ask how nature becomes an actor in social history. How are environmental objects and projects formed in such a way that they come to enable or threaten human livelihoods and lives?

In the next section of this chapter, I show how environmental history, science studies, political ecology, and cultural anthropology contribute to an emergent interdisciplinary environmental scholarship that pays close attention to "nature in the making." My goal is not to construct full reviews of these fields; instead, I examine the dialogue among them as it has raised new questions and offered new insights for environmental scholarship. Following this I offer three examples of scholarly initiatives that have developed within the intersection and overlap of these fields, as these illustrate the power and the promise of this emergent approach. First, I consider recent research on the production of scale: the making of the local, the regional, and the global. Second, I discuss investigations of the global transformations of environmental projects: How are environmental categories and practices reshaped as they are reproduced in new times and places? Third, I attend to research on the collaborative process necessary for making environmental projects happen. This research highlights both common agendas and divergences in the collaborations (such as those between foresters and villagers; activists, voters, and bureaucrats; or plants and people) that are necessary to making and maintaining social–natural environments, whether "forests," "cities," "factories," or "farms."

Four Currents and Their Confluence

Environmental historians first raised the question of nature's agency. Rivers, trees, and soils, they argued, are actors in our histories. Good historical scholarship requires attention to the doings of landscapes as well as of people. Of course, there are many other ways of framing questions in environmental history, including some that sound more familiar to anthropologists. For example: How does human action shape nature, and how does nature shape human action? Yet even these phrasings gain a particular spin when placed beside questions of the agency of nature, as scholars begin their answers with the insight that not just nature but also the form in which nature acts in relation to humans shifts historically. (Worster et al. [1990] introduces a number of key players in environmental history in a stimulating interchange on the definition and goals of the field.)

The nature of nature's agency shifts depending on the historically specific form of human and nonhuman interaction that makes up what I am calling an environmental project. Environmental historians have brought up the question of nature's agency in relation to transformations in the making of nature in different times and places over the past five hundred years (Cronon 1993). An exciting literature is growing, tracing the importance of empire building, colonial administration, capital accumulation, and nation making in creating environments that then become stubborn or willing agents in human schemes and dreams.[2] A classic example is the history of irrigation projects that channel both the flow and distribution of water—that is, the way that water is a historical agent.

Donald Worster's (1985) study of the making of public irrigation works in the U.S. West presents a number of the key themes of this literature: the importance of goals of state expansion in designing massive, landscape-changing environmental projects; the collusions among engineers, administrators, and big capital; the fortuitous social–natural catastrophes that both stimulated and revised state-sponsored landscape simplifications. Worster's study also illustrates the importance of regional consolidations and interregional connections in making new regional units of "nature." U.S. Western irrigation design drew from regional precedence (e.g., Mormon aesthetics; California gold rush law) at the same time as it borrowed from the irrigation plans and dreams of British colonial India.

Questions of regional precedence and interregional transfer are even more central in the environmental history of colonial rule. For example, historians have examined how the U.S. government's Dust Bowl policies influenced conservation in southern Africa (e.g., Beinart 1984; Showers 1989). In some areas, such as Lesotho, soil conservation projects in the 1930s and 1940s ironically caused more erosion than they prevented, in part because project managers ignored regional livelihood practices. Soil erosion, in turn, shifted the possibilities for regional livelihoods. The question of nature's agency proves particularly important here to attend to unexpected reversals and contingencies in the effects of environmental policy and landscape planning.

Environmental history brings historical nature into view; science studies draws our attention to the micropolitics of knowing and experiencing nature (Haraway 1989; Latour 1987). How do the environmental sciences discover and agree upon their objects of knowledge? Science studies points us toward the political and cultural context in which science is developed and institutionalized, as well as the political and cultural effects of scientific projects. It offers models through which we can see how facts and knowledge-making frameworks are stabilized by developing experimental protocols and research situations in which a particular kind of "nature" becomes clearly imaginable and then convincing other people of the importance and use of this kind of nature (Latour and Wolgar 1986). The agency of nature in affecting human affairs develops in tandem with human abilities to know it and manage it in particular ways.

An example of environmental science studies is Peter Taylor's (1988) research on the history of ecosystems theory, which investigates the biographical, institutional, and natural–social context in which particular models of ecosystem complexity became convincing frameworks for the analysis of the environment after World War II. Scientific frameworks move scientists as well as broader audiences in conjunction with the poetic and political imaginations they bring to bear on nature; these are features of their explanatory power (Taylor and Blum 1991). Post–World War II ecosystems modeling, Taylor argues, was convincing in part through its deployment of the technical arsenal of information sciences developed during the war combined with an aesthetics of "technocratic optimism." Furthermore, ecosystems modeling could bring political concerns for stability and management into policy-oriented understandings of landscape, as Taylor argues in his investigation of a U.S. Agency for International Development–sponsored and MIT-implemented ecosystems modeling project concerning pastoralism in the West African Sahel (Taylor 1992).

In Taylor's West African ecosystem modeling example, U.S. development objectives in Africa set many of the parameters for research; scientific projects are often tied to national and imperial aspirations. Environmental history and science studies intersect in tracing the global–local placement of environmental science; the literatures on the history of economic botany, botanic gardens, and colonial forestry are particularly rich.[3] This work too suggests the potential of science studies to illuminate the conjunction of philosophical and political stakes in environmental knowledge making.

Where science studies tends to be experimental and self-consciously provocative, political ecology offers a politically charged vision for environmental studies that is tuned to the possibilities of policy-oriented intervention. Science studies questions the categories of practitioners; political ecology uses those categories, but with an attempt to offer them a radical edge. In this spirit, political ecology shows the centrality of capital and the state in the making of landscapes and environments. (A useful review is offered by Peet and Watts [1996a].) In class-divided societies, our experience of nature is always mediated through conventions of property, which regulate our access to resources and differentiate the natural world in relation to this access, so that we know that this is the forest we exploit, or which we treasure, or from which we surreptitiously steal.[4] Land managers operate within the contraints of the political economies for which they produce; they enrich or degrade the land in relation to these constraints. International capitalism and local poverty are thus, for example, the context in which we can understand degraded or eroded soils (Blaikie 1985).

Because geographers have been important contributors to political ecology, the field has been sensitive to the connections between spatial relations and power relations (e.g., Harvey 1996). Political ecologists have been particularly alert to the effects of global inequalities on local landscapes and communities. Critical theory, cultural geography, Marxist class analysis, and world systems perspectives are used to forge critical perspectives on the ideologically charged frameworks of conservation biology's alliances with neoclassical economics. The field has developed particularly through criticisms of population-based models of environmental degradation and park-based models of conservation; this work contributes to policy as well as scholarship (e.g., Blaikie and Brookfield 1987; Hecht and Cockburn 1990; Neumann 1998; Peet and Watts 1996b; Rocheleau, Thomas-Slayter, and Wangari 1996).

Political ecologists have been active in researching the social consequences of the intervention of states and international development agencies into colonial and neocolonial Southern environments.[5] In this work, political ecologists have shown the importance of careful attention to ordinary villagers

and farmers, as these too are divided by class, gender, ethnicity, and other distinctions. Richard Schroeder's (1993) research on the Gambia, for example,
records the gender-differentiated effects of agroforestry development
schemes, which have allowed men to take over women's garden land by planting trees in the midst of women's crops. Nancy Peluso's (1992) study of the
history of Javanese teak forests describes the expansion of state authority in
the forests and the emergence of peasant resistance to state forestry planting
and harvesting policies. Haripriya Rangan investigates the loss of economic
opportunities for villagers in the Garwhal Himalayas following new anti-
logging laws that, ironically, responded to the popular Chipko "tree hugging"
movement in this region. She argues that the villagers have always been fighting for their rights to development, not forest protection (1993; 1996). These
kinds of studies investigate ambitious projects of nature making from the perspective of local human resource users.

Cultural anthropologists have contributed to this ethnographic effort,
which brings the lives of ordinary people into debates about nature. Cultural
anthropologists also extend this ethnographic perspective to study the lifeways and local knowledge of the managers and designers of environmental
projects. Cultural anthropology has a long history of studying the ways rural
people know, adapt to, and transform their environments, and this research
continues to grow richer; meanwhile, new scholarship also brings this history
of knowledge to bear on the challenge of national and international environmental projects for conservation and development (e.g., Croll and Parkin
1992). How, for example, do conservationists in the process of developing
nature reserves and the rural residents who live and work on those would-be
reserves view each other? What are the perspectives on nature of development agencies or plantation managers? How do various kinds of resource
users—for example, small boat fishermen, raft fishermen, and large-haul
fishermen—view the same resource—in this case, fish—and how do they negotiate and fight about its appropriate management and harvesting? Topics
such as these have enlivened recent anthropological discussion; while the
questions above refer specifically to research in Indonesia (e.g., Dove 1993; Li
1996; Lowe 1999; Tsing 1999; Zerner 2000), this kind of research has begun to
thrive in many locales.

In this spirit, too, cultural anthropologists have begun ethnographic study
of environmental bureaucracies, nongovernmental organizations, and scientific research initiatives.[6] Peter Brosius's research on the 1980s and 1990s environmental campaigns to defend both the Penan and their rain forest home-
place in Sarawak, Malaysia, complements his earlier Penan ethnography
(1997); the result is an ethnographic dialogue encompassing local and foreign
activists, scholars, and residents. Pauline Peters's (1994) historical exploration
of state policy making concerning common pasturage in Botswana similarly
shows the dynamic interplay of varied kinds of players and perspectives; this
interplay shapes the shifting politics and patterns of grassland, water, cattle,

and humans in the region. K. Sivaramakrishnan's (1996) research on forestry in Bengal shows the importance of careful attention to the practices of foresters; he illuminates the socially complex and historically shifting nature of the forestry bureaucracy by situating it in its regional milieu of negotiation and management. Ethnographers have also begun to describe environmental mobilizations and events (e.g., Berglund 1998; Milton 1993). These ethnographic inquiries bring cultural analysis to our understandings of environmental politics and add the richness and depth of face-to-face human interactions to our knowledge of nature in the making.

Each of these subfields adds to our ability to analyze the making of emergent environments; at the confluence where they come together to consider these questions, each is also transformed. Thus, in the process of dealing with dramatic changes in environmental orthodoxy, environmental historians have taken on cultural theory. Historians have increasingly attended to the categories and forms of knowledge through which we know and interact with nature. William Cronon's edited collection *Uncommon Ground: Toward Reinventing Nature* (1995) offers one example of an interdisciplinary interaction that addresses these new demands on environmental history. Cronon, an eminent environmental historian, chose the participants for a residential seminar to consider "nature" from a broad humanistic perspective; he included scholars in literature, philosophy, science studies, geography, architecture, history, and ecology in the group. Cronon (1992) has also contributed to an interdisciplinary wave of interest in the importance of narrative in environmental history.

In acknowledging the power of changing environmental policy, political ecologists have also embraced concerns with the formation of politically significant categories. Two recent anthologies, *Creating the Countryside* (DuPuis and Vandergeest 1996) and *Liberation Ecologies* (Peet and Watts 1996b), are examples of the new breadth of political ecology, in which poststructuralist approaches join those associated with resistance theory and political economy. Attention to cultural categories for knowing nature is brought into dialogue, in these volumes, with the study of local-to-global political and economic hierarchies, institutions, and practices. An influential special issue of the journal *World Development* on development narratives in Africa is also exemplary in this regard (Roe 1995). The authors analyze how development narratives shape landscape change even as they so often misread the landscape.[7]

Science studies in the environmental field, interacting with both environmental history and political ecology, has also developed some distinctive tendencies. In making sense of both systems and evolutionary models in the environmental sciences, science studies scholars have strayed from defining material objects and techniques, as in biological and technological science studies, to investigate environmental projects, that is, conjunctions of environmental theory and practice. This turns scholars from epistemological questions of the nature of reality toward substantive disagreements about what will count as relevant social and ecological frames and categories.

Thus, for example, one of the major "science wars" debates occurring in the environmental field concerns the question of to what extent indigenous and tribal people have historically helped to develop and maintain the forested landscapes that have become a global conservationist priority. On the one hand, conservation biologists argue that the object of both scientific concern and political advocacy should be "wildlands"; on the other, social ecologists argue that many of the forests labeled by conservation biologists as wild are products of human management. (See, e.g., Soule 1995; Hecht and Cockburn 1990; Denevan 1992.) Scholars support each side of the debate by discussing the formation of knowledge about these issues; both sides are invested in the political and practical significance of this question for conservation strategy. Furthermore, new research contrasts the knowledge-making practices of conservationists, social activists, and local resource users as these issues are played out in varied local arenas (e.g., Willems-Braun 1997; Lowe 1999).

Cultural anthropology of the environment has also grown in dialogue with these developments. Borrowing the interests and approaches of historians, science studies theorists, and political ecologists, cultural anthropologists have added their own disciplinary perspectives, such as attention to "culture" in all its varied meanings, to the mix (e.g., Milton 1996). Cultural anthropologists have also brought a concern about fieldwork methodology, particularly the challenges of fieldwork in globally interconnected yet minutely localized worlds of meaning and practice (Marcus 1995). In planning studies of environmental projects that stretch across multiple and diverse communities, cultural anthropologists have refigured ethnography in eclectic combinations with less locally specific practices for recording and interpreting texts, institutions, political relations, and natural–social landscapes. In particular, anthropologists of the environment have moved beyond community studies in both space and time by combining ethnography with various forms of "regional" historical analysis (e.g., Fairhead and Leach 1996; Sivaramakrishnan 1996; Schmink and Wood 1992).

Within these intertwined transformations, too, new kinds of shared concerns have emerged. The next section of this chapter reviews research initiatives that have developed to analyze three of these concerns: the importance of spatial scale in the political culture of environmentalism; the mobility and changing significance of environmental projects applied and reapplied in multiple locales; and the importance of collaboration in forging environmental objects and political positions. My introduction to these initiatives uses examples from South and Southeast Asia, both to give regional specificity to the work I describe and to show how exemplary studies are emerging from scholarship in this area. In both South and Southeast Asia, strong interdisciplinary literatures have grown up on colonial and postcolonial resource administration, on the one hand, and on local-to-transnational environmental movements, on the other, and these literatures have shaped the work I describe. However, I am not trying to review environmental studies in South and Southeast Asia; I am only mentioning a few essays relevant to the themes I have chosen.[8] The themes are intended as illustrations of the productiveness of new research on the changing cultural, political, and ecological shapes of environmental project making.[9]

Scale

My first example highlights research on how spatial scales are variously used to frame environmental knowledge and mobilize particular social practices. In contrast to earlier kinds of anthropology (environmental and otherwise) that reified social-spatial units from villages to habitats to social formations to establish the distinctiveness of particular cultural or ecological systems, this research makes spatial scale the object of analysis.

What, for example, does it mean to describe environmental problems as "global"? The idea of global environmental change—and particularly global climate change—has created a powerful scientific imagery and an effective political tool for environmentalism (Taylor and Buttel 1992). Naturally, something this powerful and provocative cannot go down without a fight, and the world of environmental politics is full of contests over just how the idea of the global will be determined and used in setting environmental law and policy. The disagreement between the Washington-based World Resources Institute's 1990 interpretation of global greenhouse gas emissions and the reinterpretation of the New Delhi-based Centre for Science and the Environment is a classic example of the difference perspective can make in framing "global environmentalism"; are all countries equally responsible for global warming or are there major differences in the responsibilities of the North and the South? (See Agarwal and Narain 1991; Tsing 1997; Dove 1994.) A large variety of new writing in environmental studies addresses the question of global environmental change; some of this literature tries to make globality more self-evident, while other scholarship questions its premises. The collection of articles edited by Wolfgang Sachs (1993) is particularly critical of the political uses of the "global."

One of the most exciting scholarly contributions to the debates on global environmentalism is research on the historical construction of globality. The work of historian Richard Grove (1995) on the networks that brought environmental science and politics to life from the seventeenth century to the present is exemplary here. In one insightful essay (forthcoming), for example, he argues for the origins of the notion of global climate change in correspondence between scientists of the British East India Company and their counterparts both in Great Britain and in British outposts in the Caribbean and Australia. He suggests that a series of locally experienced droughts in 1791 were connected by this scientific correspondence to produce a global framework for understanding climate that has blossomed today in institutionalized knowledge production.

Yet it is not just the global that must be produced as a framework for environmental understanding; the local is also a creative cultural product. The features and boundaries of the local are continually reformulated in relation to particular landscape-and-community–making negotiations. "Who's Local Here?" asks the Fall 1996 issue of *Cultural Survival Quarterly*, introducing discussion of the politics of participation in development. Recent scholarship has foregrounded the imposition of notions of "community" both on flora and fauna and on people as this has been encouraged by certain traditions of scholarship, on the one hand, and by development bureaucracies, on the other (e.g., Barbour 1995; Li 1996). But residents also participate in shaping "communities" during negotiations of environmental knowledge and policy. Anthropologist Susan Darlington (forthcoming) describes how Buddhist monks in Thailand have reimagined themselves as "ecology monks" to revitalize community rituals in defense of village forests. The village she studied is less than sixty years old and composed of motley immigrants, yet, working with a resident ecology monk, the villagers have formulated an indigenous village spirituality to ordain and protect a community-controlled forest.

Community construction classifies vegetation and landscape as well as people. Anthropologist Ann Gold (forthcoming) found that mesquite trees in the village she studied in India are explicitly labeled "foreign." Differentiated from native acacias to which they appear rather similar, their foreignness stimulates discussion of the divide between indigeneity and outside influence in villagers' tellings of the history of landscape change. The landscape, as villagers describe it, contains and organizes divisions between local and foreign—not by territory, but within the distribution of trees. A localizing "moral ecology" is made and remade in each interaction between village people, plants, and land.

Between the local and the global, a wide range of regional scales is called into play to explain and change our imaginings of the environment and to draw us into new practices; new research traces their viability and productiveness. For example, science historian Warwick Anderson (forthcoming) has shown how the notion of the tropics formed in the late nineteenth and early twentieth centuries through overlapping discussions of medicine, race, and environment.[10] His research focuses on the U.S.-ruled Philippines, where nineteenth-century "tropical" environmental determinisms were superceded in the twentieth century by regimes of scientific improvement, within the now naturalized parameters of "tropical" hygiene.

Once codified, the notion of the tropics has been extraordinarily productive in nurturing new understandings of both biological and cultural diversity. Where would our evolutionary perspectives be, one might ask, without the tropics? How would we create the emotive richness of the appeal of biodiversity?[11]

Movements

Another recent research trajectory: Here I highlight work on the travels and transformations of environmental projects. In contrast to earlier scholarship that assumed a neat divide between indigenous or Third World environmental knowledges and practices, on the one hand, and the Western history of development and conservation, on the other, this research explores the troubled space that connects and overlays the two. As powerfully institutionalized environmental projects are shipped from metropoles to peripheries, a tension arises between empire-building or universalistic pretensions and the translations, adaptations, or localizations that make the project succeed or fail in a particular place. The research I am describing investigates this tension—and thus the cultural and historical specificities of conservation and development.

An exemplar case is the scholarly conversation on the use and abuse of scientific forestry in India. The British colonial administration introduced German scientific forestry into India in the nineteenth century. This was a science of simplification and counting, geared to the production of timber, not to minor forest products, subsistence forest use, or the maintenance of biological diversity (Rajan 1994; Scott 1998, ch. 1). What happened to scientific forestry when it hit the Indian landscape? Scholars disagree. Sociologist Ramachandra Guha (1989) argues that by taking as its focus problems of order and exploitation, scientific forestry in India became the ultimate colonial science. Peasant resistance to forestry plans formed a significant challenge to this colonial discourse and forced it to change to take into account peasant infractions. For example, foresters finally incorporated grazing and burning into their forestry plans because peasants insisted on these practices for their livestock; unable to stop them, the foresters eventually opted for controlled versions. Forestry thus established itself as an administrative regime, molded by the conditions of colonial power and peasant struggle.

Historian Ravi Rajan (1994) disagrees, arguing that scientific forestry was continually reregularized in British empirewide meetings of foresters that homogenized the practices of metropole and periphery. Forestry techniques were taught and transferred in these empirewide discussions; thus, while forestry is indeed imperial and modernizing, there is nothing specifically "colonial" about Indian forestry. Local particularities in forestry practice were built into this centralized scientific plan, not forced upon it by Indian peasants.

Anthropologist K. Sivaramakrishnan (forthcoming) offers a third perspective in showing how forestry projects in India were transformed by the activities of foresters and the working knowledge of the landscape they developed in part through their involvement in wider issues of land administration. Sivaramakrishnan shows how the continual production of forest working plans for the regeneration of *sal* trees in Bengal challenged the uniformist designs of the central forestry administration; regionally based foresters knew, for example, that the trees would not regenerate without an uneven-aged forest canopy.

Taken together, these arguments weave a rich interdisciplinary discussion that alerts us to multiple elements of translation and localization. The conversation demonstrates the importance of the scholarly interaction of the subfields I reviewed above: environmental history, political ecology, science studies, and cultural anthropology. These authors variously highlight the importance of legacies of scientific knowledge, of administrative regimes and peasant resistance, of the awkward and shifting relations between the desired material objects—forests, trees—and the plans to produce and control them, and of the varied cultural and aesthetic standards, as well as forms of familiarity, of differently located participants in forestry development. Within the interplay of these factors, we can begin to theorize the shape and effects of the movement of environmental projects.

The benefits of this kind of focus on a single environmental project-on-the-move are enormous. Perhaps the comparable case from Southeast Asia would be scholarship debating the effects of high-input Green Revolution rice technology. Unlike the Indian forestry research, which pays considerable attention to the effects of forestry on forests, the most interesting parts of the debate on the Green Revolution in Southeast Asia has not been about plant reproduction, care, and diversity (although there is an enormous technical literature on these issues), but about the social categories sedimented by changes in the division of labor and the redefinitions of family, class, and community associated with the new rice technologies.[12]

In mapping the relationship between environmental technologies and rural social inequalities, it is particularly exciting when three prominent social scientists all work in the same district of Malaysia on the social effects of the Green Revolution, with different results. I am thinking of James Scott, Diana Wong, and Gillian Hart, all of whom worked in Malaysia's Muda District during the 1970s and 1980s. Scott's pathbreaking study (1985) found peasant resistance to the importation of new schemes of exploitation, associated with Green Revolution technologies; he focuses on the everyday "weapons of the weak" through which some peasants refuse the legitimacy of the new profit-regimes. In dialogue with Scott's study, Wong (1987) argues instead that Muda farmers only became "peasants" at this moment of capital intensification. Before the Green Revolution economy, dense networks linked households in flexible associations; when these networks were broken, male-headed households became segregated units, and only then were they motivated to engage in the forms of resistance and complaint that Scott describes as peasant heritage. Their particular class identity is made in this reorganization of family and gender. Hart (1991) continues the discussion about the making of gender and class positions. She, too, finds new inequalities between women and men, but particularly in relation to their separate positioning in the division of labor and in local politics. Male farmers are easily co-opted into the grumbling and "backstage" complaints upon which Scott focuses; women, not admitted into networks of local patronage and religious–ethnic solidarity, meanwhile stage more formal collective protests and boycotts to respond to the loss of their work as rice transplanters.

These focused conversations spread the range of tools and frameworks that scholars think to bring to our analyses. Each author attends to the local effects of a traveling environmental project by drawing attention to the class, gender, and region-making effects of new ways of organizing the natural–social landscape. Taken together, they remind us that localizations of environmental projects always have an uneven effect on resident populations, such that women and men, old and young, rich and poor—like tree species distributions—are remade in environmental transformations.

Collaborations

My third example is of a new research trajectory: the social contests and collaborations that are involved in the production of environmental objects, projects, and political positions. J. Peter Brosius's chapter in this volume on the anthropology of environmental movements reviews the literature on contest and debate in environmental politics; this chapter will not cover the same ground. The related area I will discuss is research that explores differences among *allies* rather than between opponents.

Anthropologists are used to a discussion of the divergent perspectives of groups who, endowed with long-standing and well-formulated differences in identity and interest, battle each other over political issues: villagers versus the state; frontiersmen versus natives; activists versus corporations. The new research I am interested in looks instead at how alliances rather than enmities are formed among dissimilar groups: indigenous people and urban environmentalists, Southern nationalists and Northern research foundations, fishermen and marine mammals. The environmental movement has emerged from such unaccountable and undependable alliances. So, too, in different ways, have environmental sciences and policy programs, whether for development or for conservation. Research investigating collaboration tackles both dissimilarity and congruence in the forming of environmental projects; often the object of research is a series of subtle but constitutive misunderstandings that the participants themselves are willing to overlook, or even deny, as they jointly bring the project forward.[13]

Amita Baviskar's research (forthcoming; 1995) on environmental movements involving tribal people in India is a wonderful example here. In her study of the movement that emerged to stop the Narmada Dam, and the trade union and forest protection movement that emerged from it, she found important divisions between tribal leaders and the urban environmentalists who moved to the area to support them. Their ability to work

together was essential for the movement's success, yet working together
meant coming up with common goals that would not remind them of the
deep divisions in how each group understood issues of sustainable development and tribal identity. This kind of association is always tentative and
unstable; Baviskar found that in the late 1990s, the association between the
urban activists and the tribal leaders was unraveling as the latter moved toward tribal identity politics. Contemporary tensions do not just reveal underlying differences; they also highlight the strange and fragile effectiveness
of the earlier collaboration.

Mindful of this set of concerns, Yaakov Garb (1997) and Noel Sturgeon
(1997) began a dialogue on the international uses and interpretations of the
globally influential Chipko "tree hugging" movement for forest conservation
in the Garwhal Himalayas of north India. The Chipko story has attracted great
attention internationally, inspiring environmentalist activists and scholars, yet
the uses of the Chipko story differ wildly. For Vandana Shiva (1989), Chipko
is an indigenous women's movement; this Chipko inspires ecofeminism. For
Ramachandra Guha (1989), Chipko is a peasant movement, building on centuries of anticolonial resistance; this Chipko inspires social ecology. For Anil
Agarwal (1975), Chipko is an expression of Ghandian concerns. For Haripriya
Rangan (1996), Chipko is a prodevelopment movement. If one begins to
count international appropriations, Chipkos proliferate even more freely.
Garb and Sturgeon each discuss this proliferation, arguing for the importance
of transformative "translations" as interpretations of Chipko move from context to context. Rather than searching for the "real face" of Chipko, their discussion turns us to the way that the movement's many representations engage
each other, allowing local activists and international advocates of rather different types to imagine a common object, at least for a moment. These kinds
of perhaps inappropriate and certainly misunderstanding-based collaborations are an essential feature of any social movement, whether in a village mo-
bilization or a transnational campaign.[14]

Another way of approaching issues of collaboration begins not with movement mobilizing but instead with practices that create bridges of alliance.
Nancy Peluso's (1995) research on "counter-mapping" in Kalimantan is one
excellent example. Peluso studies the use of mapping among scholarly insti-
tutes and nongovernmental organizations working with villagers to advocate
village control of forested territory. Maps become what science studies scholars have called a "boundary object," that is, an object that draws together varied interpretive communities by their common abilities to read this thing, if
in their own ways (Star and Griesemer 1989). Villagers bring long-standing
conventions for thinking about socially defined spaces to these official-
looking maps; mapmakers draw on European and colonial conventions of territoriality. The mapping works as a tool of alliance and advocacy because it
draws these separate traditions for thinking about land and rights into the
same object, the map.

Mapping has spread rapidly around the world as a tool in indigenous and tribal advocacy projects (Poole 1995). Mapping is exciting in part because it brings together the authority of the technical—enhanced by the almost magical presence of satellite and computer technology—and the authority of the traditional, the local knowledge of elders. Mapping can also inspire a participatory, community-making project, in which activist desires for community empowerment take on a concrete meaning in relation to the landscape and its familiar places.

Yet mapping projects have a different flavor in different areas. The Americas have produced particularly enthusiastic reports about the role of mapping in indigenous community advocacy. (See, for example, the articles in *Geomatics*, a special issue of *Cultural Survival Quarterly*, Winter 1995.) In the best cases, local people ask for maps and feel empowered not only by the technical training but also by their ability to enmesh their local knowledge with national land rights legislation. Maps, ideally, are boundary objects that seem solid and right to both villagers and the state. In Southeast Asia, however, scholars and activists have been concerned about the problems of mapping. Without a national legal–political context that makes the relationship between mapping and rights clear, local activists and their advocates have had to dream up ways to use maps to enhance public discussion of community rights (Tsing 1999). Boundaries between communities can cause trouble (Fox 1994), disturbing colonial precedence sometimes arises (Zerner 1994), and the symbolic charge of the map in producing favorable policy becomes open to question (Peluso 1995). In this context, the fragility of the collaborations at every level—international, national, and village; academics, advocates, elders; communities, neighbors, migrants—is especially apparent. Indeed, this fragility makes the apparent solidity of the successful North and South American collaborations particularly awe-inspiring and academically interesting. Scholarly work on understanding how effective coalitions happen has just begun.

New Questions, New Approaches

In describing these research trajectories, I am aware that I have yet to come up with the right images and vocabulary to convey their excitement and integrity. I have purposely avoided terms that, caught in current academic battles, make even humble claims appear as fighting words, because I believe that the excitement of the field I am introducing is in the eclectic combinations and half-finished frameworks that spread creativity and make disagreements productive. This leaves me with old, accepted words to convey new, emergent frames and ideas. Yet even without a dazzling vocabulary, perhaps you can hear the critical shared questions.

What is the context for the environmental problems and struggles we each know most about? As environmental rhetorics are deployed more and more freely, how do we know the difference between globe-grabbing imperialists and local allies? Is there a "locally appropriate" way to promote conservation? What are the practical implications of new forms of environmental expertise? How do local knowledges come together in building environmental movements? How do we appreciate nature's power and independence even as what we know as nature shifts in relation to our human programs?

It is the urgency of these kinds of questions that is bringing so many graduate students, as well as both young and established scholars, to research in this area. For now, the best I can do to label this emergent scholarship is to describe it as the study of nature in the making.

Notes

A shorter version of this chapter was presented at the symposium on Anthropology and the Environment at the annual meetings of the American Anthropological Association in November 1996. I am grateful to Carole Crumley for organizing the symposium and for her comments on the talk. Judith Mayer, Nancy Peluso, and K. Sivaramakrishnan each read an earlier draft of this essay, offering important clarifications and references; J. Peter Brosius, Michael Dove, Paula Ebron, and Paul Greenough also provided useful suggestions. I am grateful for their help thinking through these matters.

1. Precedents are sometimes distorted and obscured even as they become influential legacies. When historian Donald Worster traces the formation of environmental history in the 1970s, he sees the field learning particularly from the preeminent ecological anthropologists of the 1950s and 1960s, citing figures such as Julian Stewart, Marvin Harris, and Roy Rappaport (Worster 1988). In turn, environmental history has shaped the new cultural anthropology of the environment; yet, this latter field looks back to those particular anthropological ancestors, mainly through the lens of 1980s environmental history.

2. Some comparative treatments include Arnold (1996); Beinart (1989); Beinart and Coates (1995); Grove (1995); and Grove, Damodaran, and Sangwan (1998).

3. Grove (1995), Brockway (1979), MacKenzie (1990), Juma (1989), Rajan (1994).

4. The centrality of property and other access conventions in creating social–natural landscapes is discussed in Scott (1985) and Peluso (1996).

5. See also Ramachandra Guha's "social ecology" (1994).

6. New ethnographic research on environmental science is currently coming to fruition; I think, for example, of Myanna Lahsen's research on climate change and Corinne Hayden's (2000) research on biodiversity.

7. James Fairhead and Melissa Leach's *Misreading the African Landscape* (1996) is one of the few book-length considerations of this kind of problem. Fairhead and Leach argue that authoritative understandings of deforestation in Guinea, West Africa, have badly misread the historical record even as they have led to powerful policy directives.

8. Some of the essays derive from the conference on Environmental Discourses and Human Welfare in South and Southeast Asia, held in Hilo, Hawaii, in December 1995; see Greenough and Tsing (forthcoming).

9. For South and Southeast Asian environmental project-making, see also Arnold and Guha (1995); Grove, Damodaran, and Sangwan (1998); Li (1999).

10. See also Arnold (1996).

11. Consider, for example, the opening chapter of biodiversity advocate Edward O. Wilson's *The Diversity of Life,* which places Wilson and his readers in a tropical rain forest full of insects, bats, and orchids, waiting for a storm. Traditions of studying and narrating the tropics create the dramatic force for the book's moral–intellectual claim: "It is diversity by which life builds and saturates the rain forest . . ." (1992: 11).

12. There are notable exceptions in which research attends to both plants and human social relations, for example, James Fox's on rice strain simplifications (1991) or Virginia Nazarea Sandoval's on hidden heirloom rice varieties in Green Revolution fields (1995).

13. See Keck and Sikkink (1998) and Rocheleau, Thomas-Slayter, and Wangari (1996).

14. In their introduction, Grove, Damodaran, and Sangwan (1998) show how disagreements about the Chipko movement also stimulated scholarship on the history of Indian forests.

References

Abraham, Itty. 1998. *The Making of the Indian Atomic Bomb: Science, Secrecy, and the Postcolonial State.* London: Zed Press.

Agarwal, Anil. 1975. "Ghandi's Ghost Saves the Himalayan Trees." *New Scientist* 67:386–87.

———, and Sunita Narain. 1991. *Global Warming in an Unequal World: A Case of Environmental Colonialism.* New Delhi: Centre for Science and Environment.

Anderson, Warwick. Forthcoming. "The Natures of Culture: Environment and Race in the Colonial Tropics." In Greenough and Tsing, eds., *Imagination and Distress in Southern Environmental Projects.*

Arnold, David. 1996. *The Problem of Nature: Environment, Culture, and European Expansion.* Oxford: Blackwell.

———, and Ramachandra Guha, eds. 1995. *Nature, Culture, and Imperialism: Essays on the Environmental History of South Asia.* Delhi: Oxford University Press.

Barbour, Michael. 1995. "Ecological Fragmentation in the Fifties." In William Cronon, ed., *Uncommon Ground,* 233–55. New York: Norton.

Baviskar, Amita. 1995. *In the Belly of the River: Tribal Conflicts over Development in the Narmada Valley.* Delhi: Oxford University Press.

———. Forthcoming. "Tribal Politics and Sustainable Development." In Greenough and Tsing, eds., *Imagination and Distress in Southern Environmental Projects.*

Beinart, William. 1984. "Soil Erosion, Conservationism, and Ideas about Development: A Southern African Exploration, 1900–1960." *Journal of Southern African Studies* 11(1): 52–83.

———. 1989. "Introduction: The Politics of Colonial Conservation." *Journal of Southern African Studies,* Special Issue on the Politics of Conservation in Southern Africa, 15(2): 143–61.

———, and Peter Coates. 1995. *Environment and History: The Taming of Nature in the U.S.A and South Africa.* London: Routledge.

Berglund, Eeva. 1998. *Knowing Nature, Knowing Science.* Cambridge U.K.: White Horse Press.

Blaikie, Piers. 1985. *The Political Economy of Soil Erosion.* London: Methuen.

——, and Harold Brookfield, eds. 1987. *Land Degradation and Society.* London: Methuen.

Brockway, Lucille. 1979. *Science and Colonial Expansion.* New York: Academic.

Brosius, J. Peter. 1997. "Prior Transcripts, Divergent Paths: Resistance and Acquiescence to Logging in Sarawak, East Malaysia." *Comparative Studies in Society and History* 39(3): 468–510.

Croll, Elisabeth, and David Parkin, eds. 1992. *Bush Base: Forest Farm: Culture, Environment, and Development.* London: Routledge.

Cronon, William. 1992. "A Place for Stories: Nature, History, and Narrative." *Journal of American History* 78(4): 1347–76.

——. 1993. "The Uses of Environmental History." *Environmental History Review.* (Fall): 1-22.

——, ed. 1995. *Uncommon Ground: Toward Reinventing Nature.* New York: Norton.

Darlington, Susan. Forthcoming. "Practical Spirituality and Community Forests: Monks, Ritual and Radical Conservatism in Thailand." In Greenough and Tsing, eds., *Imagination and Distress in Southern Environmental Projects.*

Denevan, William. 1992. "The Pristine Myth: The Landscape of the Americas in 1492." *Annals of the Association of American Geographers* 82(3): 369–85.

Dove, Michael. 1993. "A Revisionist View of Tropical Deforestation and Development." *Environmental Conservation* 20(1): 17–24.

——. 1994. "North–South Differences, Global Warming, and the Global System." *Chemosphere* 29(5): 1063–77.

DuPuis, Melanie, and Peter Vandergeest, eds. 1996. *Creating the Countryside: The Politics of Rural and Environmental Discourse.* Philadelphia: Temple University Press. Historical Ecology, and the Renegotiation of Nature in Central Seram." In Tania Murray Li, ed., *Transforming the Indonesian Uplands: Marginality, Power, and Production.* Singapore: Hardwood.

Fairhead, James, and Melissa Leach. 1996. *Misreading the African Landscape.* Cambridge: Cambridge University Press.

Fox, James. 1991. "Managing the Ecology of Rice Production in Indonesia." In Joan Hardjono, ed., *Indonesia: Resources, Ecology, and Environment,* 61–84. Singapore: Oxford University Press.

Fox, Jefferson. 1994. "Mapping Customary Lands: A Tool for Forest Management." Paper delivered at the annual meeting of the Association for Asian Studies, Boston, Mass.

Garb, Yaakov. 1997. "Lost in Translation: Toward a Feminist Account of Chipko." In Joan Scott, Cora Kaplan, and Debra Keates, eds., *Transitions, Environments, Translations,* 273–84. New York: Routledge.

Gold, Ann. Forthcoming. "Foreign Trees: Lives and Landscapes in Rajasthan." In Greenough and Tsing, eds., *Imagination and Distress in Southern Environmental Projects.*

Greenough, Paul, and Anna Tsing, eds. Forthcoming. *Imagination and Distress in Southern Environmental Projects.*

Grove, Richard. 1995. *Green Imperialism.* Cambridge: Cambridge University Press.

——. Forthcoming. "The East India Company, the Australians, and the El Niño: Colonial Scientists and the Discourse of Climatic Change and Teleconnections between 1770 and 1930." In Greenough and Tsing, eds., *Imagination and Distress in Southern Environmental Projects.*

——, Vinita Damodaran, and Satpal Sangwan, eds. 1998. *Nature and the Orient: Essays on the Environmental History of South and Southeast Asia*. New Delhi: Oxford University Press.

Guha, Ramachandra. 1989. *The Unquiet Woods: Ecological Change and Peasant Resistance in the Himalaya*. Berkeley: University of California Press.

——, ed. 1994. *Social Ecology*. Delhi: Oxford University Press.

Haraway, Donna. 1989. *Primate Visions: Gender, Race, and Nature in the World*. London: Routledge.

Hart, Gillian. 1991. "Engendering Everyday Resistance: Gender, Patronage, and Production Politics in Rural Malaysia." *Journal of Peasant Studies* 19(1): 93–121.

Harvey, David. 1996. *Justice, Nature, and the Geography of Difference*. Cambridge, Mass: Blackwell.

Hayden, Corinne. 2000. "When Nature Goes Public: An Ethnology of Bio-Prospecting in Mexico." Ph.D. dissertation, University of California, Santa Cruz.

Hecht, Susanna, and Alexander Cockburn. 1990. *The Fate of the Forest: Developers, Destroyers, and Defenders of the Amazon*. New York: HarperCollins.

Johnson, Stanley. 1993. *The Earth Summit*. London: Graham and Trotman.

Juma, Calestous. 1989. *The Gene Hunters: Biotechnology and the Scramble for Seeds*. Princeton: Princeton University Press.

Keck, Margaret, and Kathryn Sikkink. 1998. *Activists beyond Borders: Transnational Advocacy Networks in International Politics*. Ithaca, N.Y.: Cornell University Press.

Kuletz, Valerie. 1998. *The Tainted Desert: Environmental Ruin in the American West*. New York: Routledge.

Latour, Bruno. 1987. *Science in Action: How to Follow Scientists and Engineers Through Society*. Cambridge, Mass.: Harvard University Press.

——, and Steve Wolgar. 1986 (1979). *Laboratory Life: The Construction of Scientific Facts*. 2nd ed. Princeton, N.J.: Princeton University Press.

Li, Tania. 1996. "Images of Community: Discourse and Strategy in Property Relations." *Development and Change* 27(3): 501–27.

——, ed. 1999. *Transforming the Indonesian Uplands: Marginality, Power, and Production*. London: Harwood Academic Press.

Lowe, Celia. 1999. "Cultures of Nature: Mobility, Identity, and Biodiversity Conservation in the Togean Islands of Sulawesi, Indonesia." Ph.D. dissertation, Yale University.

——. 2000. "Global Markets, Local Injustice in Southeast Asian Seas: The Live Fish Trade and Local Fisheries in the Togean Islands of Sulawesi, Indonesia." In Zerner, ed., *Peoples, Plants, and Justice*. New York: Columbia University Press.

MacKenzie, John, ed. 1990. *Imperialism and the Natural World*. Manchester: Manchester University Press.

Marcus, George. 1995. "Ethnography in/of the World System: The Emergence of Multisited Ethnography." *Annual Review of Anthropology* 25: 95–117.

Milton, Kay. 1993. *Environmentalism: The View from Anthropology*. London: Routledge.

——. 1996. *Environmentalism and Cultural Theory*. London: Routledge.

Nazarea Sandoval, Virginia. 1995. *Local Knowledge and Agricultural Decision Making in the Philippines*. Ithaca, N.Y.: Cornell University Press.

Neumann, Roderick. 1998. *Imposing Wilderness: Struggles over Livelihood and Nature Preservation in Africa*. Berkeley: University of California Press.

Peet, Richard, and Michael Watts. 1996a. "Liberation Ecology: Development, Sustainability, and the Environment in an Age of Market Triumphalism." In Peet and Watts, eds., *Liberation Ecologies: Environment, Development, Social Movements.* New York: Routledge, 1–45.

——, eds. 1996b. *Liberation Ecologies: Environment, Development, Social Movements.* New York: Routledge.

Peluso, Nancy. 1992. *Rich Forests, Poor People: Resource Control and Resistance in Java.* Berkeley: University of California Press.

——. 1995. "Whose Woods are These? Counter-Mapping Forest Territories in Kalimantan, Indonesia." *Antipode* 27(4): 383–406.

——. 1996. "Fruit Trees and Family Trees in an Anthropogenic Forest: Property Rights, Ethics of Access, and Environmental Change in Indonesia." *Comparative Studies in Society and History* 38(3): 510–48.

——. Forthcoming. "Territorializing Local Struggles for Resource Control: A Look at Environmental Discourses and Politics in Indonesia." In Greenough and Tsing, eds., *Imagination and Distress in Southern Environmental Projects.*

Peters, Pauline. 1994. *Dividing the Commons: Politics, Policy, and Culture in Botswana.* Charlottesville: University of Virginia Press.

Poole, Peter. 1995. *Indigenous Peoples, Mapping, and Biodiversity Conservation.* Washington, D.C.: Biodiversity Support Program.

Rajan, Ravi. 1994. "Imperial Environmentalism: The Agendas and Ideologies of Natural Resource Management in British Colonial Forestry, 1800–1950." Ph.D. dissertation, Oxford University.

Rangan, Haripriya. 1993. "Of Myths and Movements: Forestry and Regional Development in the Garwhal Himalayas." Ph.D. dissertation, University of California, Los Angeles.

——. 1996. "From Chipko to Uttaranchal: Development, Environment, and Social Protest in the Garwhal Himalayas, India." In Peet and Watts, eds., *Liberation Ecologies: Environment, Development, Social Movements.* New York: Routledge, 205–26.

Rocheleau, Diane, Barbara Thomas-Slayter, and Ester Wangari, eds. 1996. *Feminist Political Ecology.* London: Routledge.

Roe, Emery, ed. 1995. *World Development,* Special issue, 23(6): 1005–69.

Sachs, Wolfgang, ed. 1993. *Global Ecology: A New Arena of Political Conflict.* London: Zed Press.

Schmink, Marianne, and Charles Wood. 1992. *Contested Frontiers in Amazonia.* New York: Columbia University Press.

Schroeder, Richard. 1993. "Shady Practice: Gender and the Political Ecology of Resource Stabilization in Gambian Orchards/Gardens." *Economic Geography* 69(1): 319–65.

Scott, James. 1985. *Weapons of the Weak: Everyday Forms of Peasant Resistance.* New Haven, Conn.: Yale University Press.

——. 1998. *Seeing Like a State.* New Haven, Conn.: Yale University Press.

Shiva, Vandana. 1989. *Staying Alive: Women, Ecology, Development.* London: Zed Books.

Showers, Kate. 1989. "Soil Erosion in the Kingdom of Lesotho: Origins and Colonial Response, 1830s–1950s." *Journal of Southern African Studies* 15(2): 263–86.

Sivaramakrishnan, K. 1996. "Forest Politics and Governance in Bengal, 1794–1994." Ph.D. dissertation, Yale University.

——. Forthcoming. "Scientific Forestry and Genealogies of Development in Bengal." In Greenough and Tsing, eds., *Imagination and Distress in Southern Environmental Projects.*

Soule, Michael. 1995. "The Social Siege of Nature." In Michael Soule and Gary Lease, eds., *Reinventing Nature? Responses to Postmodern Deconstruction*, 137–70. Washington, D.C.: Island Press.

Star, S. L., and J. R. Griesemer. 1989. "Institutionalized Ecology, 'Translations,' and Boundary Objects: Amateurs and Professionals in Berkeley's Museum of Vertebrate Zoology, 1907–39." *Social Studies of Science* 19: 387–420.

Sturgeon, Noel. 1997. "Strategic Environmentalisms." In Joan Scott, Cora Kaplan, and Debra Keates, eds., *Transitions, Environments, Translations*, 285–91. New York: Routledge.

Taylor, Peter. 1988. "Technocratic Optimism, H. T. Odum, and the Partial Transformation of Ecological Metaphor after World War II." *Journal of the History of Biology* 21(2): 213–44.

——. 1992. "Re/Constructing Socio-Ecologies: System Dynamic Modeling of Nomadic Pastoralists in Sub-Saharan Africa." In Adele Clarke and Joan Fujimura, eds., *The Right Tool for the Job: At Work in Twentieth-Century Life Sciences*, 115–48. Princeton, N.J.: Princeton University Press.

——, and Ann Blum. 1991. "Ecosystems as Circuits: Diagrams and the Limits of Physical Analogies." *Biology and Philosophy* 6: 275–94.

Taylor, Peter, and Frederick Buttel. 1992. "How Do We Know We Have Global Environmental Problems? Science and the Globalization of Environmental Discourse." *Geoforum* 23(3): 405–16.

Tsing, Anna. 1997. "Environmentalism: Transitions as Translations." In Joan Scott, Cora Kaplan, and Debra Keates, eds., *Transitions, Environments, Translations*, 253–72. New York: Routledge.

——. 1999. "Becoming a Tribal Elder and Other Green Development Fantasies." In Li, ed., *Transforming the Indonesian Uplands: Marginality, Power, and Production*. London: Harwood.

Willems-Braun, Bruce. 1997. "Buried Epistemologies: The Politics of Nature in (Post)colonial British Columbia." *Annals of the Association of American Geographers* 87(1): 3–31.

Wilson, Edward O. 1992. *The Diversity of Life*. Cambridge, Mass: Harvard University Press.

Wong, Diana. 1987. *Peasants in the Making: Malaysia's Green Revolution*. Singapore: Institute of Southeast Asian Studies.

Worster, Donald. 1985. *Rivers of Empire: Water, Aridity, and the Growth of the American West*. New York: Oxford University Press.

——. 1988. "Doing Environmental History." In Donald Worster, ed., *The Ends of the Earth: Perspectives on Modern Environmental History*, 289–307. Cambridge: Cambridge University Press.

——, et al. 1990. "A Roundtable: Environmental History." *Journal of American History* 76(4): 1087–147.

Zerner, Charles. 1994. "Through a Green Lens: The Construction of Customary Environmental Law and Community in Indonesia's Maluku Islands." *Law and Society Review* 28(5): 1079–122.

——. In press. "Sounding the Makassar Strait: The Political Economy of Authority in an Indonesian Marine Environment." In Charles Zerner, ed., *Culture and the Question of Rights in Southeast Asian Environments*. Raleigh, N.C.: Duke University Press.

Zerner, Charles, ed. 2000. *People, Plants, and Justice*. New York: Columbia University Press.

2

Linking Language and Environment:
A Coevolutionary Perspective

Luisa E. Maffi

Human languages are memories of human inventiveness, adaptation, and survival skills.

—Peter Mühlhäusler

The voice of the land is in our language.

—National First Nations Elders/Language Gathering, M'igmaq Nation

Words have power. Languages connected to place help us to respect local knowledge, to ask and answer the tough questions about how the human and nonhuman can live together in a tolerant and dignified way. They can help us extend our sense of community, what we hold ourselves responsible for, what we must do to live right and well.

—Nancy Lord

There is a fire burning over the Earth, taking with it plants and animals, cultures, languages, ancient skills, and visionary wisdom. Quelling this flame and reinventing the poetry of diversity is the most important challenge of our times.

—Wade Davis[1]

Interest in the links between language and the environment is not new in the history of anthropology, although until fairly recently it has been sparse. In the North American anthropological tradition, one can go at least as far back as 1912 to find such interest expressed in the writings of Edward Sapir. Sapir saw the interaction between language and the environment as mediated by human cognition and social life and expressed through linguistic features. In his work on Native American languages, he noted the ways in which the vocabulary of a language encodes and inventories, among other things, the characteristics of the local landscape and its flora and fauna and thus "bears the stamp of the physical environment in which the speakers are placed," while reflecting "the interest of the people in such environmental features." He also noted that "there are natural limits set to the variability of lexical materials in so far as they give expression to concepts derived from the physical world" because of the universal distribution in time and place of many of the elements that make up the physical environment.[2] Another pioneer of North American anthropology, Alfred Kroeber, studied the relationships between Native American culture areas and the natural areas (today we would say ecosystems) of the North American continent, although he had a more marginal interest than Sapir in the role of language in human–environment relationships.[3] These early studies are foundational each in its own right, yet they did not give rise to a steady stream of research on language– (and/or culture–) environment relations, although they foreshadowed aspects of the work that would be carried out several decades later by ethnobiologists, ethnoecologists, and human ecologists, as well as researchers interested in indigenous place-naming.

Focused attention to the links between language and the environment has been developing recently in part as an outcome of these latter lines of research, in part stemming from work carried out in linguistics on the notion of "linguistic ecologies," and in part still as the result of studies devoted to the current "extinction crisis" experienced by the world's linguistic diversity and to the relationships between this linguistic diversity loss and the concurrent worldwide loss of biodiversity. Interest in this topic is growing, especially as there is increasing recognition, on the one hand, of the value of the traditional ecological knowledge and practices of indigenous and tribal peoples and of the extent to which such knowledge and practices are developed, encoded, and transmitted through language, and, on the other, that traditional knowledge and practices, along with the languages that carry them, are being placed at risk by the same global and local socioeconomic and political processes that are threatening the integrity and the very survival of indigenous and tribal cultures. At this point, a picture of language–environment interrelations is beginning to emerge at various degrees of resolution, from a global to a local scale, and at various levels of analysis, from the macro to the micro.

This chapter reviews some of the main aspects of this emerging picture, beginning with global correlations and then "zooming in" at progressively higher degrees of resolution, examining at each step how these correlations might be said to represent a form of "coevolution" between language and the environment (sections 1, 2, 3).[4] In addition to providing a convenient way of organizing the various threads of this research field, the structure of the chapter is intended to highlight the point that the study of language–environment correlations offers a significant way of "linking levels of analysis"—a concern that has become central in ecological anthropology. Research at each level feeds into, and illuminates, findings at other levels. Following this overview, the chapter goes on to describe ways in which knowledge about the natural world is linguistically encoded (section 4) and to consider issues related to the erosion of this linguistically encoded knowledge (section 5). The chapter concludes by contemplating prospects for the maintenance and revitalization of such key aspects of indigenous and tribal cultures (section 6).[5]

1. Linguistic and Biological Diversity: Global Correlations

Starting with a planetary view, global cross-mappings of the world's biological and linguistic diversity, produced by conservationist David Harmon, show remarkable overlaps between these two forms of diversity: in particular, between countries with high endemism for vertebrates, flowering plants, and birds and countries with high numbers of endemic languages (*endemic* meaning, for both species and languages, "being restricted in range to a single region").[6] Furthermore, ten of the twelve biological megadiversity countries (i.e., countries identified as likely to contain a large percentage of global species richness) also figure among the top twenty-five for endemic languages. There are exceptions (e.g., Papua New Guinea—the country with the highest linguistic diversity and endemism in the world, with more than eight hundred different languages, mostly uniquely spoken in it—does not figure among the twelve megadiversity countries). Yet, on a global scale, there is no overlooking the overall trend for biological and linguistic diversity, and particularly endemism at the two levels, to coincide in the same parts of the world.

What may account for these correlations? Harmon points to several physiographic features of the Earth's surface that might comparably affect biodiversity and linguistic diversity (and especially endemism in both cases): (1) Extensive landmasses with a variety of terrains, climates, and ecosystems; (2) Island territories, especially with internal geophysical barriers; (3) Tropical climates, fostering higher numbers and densities of species. Harmon notes that these circumstances favor speciation and that in all such cases high biodiversity and species endemism are common. He suggests that, under the same conditions, and at the low population densities that were prevalent before European expansion, communicative isolation among small-scale human groups may have occurred, giving rise to many different local languages. From this perspective, then, a coincidence of biological and linguistic diversity would arise in parallel, due to the same independent set of geographical and climatic characteristics.

While the above circumstances per se might be seen as providing a plausible historical account of this concurrence, Harmon points out that these same circumstances might have favored an additional phenomenon that might in turn have contributed to fostering the biodiversity–linguistic diversity correlations: a process of coevolution of small-scale human societies

Table 2.1   Endemism in Languages Compared with Rankings of Biodiversity (From Harmon 1998)

| Country | Rank, Total Number of . . . | | | | On megadiversity list? |
	Endemic Languages	Endemic Vertebrates	Flowering Plants	Endemic Bird Areas (EBAs)	
Papua New Guinea	1st	13th	18th	6th	
Indonesia	2nd	4th	7th	1st	yes
Nigeria	3rd				
India	4th	7th	12th	11th	yes
Australia	5th	1st	11th	9th	yes
Mexico	6th	2nd	4th	2nd	yes
Cameroon	7th	23rd	24th		
Brazil	8th	3rd	1st	4th	yes
Democratic Republic of Congo	9th	18th	17th		yes
Philippines	10th	6th	25th	11th	
USA	11th	11th	9th	15th	
Vanuatu	12th				
Tanzania	13th	21st	19th	14th	
Sudan	14th				
Malaysia	15th		14th		yes
Ethiopia	16th	25th			
China	17th	12th	3rd	6th	yes
Peru	18th	8th	13th	3rd	yes
Chad	19th				
Russia	20th		6th		
Solomon Islands	21st	24th			
Nepal	22nd		22nd		
Colombia	23rd	9th	2nd	5th	yes
Côte d'Ivoire	24th				
Canada	25th				

SOURCES: ENDEMIC LANGUAGES: D. HARMON. 1995. "THE STATUS OF THE WORLD'S LANGUAGES AS REPORTED IN ETH-
NOLOGUE," SOUTHWEST JOURNAL OF LINGUISTICS 14: 1–33. ENDEMIC VERTEBRATES: B. GROOMBRIDGE, ED. 1992.
GLOBAL BIODIVERSITY: STATUS OF THE WORLD'S LIVING RESOURCES. LONDON: CHAPMAN AND HALL. FLOWERING
PLANTS: GROOMBRIDGE (1992). EBAS: A. J. STATTERSFIELD ET AL., EDS. 1998. ENDEMIC BIRD AREAS OF THE WORLD:
PRIORITIES FOR BIODIVERSITY CONSERVATION. CAMBRIDGE, U.K.: BIRDLIFE INTERNATIONAL. MEGADIVERSITY COUN-
TRIES: MCNEELY ET AL. 1990. CONSERVING THE WORLD'S BIOLOGICAL DIVERSITY, GLAND/ WASHINGTON, D.C.:
IUCN/WRI/CONSERVATION INTERNATIONAL/WWF-US/THE WORLD BANK.
NOTES: FIGURES FOR ETHIOPIA INCLUDE ERITREA. ENDEMIC VERTEBRATE FIGURES FOR CHINA, PAPUA NEW GUINEA AND
USA DO NOT INCLUDE REPTILES BECAUSE THE NUMBER OF ENDEMIC SPECIES IS NOT REPORTED IN THE SOURCE TABLE.
FLOWERING PLANT SPECIES INCLUDE BOTH ENDEMICS AND NON-ENDEMICS. "MEGADIVERSITY COUNTRIES" HAVE BEEN
IDENTIFIED AS THOSE LIKELY TO CONTAIN A LARGE PERCENTAGE OF GLOBAL SPECIES RICHNESS. THE TWELVE LISTED WERE
IDENTIFIED ON THE BASIS OF SPECIES LISTS FOR VERTEBRATES, SWALLOWTAIL BUTTERFLIES, AND HIGHER PLANTS.

with their local ecosystems and the plant and animal species found in them.
This is the connection implied in the notion of "ecosystem peoples" first
developed three decades ago by geographer Richard Dasmann to refer to

small-scale human communities that draw direct sustenance from local ecosystems, relying on the environment for food, fruit, medicine, construction materials, and other products essential for their subsistence and their physical and spiritual well-being.[7] Not only do such societies develop extensive and detailed knowledge of local flora, fauna, and ecological relations, they also learn how to use local natural resources sustainably, so that the resources continue to reproduce themselves and support human life. Furthermore, they learn to manage these resources by means of a number of practices (such as natural forest management, cultivation, and the use of fire) that actually affect the biodiversity found in place, modifying it, enhancing it, or even creating it. Therefore, this biodiversity depends on humans to be and/or stay in place; on the other hand, humans come to depend on this biodiversity for their own survival.[8] What has been said of Australian Aboriginal tribes could be said in hundreds of other cases of indigenous and tribal peoples around the world: "Coincidences of tribal boundaries to local ecology are not uncommon and imply that a given group of people may achieve stability by becoming the most efficient users of a given area and understanding its potentialities."[9] It has also been observed that language and ethnicity have a spatial dimension, one that is intimately related to use of the environment: "each ethnic group has its own way of acting over its environment to conveniently fit in space. There are undoubtedly ethnic regions and the criterion for their delimitation is language."[10]

The role of language in these processes is perhaps best stated by linguist Peter Mühlhäusler: "Life in a particular human environment is dependent on people's ability to talk about it."[11] Over time, as human communities interact closely with the local environment, modifying it as they adapt to life in specific ecological niches, the knowledge they acquire about the environment and how to use and manage it for individual and group survival becomes encoded and transmitted through the local languages. From this perspective, linguistic and biological diversity are no longer the parallel products of external factors that independently affect both; rather they are intimately related and mutually reinforcing. In this connection, Mühlhäusler's notion of "linguistic ecologies" portrays networks of relationships that encompass not only the linguistic and social environment, but also the physical environment, within a worldview in which physical reality and the description of that reality are not seen as separate phenomena, but instead as interrelated parts of a whole.[12]

The issue of the coevolution of linguistic, cultural, and biological diversity has also been taken up by ecological anthropologist Eric Smith.[13] He has similarly examined ways in which cultural diversity might directly enhance biodiversity and vice versa; conversely, he has noted a correlation between low-diversity cultural systems and low biodiversity, suggesting that cultural diversity may require small-scale, localized socioeconomic systems, while large-scale systems lead to a reduction in cultural diversity, through processes that also have profound ecological consequences.

2. Linguistic and Biological Diversity: Areal and Regional Correlations

How do these correlations between biodiversity and linguistic and cultural diversity fare when one moves from a global to a regional scale? Smith has probed the issue by taking Native North America as an areal test case.[14] For Native North American culture areas, he finds that measures of linguistic diversity and cultural diversity independently correlate with some measures of biodiversity (floral diversity), although not others (faunal diversity). On the other hand, measures of linguistic diversity and cultural diversity for Native North America do not correlate well with each other, given the existence of cases of cultural similarity between linguistically diverse groups (e.g., Plains Indians), as well as cases of cultural divergence between linguistically related groups (e.g., Athapaskan speakers)—which Smith attributes to differential adaptations.

Smith's findings highlight the point that, while correlations between linguistic, cultural, and biological diversity are significant on a global scale, individual cases must be carefully examined in light of the specific factors at play. This requires historical data on population movements and contacts (including displacement or extinction of ethnolinguistic groups) and processes of environmental change. Furthermore, measures of linguistic and cultural diversity that have traditionally been employed by anthropologists have tended to be based on the identification and comparison of general traits.[15] These are not best suited for revealing the linguistic and cultural distinctiveness that may have developed, in response to specific local circumstances, even among human groups belonging to the same broadly defined cultural area or whose languages are genetically related.[16] This stresses the need for more fine-grained ways to define and identify linguistic and cultural diversity and their relationships with biodiversity at this higher degree of resolution—ways that take into account the variety of ecological as well as sociocultural circumstances under which, historically, human–environment adaptations occur.

For instance, a study of linguistic diversity in West Africa, carried out by Daniel Nettle, reveals that the diversity of languages in that region follows an ecological gradient: the number and size of ethnolinguistic groups correlates with the region's ecoclimatic zones, going from higher numbers of smaller groups in the tropical rain forests of the south to lower numbers of larger groups in the arid north.[17] The explanation of this finding, according to Nettle, lies in the notion of "ecological risk"—the extent of variation in the availability of food supplies according to ecoclimatic conditions, leading to the adoption of different socioeconomic strategies by the region's ethnolinguistic groups: small-scale, localized social networks where the food supply is reliable (such as in the rain forests) versus long-range, extended networks where a steady stream of food resources cannot be counted on (such as in the arid zones).

Interestingly, a comparable situation on a smaller geographical scale is found by Jane Hill in a study of dialectal variation in Tohono O'odham (a

Uto-Aztecan language spoken in Arizona).[18] In this case, the differential soci-olinguistic characteristics of two dialect communities of Tohono O'odham are found to correlate with the extent to which each community can make secure claims over vital resources such as water. Of the two communities, the one that has access to a steady supply of water throughout the year favors a "local-ist" sociolinguistic stance that tends to reduce the amount of internal linguis-tic variation and innovation; the community that has more limited, and sea-sonally variable, access to water, and thus has a history of moving around more frequently, favors a "distributed" stance that leads to greater linguistic variation and innovation.

Other studies at a regional level reveal the highly localized nature of some human–environment adaptations. A comparative investigation of the ecolog-ical practices of four small indigenous groups of the Brazilian Amazon (Parakaná, Araweté, Mayoruna, and Matis) who have a relatively short history of contact with the outside world, carried out by biological anthropologist Katharine Milton, shows remarkable differences in cultural and ecological knowledge and practices even between neighboring groups pertaining to the same linguistic stock.[19] Milton finds a diversity of staple crops and preys, dif-ferent uses of forest products for foods and medicines, variation in basic tech-nologies, and so forth, with one indigenous society often making no use of a commonly available plant or animal species that figures heavily in the cultural practices of another. This suggests to her, on the one hand, that the biological richness of the neotropical forest is reflected in the diversity of local adapta-tions and, on the other, that some of the variation (e.g., in the use of foods) may be reinforced by cultural factors, such as use as a marker of identity and of group boundaries.

An in-depth biogeographical study of a single bioregion, the Pacific North-west Coast of North America, brings in the history of human relationships with the bioregion as one of the key forces shaping (and being shaped by) the environment, with special reference to its original Native American occu-pants.[20] This study finds that, while Northwest Coast Indians are very diverse linguistically, their languages and cultural traditions also have many elements in common (probably due to long historical contact among the different groups and diffusion of linguistic and cultural features among them). How-ever, apart from its overall common ecological characteristics, this bioregion presents a high variety of local ecosystems and, as a consequence, local sub-sistence economies may also vary considerably from place to place. This di-versity is considered fundamental to understanding the Northwest Coast as a human environment.

Of the latter two studies, neither goes on to pursue an in-depth investiga-tion of the linguistic correlates of these different local adaptations; however, one may expect for this diversity of adaptational knowledge to be reflected in the various local languages, beyond any regional common features they may share. This points to the need for additional studies conducted at this degree of resolution that will map biodiversity, linguistic diversity, and cultural diversity at a regional level, with a specific focus on local ecological knowledge and the linguistic expression of local relationships with the environment.

3. Language and the Environment: Local Correlations

Recently, in part under the influence of ecosystem and bioregional approaches in biology and biodiversity conservation, ethnobiologists and ethnoecologists have become interested in mapping the biogeographical distribution of traditional environmental knowledge: in other words, in actually plotting this knowledge onto the land (the actual territory occupied by a given human community and/or over which community members range in their customary subsistence activities), with the aid of advanced mapping technology such as GPS/GIS.[21] Initial research shows that indigenous systems of classification of local ecological features, as expressed in linguistically encoded concepts, not only match the classifications of Western scientists, but in fact go significantly beyond them in depth and detail of recognition of relevant features.

For instance, a study of forest ecology in the Peruvian Amazon, carried out by ethnobiologist Glenn Shepard and ecologists Douglas Yu and Bruce Nelson, reveals that the local Matsigenka indigenous people recognize all forest types currently known to ecologists working in the region, as well as numerous biotopes not known to ecologists.[22] Many of the latter represent subtle variations in vegetation types that are not detectable on satellite images of the region, so that ethnobotanical knowledge also provides a means for "groundtruthing" the information on forest diversity obtained through such images. A rich oral tradition, along with a strong "spiritual ecology," sustains the Matsigenka's biogeographic knowledge. As more such "cognitive biogeographic" studies become available, it is likely that they will increasingly show remarkable degrees of isomorphism between given ecological niches (plants, animals, floral and faunal associations and interactions) and humans' cognitive maps of them—each shaped by and shaping the other over the history of local human populations.

Another way in which human relationships with local ecosystems are cognitively and linguistically codified is through place-naming. In his work with the Sahaptin of the Columbia Plateau of North America, ethnobiologist Eugene Hunn has stressed the ecological context in which indigenous place-naming occurs, along with the individual and cultural significance of this activity for indigenous peoples, "as a framework for cultural transmission and moral instruction, as a symbolic link to their land, and as a ground for their identity."[23] Hunn indicates that indigenous place-names tend to be vividly descriptive, either of some perceptible feature of a given aspect of the landscape, or of some meaningful association between people and a given site. In Sahaptin, places are named most often from organisms found in those places, as well as from observed ecological associations, animal behaviors, and topographic features. In all cases, place-names describe "places where things happen" within the local environment, so that "plotting the distribution of named places in Sahaptin is one means to appreciate the ecological niche occupied by local Indian peoples" as well as the intensity of cultural focus a region enjoys.[24] Place-names (and the same applies to plant and animal names or names for floral and faunal associations) thus come to represent entries in their users' "mental encyclopedia."

Hunn has also elaborated a measure of "toponymic density," the number of place-names per square mile within the recognized territory of a given indigenous group.[25] He points out that the distribution of place-names across the territory (such as, in the case of the Sahaptin, concentration of names along rivers and streams) may reveal important features of settlement patterns and subsistence. Through a comparative study of place-names in twelve cultures from different parts of the world, he has also found that the extension of the area over which place-names are distributed is inversely proportional to the population density of a given group. This in turn correlates with mode of subsistence (with hunter-gatherers ranging over a much larger territory than subsistence farmers). He describes this correlation as the level of "cognitive resolution" of a given group's landscape. These findings add to the emerging picture of the ecological and sociocultural correlates of the distribution of languages and linguistic features discussed in the previous section.

Named landmarks convey and evoke knowledge (often in the form of traditional narratives, songs, etc.) both about the physical environment and daily human activities, historical events, social relations, ritual, and moral conduct. As linguistic anthropologist Keith Basso puts it, "wisdom sits in places."[26] Landscapes are linguistically woven networks of such places of knowledge and wisdom and thus can be said to be anthropogenic (human-made), not only in the sense that they are physically modified by human intervention, but also because they are symbolically brought into the sphere of human interactions by language—by the words, expressions, stories, legends, and songs that encode and convey human relationships with the environment and inscribe the history of those relationships onto the land.[27]

Yet another way in which human–environment relationships can be expressed and symbolized through language is the metaphorical application of human anatomical concepts to the land, which, as Hunn suggests about the Sahaptin, is indicative of a tendency to "embody the landscape." In a study among the Highland Maya of Chiapas, Mexico, linguistic anthropologist Luisa Maffi found that metaphorical extension from the human body to the land can also occur at the level of human physiology.[28] Two major ethnoecological categories in terms of which the Highland Maya conceptualize their territory—labeled "warm country" and "cold country"—do not simply designate physiographic features of the land. Rather, they are based on an analogy with notions of the healthy versus diseased human body, especially in terms of generativity, and refer to the differential fertility and productivity of the land. This metaphorical extension of warmth/fertility vs. cold/barrenness from the human body to concepts of the land may occur (as also found elsewhere in Native America) through the connection of agricultural and seasonal cycles and the female reproductive cycle to lunar cycles, as well as via the identification of the earth with a woman's womb. This gives a very real sense to the Native American notion of "Mother Earth," and portrays a connection between humans and the land that is at one and the same time as primordially physiological and as powerfully symbolic as an umbilical cord.

4. The Linguistic Encoding of the Natural World

The nature and dynamics of the interactions between biodiversity and human languages and cultures are perhaps best studied at this local level, through the observation of the ways in which languages encode local ecological knowledge: knowledge about plant and animal species, the nonliving features of the landscape, and their mutual relationships, as well as concepts about human–environment interactions.

Over the past fifty years, much work in ethnobiology has been devoted to the study of indigenous systems of categorization and naming of natural kinds. The most comprehensive treatment of this topic to date has been provided by Brent Berlin.[29] Based on comparative evidence, Berlin has proposed that in traditional societies the classification and naming of natural kinds are governed by a number of general, cross-culturally recurrent principles.[30] These principles stipulate that, the world over, ethnobiological systems are based on the perceptual recognition of salient discontinuities as well as affinities in nature and on keen observation of the morphological and behavioral characteristics of local plant and animal species. Such recognition and observation, Berlin argues, are reflected in the classification of natural kinds that commonly takes the form of hierarchically organized folk taxonomies. In most cases described in the literature, these folk taxonomies reveal a considerable degree of correspondence with Western biosystematic taxonomies.

Berlin also notes that ethnobiological nomenclature normally matches and reflects the taxonomic organization of named plant and animal species. His principles identify a number of crosslinguistic regularities in the lexical structure of folk names for plants and animals that also correlate with the position of folk taxa at given classificatory ranks in the local biotaxonomic hierarchies. In addition, Berlin points out that by and large the naming of folk taxa is linguistically nonarbitrary, in that it is generally descriptive of salient morphological, ecological, or behavioral features of the taxa in question. Particularly in the case of animal nomenclature, Berlin shows that a cross-culturally recurrent feature is the use of onomatopoeia and other forms of sound symbolism. For animals that emit calls or noises (such as birds, amphibians, and insects), it is frequent for their folk names to be linguistic renderings of the their characteristic sounds (onomatopoeia). A subtler form of sound symbolism found in animal names associates certain features of the named organism with sounds that are perceived by analogy as conveying those same features. For instance, in many languages largeness or slow movement of given organisms recurrently correlate with presence in their folk names of low-frequency sounds such as the vowel [a], while smallness or rapid movement correlate with presence of high-frequency [I].[31] A higher level of resolution could hardly be reached, in noting the intimate bond between language and the environment, than in this non-arbitrary association of salient features of named biological organisms with a language's individual sounds.

Linking back from micro- to macro-associations between language and the environment, Berlin has also undertaken a study of the individual development of folk taxonomic systems as rooted in biogeography.[32] Based on the assumption that each person first learns about the natural kinds found in the localized ecosystem in which he or she becomes socialized and enculturated, Berlin finds evidence that these more familiar organisms cognitively recognized in early life then become the prototypes, or exemplars, of the folkbiological categories that individuals use as adults. When they begin to move around in surrounding areas and encounter unfamiliar organisms, adult individuals may notice perceptual affinities to the prototypes they have stored in mind, and assimilate them to the familiar kinds as "similar to" them—a recognition that can be given overt linguistic expression by calling the new species "like x" (where x is the familiar species).[33] In this sense, Berlin remarks, the individual's classification can be said to be both natural (i.e., based on recognition of perceptual affinities) and comprehensive (i.e., given enough experience, it can go well beyond a localized ecological niche and potentially extend over all or most of the species found in a given bioregion).

Berlin's approach argues for the prevailing role of perceptual factors in ethnobiological classification and naming over practical criteria (such as use for food or medicine, or other economic value)—although he acknowledges that, for domesticated or otherwise culturally significant plant and animal species, taxonomic and nomenclatural principles may diverge from his general principles, if in specifiable ways. Folk generics[34] of high cultural significance tend to have short and semantically unanalyzable names; also, a larger number of subgeneric taxa are normally recognized in the case of domesticated or otherwise economically important plant and animal species.[35] It is a matter for continuing debate among ethnobiologists to what extent the singling out of species in the local environment for classification and naming in traditional societies is driven by "intellectualist" versus "utilitarian" criteria.[36] In this debate, intellectualist criteria are seen as driven by humans' "intellectual curiosity" and as leading to recognition of natural kinds on the basis of "perceptual salience"; utilitarian criteria are considered to be driven by "subsistence value" and to lead to recognition of natural kinds based on "cultural salience."

However, there is evidence that perceptual and cultural salience interact in ethnobiological categorization. Hunn has found that perceptual criteria appear to be prevalent if one includes among them the ecological salience of an organism (as marked by the organism's biogeographic distribution compared to the distribution of the local human population, or by the organism's behavioral habits) and if morphological (phenotypic) salience is understood particularly in terms of the organism's size.[37] On the other hand, Hunn notes that exceptions to the general trend toward prevalence of perceptual criteria mostly correspond to organisms having high local cultural salience, organisms that will be singled out even if they may not be especially salient perceptually. These two dimensions also mutually interact, for example, with higher overall salience of a given set of organisms (mammals, fish, etc.) if there is a cultural focus on that set—although, within the set, recognition of organisms still follows perceptual criteria. It is likely that a satisfactory account of the bases for human classification and naming of nature will be found through a better understanding of the interactions between these and other relevant factors.

At the same time, a full understanding of the linguistic encoding of traditional ecological knowledge requires going well beyond plant and animal nomenclature. As we have already seen, ethnobiologists are devoting increasing attention to recording native terminologies for ecological or habitat features. In the process, it is becoming apparent that the linguistic expression of ecological knowledge and of human attitudes toward the environment is not only found in the words people use to name natural kinds, floral and faunal associations and interactions, and geographical features of the landscape; it is also spread in subtle ways throughout the linguistic system, in all aspects of grammar and language use.

In light of recent definitions of traditional ecological knowledge, linguist Andrew Pawley points out that much of this knowledge (where "knowledge," he notes, should be understood as including "perceptions" and "beliefs") is in fact not about entities per se, such as natural kinds; it is about natural processes and relations among entities, as in the perceived ecological relationships among the plants and animal species in a given local ecosystem, and between humans and the ecosystem.[38] This kind of knowledge, Pawley maintains, is not simply conveyed by nomenclature. It is conveyed by more complex means, that is, via speech formulas that the group's members regularly use in conversation: culturally conventionalized ways of talking about certain subject matter, expressing spatial, temporal, causal relations, and so forth. These speech formulas can go from set phrases to specified ways of building sentences or even whole discourses, narratives, etc. In other words, to convey ecological knowledge speakers make use of the whole tool kit their language puts at their disposal (and to identify this knowledge, the analyst must become familiar with the whole tool kit).[39] Pawley illustrates these points with examples drawn from Kalam (Papua New Guinea) discourse about plants and animals, their habitats, their mutual relationships, vegetational formations, and so forth, showing how this discourse is replete with idioms—highly conventionalized expressions that conveniently package enormous amounts of cultural knowledge about the environment.

David Wilkins makes analogous observations in his study of the linguistic expression of human–environment relationships among the Mparntwe Arrernte (a group of Australian Aborigines).[40] Wilkins finds that the interdependence between kinship, land, and "Dreamtime" totemism among Aborigines (as recognized by ethnographers as well as overtly expressed in Aboriginal philosophy) is reflected in a wide variety of features of the Mparntwe Arrernte language, drawn from both language structure and language use. He calls this recurrent pattern of linguistic expression an "ethno-semantic regularity" that embodies a holistic and mutual link between people, plants, animals, places, and the spiritual or supernatural. Wilkins suggests that the more important a given theme has been for a cultural group, and the longer it has been embedded in the group's social life, the more likely it is to have "worked itself into the fabric of the language," manifesting itself not only in the lexicon, but also in grammar and language use.

Nancy Lord synthesizes these concepts in speaking of the Dena'ina Athabaskan language of the Cook Inlet (Alaska) as a "coevolutionary tongue," a language that confirms the landscape at one and the same time that the landscape shapes it:[41] dictating, for instance, not only an ample vocabulary for talking about salmon and other fish, vegetation, streams, and trails, but also extensive development of grammatical devices for expressing "direction, distances, and relative positionings—very important in a semi-nomadic culture where people needed to be very clear about where they were and where they needed to go for food and other necessities." And even individual words may signify much more about human perceptions of the environment than the mere recognition of individual natural objects:

> When the rain stops . . . [t]he air is fragrant with plant oils and wet earth, and all the leaves and grasses are magnified by the droplets caught in their creases and dangling from the tips. A warm white light suffuses the breaking clouds; its shafts pierce the mosaic of green and gray inlet waters. There's a Dena'ina word for this—this fresh-scrubbed, brightened, new-world look. *Htashtch'ul.*

The study of these pervasive forms of coevolution between language and the environment clearly has much to offer to the understanding of human–environment relationships. It also provides a fertile ground for cooperation between linguists and ecological anthropologists. So far, such cooperation has been limited, however—although this is beginning to change. In a passage that deserves being quoted at length, Jeffrey Wollock, a historian of the language sciences, gives the following account of this state of affairs:

> Modern theories of linguistics cannot begin to explain the connections between linguistic diversity and biodiversity, because, being structurally oriented, they

deal with languages as autonomous, self-contained systems—grammars. When linguistic theory extends to semantics, this is rarely seen as anything but a self-contained, self-referential system (a "text"). Even pragmatics, the study of the relation between linguistic systems and their users, does not necessarily get us beyond the text. Modern linguistic theory, obsessed with the nominalist conception of language as a purely arbitrary system of signs, cannot handle the idea that there are really-existing systems outside of language and outside of man, to which language bears a definite relation. Nature, if considered at all, is [seen as] an abstraction, a sociolinguistic construct. . . . It is only when we shift our perspective from language as grammar . . . to language as a pattern of human action, used by human beings with bodies as well as minds and connected with other actions within the social and natural world, that it becomes possible to talk adequately about how linguistic diversity is related to biodiversity.

Each culture has an established policy as to the actions and forbearances that are good (or bad) to do on the land which it holds under its jurisdiction. Traditional cultures believe they have received this in the form of instructions from a superhuman agent and they have often formalized these as a covenant with that agent and/or all other species in the community. . . . That such a world-view is not simply a linguistic construct but an adequate reflection of extra-linguistic (ontological) reality is being experimentally demonstrated by the history of the very phenomenon in question, i.e., the growing correlation of high linguistic diversity and biodiversity with the territories of more traditional cultures, and of low diversity with "developed" cultures, which have internalized the idea of nature as a mere construct.[42]

5. The Erosion of Languages and Ecological Knowledge

The central role of language, and of whole linguistic systems, in encoding and transmitting ecological (and, of course, other) knowledge stresses the fundamental importance of continued vitality of local languages as a means for sustaining the integrity of local ecological knowledge systems, and thus of local environments and the communities that depend on them for their subsistence. Yet indigenous and tribal languages around the world and the knowledge they convey are rapidly undergoing dramatic erosion.

The ecological and cultural consequences of the global and local socioeconomic processes that are disrupting traditional ways of life are everywhere to be seen, in the progressive depletion of the world's forests and ranges, deterioration of water and air quality, and humans' increasing inability to live sustainably and harmoniously on earth. Less visible, yet no less dramatic in their nature and their consequences, are the processes of decay that are affecting languages and linguistically encoded knowledge, including ecological knowledge. Because in most cases indigenous knowledge is only carried via oral tradition, when a shift toward "modernization" and dominant languages occurs and local oral tradition is not kept up in the native language, traditional knowledge also becomes lost. And much of the traditional knowledge that becomes lost is ecological knowledge. Due to its place-specificity and close links to local modes of subsistence, ecological knowledge is one of the cultural domains more at risk when people are removed from their traditional environments or become alienated from traditional ways of life. Generally, local knowledge does not "translate" well into the majority language to which indigenous language speakers switch; the replacing language does not represent a readily interchangeable vehicle for linguistic expression and cultural maintenance. Furthermore, with the new dominant language comes a new, equally dominant cultural framework, along with strong pressure for its adoption. The rapid and dramatic erosion of this knowledge can be observed throughout the world, as people begin to lose their close links with nature, heralded by the loss of the linguistic tools needed to express and communicate it. In the words of linguist Stephen Wurm, a local language

> will lose a number of its characteristics which are rooted in the traditional culture of its speakers. . . . It no longer reflects the unique traditional and original world-view and culture of its speakers which has been lost, but more that of the culturally more aggressive people who have influenced its speakers.[43]

In describing language decay, linguistic anthropologist Jane Hill has stressed that the processes involved in it are distinct from processes of natural language change.[44] In the latter case, a language may undergo structural reduction at some level, but this is normally compensated by elaboration at some other level (so that overall the language maintains a sort of "steady state"). Instead, language decay consists in the radical, largely uncompensated erosion of both the structural features of a language (from its phonology to its grammar to its lexicon) and the functional domains of language use (ways of speaking, interactional frames, storytelling, and other forms of communication). In other words, language decay consists in a unidirectional loss of both structural and functional complexity. Hill also points out that these phenomena occur not only due to the disruption of normal intergenerational transmission of a given language, but also because of the progressive reduction of the range of contexts available for language use. Therefore, these phenomena are observed not only in younger generations that are learning the language imperfectly, but also in once-fluent adults who are no longer using their language as frequently and in as many different situations as before.

Underlying language and knowledge erosion, in both children and adults, is what Gary Nabhan and Sara St. Antoine have called the "extinction of experience," the radical loss of direct contact and hands-on interaction with the surrounding environment.[45] Among the O'odham of the Sonoran Desert in the southwestern United States, Nabhan and St. Antoine observed disruption of intergenerational transmission in school-age children. None of these children was fluent in O'odham, although they heard it spoken at home; nor did they did go out into the desert as a part of their everyday activities. Most of them were not being exposed to traditional storytelling and other forms of oral tradition in their interactions with their parents, grandparents, and other elders. A majority of them indicated that their main sources of information (and of authoritative knowledge) were school and television. The children were able to give the O'odham names for only one-third of the most common plants and animals found in the local environment—while having no trouble giving the English names for African megafauna seen on television documentaries.

Comparable difficulties in naming commonly occurring plants and animals were found by Jane Hill and Ofelia Zepeda among some of the O'odham elders they tested.[46] A sizable number of speakers over fifty years of age were tested for their ability to name a set of plants and animals commonly occurring in their Sonoran Desert environment (represented by easily identifiable pictures). While some of the elders had no trouble naming all the species (and in fact also volunteered much additional information about them evoked by the pictures), and others were able to name almost all of them (sometimes with some prompting), a third group had great difficulty with the task. Notably, this last group included some of the people with the highest degree of formal education in the sample, who had lived away from the O'odham reservation for long periods of time. These people were still fairly fluent in the language (while being bilingual in English) but due to their extended absence had lost the context of use of the O'odham biosystematic lexicon. Furthermore, English did not provide them with an alternative vehicle for maintaining this knowledge, since even the local variant of English makes far fewer distinctions than the O'odham do among the local flora and fauna. Hill suggests that this loss in biosystematic lexicon may lead to alienation from traditional forms of knowledge. She finds that the latter trend may also be reinforced by the loss of traditional oratory and ritual narrative, both of which have virtually disappeared even among elders. The traditional knowledge that was encoded in these genres of speech becomes lost along with the ability to perform the genres.

The extinction of experience, then, has much to do with processes of acculturation that promote language shift and cultural assimilation. How radical this language and knowledge loss can be even in a domain as basic as that of subsistence is illustrated by linguist Nancy Dorian with an example from an obsolescent language of Europe, Scottish Gaelic, spoken by fisherfolk in the East Sutherland region of Scotland.[47] Dorian has found that formerly fluent or partially fluent Scottish Gaelic speakers who no longer practice fishing or fishing-related activities as their source of subsistence may not only have trouble with impromptu recall of Gaelic names for kinds of fish, kinds of boats, terms for sailing and for fish processing, and even the word for *season*; they may continue to have trouble remembering the words and using them appropriately in context even after being reminded of what the words are. As

Dorian points out, this suggests that not even early intimate familiarity with basic local subsistence lexicon in one's native language necessarily guarantees that lexical items from this domain will later be easily retrieved from memory, once socioeconomic circumstances have driven people away from their traditional mode of subsistence and the local language.

In some cases, external forces responsible for language and knowledge erosion may spark endogenous processes that compound the effects of the external factors. For instance, in her work with the Alune people of the island of Seram, in eastern Indonesia, linguist Margaret Florey has found that loss of the Alune language and knowledge about the environment—due to religious conversion, formal schooling (in Indonesian and Malay), and profound political and economic changes—is accelerated by the reinterpretation of knowledge by younger Alune.[48] Such reinterpretation is occurring for instance in the use of incantations traditionally employed in Alune healing practices in association with the administering of medicinal plants. Use of these incantations and of the related medicinal knowledge and practices in Alune villages has already been suppressed through conversion to Christianity, leading to the abrupt interruption of knowledge transmission. In addition, while some younger Alune are still using incantations, they have reinterpreted their function as a means for self-defense and harming others, have changed their structure, and have begun reciting them in Malay (the local majority language). The joint effect of these processes is radical language and knowledge loss in a domain as vital as that of health care. Younger Alune no longer rely on local medicinal knowledge but resort to (poor quality) Western medical care.

In other cases, the loss of traditional language and culture may be hastened by environmental degradation caused by externally driven socioeconomic changes. Felipe Molina, a tribal scholar from the Yoeme (Yaqui) people of Arizona's Sonoran Desert, has found that the performance of Yoeme ritual is being hampered by the disappearance from the local desert ecosystem of many plant species that were traditionally employed in religious ceremonies.[49] This is due to increasing settlement of the desert by non-Yoeme and to unsound harvesting of many plants or their eradication as the land is being converted to nontraditional uses. Traditional ritual is one of the main contexts for the teaching of the Yoeme Truth and in particular of the intimate spiritual and physical connection with and respect for nature, the wilderness world.

> Yaquis have always believed that a close communication exists among *all* the inhabitants of the Sonoran desert world in which they live: plants, animals, birds, fishes, even rocks and springs. All of these come together as a part of one living community which Yaquis call the *huya ania*, the wilderness world. . . . Yaquis regard song [as a part of ritual] as a special language of this community, a kind of "lingua franca of the intelligent universe."[50]

The elders' inability to perform ritual correctly due to environmental degradation compounds other effects of socioeconomic change (such as schooling in English that induces language shift in children) in precipitating language and knowledge loss. This creates a negative feedback loop that in turn affects the local ecosystem.

In the face of worldwide erosion of indigenous languages and linguistically encoded traditional knowledge about the environment, it becomes essential to gain a systematic understanding of local patterns and processes leading to these phenomena. Ecological anthropologist Stanford Zent has devoted himself to this pursuit in relation to ethnobotanical knowledge loss among the Piaroa indigenous people of Venezuela.[51] Zent's focus is on field methods that make it possible to systematically document and measure knowledge loss and to identify relevant factors. He has measured ethnobotanical knowledge variation among the Piaroa by means of various survey, interview, and statistical techniques that reveal a dramatic decline in knowledge among younger Piaroa individuals, as well as a negative correlation between ethnobotanical knowledge and the social variables of bilingualism and formal schooling. Notably, Zent has also found a correlation between the ability to provide the Piaroa name for a given plant species and the correct identification of the cultural uses of that species. This pinpoints the key role of ethnobotanical nomenclature in anchoring knowledge about the plant and animal species in the local environment. Having a name for a given species does not only signify conceptual recognition of that species; it also allows the retrieval of cultural knowledge about it (as well as other mental operations having to do with the species in question, such as ecological reasoning; see below). Zent's findings clearly indicate that the erosion of native-language taxonomies is directly linked to erosion of local knowledge and again points to the need to maintain the integrity of linguistic systems if knowledge systems are to persist.

While the current magnitude of these phenomena of language and knowledge loss among indigenous groups is evident, documenting them over time is difficult, due to lack of historical records in most cases. Thus, it is interesting to consider a study of diachronic change in folkbotanical terminology in one of the world's dominant languages, English, for which ample documentation exists. This study, carried out by cognitive psychologists Phillip Wolff and Douglas Medin, is based on the on-line version of the *Oxford English Dictionary*, which contains a vast body of citations of words in context from the twelfth century on.[52] The authors set out to test the hypothesis that, with modernization, knowledge of natural kinds has devolved and that this may be due not only to decreasing exposure to the natural world, but also to diminished "cultural support" (the extent to which a society promotes a given domain of knowledge). Focusing on the life-form "tree," Wolff and Medin use as a measure of cultural support the extent to which trees are mentioned in written sources over the history of British English. They also investigate at what level of specificity trees are mentioned: whether the life-form rank (tree), the folk generic rank (spruce, oak), or the specific rank (blue spruce, post oak). Overall, mention of tree terms over time increases until the nineteenth century then drops dramatically in the twentieth. Mention of trees at all three levels of specificity follows a similar pattern. The turning point appears to be the Industrial Revolution, when England's population became increasingly urban and cut off from the natural environment. However, the decline in the twentieth century is less marked for folk generics than the other two ranks. Wolff and Medin speculate that, rather than to the presence of a subset of tree specialists, this lesser decrease in specific terms may be due to the lingering of labels in the language after the knowledge about their referents has eroded, so that these terms may represent "loose categories," decoupled from their actual referents in the world. Loss of the labels may come next—while at the same time, whatever traces of the knowledge may still be indirectly carried in the language may offer hope for its future reacquisition.

Previous research had already identified the tendency for people in industrial societies (apart from specialists) to have limited knowledge of plant and animal species, even those found in the local urban environment, and to tend to refer to species at the level of life-forms (such as "tree" or "bird"). The study by Wolff and Medin confirms these earlier findings but also adds an important historical perspective to them. In turn, it may be useful to further add to this perspective by considering the possible historical circumstances of the loss of folkbiological terminology in English. An investigation of changing attitudes toward nature in England between 1500 and 1800 shows that many of the same factors that currently operate on indigenous and minority languages were at work in stamping out local knowledge in England.[53] As the use of Latin binomials was being promoted by trained biologists, vernacular names for plants and animals were being stigmatized and fell into disuse or increasingly became the limited province of "backward" rural populations. Local agricultural and plant medicinal knowledge was also being ridiculed and neglected. The emergence and imposition of more authoritative linguistic and cultural models leading to a reduction of linguistic and cultural diversity has thus also characterized the internal history of the English language and English society.

Other research shows that what may also be lost in urban populations in industrial countries is the ability for ecological reasoning.[54] In a comparison of reasoning about natural kinds among urban people in the United States and Itzaj Maya Indians from the Petén region of Guatemala, Scott Atran and Douglas Medin found, on the one hand, that these two groups followed essentially the same taxonomic principles in the classification of the local flora and fauna (confirming the universal bases of folkbiological taxonomies). On the other hand, they found both similarities and differences between the two groups in a variety of tasks that implied reasoning about the relationships among natural kinds. In some of these tasks, and particularly in those that required the application of the "principle of diversity,"[55] the Itzaj diverged from U.S. people in that ecological knowledge took over taxonomic knowledge in leading the inferences the Itzaj drew. They "knew too much" about the actual ecological relations among the species in their environment to be willing to apply taxonomic criteria in the abstract. Some of the differences in reasoning observed among the Itzaj compared to U.S. people were also due to the Itzaj applying criteria based on the cultural salience of the species in question (although not necessarily in purely utilitarian terms; e.g., they consider the jaguar as symbolically as well as ecologically salient).

Unfortunately the Itzaj are culturally and linguistically highly at risk. Their language is one of those that linguists would classify as "moribund"—no longer being passed on to younger generations. There are only about fifty fluent speakers of Itzaj Maya left, and none of the children are learning the language; they are monolingual in Spanish. Many of the Itzaj cultural traditions still survive, including their mode of subsistence and ecological knowledge. They also have established their own small biosphere reserve in which to continue their own way of tending to the environment. However, it is a fragile situation being constantly encroached upon from all sides, both from outside and from forces within the same area. Itzaj-speaking adults worry that as their children are not learning Itzaj and not "walking alone in the forest" anymore, traditional knowledge about the environment and human interactions with it will be lost along with the language. Yet, as the Itzaj also undertake efforts to revive their language, there is some hope arising precisely from the links between language and the environment. So far, it appears that the most successful way to awaken Itzaj children's interest in their ancestral language has been through a focus on the plant and animal world.

6. Languages and Ecological Knowledge: Prospects for Persistence and Revitalization

The Itzaj are not alone in their efforts. Scores of indigenous communities around the world are at work to ensure the continued viability of their languages and ways of life, which are threatened by encroachment by majority languages and dominant cultures, or to revitalize ancestral languages and cultural traditions. Commonly, language and culture maintenance and revitalization go hand in hand with the reaffirmation of traditional relationships with the environment, as well as with the struggle for land and resources rights and linguistic, cultural, and other human rights. Indigenous organizations are increasingly making their voices heard at the main fora in which international instruments for the protection of biodiversity and cultural and linguistic diversity are being developed: from the Convention on Biological Diversity (that acknowledged the important role of traditional ecological knowledge and natural resource management practices for biodiversity conservation) to the draft UN Declaration on the Rights of Indigenous Peoples and the draft Universal Declaration of Linguistic Rights, to cite only a few of the main ones. International conservation organizations such as the United

Nations Environment Programme, the International Union for Conservation of Nature and Natural Resources, and the World Wide Fund for Nature have been taking note in the elaboration of their policies and conservation plans. Among professional organizations, the International Society of Ethnobiology, in its Code of Ethics, explicitly affirms the existence of an "inextricable link" between cultural, linguistic, and biological diversity—a link residing in indigenous peoples' knowledge of, and stewardship over, a large part of the world's most diverse ecosystems. Academic and research institutions are beginning to recognize the need for interdisciplinary, integrated work on the diversity of life, in both nature and culture—or biocultural diversity, as it is now being called.

No doubt, it is still an uphill battle against the political and economic forces that lie behind the biocultural diversity crisis—in our times, mainly the forces of globalization—and the sociocultural attitudes and behaviors they induce. Yet these developments, and the growing awareness of the links between language, knowledge, and the environment, offer some hope. Perhaps, deep inside human consciousness lies something akin to what E. O. Wilson has described as "biophilia"—an innate human need for contact with a diversity of life-forms[56]—or what traditional peoples around the world usually conceptualize as an intrinsic spiritual connection between humans and nature. Perhaps, this connection is established and evoked, and can be brought back, by language.

Notes

1. The epigraphs are from Mühlhäusler (1995: 156); a T-shirt of the National First Nations Elders/Language Gathering, M'igmaq Nation; p. 69 of N. Lord, 1996, "Native Tongues," *Sierra* 81(6): 46–69; and p. 279 of W. Davis, 1998, *Shadows in the Sun* (Washington, D.C./Covelo, California: Island Press/Shearwater Books).

2. Sapir (1912: 228, 229, 232). In that article, Sapir argued that language–environment relationships could be found by and large only in the lexicon of a language, to the exclusion of grammar and phonology. More recent work reviewed later in this chapter shows otherwise.

3. See Kroeber (1939).

4. For an extensive overview of this field, see Maffi (in press), based in part on the working conference "Endangered Languages, Endangered Knowledge, Endangered Environments," held in Berkeley, California, October 25–27, 1996.

5. This chapter draws in part from sections of Maffi, Skutnabb-Kangas, and Andrianarivo (1999), as well as the introduction to Maffi (in press).

6. See Harmon (1996, 1998). As with biodiversity, there are various definitions of linguistic diversity. Most commonly, however, the number of different languages spoken on earth is used as a measure of global linguistic diversity. This is parallel to the use of "species richness" (number of different species) as a way of gauging global biodiversity. The estimate most widely accepted by linguists is that there are five thousand to seven thousand oral languages spoken today on the five continents. In recent work,

the diversity of human languages has also been commonly used as the best available proxy for human cultural diversity. There are many instances in which distinctiveness of languages does not correspond to distinctiveness of cultures, or sameness of language to sameness of culture. However, as Harmon (1996: 5) argues, language is the carrier of many cultural differences, and using language as a proxy "affords us the best chance of making a comprehensible division of the world's peoples into constituent cultural groups" and of identifying general trends. A fuller account of biodiversity should take into consideration "interaction biodiversity"—the interactions among species (see: J. N. Thompson, 1996, "Evolutionary Ecology and the Conservation of Biodiversity," *Trends in Ecology and Evolution* 11: 300–3). Likewise, in the case of linguistic diversity, attention should be given to the interactions among languages (part of what is involved in the notion of "linguistic ecologies" described later in this chapter).

7. See R. Dasmann, 1964, *Wildlife Biology* (New York: Wiley).

8. The work of ethnobiologists and ethnoecologists, reviewed later in this chapter, has provided ample documentation of these phenomena.

9. N. B. Tindale, 1974, *Aboriginal Tribes of Australia* (Berkeley: University of California Press), 133.

10. H. Isnard, 1999, "Preface to the First [1976] Edition," in R. J. L. Breton, *Atlas of the Languages and Ethnic Communities of South Asia*, updated edition (London: Sage), 11.

11. Mühlhäusler (1995: 155).

12. See Mühlhäusler (1996).

13. See E. A. Smith, "On the Coevolution of Cultural, Linguistic, and Biological Diversity," in Maffi (in press).

14. See E. A. Smith, "On the Coevolution." Comparable cross-mappings have been done for Central America by M. Chapin (1992, "The Co-existence of Indigenous Peoples and Environments in Central America," *Research and Exploration* 8(2) [map]) and for South America by M. Lizarralde ("Biodiversity and Loss of Indigenous Languages and Knowledge in South America," in Maffi [in press]).

15. See, e.g., G. P. Murdock, 1981, *Atlas of World Cultures* (Pittsburgh, Pa.: University of Pittsburgh Press).

16. But see Kroeber (1939). In that work, Kroeber's approach to the study of culture areas was holistic (i.e., focused on culture wholes rather than cultural traits or complexes), as well as squarely ecological and historical.

17. See D. Nettle, 1996, "Language Diversity in West Africa: An Ecological Approach," *Journal of Anthropological Archaeology* 15: 403–38.

18. See J. H. Hill, 1996, "Languages of the Land: Toward an Anthropological Dialectology." The David Skomp Distinguished Lectures Series in Anthropology. Indiana University, Dept. of Anthropology, 21 March 1996.

19. See K. Milton, "Aspects and Implications of Ecological Diversity in Forest Societies of the Brazilian Amazon," in Maffi (in press).

20. See P. K. Schoonemaker, B. von Hagen, and E. C. Wolf, eds., 1997, *The Rain Forests of Home: Profile of a North American Bioregion* (Covelo, Calif.: Island Press). Also, E. L. Kellogg, ed., 1995, *The Rain Forests of Home: An Atlas of People and Place.* Part 1: *Natural Forests and Native Languages of the Coastal Temperate Rain Forest* (Portland, Ore./Washington, D.C.: Ecotrust/Pacific GIS/Conservation International).

21. GPS = global positioning satellite; GIS = global information system.

22. See Glenn Shepard, Douglas W. Yu, Bruce Nelson, M. Lizarralde, M. Italiano, "Ethnobotanical Ground-Truthing and Forest Diversity in the Western Amazon," in preparation for *Ethnobotany and Conservation of Biocultural Diversity* (L. Maffi and T. Carlson, eds.). To be submitted to the series *Advances in Economic Botany* (Bronx, N.Y.: Botanical Garden Press).

23. Hunn (1996: 4).

24. Hunn (1996: 18).

25. See Hunn (1994).

26. See Basso (1996).

27. See Maffi (1998).

28. See L. Maffi, 1999, "Domesticated Land, Warm and Cold: Linguistic and Historical Evidence on Tzeltal Maya Ethnoecology," in Blount and Gragson (1999), 41–56.

29. See Berlin (1992).

30. One may wish to go back to this chapter's introduction and consider again Sapir's early statements about the limits in the variability of the lexical materials expressing concepts derived from the physical world.

31. See Berlin (1992); also B. Berlin, 1997, "Tapir and Squirrel: Further Nomenclatural Meanderings toward a Universal Sound-Symbolic Bestiary." Paper presented at the twentieth Annual Meeting of the Society of Ethnobiology, University of Georgia, Athens, March 26–29, 1997.

32. See B. Berlin, 1999, "How a Folkbotanical System Can Be Both Natural and Comprehensive: One Maya Indian's View of the Plant World," in Medin and Atran (1999), 71–89. Also B. Stross, 1973, "Acquisition of Botanical Terminology by Tzeltal Children," in M. S. Edmonson, ed., *Meaning in Mayan Languages* (The Hague: Mouton), 107–41.

33. Berlin (1999) points out that it does also happen that the individual finding him/herself in an unfamiliar environment will learn and adopt the names that the locals give the organisms in question.

34. According to Berlin (1992), in ethnobiological taxonomies, the "folk generic" rank includes taxa that are perceptually salient and identifiable without close scrutiny. These taxa may be among the first ones learned by children; they are named by primary lexemes, and their names tend to occur more often in everyday discourse and to be mentioned first in eliciting taxonomies. They appear to constitute the "basic level" of ethnobiological categorization and to correspond closely to biological genera or species.

35. See also B. Berlin, 1999, "Lexical Reflections on the Cultural Importance of Medicinal Plants among Tzotzil and Tzeltal Maya," in Blount and Gragson (1999), 12–23. Here, Berlin observes that cultural consensus concerning the use of given medicinal plants leads to lesser dialectal variation in the naming of these plant species.

36. See Berlin (1992); T. E. Hays, 1982, "Utilitarian/Adaptationist Explanations of Folk Biological Classification: Some Cautionary Notes," *Journal of Ethnobiology* 2: 89–94; E. S. Hunn, 1982, "The Utilitarian Factor in Folkbiological Classification," *American Anthropologist* 84: 830–47.

37. See E. S. Hunn, 1999, "Size as Limiting the Recognition of Biodiversity in Folk-biological Classifications: One of Four Factors Governing the Cultural Recognition of Biological Taxa," in Medin and Atran (1999), 47–69. In light of the special relevance of the size criterion, it is interesting to refer back to Berlin's finding about the widespread sound-symbolic representation of size in ethnozoological nomenclature.

38. See A. Pawley, "Some Problems of Describing Linguistic and Ecological Knowledge," in Maffi (in press).

39. At the same time, this is not to suggest that verbal communication, even in this expanded sense, is all that is involved in conveying human relationships with the environment. A fuller account should also include nonverbal aspects of communication, such as gesture. And, of course, there are aspects of human–environment relationships that do not involve communication at all. The focus here is on those numerous aspects that do.

40. See D. Wilkins, 1993, "Linguistic Evidence in Support of a Holistic Approach to Traditional Ecological Knowledge," in N. M. Williams and G. Baines, ed., *Traditional Ecological Knowledge: Wisdom for Sustainable Development* (Canberra: Centre for Resource and Environmental Studies, Australian National University), 71–93.

41. See N. Lord, "Native Tongues," 46 and 69.

42. J. Wollock, 1997, "How Linguistic Diversity and Biodiversity Are Related," *Terralingua Discussion Paper* #5. Available on the World Wide Web at <http://cougar. ucdavis.edu/nas/terralin/home.html>. See also J. Wollock, "Linguistic Diversity and Biodiversity: Some Implications for the Language Sciences," in Maffi (in press).

43. S. A. Wurm, 1991, "Language Death and Disappearance: Causes and Circumstances," in R. H. Robins and E. M. Uhlenbeck, eds., *Endangered Languages* (Oxford: Berg), 7.

44. See J. H. Hill and O. Zepeda, "Dimensions of Attrition in Language Death," in Maffi (in press).

45. See Nabhan and St. Antoine (1993).

46. See J. H. Hill and O. Zepeda, "Dimensions of Attrition."

47. See N. Dorian, 1997, "Lexical Loss among the Final Speakers of an Obsolescent Language: A Formerly Fluent Speaker and a Semi-Speaker Compared," *Terralingua Discussion Paper* #2. Available on the World Wide Web at <http://cougar.ucdavis. edu/nas/terralin/home.html>.

48. See M. J. Florey and X. Y. Wolff, 1998, "Incantations and Herbal Medicines: Alune Ethnomedical Knowledge in a Context of Change," *Journal of Ethnobiology* 18(1): 39–67. Also M. Florey, "Threats to Indigenous Knowledge: A Case Study from Eastern Indonesia," in Maffi (in press).

49. See F. Molina, "Wa Huya Ania ama vutti yo'oriwa: The Wilderness World Is Respected Greatly: The Yoeme/Yaqui Truth from the Yoeme Communities of the Sonoran Desert," in Maffi (in press).

50. L. Evers and F. S. Molina, 1987, *Maso Bwikam/Yaqui Deer Songs: A Native American Poetry* (Tucson: University of Arizona Press), 18. In this connection, Evers and Molina (1987: 201) refer to K. W. Luckert's description (in his 1975 *The Navajo Hunter Tradition* [Tucson: University of Arizona Press]) of "man's primeval kinship with all creatures of the living world" as "perhaps the most basic [form of human awareness] in the history of man's religious consciousness—at least the oldest still discernible coherent world view."

51. See S. Zent, 1999, "The Quandary of Conserving Ethnoecological Knowledge: A Piaroa Example," in Blount and Gragson (1999), 90–124; S. Zent, "Acculturation and Ethnobotanical Knowledge Loss among the Piaroa of Venezuela: Demonstration of a Quantitative Method for the Empirical Study of TEK Change," in Maffi (in press).

52. See P. Wolff and D. Medin, "Measuring the Evolution and Devolution of Folkbiological Knowledge," in Maffi (in press).

53. See K. Thomas, 1983, *Man and the Natural World: Changing Attitudes in England 1500–1800* (Harmondsworth: Penguin).

54. See S. Atran and D. L. Medin, 1997, "Knowledge and Action: Cultural Models of Nature and Resource Management in Mesoamerica," in M. H. Bazerman, D. M. Messick, A. E. Tenbrunsel, and K. A. Wade-Benzoni, eds., *Environment, Ethics, and Behavior* (San Francisco: New Lexington Press), 171–208.

55. In the psychological study of induction processes, the principle of diversity states that "The more diverse the premises, the stronger the conclusion" (see D. Osherson, E. Smith, O. Wilkie, and E. Shafir, 1990, "Category-based Induction," *Psychological Review* 97: 185–200). According to this principle, it may be expected that a property shared by a mouse and a horse will more likely be attributed to all mammals than a property shared by a mouse and a hamster.

56. See E. O. Wilson, 1984, *Biophilia* (Cambridge, Mass.: Harvard University Press).

References

Basso, K. H. 1996. *Wisdom Sits in Places: Landscape and Language among the Western Apache.* Albuquerque: University of New Mexico Press.

Berlin, B. 1992. *Ethnobiological Classification: Principles of Categorization of Plants and Animals in Traditional Societies.* Princeton, N. J.: Princeton University Press.

Blount, B., and T. Gragson, eds. 1999. *Ethnoecology: Knowledge, Resources and Rights.* Athens, Georgia: Georgia University Press.

Harmon, D. 1996. "Losing Species, Losing Languages: Connections between Biological and Linguistic Diversity." *Southwest Journal of Linguistics* 15: 89–108.

———. 1998. "Sameness and Silence: Language Extinctions and the Dawning of a Biocultural Approach to Diversity. *Global Biodiversity* 8(3): 2–10.

Hunn, E. S. 1994. "Place-names, Population Density, and the Magic Number 500." *Current Anthropology* 35(1): 81–85.

———. 1996. "Columbia Plateau Place-Names: What Can They Teach Us?" *Journal of Linguistic Anthropology* 6(1): 3-26.

Kroeber, A. L. 1939. *Cultural and Natural Areas of Native North America.* Berkeley: University of California Press.

Maffi, L. 1998. "Language: A Resource for Nature." *Nature and Resources: The UNESCO Journal on the Environment and Natural Resources Research* 34(4): 12–21.

———, ed. In press. *On Biocultural Diversity: Linking Language, Knowledge, and the Environment.* Washington, D.C.: Smithsonian Institution Press.

Maffi, L., T. Skutnabb-Kangas, and J. Andrianarivo. 1999. "Linguistic Diversity." In D. Posey, ed., *Cultural and Spiritual Values of Biodiversity,* 21–57. London/Nairobi: Intermediate Technology Publications/UN Environment Programme.

Medin, D. L., and S. Atran, eds. 1999. *Folkbiology.* Cambridge, Mass.: MIT Press.

Mühlhäusler, P. 1995. "The Interdependence of Linguistic and Biological Diversity." In Myers, D., ed., *The Politics of Multiculturalism in the Asia/Pacific,* 154–61. Darwin, Australia: Northern Territory University Press.

———. 1996. *Linguistic Ecology: Language Change and Linguistic Imperialism in the Pacific Rim.* London: Routledge.

Nabhan, G. P., and S. St. Antoine. 1993. "The Loss of Floral and Faunal Story: The Extinction of Experience." In S. R. Kellert and E. O. Wilson, eds., *The Biophilia Hypothesis,* 229–50. Washington, D.C.: Island Press.

Sapir, E. 1912. "Language and Environment." *American Anthropologist* 14: 226–42.

Cognitive Anthropology
and the Environment

Willett Kempton

Since its inception, cognitive anthropology—the subfield of anthropology concerned with human thought—has explored human–environment relations. This chapter reviews what cognitive anthropology and related areas contribute to understanding the relationships between human societies and the environment. "Cognitive anthropology" is defined clearly in a recent and excellent review of the field:

> Cognitive anthropology is the study of the relation between human society and human thought. The cognitive anthropologist studies how people in social groups conceive and think about the objects and events which make up their world—including everything from physical objects like wild plants to abstract events like social justice. (D'Andrade 1995: 1)

This review begins with one of the domains cited by D'Andrade—wild plants—a domain that was central to the development of cognitive anthropology and is also of current import to the anthropology of human–environment relationships.

In indigenous societies, wild plants, and to a lesser extent animals, are extensively named and classified, and a large variety of them are utilized. This review will begin with early studies of indigenous classification of living species, then move to more recent work in ethnopharmacology—the study of traditional medicine utilizing preparations from natural substances (typically, wild plants). In addition to ethnopharmacology's anthropological interest, many "modern" pharmaceuticals directly copy their use from indigenous societies, and ethnopharmacological knowledge continues to be an important source of new medical treatments in state societies. Of course, the transfer of indigenous knowledge to global markets raises concerns about the intellectual property rights of indigenous peoples. I also review studies of indigenous resource management, which has demonstrated that mental constructs, social norms, and ritual practices regulate exploitation of ecosystems to within their sustainable yield—in some societies but not others. More recent research, based on the cognitive concept of "cultural models," has revealed elaborate cultural models of ecosystems, both in state societies and in indigenous societies, and in both cases these models affect behavior toward the environment. Taking a different tack, this review will also cover cognitive anthropological work in state societies, which includes the study of identity and the environmental movement and how support or opposition to environmental policy develops.

In the process of this loosely chronological review of topics, we shall also follow cognitive anthropology from its beginnings as a theoretical perspective focused on classification and naming to its development of more complex theories of cognition, including cultural models, cognition in practice, socially distributed cognition, and identity. A concluding section suggests emerging research questions.

Why Indigenous Societies Are Important for Understanding Human–Environment Relationships

In reviewing cognitive anthropology and the environment, this text will group together one important subset of societies under the rubric *indigenous societies* and distinguish them from state societies. This is not a distinction particularly important in cognitive anthropology, but it is important for understanding human–environment relationships. Here, *indigenous* is used in a specific way—to refer to societies with millennium-scale continuity of culture, place, and resource use. That is, societies that have existed in the same region and interacted in similar ways with the same natural environment for many centuries. As we shall see, under these conditions we find well-developed and sophisticated cognition of the natural world. Given humanity's history and twentieth-century development, contemporary indigenous societies also happen to have additional characteristics—they are small scale, are relatively isolated, and use what might be called "low technology"—but these additional characteristics have little bearing on this discussion. By contrast, no state-level societies meet this definition of indigenous, as—in the current historical epoch—their current interactions with the natural world have only shallow historical depth. Also, since the vast majority of the members of state societies have only limited interactions with the natural world, they provide a contrasting case of degraded environmental cognition.

Cognition in contemporary nation-state societies is of a second interest, beyond being a degraded case of classification of the natural world. This second interest becomes important for anthropologists who move beyond detached research to apply their findings to social activism. At that point a conscientious scholar may ask, for example, How can we reduce the impact of global markets and "development" upon local environments and indigenous peoples? To be effective in states where public opinion matters, the activist or political agent must understand public support for various policies. Thus, this chapter reveals how anthropological findings contrast with beliefs among the lay public in the United States. As we shall see, some anthropological findings have already filtered out to the general public, so that anthropology to date has already affected the possibilities for political changes bearing upon the human–environment relationship.

Folk Classification of Biological Species

Classic "cognitive anthropology" was founded on studies of classification systems, based on two primary examples: biological species and kinship. The first of these two, the study of folkbiological classification and knowledge, or "ethnobiology," we can see now, in retrospect, as having been a pivotal early foray into the study of human–environment relationships.[1]

The justification for ethnobiological research rested on three assumptions. The first assumption was that if a community or language group had extensive systems of terminology for a domain (say, mushrooms or manioc), that domain must be culturally important to them. Second, names and categories used to organize that domain were expected to provide clues about the history and development of that community's classification system and about their uses of the plants or animals. The third assumption was that individual studies of particular cultures, when compared, would ultimately lead to generalizations about panhuman mental processes and the total range of possible types of cultural knowledge.

Early ethnobiological studies quickly demonstrated that indigenous societies have extensive named categories for the plants and animals around them (e.g., Conklin 1954; Berlin, Breedlove, and Raven 1974; Bulmer 1974). For the relativistically trained field-workers of the time, a surprising and carefully confirmed early finding was that the species- and genus-level categories corresponded quite closely to those of Linnean biology. The number of categories was impressive—indigenous languages commonly have 1,000 to 2,000 names for plants and animals, with some of those named categories being subdivisions of others.[2] As human classification systems go, 1,000–2,000 is an extraordinary number. If we accept the first premise above about cultural importance, these large numbers of named categories suggest that biological species are extremely important to indigenous peoples, more important than any other domain.[3]

As one might expect, systems of names and categories are often more extensive when the species or genera have functional utility. It was not expected before detailed studies were done, and it is perhaps of greater interest, that indigenous peoples also categorize and name many species of little or no functional importance or cultural significance. Apparently many of these species are named and subdivided simply because they are attractive or interesting. For a comprehensive review of research and findings on ethnobiological classification, see Berlin (1992).

Branches of the ethnobiological research tradition have more recently shown that residents of industrialized state societies have far fewer terms for biological kinds than do indigenous peoples. This has most frequently been documented in scattered small studies of convenience samples in the United States (Dougherty 1978). It has also been confirmed, with data of much greater time depth, by using the *Oxford English Dictionary* to trace usage from the fourteenth to the twentieth centuries (Wolff and Medin in press). Medin shows clear "devolution" in the use of terms for biological kinds. This devolution occurs over a multicentury period corresponding to massive social transformations and increasing isolation of these cultures from the natural world. Lack of biological categories is not monolithic in state societies. Natural resource-using groups may have extensive classification and nomenclature, at least within specific segments of the living world. For example, not only do fishermen have more extensive classification of fish species than nonfishermen, but also the types of categories and the criteria for classification are different among commercial fishermen, sport fishermen, and nonfishermen (Boster and Johnson 1989). Naturalists, whether professional or amateur (such as bird-watchers), would be other examples. In each case a small subgroup has, for limited domains, a classification system much more developed than that of other members of the same state society.

Folkbiological classification's core insight for understanding culture and the environment has been that social groups in close contact with the natural world—our most impressive examples being indigenous peoples, but also some subgroups in state societies—live in the environment not only in a physical sense. They also carry in their minds elaborate mental apparatus for classifying the natural world, identifying biological kinds, and referring to them linguistically. They apparently have these cognitive and linguistic resources primarily in order to utilize plant and animal resources from the natural world, but also just for observing, enjoying, or commenting upon their environment.

These findings from folkbiology become more important as we examine how this knowledge of the natural world is used by indigenous peoples, both to tap biological resources and to regulate their own human environmental impact. The next two sections give an example of each: the use of plant materials for medicines and the social and cognitive mechanisms that regulate the exploitation of the natural world.

Ethnopharmacology: An Example of
Cultural Knowledge of Natural Resources

All societies use biological materials, as food, fuel, tools, shelter, and many other things. This section concentrates on one area of utilization: medicinal uses of plant materials in indigenous societies. Medicinal uses are interesting both because they involve complex cultural knowledge and because they have had, and will continue to have, great practical value to humanity.

That diverse cultures use biologically derived substances as medicine and as psychoactive ingredients in ritual has been known since long before there was a field called cognitive anthropology. Cognitive anthropologists, working in conjunction with botanists, pharmacologists, and/or physicians, have since examined these systems of disease diagnosis and treatment in detail. Indigenous knowledge in this area can be copious. For example, documenting the diagnosis and treatment of just one group of diseases (gastrointestinal) in a single Maya culture required an entire 577-page volume (Berlin and Berlin 1996).

Ethnobotanical knowledge is increasingly being seen by state societies as having immense practical significance: many "modern" medicines are derived from traditional ethnobotanical and ethnopharmacological knowledge. Specifically, of all drug prescriptions written between 1959 and 1980 in the United States, 25 percent were derived from botanical species, and 74 percent of those (20 percent of all prescriptions) were plants used ethnomedically for the same therapeutic purpose (Farnsworth et al. 1985). In other words, 20 percent of U.S. drug prescriptions directly imitate indigenous medicine—the same drug is used for the same purpose (some directly extracted from plants, others synthesized). Furthermore, ethnopharmacological investigation is now a recognized source of new medicines for state societies—a recent review predicts that wild plants "will continue to serve as the source of the new pharmaceuticals of the future" (Janetos 1997: 16).

Pharmacological researchers (from state societies) search for new medicines, sometimes by seeking the knowledge of members of indigenous societies. Indigenous people's knowledge is valuable to pharmacological researchers in knowing what plants are biologically active; how to prepare the plant materials; and, to a lesser extent, which human diseases they cure. *For the pharmacological field researcher, it is more practical to ask the people who know than to experiment randomly with multiple preparations of many plants against many diseases.* The popular concept of indigenous pharmacological knowledge is that its distribution parallels that of medicine in state societies, that is, the knowledge is held by a specialist, called a shaman, curer, or healer, within the indigenous society. This has also been suggested by the work of some of the botanists and pharmacologists working in these areas, whose field interviewing is primarily with shamans (e.g., Plotkin 1994). But several ethnographic investigations in which interviews were carried out with all members of indigenous communities find that treatments for common physical disorders (that is, those based on observable physical symptoms) are commonly known by most adults; the shaman's additional specialized knowledge is sought only for those disorders presumed to be based on supernatural agents (Schultes and von Reis 1995; Stepp 2000).

In fact, few of the recent ethnopharmacological studies have yet resulted in commercial pharmaceuticals. A contrasting view to the optimistic one is given by Wade Davis (quoted in Christensen 1999): Westerners, "starting with the Spanish conquistadores, quickly picked up the most obviously efficacious and economically valuable medicines, like coca . . . quinine, and . . . curare," leaving little more. Davis feels that in the modern attempt to tap indigenous knowledge, "the rhetoric ran away from reality. . . . [W]e have not found new drugs." So the idea of *new* medicines from the rain forest, although plausible, intriguing, and taken for granted in lay thinking (see below), has not yet been proven. (This lack of results so far must be interpreted in the light of the large time lags, up to twenty years, between when a novel compound is discovered and its appearance as an approved, mass-produced drug.)

There are two ways in which indigenous pharmacology is brought into debates within state societies. One involves the intellectual property rights of indigenous knowledge and the other concerns ethnopharmacological knowledge as a justification for forest protection and cultural survival.

The transfer of ethnopharmacological knowledge raises issues of justice and ethics. One could argue that ethnopharmacological research is free of such questions because knowledge is being disseminated rather than raw materials being taken. The small amount of sample material taken for initial testing is usually compensated, this argument goes, and the few biological substances that prove valuable will be synthesized for mass use, not extracted. Ethnopharmacological research does not necessarily damage traditional societies. It differs from widespread extractive exploitation such as, say, clearcutting the forests or depleting the fisheries that indigenous peoples depend upon. On the contrary, ethnopharmacological field research can demonstrate the value of traditional ways, such as the example of a shaman whose status was restored among his or her people (see, e.g., Cherry and Plotkin 1998).

These arguments of nonharm inadequately address the issue. Principles of patent law, copyright law, and intellectual property law, along with explicit international agreements deriving from the 1992 United National Convention on Environment and Development, oblige some form of compensation to the indigenous source of knowledge. Unfortunately, to date this obligation has been rarely fulfilled in practice (Posey 1996). For an interesting indigenous perspective on these issues, which separates "intellectual contributions" of indigenous peoples from any commercial value, see Fundación Sabiduría Indígenena and Kothari (1997). The contrasting perspective is that it is a very long and expensive road (tens of million of dollars) from an indigenous practice that works in the forest to extracting and proving the biological component and making a synthetic pill that works in a very different cultural context. In fact, the primary commercial firm working exclusively in this area, Shaman Pharmaceuticals, in 1999 abandoned the search for drugs from the rain forest, reorganized with more modest goals and activities, and is now only selling dietary supplements (Christensen 1999). Some participants cite activist calls for compensation and the resulting suspicion by shamans as one factor in the collapse of what was surely the most culturally sensitive firm working in this area (Christensen 1999), leaving only the large pharmaceutical firms. (Others say the daunting cash requirements, or lack of efficacy of the treatments being tested, were sufficient to explain the company's demise.)

The second concept that brings indigenous pharmacological practice into debates in state societies is the medical value of tropical plants as an element in Western ideologies supporting environmental protection. Unfortunately, the public has of yet received only the biological part of this picture, not the anthropological component. In the United States, a survey by Kempton, Boster, and Hartley found that over 80 percent agreed with the statement: "There are probably thousands of medicinal and other useful plants that are unknown to science . . ." (Kempton, Boster, and Hartley 1995: 104). That is, U.S. residents recognize that the plant world is a source of pharmacological resources, and this recognition—touted by environmental groups—may augment voter support for tropical forest protection. However, from interview data from the same study, it appears that voters do not understand that indigenous knowledge is an essential part of the picture. For example, consider this reported informant statement:

> On destruction of the tropical rain forest . . . thousands of plants . . . are unclassified and unknown to man right now that might have possible medical benefits . . . that are undiscovered as of yet. (informant quoted in Kempton, Boster, and Hartley 1995: 105)

Note in the above quotation that these plants are claimed to be "unknown to man" with "undiscovered" medicinal benefits. The popular view supports activism to protect species-rich environments, but not particularly activism to protect traditional cultures. Key elements missing from the popular view are the fact that indigenous people are there in the rain forest (or wherever); they already know which plants are medicinal and how to use them; it is far more efficient to ask them than to randomly pull plants for testing; their ancestors created and maintained that knowledge; they today bear that cultural knowledge and quite possibly maintain the plants as well; and they have some forms of rights to that knowledge.

Going beyond the above-reviewed findings, a research question that seems to me essential is, inexplicably, rarely raised in this literature: How is ethnopharmacological knowledge created by indigenous societies? Could it be by trial and error? Because of the huge number of permutations of plant, preparation method, and disease, and because many plant extractions, including important medicinal ones, are toxic, trial and error seems implausible. Within this research question, a subquestion, to my knowledge unasked to date, is Do members of these societies have an ongoing, if occasional, process of learning new treatments? Or is there an Isaac Newton or Marie Curie who comes along every, say, five hundred years, whose discoveries are carefully preserved by chains of apprentices? If the latter is the process of invention—the occasional great discoverer—it may be lost forever. This is due to the small number of practitioners today and their declining status in their communities. Given the evidence that ethnomedical knowledge is widely shared in indigenous societies, the former case—incremental discoveries—seems more likely. In that case, there is hope for discovering how the process works by long-term studies of surviving ethnopharmacological practice. Such a course of ethnographic research offers the exciting possibility of discovering more about the nature of indigenous basic research science and perhaps gaining a healthy contrasting perspective to our own society's hyperspecialization of knowledge and research.

Cognition That Limits Destruction of Ecosystems

A related set of questions derives from studies of how societies regulate their utilization of ecosystems. This chapter initially defined indigenous societies as those which have passed centuries interacting in similar ways with the same environment. From their multicentury life spans, it follows that such societies could not be destroying the environment they depend upon. In fact, many specific mechanisms for limiting environmental damage have been documented. This research has been carried out by people who would be identified primarily as cultural ecologists and secondarily—if at all—as cognitive anthropologists. For example, Rappaport (1968) showed that religious practice and ritual regulated the slaughter of pigs and the swidden cycle, providing nutrition when needed while maintaining the long-term carrying capacity of the land. Rappaport combined analysis of the ecology, religion, and what he called "cognized models," the latter being the ways in which thought processes led to ecological management. Rappaport's analysis of cognized models employed theoretical constructs similar to those of cognitive anthropology, but he did not explicitly make that link.

As the second of many potential examples, Chernela (1982, 1987) has shown that the Tukano (in the Northwest Amazon) apply their cultural model of clans, vengeful ancestors, and clan "sitting places" to their river fishing activities. As a result of their cultural models and religious prohibitions, fishing and agriculture are restricted in just the areas (e.g., spawning grounds) that must be restricted for sustainable resource management. Again, cognitive structures that might be labeled "religious" are functioning to regulate human activities so as to protect natural resources essential to livelihood.

In a third type of example, it is clear that most indigenous societies effectively manage common property, setting levels of extraction that achieve *sustainable* use. This is well documented by, for example, McCay and Acheson (1987).

The claim that any particular society manages its environment sustainably must be examined empirically and critically. Several cogent critiques illustrate that this finding is often overextended (e.g., Diamond 1986). Technologically primitive peoples have destroyed some local environments, although they may not be "indigenous peoples" in that the cases of environmental destruction often involve a society of recent "in-migrants," or a society causing substantial ecological changes at the dawn of a long period of ecological stability.

The anthropological finding of *sustainable* resource management has already filtered out to popular culture. For example, many of Kempton, Boster, and Hartley's American informants express the idea in terms such as

> the way native peoples have lived . . . you almost always see that they had this great understanding, sort of an intuitive understanding . . . they never took too much and they never wiped out a certain animal that they liked to eat. (informant quoted in Kempton, Boster, and Hartley 1995: 58)

In Kempton, Boster, and Hartley's U.S. sample (1995: 58), three-quarters agreed with a statement that "Indians were completely in balance with their environment . . . and didn't alter it." This cultural model is more specifically about ecological management practices than the related stereotype of Native Americans' ideology or religion as being pro–environmental protection. I suspect, but have not demonstrated, that the savage as environmental manager comes after human–ecological studies were done, postdating the "ecologically correct savage" stereotype.

It is easy to pick at both the factual and conceptual basis of this bit of American folk wisdom, and it may even be appropriate to repudiate it (as Diamond 1986 and Stearman 1994 do) when such romanticism creeps into the writing of scholars. Nevertheless, I suspect that anthropology can take some credit for the public's knowledge that undisturbed indigenous peoples—in most cases—have long-term sustainable environmental management practices. The practical correlate is that anthropological studies of indigenous practice might offer some clues to sustainable management—which environmentally oriented policymakers see as a pressing but elusive goal of today's state societies. (When teaching environmental policy seminars, I myself use one or two human ecology readings to shift the debate from "Is an ecologically sustainable society possible?" to "Okay, that's one way sustainability works; now, how would our society do it?")

As in the case of ethnopharmacology, we can again ask how indigenous societies develop their own ecological knowledge and their practices of ecological management. Careful observation by indigenous thinkers may be plausible and sufficient in some cases, for example, noting that fishing in a spawning area leads to a lower catch later in the season. But for less explicit knowledge that works well in practice, for example, religious prohibitions leading behavior to fit sustainable management, the origins are not so obvious and are more intriguing. Here it seems impractical to conduct research—too much time would be required, in a near-pristine society—but the above suggested study—how ethnopharmacological knowledge is created—might lend some clues.

Conservation Biology, Linguistic Diversity, and Cultural Diversity

Recently, a link has been made between cultural and linguistic diversity and the desire to preserve biological diversity. This development draws on the observation that areas of the world with high biological diversity, such as the Amazon Basin, Mesoamerica, and Papua New Guinea, also tend to have high cultural and linguistic diversity. Several hypotheses have been advanced to explain these connections—some posing biological diversity, others linguistic and cultural diversity, as the causal factor. Some of the scholars entering this new area are motivated by the theoretical and research challenges, others bring more of an activist and preservationist perspective (Maffi 1997; this volume).

The language–knowledge–environment connection is a logical extension of many of the findings reviewed in this chapter, at the same time merging the sometimes-divergent activist goals of cultural survival and biological conservation. This connection, if valid, also reinforces the case for linguistic preservation. In addition to asserting value for each of the three—language, cultural knowledge, and biodiversity—this recent body of literature posits major connections among them, as follows:

1. Indigenous peoples possess extensive knowledge of the biological world, including classification, use knowledge (described above), and ecological knowledge (described below). Significant proportions of both use knowledge and ecological knowledge are not known to Western science and have scientific and/or economic value to state societies.

2. Sociolinguistically, when children stop learning their community's traditional language, indigenous biological knowledge is soon lost. Thus, efforts toward language revitalization (e.g., Bernard 1992; also see work by Leanne Hinton), typically promoted for cultural and community preservation, also result in preserving biological and ecological knowledge. This also means that for practical reasons, a better understanding of the process of language loss becomes important. For example, why is it that some communities maintain their traditional language in the face of extensive contact over centuries (examples of such endurance include Hopi and Zapotec), whereas the language of other communities is lost a generation or two after contact?

3. Biologically rich environments are often occupied by indigenous peoples with sustainable resource use methods. Thus, continuance of those people

and their way of life is less likely to damage those environments; displacement of those peoples or "modernization" of their way of life is more likely to damage those environments.

The above observations and connections have a policy implication. They provide further justification to governments, international organizations, and environmental activists to strive not just for preservation of biologically rich environments, but also to strive for self-determination of the peoples who live in those environments.

Apart from any arguments based on "scientific or economic" value, many would focus on ethical or expressive arguments for cultural and linguistic preservation. I would myself make this argument as follows: Indigenous languages and cultures are valuable in their own right. Diversity of languages and cultures is part of what makes us human. If the whole planet were to become one people, speaking one language, our essential humanity would be diminished.[4] Whether arguing on ethical or functional grounds, the co-occurrence of biological, cultural, and linguistic diversity bolsters the case for preservation and cultural survival.

Cultural Models of the Environment and Traditional Ecological Knowledge

In the past five years or so, a substantial advance has occurred in the alliance of the theoretical development of "cultural models" with a topical interest in ecological relationships. Rather than asking how a culture classifies the natural world, this new approach asks: *What mental constructs does a culture use to understand and predict the ways in which species interact with each other and with human perturbations?* We call these mental constructs "cultural models" (Holland and Quinn 1987). They are *models* because they provide more than a category and name; they connect parts and emulate relationships among them. Furthermore, these models enable prediction and explanation. And they are *cultural* because they are shared and reproduced within a culture. Some of the studies reviewed in this section are ethnographic descriptions of knowledge of specific behavior and interrelationships among species. Going by names such as TEK (traditional ecological knowledge) or TEKMS (traditional ecological knowledge and management systems), these studies (e.g., see Berkes 1999; Johannes 1990) are well grounded in ecological and biological principles (see below) but do not use recent theoretical constructs from cognitive anthropology such as cultural models, which allow higher levels of generalization.

Findings of indigenous knowledge of individual species interactions show that indigenous peoples possess ecological knowledge unknown to Western biology. For example, Gary Nabhan (1996) has identified indigenous knowledge of complex interactions between flora and fauna—such as flowers and pollinators—"that biologists are only now beginning to notice and study."

This knowledge is used by these people to maintain biological diversity in their local environments. In another example, Palauan fishermen described to Johannes the precise spawning aggregations of fifty-five food-fish species on their tiny cluster of islands—they knew of more than twice as many fish species exhibiting lunar spawning periodicity in Palau as the scientific literature had previously described for the entire world (Johannes 1980). "Discovered" now by visitors from state societies, this knowledge is valuable for scientific, resource management, and commercial reasons in developed countries, as well as for environmental impact assessment in the regions where the knowledge was developed.

More recently, cultural models have been shown to apply at a much higher level of generality than specific ecological knowledge of individual species. Despite its importance, this has, to my knowledge, been done in detail for only one society. Atran and Medin (1997) have documented a general indigenous cultural model of ecosystem interactions (also see Medin and Atran 1999). Working in a Lowland Maya group, they used a series of questions—about dependencies and relationships—rather different from prior classification-oriented ethnobiological research. They asked which species "are most necessary for the forest to live" and about dependencies between species. In each case they asked their informants to "justify their answers at every point."

Atran and Medin conclude that the indigenous Maya in the area (as compared with recent Ladino immigrants) have a "more or less sustainable model of the forest." The Maya model is sophisticated and leads to sustainable management of Maya agriculture:

> Thus far, there appear to be four outstanding candidate elements of the Maya model: 1) selecting crucial input (that is, relevant species) jointly on the basis of perceptual (morphology), cultural (function), and ecological (dominance) salience; 2) inferring recycling through the reciprocal interactions between humans, plants, and animals; 3) inferring the substitutability of agents through the image of the forest as the "Maya house"; and 4) performing in accordance with an effective understanding of the forest through milpa practices that emulate and maintain forest biodiversity and the recycling of nutrients. (Atran and Medin 1997: 198)

Atran and Medin contrast their findings for both Maya and Ladinos with the cultural model of Americans found by Kempton et al. (discussed subsequently):

> Indeed, the whole organic metaphor of nature that is current in popular Western thinking about ecology seems to be entirely alien to these people. Ladinos never describe the forest as a living being, consisting of essential parts that are necessarily dependent upon one another, where some parts—or species—are so essential that the whole dies without them (Kempton, Boster, and Hartley 1995). Among Ladinos, there is no view of the environment as being similar to the human body, which consists of integrated parts that vitally depend upon one another.... This is basically true for Maya as well.... (Atran and Medin 1997: 187)

Rather than a body or essentially interdependent parts,

> Instead, the model that both Maya and Ladino informants tend to use when they imagine the forest is more like a house or household. In fact, the Maya cosmos is classically represented as a house (*itzam-naj*, "*itzam*-house"). In this worldview, the parts are vitally linked to one another but not in any essential way. The kitchen and living room may be more important than the storage room or pantry, but you could always sleep in the rafters or cook in the pantry if you had to. Unlike the popular view of ecology current in the US and Europe, neither the Maya nor the Ladinos conception of the environment is something akin to a delicately balanced house of cards. Rather, the Maya and the Ladinos see the forest as naturally robust and recoverable, unless subject to sustained external disruption. In this, their views may be closer to ecological science than North American lay thinking. (Atran and Medin 1997: 188)

Atran and Medin also conclude that Maya ecological knowledge "is not only crucial to Maya reasoning about the natural world but also to behavior with respect to the biological environment." That is, it has an effect on how the Maya manage and sustain their environment. The immigrants to the same area, although sharing much of the ecological model, differ in critical respects that tend to lead them to unsustainable management. Given the practical importance of these findings, it would seem vital to further investigate cultural models of the environment in a wider range of cultures.

The U.S. cultural models referred to by Atran and Medin were discovered by Kempton, Boster, and Hartley (1995) and have subsequently been documented in several European countries. Regarding ecosystem interactions, this cultural model of Western state societies includes the concepts of "chain reactions" and "balance of nature."

> Most of our interviewees had a clear model of interdependencies in nature. They expect that perturbations, like removing or adding a species or changing climate, will cause other significant changes. Many informants refer to these interactions using the term *chain* or *chain reaction*, lay terminology that seems to derive both from the physics terminology for nuclear reactions and from the biological term *food chain*. The term *balance* is also used frequently in this context, presumably referring to a *balance of nature*. (Kempton, Boster, and Hartley 1995: 43–44; italics in original)

Kempton, Boster, and Hartley also find cultural models of human-caused environmental damage. For example, one important cultural model is *pollution*. These cultural models are inferred from analysis of lengthy texts produced in semistructured interviews with a variety of Americans. For example, a resort proprietor in Maine produced the following in response to a general question about the environment (the question did not mention pollution):

> Now they're polluting the air by burning the garbage. And they say that they have equipment that prevents the air from being polluted as a result of the garbage

being burned. On the other hand, the people say that their cars are losing their paint in the immediate area of the incinerator and that the paint is peeling off the houses, and I suspect that in due course, several years down the road, they will discover that the incidence of cancer around the incinerator, which fortunately is located some distance from us here, is on the upswing. (informant statement, quoted in Kempton, Boster, and Hartley 1995: 64)

This type of text is used to infer cultural models. No link between peeling paint and cancer can be directly observed; the link is presumably through a cultural model. Kempton et al. concluded from statements such as the above, along with other similar interview data, that a common American pollution model includes the following elements:

1. Pollution consists of artificial chemicals, not natural substances.
2. These chemicals are toxic to humans and other life, although health effects may not be observed until much later.
3. Sources of these artificial chemicals are predominately industrial and automotive.
4. Pollution is fixed by installing additional filtering equipment.

This partial list of elements of this pollution model may seem unsurprising or even obvious to Western readers who share it. It is of relevance to current policy debates because, as Kempton, Boster, and Hartley illustrate in detail, every element of it is misleading for understanding certain new environmental problems such as global climate change (1995:136–53). Furthermore, some elements of the cultural model seem to have been deliberately exploited in the United States to mislead voters about possible policies to respond to climate change (1995: 152–53). The lesson is that while cultural models can greatly facilitate understanding and reasoning, they can also impede understanding and can be exploited to mislead.

I will digress briefly for an important methodological point. Research on traditional ecological knowledge cannot be done without either collaboration with biologists and ecologists or the unusual combination of an anthropologically trained field researcher who also has extensive knowledge of those other areas. This is especially true of specific species interactions, but is also true of studies of general cultural models of ecosystems (the Kempton, Boster, and Hartley analysis was completely rewritten after review by several ecologists). There are several reasons for this:

Biologically unsophisticated [ethnographic] researchers are not well equipped to determine what portions of the information they obtain are new, important, already well-known or implausible. Nor can they frame the appropriate questions to pursue promising biological leads opened up by the local expert. Some older anthropological writings are loaded with tantalizing bits of information on traditional ecological knowledge which were not explored further. This is because the researcher was untrained in the appropriate environmental subjects and therefore unaware of the potential significance of such information. Opportunities to record very large quantities of valuable traditional ecological knowledge have been lost irretrievably for this reason. (Johannes 1993; this quotation from draft pages 5–6)

This methodological point, the essential need for multiple disciplines of knowledge being applied in the field, is also essential to the prior discussions of ethnobiology and ethnopharmacology. The argument cuts both ways, of course. Ecologists, pharmacologists, or plant taxonomists are not equipped to even elicit traditional knowledge in the native language, much less think about how it fits into culture and practice, the social distribution of this knowledge, why it may function despite its form being different from Western science, or how indigenous societies develop this knowledge.

Environmental Groups, Identity, and Shared Cultural Models

Moving cognitive anthropology from the individual level to the group level is, on the one hand, at the cutting edge of cognitive anthropology and, on the other hand, embarrassingly long overdue. Interesting studies of cognition in social groups include Hutchins's (1995) evidence for cognition distributed across individuals on a ship and Holland and Eisenhart's (1990) work on college women's socialization into the world of romance. Following the topical focus of this review, here I am concerned with group cognition only if related to environmental issues. Two approaches are reviewed here: Douglas's "cultural theory" and identity in the environmental movement.

The "cultural theory" approach derives from Mary Douglas, subsequently developed by Michael Thompson (Schwartz and Thompson 1990), Steve Rayner (1994), and others. This approach posits that environmental groups (and other groups) exhibit three kinds of solidarity—market or individual, egalitarian, and hierarchical—and that this is true cross-culturally. Each of these types of social solidarity is reinforced by a particular view of nature: the "cornucopian," which sees nature as stable and robust in the face of perturbations; the "catastrophic," which posits that small human changes in nature can cause ecological collapse; and the "manageable," which expects nature can recover from small changes, but that large ones may be destabilizing (see illustrative figures in Schwartz and Thompson 1990).

These alternative views of nature are not derived directly from data and derive from theory that is only shallowly cognitive at best. Nevertheless, their acceptance in several literatures indicates that these alternative views at least have face validity in delimiting the views of nature held by different groups in Western society.

The cornucopian view, an environment safe from serious human perturbation, is described by Rayner as follows:

> The market kind of solidarity is supported by a view of nature as *cornucopian* (Cotgrove 1982), a flexible resource providing endless inputs for human . . . growth, creativity and consumption. This view of nature can be represented by the icon of a ball in a cup. If the ball is perturbed, it tends to return to its original position. (Rayner 1994: 68)

The second view of nature is catastrophic:

> egalitarian solidarities tend to promote *catastrophic* conceptualizations of nature. . . . The appropriate icon here is a ball balanced precariously on an upturned cup, where any perturbation would result in an irretrievable loss of system stability. The notion that nature is extremely fragile adds urgency. . . . (Rayner 1994: 69)

The third view, consistent with hierarchical solidarity, is that nature is stable within limits, although those limits may not be totally predictable in advance. Limited human perturbation is safe, but too much can trigger catastrophic change. This view also justifies the need for technocratic managers, needed to predict just how much perturbation is safe.

This set of "views" has some intuitive appeal for explaining differences among various peoples' and groups' views of nature. However, it is essentially a classification scheme for sorting and naming aspects of groups and individuals. It is not like most of the previously reviewed areas, in which methods of investigation are productive of new observations about cultural groups and their views of nature.

A different approach to environmental groups, the basis of current work by Holland and myself (Holland and Kempton 1996), treats identity as a central concept in group formation and motivation for action. This perspective advances the concept of "identity" as a key link between collective cultural forms and individual action. That is, individuals form identities in the context of social movements, and these identities mediate changes in individual behavior.

As one crude index that identity has become important in the environmental movement, almost three-quarters of adult Americans have identified themselves in Gallup polls as "environmentalists," suggesting that environmentalism has become linked to personal identity (see Kempton, Boster, and Hartley 1995: 4–5). Can such identities affect behavior? Our research focuses on the dynamics of the movement—the struggle of pro- and anti-environmental groups—and how individuals elaborate their environmental concerns and translate them into action in and against this movement. Through participant observation in contrasting groups, semistructured interviewing, and personal involvement narratives, we are examining development of an individual's identity as an "environmentalist," different types of environmental identity, concepts of environmental action, and the social and cognitive processes through which such identities lead to changes in individual behavior. Our initial findings are that, as a result of environmental group membership and action, individuals go through a set of reformations of themselves and that members' own identities, reformulations, and environmental actions vary significantly across groups (Kitchell et al. 2000).

Potential Anthropological Research Areas of Environmental Consequence

This review has suggested several critical research areas of theoretical interest and practical importance. Three are outlined in this section.

The Atran and Medin (1997) findings of Maya ecological models, especially when contrasted with the Kempton, Boster, and Hartley (1995) findings from Western state societies, call our attention to the possibility of vastly different models of the environment across cultures. Both studies provide evidence that these cultural models affect behavior—whether managing milpas or supporting national environmental policy. Therefore, it would seem of theoretical interest and of great practical importance to study and better understand cultural models of the environment in a larger set of societies, especially the fast-disappearing indigenous societies still practicing traditional ecological management.

Second, as noted earlier, regions with high linguistic and cultural diversity are typically also biologically rich, with high biodiversity and many endemic species. Indigenous ecological knowledge is valuable for several reasons: It is used to manage the local environment sustainably, it represents biological knowledge in some cases unknown to Western science, it points toward medicinal plants of pharmacological value, and—as a perishable aspect of the human experience—it is priceless and its loss would be tragic. Preserving some of these languages and the cultural integrity would be easier if we better understood the processes and forces that encourage or impede the transfer of indigenous knowledge within societies.

At Maffi's conference on this biological, linguistic, and cultural diversity, two indigenous activists described their struggles to preserve their language and indigenous knowledge. They spoke poignantly of their efforts to stop the loss, efforts underfunded but often strongly supported by their communities (e.g., Majnep with Pawley in press). Yet to my ear, most of the efforts were a rearguard defense—tape recording the knowledge of their elders, starting a one-month summer school to teach this knowledge, publishing a book of ethnobotanical wisdom. All proceeded without any systematic way to understand or affect the central processes, namely, Why do children focus on the national language to the exclusion of their ancestors' tongue? On the teacher from the city to the exclusion of their elders' wisdom? On the new pharmacist (who indiscriminately passes out antibiotics for everything from the flu to TB) to the exclusion of the shaman who can diagnose and treat several score problems in the local area?[5] And why do their parents believe they should strive to withhold speaking the language at home, in the name of furthering their children's economic success? These are the processes to which well-conceived research could bring missing tools to indigenous activists who desperately need them. (To be clear, I mean that learning how to facilitate or restore the transfer of indigenous knowledge is necessary research but not by itself a sufficient social program. Other needs include developing writers in the language and political action to support native people's resistance against encroachment on their land, culture, and local resources.)

A third research area for cognitive anthropology follows from the second one. To an appalling degree, we do not have a clue as to how indigenous knowledge of the environment is produced. Trial and error could be an explanation for how indigenous people find the most flexible saplings for bows or find which rocks break into the best points. And the classification and naming of plants and animals is already reasonably well understood (reviewed in Berlin 1992). But how is more complex indigenous knowledge developed? Two areas seem interesting and important—*ethnopharmacological knowledge* and *sustainable environmental management.*

The problem of how ethnopharmacological knowledge develops is perplexing. How, among thousands of named plants and dozens of preparation methods, could indigenous societies have developed the knowledge of which ones, prepared in which ways, should be used to treat specific diseases?[6] We don't even know the rudiments of an answer. For example, is there a low level of continuous knowledge development? Or does an occasional innovator appear, say after centuries of pharmacological stasis, whose knowledge is carefully maintained by subsequent generations? Is the process based more on experimentation or theory (where the symbols of the theory might seem to Westerners more like religion or cosmology than pharmacology), or both? As indigenous societies disappear and shamans are locally stigmatized, this process is disappearing from the earth—and we will be left never knowing.

In the case of indigenous environmental management, the questions are similar. How do societies come to develop sustainable practices? Some scholars have cited social evolution—societies that did not husband their resources had to change or die. I personally do not find such a coarse mechanism plausible when we look at such systems in detail; there are too many cases of people going out of their way to preserve ecosystem elements that could not be easily inferred to be important. Furthermore, those indigenous people produce explanations seemingly unrelated to modern biology but which effectively guide management sustainably (see the Atran and Medin examples above, or Chernela 1987). How did these beliefs, myths, religious practices, and other regulatory mechanisms come into being?

Conclusion

Cognitive anthropology has been, since its origins in ethnobiology, an anthropological subfield important to what might now be called "environmental anthropology." The average indigenous forest dweller can distinguish and name thousands of biological kinds—this fact should still command respect, even if it were the only remarkable thing about indigenous environmental knowledge. It is not. The past decades have seen increasing studies documenting indigenous knowledge of biologically active plants and their medicinal uses, an explicit recognition that current Western pharmacology owes indigenous practice a great debt, a more systematic attempt to learn more from indigenous healers, and a necessary attendant debate on how to do so ethically. Most indigenous societies also practice effective common-property resource management, an existence proof of the contemporarily expressed, but seemingly elusive, goal of sustainable environmental management. In the past few years, two studies—one of Americans and one of Lowland Maya—have revealed elaborate cultural models of ecological relationships and suggest that these cultural models affect environmental behavior in both the city and the rain forest.

After centuries of denigrating, exploiting, and wantonly destroying indigenous societies, these societies now seem to offer important elements of what is sought by state-level societies, at least in the environmental arena. Ironically, their value is being recognized just as the triple threat of global markets, global culture, and ecological destruction seem to limit these societies' remaining lifetimes to a few decades at most. The importance of their knowledge is recognized only in the area of pharmacology. More important in my view, most truly indigenous societies have extensive environmental knowledge shared widely by their members, unbelievably efficient use of resources (by Western standards, see Kempton n.d.), and the ability to manage their environment on a long-term, *sustainable* basis. One can hope that a few anthropologists will be motivated to marshal the resources to better understand this diverse wisdom and practice soon. We might find some guidance toward making state societies more environmentally sustainable. And, more difficult, we might learn a little more that could help stay the extinction of the last flickering candles of true cultural diversity.

Acknowledgments

A preliminary draft of this chapter was presented in the session "Human Dimensions of Environmental Change: Anthropology Engages the Issues," organized by Carole Crumley, at the Annual Meeting of the American Anthropological Association, San Francisco, November 20–24, 1996. I am grateful to several members of the panel and of the audience for suggestions that have improved this paper. Tom Carlson of Shaman Pharmaceuticals (now Shaman Botanicals.com) helped with the discussion of the reliance of "modern" medicine on ethnobotany. The paper has been improved by the ideas and criticisms of Brent Berlin, Carole Crumley, John Rick Stepp, Jennifer Collier of AltaMira, and several anonymous reviewers, none of whom are responsible for errors herein.

Notes

1. Ethnobiology can be divided into ethnobotany and ethnozoology, the study of the cultural knowledge of plants and of animals, respectively. Classification of plants by indigenous societies has always been found to be more extensive, presumably because of the greater number of plants and their greater total biomass. Correspondingly, ethnobotanical studies predominate in the literature.

2. For example, Hanunóo have 1,800 specific plant names (Conklin 1954), the Ndambu have over 1,000 plant names (Hayes 1974), and the Aguaruna have 563 generic names and 296 specific names within some of those generics (Berlin 1976).

3. How can the reader get a perspective on 1,000 to 2,000 names for types of plants and animals? To benchmark this number against a domain that may be more familiar to many readers, Holland and Eisenhart (1990) found that American college students possessed about two hundred named categories for members of the opposite sex. If we may use the count of named categories as a very crude measure of cultural importance, that would mean that categorizing and talking about biological species is something like five times as important to indigenous peoples as categorizing and talking about the opposite sex is to American college students. Now that's impressive!

4. I have constructed this argument after hearing various comments made at a conference on endangered languages, cultures, and environments (Maffi 1997), and I'm not sure what proportion of it—if any—is original. The reader should be advised that it is a statement of my own values; unlike most of this chapter it is not a finding that can be derived from the literature and anthropological findings presented here.

5. As one clue to how one might slow the loss, one of the effects of having Western pharmaceutical "prospectors" work with a shaman is that local youngsters for the first time realize that there is some value to that knowledge. The local shaman is elevated in status in their eyes and for the first time becomes interested in learning what he or she knows themselves (personal communication, Thomas Carlson, director of Ethnobiomedial Field Research, Shaman Pharmaceuticals; one case is also documented in Cherry and Plotkin 1998).

6. The question of how ethnopharmacological knowledge developed is similar in form to the earlier question of why most indigenous diets are nutritionally well balanced. However, in the case of diet a cultural explanation has been less compelling subsequent to the observation that both animals and human infants by themselves pick balanced diets (given a diversity of foods available, and in the absence of refined sugar). This finding suggests a biological basis in the senses of taste and smell. No such biological explanation seems possible to explain ethnopharmacology or indigenous resource management.

References

Atran, Scott, and Douglas Medin. 1997. "Knowledge and Action: Cultural Models of Nature and Resource Management in Mesoamerica." In Max H. Bazerman, David Messick, Ann Tenbrunsel, and Kimberly Wade-Benzoni, eds., *Environment, Ethics, and Behavior: The Psychology of Environmental Valuation and Degradation*. San Francisco: New Lexington Press.

Berkes, Fikret. 1999. *Sacred Ecology: Traditional Ecological Knowledge*. Philadelphia: Taylor and Francis.

Berlin, Brent. 1976. "The Concept of Rank in Ethnobiological Classification." *American Ethnologist* 3: 381–99.

———. 1992. *Ethnobiological Classification: Principles of Categorization of Plants and Animals in Traditional Societies*. Princeton, N.J.: Princeton University Press.

———, Dennis E. Breedlove, and Peter H. Raven. 1974. *Principles of Tzeltal Plant Classification: An Introduction to the Botanical Ethnography of a Mayan-Speaking Community of Highland Chiapas*. New York: Academic.

Berlin, Elois Ann, and Brent Berlin. 1996. *Medical Ethnobiology of the Highland Maya of Chiapas, Mexico: The Gastrointestinal Diseases*. Princeton, N.J.: Princeton University Press.

Bernard, H. Russel. 1992. "Preserving Language Diversity." *Human Organization* 51(1): 82–89.

Boster, James, and Jeffrey C. Johnson. 1989. "Form or Function? A Comparison of Expert and Novice Judgments of Similarity among Fish." *American Anthropologist* 91(4): 866–89.

Bulmer, Ralph. 1974. "Folk Biology in the New Guinea Highlands." *Social Science Information* 13: 9–28.

Chernela, Janet M. 1982. "Indigenous Forest and Fish Management in the Uaupes Basin of Brazil." *Cultural Survival Quarterly* 6(2): 17–18.

———. 1987. "Endangered Ideologies: Tukano Fishing Taboos." *Cultural Survival Quarterly* 11(2): 50–52.

Cherry, Lynne, and Mark Plotkin. 1998. *The Shaman's Apprentice*. San Diego: Harcourt Brace.

Christensen, Jon. 1999. "A Romance with a Rain Forest and Its Elusive Miracles." *New York Times*, 20 Nov 1999, p. D3.

Conklin, Harold C. 1954. "The Relation of Hanunóo Culture to the Plant World." Ph.D. dissertation, Yale University.

D'Andrade, Roy. 1995. *The Development of Cognitive Anthropology*. Cambridge: Cambridge University Press.

———, and Claudia Strauss. 1992. *Human Motives and Cultural Models*. New York: Cambridge University Press.

Diamond, Jared M. 1986. "The Environmentalist Myth." *Nature* 324 (6 November): 19–20.

Dougherty, Janet. 1978. "Salience and Relativity in Classification." *American Ethnologist* 5(1): 66–79.

Farnsworth, Norman R., Olayiwola Akerele, Audrey S. Bingel, Diaja D. Soejarto, and Zhengang Guo. 1985. "Medicinal Plants in Therapy." *Bulletin of the World Health Organization* 63(6): 965–81.

Fundación Sabiduría Indígena, and Brij Kothari. 1997. "Rights to the Benefits of Research: Compensating Indigenous Peoples for Their Intellectual Contribution." *Human Organization* 6(2): 127–37.

Hayes, A. Terrence. 1974. *Mauna: Explorations in Ndumba Ethnobotany*. Ann Arbor, Mich.: University Microfilms International.

Holland, Dorothy C., and Margaret A. Eisenhart. 1990. *Educated in Romance: Women, Achievement, and College Culture*. Chicago: University of Chicago Press.

———, and Willett Kempton. 1996. "Identities and Worlds of Environmental Action." Paper presented at Society for Applied Anthropology annual meetings, Baltimore, 29 March.

Holland, Dorothy C., and Naomi Quinn. 1987. *Cultural Models in Language and Thought*. London: Cambridge University Press.

Hutchins, Edwin. 1995. *Cognition in the Wild.* Cambridge, Mass.: MIT Press.

Janetos, Anthony C. 1997. "Do We Still Need Nature? The Importance of Biological Diversity." *Consequences: The Nature and Implications of Environmental Change* 3(1): 17–26.

Johanes, J. E. 1980. "Using Knowledge of the Reproductive Behavior of Reef and Lagoon Fishes to Improve Yields." In J. Bardach, J. Magnuson, R. May, and J. Reinhart, eds., *Fish Behavior and Fisheries Management (Capture and Culture).* Manila: ICLARM.

Johannes, Robert E. 1993. "Integrating Traditional Ecological Knowledge and Management with Concepts and Cases." Ottawa: International Program on Traditional Ecological Knowledge and International Development Research Centre.

———, ed. 1990. *Contribution of Traditional Knowledge to Environmental Science.* International Union for the Conservation of Nature and Natural Resources, IUCN Conservation Science Series No 1.

Kempton, Willet. n.d. "A Cross-cultural Perspective on Consumption and the Environment." (Manuscript available from the author.)

———, James S. Boster, and Jennifer Hartley. 1995. *Environmental Values in American Culture.* Cambridge, Mass: MIT Press.

Kitchell, Anne, Willet Kempton, Dorothy Holland, and Danielle Tesch. 2000. "Identities and Actions within Environmental Groups." *Human Ecology Review* 7(2).

Levinson, Bradley A., Douglas E. Foley, Dorothy C. Holland, eds. 1996. *The Cultural Production of the Educated Person: Critical Ethnographies of Schooling and Local Practice.* Albany: State University of New York Press.

McCay, Bonnie J., and James M. Acheson, eds. 1987. *The Question of the Commons: The Culture and Ecology of Communal Resources.* Tucson: University of Arizona Press.

Maffi, Luisa. 1997. "Language, Knowledge, and the Environment: Threats to the World's Biocultural Diversity." *Anthropology Newsletter* 38(2): 11 (Feb 1997). [Describing a conference in Berkeley, Calif., 25–27 Oct 1996.]

———, ed. In press. *Language, Knowledge, and the Environment: The Interdependence of Biological and Cultural Diversity.* Washington, D.C.: Smithsonian Institution Press.

Majnep, Saem, with Andrew Pawley. In press. "On the Value of Ecological Knowledge to the Kalam of Papua New Guinea: An Insider's View." In Luisa Maffi, ed., *Language, Knowledge, and the Environment: The Interdependence of Biological and Cultural Diversity* (Washington, D.C.: Smithsonian Institution Press), chapter 20.

Medin, Douglas L., and Scott Atran. 1999. *Folkbiology.* Cambridge, Mass.: MIT Press.

Nabhan, Gary. 1996. "Indigenous Knowledge and Management of Plant/Animal Interactions in Aridoamerica." Paper presented at Endangered Languages, Endangered Knowledge, Endangered Environments Conference, organized by Luisa Maffi. Berkeley, Calif., 25–27 Oct 1996.

Plotkin, Mark J. 1994. *Tales of a Shaman's Apprentice: An Ethnobotanist Searches for New Medicines in the Amazon Rain Forest.* New York: Penguin.

Posey, Darrell A. 1996. "Protecting Indigenous Peoples' Rights to Biodiversity." *Environment* 38(8): 7–9, 37–45.

Rappaport, Roy A. 1968. *Pigs for the Ancestors: Ritual in the Ecology of a New Guinea People.* New Haven, Conn.: Yale University Press.

Rayner, Steve. 1994. "A Conceptual Map of Human Values for Climate Change Decision-making." Paper presented at the IPCC Working Group III Workshop on Equity and Social Considerations Related to Climate Change. Nairobi, Kenya, July 1994.

Schultes, R. E. 1994. "Amazonian Ethnobotany and the Search for New Drugs." *Ethnobotany and the Search for New Drugs* 185: 106–12.

———, and S. von Reis, eds. 1995. *Ethnobotany: Evolution of a Discipline.* Portland, Ore.: Timber Press.

Schwartz, M., and Michael Thompson. 1990. *Divided We Stand: Redefining Politics, Technology and Social Choice.* New York: Harvester.

Stearman, A. M. 1994. "Only Slaves Climb Trees—Revisiting the Myth of the Ecologically Noble Savage in Amazonia." *Human Nature—An Interdisciplinary Biosocial Perspective* 5(4): 339–57.

Stepp, John R. 2000. "Highland Maya Medical Ethnobotany in Ecological Perspective." Ph.D. dissertation, University of Georgia, Athens.

Wolff, Phillip, and Douglas L. Medin. In press. "Measuring the Evolution and Devolution of Folkbiological Knowledge." In Luisa Maffi, ed., *Language, Knowledge, and the Environment: The Interdependence of Biological and Cultural Diversity* (Washington, D.C.: Smithsonian Institution Press), chapter 12.

Archaeology and Environmental Changes

Donald L. Hardesty and Don D. Fowler

In this chapter we explore how archaeology may contribute to "concepts and principles applicable to contemporary environmental issues" (Crumley 1996: 1). We see the practice of archaeology as a holistic continuum, hence we ignore subcategories such as "prehistoric," "historic," or "classical" archaeology. Archaeological interpretation for certain world areas and periods may be document-aided; that is, readable written documents may be available, ranging from Sumerian cuneiform tablets to Egyptian papyrus scrolls; to Maya glyphs and Aztec codices; to newspapers, personal letters, and diaries. Other areas or periods are sans documents; that is, no documents exist, or they cannot presently be read, as for example those of the ancient Indus civilization.

We address two topics. First, we discuss environmental archaeology as previously practiced and note its limitations. Second, we propose an expansion of environmental archaeology well beyond its current common boundaries, urging that it should be centrally concerned both with writing "landscape histories," or "ecohistories," at various scales and time depths, and investigating past environmental meanings, insofar as they may be recoverable.

The relevance of archaeology to an understanding of contemporary environmental (and other) issues is perhaps best expressed by Carver's (1991: 1–2) discussion of the relationships between past and present:

> A few moments' reflection . . . will suggest that ignoring the past is not an acceptable way of examining the present, nor is ignorance of history a recipe for contemporary bliss. The present is not a succession of fresh moments into which we can insert our views and actions as we like. Rather it is merely the past as far

as it has yet proceeded. Thus the question of what the present is—what is the case at this particular moment—is really a historical question and not separable from a narrative of past ideas and events. Research into the past is not a way of explaining how we got to the present we are in. . . . Rather, there is no knowledge of the present that is not constructed from ideas that were generated in the past. Moreover, they were not generated strictly in one's own past but were acquired or adopted through the kinds of communication that characterize our social life. . . . It follows from this that any examination of present problems is itself an examination of past ideas and events. Or rather, because the present is constantly precipitating out of those ideas and events, any examination of the present is essentially a reexamination of those ideas and events from the past that we take the present to be.

If we accept Carver's view that the present is a precipitate of past ideas and events, then environmental archaeology, concerned as it is with the totality of the human past on a worldwide scale, should certainly be able to contribute to "concepts and principles applicable to contemporary environmental issues."

Archaeology and Archaeological Method

Archaeology is concerned with the things, relations, processes, and meanings of past sociocultural/environmental totalities and their temporal and spatial boundaries, organization, operation, and changes over time and across the world. The central methodological question in archaeology is "How do you get from the distributions of artifacts, ecofacts [plant and animal remains], and geofacts [soils, sediments, minerals], and their relationships on and in the ground, to valid statements about past human behavior within specific theoretical frameworks?" (Fowler 1996: 70). The nature of the archaeological record imposes certain limits. As the late David Clarke (1979: 100) once put it, archaeology is "the discipline with the theory and practice for the recovery of unobservable hominid behavior patterns from indirect traces in bad samples." Or, put another way, "archaeologists never get to play with a full deck" (Catherine Fowler, personal communication).

One consequence of the partial deck problem is that archaeological inferences are always uncertain to some degree, and the uncertainty increases as one recedes farther and farther into "deep time." Archaeologists must often rely on analogies drawn from history and ethnography and then make inferences from those analogies. As an example: "The people of Tribe Z were observed using tools shaped thusly to do certain tasks; similarly shaped tools found archaeologically likely were used for the 'same' or analogous tasks by their makers." How far back in time such analogies may be extended is discussed later.

Archaeology and Environment

Archaeologists have long been concerned to understand human–environment interactions. Most contemporary archaeological understandings of these interactions have their roots in Julian Steward's (1955) concept of "cultural ecology." Prior to the 1940s, biologists defined "ecology" in terms of physical, biochemical, and behavioral interactions within the natural world, or subsets of it. They saw the realm of human culture as somehow outside, separate from, or irrelevant to the processes going on within the natural world. Steward pointed out that humans and their culturally determined behaviors interact continually and in complex ways with the "natural world"; indeed, the two cannot be separated. Once humans enter a region, it is no longer a pristine natural world. The "natural world" is a cultural construct and does not exist absent of human definition of it.

The key question in cultural ecology is "How has each group of humans lived on a particular landscape, or in a particular environment, at a particular past time?" More specifically, what plant and animal resources were there, and how did people gather, grow, hunt, or herd them to get their groceries? What other material resources, stone, metals, and fibers were available, and how were they used? More generally, how did "the environment" affect human activities, and how did humans affect the environment? By the 1950s, questions framed this way were being asked by archaeologists working in Africa, Europe, the Near East, and Mesoamerica (e.g., Butzer 1971, 1976; J. D. Clark 1960).

Steward's (1955) cultural ecology concept also provided a methodological framework for testing his theory of multilinear evolution, which predicts that human populations adapt to similar environments in much the same ways. Therefore, he thought, the evolutionary trajectories of human populations living in similar environments will converge over time. Steward focused on *adaptation*, which he defined as the "dialectical" interplay between "culture core" and environment. A culture core consists of those features "most closely related to subsistence activities and economic arrangements" (Steward 1955: 37). He thought that particular cultural practices originated in processes of environmental adaptation and that similar practices would reoccur in similar environments. An example is irrigation agriculture in arid and semiarid environments. Steward also held that ideology and meaning were not involved in human–environment interactions; such "epi-phenomena" were explainable only by history. Steward's approach set a programmatic agenda for archaeologists: first, reconstruct the modes of production of past human populations and the environments in which they lived; second, analyze the interplay between the two; third, identify those features whose origins can be explained by adaptation.

Systems Models and Archaeology

By the late 1930s, some scientists and engineers in various fields, such as ecology, operations research, electronic communications, advanced military technologies, and statistics, were thinking in "systems" terms. "Systems" thinking ultimately derives from what is called the "*organismic analogy.*" That is, the world (or subsets of it) is seen as analogous to an organism. An organism has anatomy and physiology or, more generally, structure and functions. The parts and processes of an organism in toto can be seen as a "system" or can be analyzed as operating like a system. Human societies may be seen as being analogous to an organism, with various institutions (structure) and social interactions (functions) making up a "social system."

By the late 1930s, ecologists had adopted the organismic analogy and were thinking of the natural world, or subsets of it, as dynamic biochemical and biophysical systems. By the 1940s, engineers were thinking about telecommunications, computers, weapons, and assembly lines as dynamic systems of human–machine interactions and information processing. By the 1950s, some scientists and engineers began trying to generalize—to move toward a *general theory of systems.* Physical, chemical, biochemical, ecological, social, and sociotechnic phenomena, such as information processing machines, and other human–machine interactions were all seen as "organized systems." The Society for General Systems Research was founded in 1954–55 to investigate commonalities in the structure, function, and evolution of such organized systems.

By the mid-1960s, some archaeologists and anthropologists had adopted a "systems viewpoint" and were exploring the applications of "systems models" to problems of human–environment relationships. Rather than defining human–environment interactions as simple cause and effect linear relationships, as Steward had done, systems models analyzed the relationships in terms of "complexity," "feedback loops," "self-regulation mechanisms," "equilibrium processes," and "deviation amplifying processes" (Trigger 1971).

Archaeologists redefined "*environment*" as sets of ecological processes, including human activities, interacting within nested "systems." They used this framework to explain such things as the origins of food production. Kent Flannery (1968), for example, developed an "opportunistic" ecosystems model that explored how humans' interaction with plants ultimately led to food production in Mesoamerica. He assumed that early hunter-gatherers, or foragers, depended upon a few abundant and reliable plants and animals for food and fiber. These resources, which included the wild progenitor of maize, occurred in a variety of microenvironments and at times of the year that structured the foragers' annual subsistence round. Long-term and gradual genetic changes in ancestral maize increased its productivity and led to its greater use as food. This eventually created scheduling conflicts for people that forced them to drop some of the other subsistence resources from their diet. Such systemic interactions ultimately led to the evolution of Mesoamerican farming, according to Flannery. Here *ecological processes* were seen as centrally operative in human–environment interaction.

The dictionary defines "*process*" as "a continuing development involving many changes" (*Webster's* 1960: 1161). A major aim of science is to seek out and understand the general processes—the operating rules, the "software," if you will—that drive continuing development and change in the universe. Social scientists, including archaeologists, have long sought to define general processes that make humans behave as they do by assuming that such processes are qualitatively "the same as" processes operative in the natural world. Ecosystem modeling in archaeology is one processual approach to understanding human–environment interactions.

Archaeologists have also sought other general processes to explain human–environment interactions. One approach, usually called evolutionary ecology, continues to see environmental adaptation as the primary cause of cultural change but recognizes that individual decision-making factors enter into the process. Robert Kelly (1995) provides a general overview of this approach, which has focused principally on hunter-gatherers. A basic assumption is that such folk, past and present, tend to forage "optimally." That is, they make decisions about where and what foodstuffs to forage, for that will provide them with the greatest number of calories for the least amount of effort. Ideally, they gain more calories than they expend in searching and collecting. A good example is E. A. Smith's (1991) study of the foraging strategies of the Inujjaumiut people in the Arctic. But, whether this behavior is somehow process-driven or is a matter of cultural preference and human agency (see below) remains to be demonstrated both ethnographically and archaeologically. A similar approach uses Darwinian selection processes to explain how adaptive changes take place (Teltser 1995), but the issues of cultural preferences and human agency remain here as well.

Another set of approaches focuses on social processes rather than environmental adaptation to explain cultural change. For example, Barbara Bender (1978) discusses social interactions (rather than cultural–environmental interactions) that may have caused the transition from hunter-gatherers to farmers. McGuire (1992) uses a Marxist perspective that considers the social dynamics of modes of production as the prime mover of cultural change. The so-called "world systems" paradigm sees the cause of change in the social relations of economic exchange (Falk 1991; Orser 1996; Sanderson 1995; Wallerstein 1976–89). In these processual approaches, environment became an "epi-phenomenon" rather than a cause of culture change. Finally, there is the recent application of concepts of risk assessment and management coupled with the investigation of past sociopolitical complexity. So far, these studies are principally programmatic, and their utility to environmental archaeology remains to be developed.

Thus, between the 1950s and the 1990s, viewing culture as a "means of adaptation" to environment led to the development of various materialist, functionalist, processual, and systemic ways of thinking about human–environment interactions. But other archaeologists found fault with these approaches and reintroduced the concept of "*agency*" into archaeology. "Agency" is defined as "1. action, power; 2. means, instrumentality" (*Webster* 1960: 27). In anthropological parlance, agency rejects or holds in abeyance the idea that human actions are somehow caused only by unconscious forces or processes inherent in the universe, society, or cultural–environmental interaction. Rather, humans make conscious goal-based decisions and act upon them. For example, Elizabeth Brumfiel (1992) cogently argues against the use of the processual ecosystem approach. She objects to the idea that human cultures are merely "adaptive systems." In her view, cultures are "behavioral systems," which are "the composite outcomes of negotiation between positioned social agents pursuing their goals under both ecological and social constraints." She further objects to the use of whole populations as the analytical unit in ecological studies, arguing that such usage "obscure[s] the visibility of gender, class, and faction in the prehistoric past."

Others had earlier moved away from materialistic explanations of social and cultural change to more cognitive or ideational approaches that focus on how human groups transform nature into culture. James Deetz (1977) used a "structuralist" approach derived from the work of the French anthropologist Claude Lévi-Strauss to interpret major chronological changes in the architecture, foodways, and mortuary art of seventeenth- and eighteenth-century New England. Mark Leone (1984) emphasized the symbolic and ideological "meaning" of landscapes within a cultural context, for example the formal gardens in colonial Annapolis, Maryland (see below). It is apparent from our rapid and incomplete historical review that fashions in archaeological orientations and pursuits have changed rapidly over the past three decades (Fowler 1993; Yoffee and Sherratt 1993). During the same time, philosophers of science also came to understand that empirical data are not "given," but "theory-laden," that is, "collected and interpreted in the light of some theoretical framework or other" (Hesse 1992: 107). This recognition is built into our definition of archaeological method stated earlier: "How do you get from . . . to . . . within a specific theoretical framework?"

Environmental Archaeology and Landscape History

Previous environmental archaeology approaches typically ignored history in explanations of human–environment interaction. During the same period of time, other environmental sciences, such as biological ecology, also took an ahistorical approach to the explanation of diversity and change in the natural world. But the 1980s and 1990s brought a new recognition of the importance of history in explaining both the natural and human worlds. Stephen Pyne's (1995) *World Fire: The Culture of Fire on Earth,* for example, uses history to explain how fire affects the development of macroscale continental and regional biomes. Carole Crumley (1994) and others turned their attention to the use of historical analogs in interpreting the archaeological record of human–environment interactions. We believe that an expanded environmental archaeology should take a similar historical approach.

In our view, environmental archaeology is first and foremost a historical discipline, both historical science and humanistic history. As historical science, archaeology should seek, document, and account for apparent regularities (both of historical "events" and "processes") in interactions between humans and their environments. Questions include: What are the ongoing interactive relationships between humans and their environments over time? Are any of those relationships "determinate," or merely "influential" or "conditional"? As humanistic history, archaeology is concerned with environmental meanings and their historical contexts. What did environments mean to past peoples, and how did those meanings influence *decisions* they made about using and changing those environments?

An expanded environmental archaeology thus has two tasks. First, to write landscape histories, or ecohistories (we use the terms interchangeably), at various scales and from various perspectives. That is, to search landscapes for historical evidence of how they were created and changed by both human activity and natural processes and the synergistic interactions between them. The second task is to seek out the "meanings" beneath the decisions of individual actors involved in human–environment interplay. Such an archaeology derives from Carole Crumley's (1994: 5–6) approach to landscapes and human activities thereon. She defines *landscape* as "the material manifestation of the relation between humans and the environment" and *historical ecology* or *landscape history* as "the study of past ecosystems by charting the change in landscapes over time." She also notes that in such studies,

> the operant relationship between humans and the environment is assumed to be dialectically interactive. . . . Reliable and widely available evidence for the historical interrelatedness of humans and the environment may be read in the *landscape.* . . . By inference, *changing human attitudes* toward the environment may also be identified and their effects studied . . . it is, after all, *decisions—both conscious and unconscious*—and their effects that impact human lives and livelihood and change the face of the earth. (Crumley 1994: 6, emphasis added)

With the foregoing section as background, we turn first to landscape histories, or ecohistories, and then to problems of meaning.

Writing Ecohistories

Landscape histories, or ecohistories, may be either coarse-grained or fine-grained. Coarse-grained ecohistories are those covering relatively long time periods and fairly large geographical scales, such as regions. Ecohistories of major civilizations are also, necessarily, coarse-grained. Environmental archaeologists and others who study past environments have long paid close attention to climatic changes and how those changes impact landscapes and the peoples living on them. A century and more of intensive archaeological and paleoenvironmental research has produced ecohistories of varying degrees of "graininess" for all the ancient "primary" civilizations of Egypt, Mesopotamia, the Indus Valley, China, Mesoamerica, and Highland South America. Each ecohistory is a record of complex interactions between climatic change and environmental changes wrought both by climate and human activities on the land; each provides a background to the waxing and waning of the various civilizations. For example, the Sumerian, Akkadian, and subsequent civilizations in the Tigris and Euphrates River Basin in present-day Syria, Iraq, and western Iran and the Indus, or Harappan, civilization in the Indus River Basin in present-day Pakistan and western India were all negatively impacted by deforestation, overgrazing, and salinity built up from long-term irrigation. These problems, coupled with climatic changes, radically altered the landscapes in both regions. The ecohistories of both regions reflect a general trend of environmental degradation over several millennia.

In other regions, ranging from semiarid to temperate to tropical, long-term climatic cycles produced ecological changes that impacted cultures in both positive and negative ways. For example, in the North American Southwest, climatic changes, coupled with cycles of erosion and aggradation, directly influenced the distribution of people across the landscape. Periods of drought were accompanied by erosion of arable lands and abandonment of marginal areas. Wetter climates were accompanied by aggradation, and populations expanded back into marginal areas (Cameron 1995; Cordell 1997). On a broader scale, Karl Butzer (1996) summarizes archaeological studies of farming in the Mediterranean region and in Mesoamerica to document parallel long-term trends such as periods of climatic instability coupled with ecological damage, which directly impact farming practices and population distributions. Butzer's study complements another study by Joel Gunn (1994), who documents the responses of human groups to climatic fluctuations over the past two millennia in two regions: western Europe and the Maya lowlands. He correlates alternative periods of global cooling and warming with the appearance and disappearance of empires in the two regions. Interestingly, the correlation is reversed: Maya empires flourished when those in western Europe declined, and vice versa.

Fine-grained Ecohistories

Fine-grained ecohistories are documented at microscales, for example, ecological life histories of individuals, co-residential households, or communities. Fine-grained ecohistories often document human–environment interactions resulting from specific events such as volcanic eruptions, floods, fires, or the introduction of exotic biota. One example is the variable responses of prehistoric farmers in the American Southwest to the volcanic eruption of Sunset Crater beginning in 1064 C.E. (Sullivan and Downum 1991). The eruption, which initially caused crop failures, drove some people out of the region, but others remained and coped with the event by taking advantage of social alliances and storage facilities. Later, the ash-rich soil made possible an increase in crop production.

Archaeological Ecobiography

Fine-grained ecohistories also may be *actor-based*, following Brumfiel's (1992) argument that individuals, not whole populations, make decisions that affect ecological interactions. Her point is well-taken. We should make every effort to write archaeological ecobiographies, or life histories of individuals or other decision-making units such as co-residential households, where possible. Tracing the behavioral trajectories of humans seeking to accomplish goals through a historical context of ecological and social constraints and opportunities should be an important part of documenting fine-grained archaeological ecohistories. Writing archaeological ecobiographies necessarily involves the integration of documentary biographical data, oral histories, and archaeological remains of households. In some cases in the American West, for example, it is possible to track the archaeological record of specific individuals as they move from one place to another (Brooks 1995; King 1993). More frequently it is possible to follow the trajectory of changes in the organization of specific co-residential households, for example, Ruth Tringham's (1991) excellent life history studies of Neolithic households in central Europe.

"Nested Patches" in Landscape Histories

Ecohistories may include patterns and processes of human–environment interaction that are discernible at quite different geographical and chronological scales. Often, they may be thought of as being "nested" in a fashion analogous to the "nesting" of ecosystems within ecosystems (O'Neill et al. 1986). Thus, some human–environment interactions take place at the scale of localities, others at a regional scale, and yet others at a global scale. For example, the Comstock mining district in and around Virginia City, Nevada (Hardesty 1995), is a mining landscape on a local scale. However, the industrialized Comstock Lode served as a control center for a regional network made up of

several localized clusters of people and economic activities, such as ore processing mills along the Carson River, forests in and around the Lake Tahoe
basin and on the Virginia Mountains for mine timbers and charcoal for
process heat, and farms and ranches in adjacent valleys to provide food and
draft animals. These localized clusters were separated from the Comstock
mines and from each other by several miles. Together, they can be conceptualized as individual ecogeographical "patches," each with a distinct ecohistory
yet nested within a regional ecosystem linked together by Comstock industrial
mining. At the same time, the Comstock was very much part of a macro economic and political network or world system that operated on a global scale.
Each "patch," and the interactions of the related patches within the larger
whole, were the outcomes of hundreds and thousands of individual decisions
made by hundreds of people in the Comstock region and in distant places,
such as San Francisco, New York, and London.

Environmental Archaeology of the Modern World

The archaeological record is a particularly strong document of environmental
change taking place over the past five hundred years, a period of time that historians refer to as the "modern world" (Wallerstein 1976–89). Landscapes of
the modern world reflect dramatically changed ecological relationships,
scales, physical and sociohistorical structures, and boundaries. Alfred Crosby's
(1986) magisterial *Ecological Imperialism: The Biological Expansion of Europe,
900–1900* documents how European plants, animals, and diseases radically altered ecologies and often devastated or destroyed animal and human populations in Africa and Australasia and throughout the Pacific Ocean over the past
millennium. Patrick Kirch's (1992) archaeological and documentary study of
environmental change in the Anahulu Valley on the Hawaiian island of O'ahu
is an excellent case study of Crosby's thesis. Kirch describes two episodes of
major ecological change in the valley. The first began in the third century C.E.
with the introduction of irrigation taro farming and husbandry of pigs and
dogs by seafaring Polynesian colonizers. This rapidly transformed the pristine
forest into a "mosaic of gardens and second-growth vegetation." Captain
James Cook's arrival in Hawaii in 1778 signaled the beginning of a second
episode of rapid ecological change. The exotic "portmanteau biota" (Crosby
1986: 89–90), the plants, animals, and diseases introduced by the Europeans
who followed Cook to Hawaii, had transformed the valley into a modern
world landscape by the late nineteenth century. Kirch's study of the Anahulu
Valley landscape clearly shows why unique historical events must be considered in the interpretation of local environmental change. But even more important is his conclusion that the ecohistory of this localized landscape cannot be understood without taking into account the global scale of historical
events in the modern world.

Another example of the usefulness of the archaeological record in documenting modern world ecological change comes from Deagan's (1996) discussions of the environmental archaeology of American colonization. She reaches several interesting conclusions. First, traditional European foodways did not change along ethnic and national lines, as might be expected. Rather, foodways changed as people adapted to local environments, especially by increasing the use of those domestic animals most suitable for local habitat conditions. Second, the foodways of the indigenous people of the Americas, such as those in the missions and villages of Spanish-colonial Florida, changed very little as a result of European influence. Third, African American slaves actively combined plants and animals from America, Europe, and Africa to create a new and distinctive food complex.

The evolution of modern world landscapes also involves the processes of urbanization and industrialization. Archaeological ecohistories of urban places document the interactions of city dwellers with their environments. For example, the studies of New England's urban landscapes conducted by Steven Mrozowski, Mary Beaudry (1986, 1988), and their colleagues found that the earliest city landscapes included urban household gardens used for food production. The later growth and development of cities, however, resulted in the movement of domestic residences to the suburban fringe, with formal yards replacing household gardens and the abandonment of gardens entirely in the city center.

Environmental archaeology also is a significant source of information about ecological change brought about by industrialization within a world systems context. A fine-grained example is Eugene Hattori and Marna Thompson's (1987) study of pinyon-juniper woodlands in the Cortez mining district of central Nevada between 1863 and the early twentieth century. The woodlands were used for building materials and household fuel and converted to charcoal for process heat in the smelters. Conventional wisdom, folk history, and photographs of areas immediately around the Cortez mills held that the pinyon-juniper woodland had been clear-cut for a radius of about 60 miles. However, Hattori and Thompson conducted an intensive dendrochronology study, using living trees, stumps, and a wide variety of wooden artifacts and structural elements. They developed an absolute chronology of woodland use and demonstrated that the area was never clear-cut, that about 10 percent of still-living trees survived from the period of heavy deforestation, and that the woodland rather rapidly reestablished itself after 1897 when fuel and milled lumber began to be imported.

Another example is the work of Ronald Reno (1996), who conducted an intensive study of the charcoal burning industry in central Nevada. The charcoal was used for process heat in the smelters of Eureka, Nevada, from 1869 to about 1900. Almost all the charcoal was produced by *carbonari*, Italian immigrant men. The charcoal industry had a major impact on the ecology of the region. Reno documented the ecohistory of the region before, during, and after the period of smelting using charcoal. He demonstrated that such re-gional ecohistory must be understood within broader contexts of industrial archaeology, mining history, ethnicity and migration patterns, and ultimately world capitalism.

The Problems of Meanings

We turn now to problems of meanings. We use the plural because of the broad range of archaeological phenomena involved and the equally broad range of problems raised by attempts to "recover" meanings. In document-aided ar-chaeological situations, recovery of meaning at all levels of scale, from cityscapes to backyards, is an integral part of interpretation.

Ideology plays a prominent role in creating religious, social, and political contexts and assigning meanings to them. Ideologies serve the political pur-poses of social groups or individuals to legitimize power and authority and/or rationalize inequalities among classes or other social groups. They also define the relationships between humans and the supernatural, or transcendent, as those are understood in any particular culture. The uses of monumental ar-chitecture and urban landscapes as expressions of religious and/or political ideology and power have been understood since the first cities were built. The pyramids and temples of ancient Egypt; the ziggurats and their surrounding plazas in ancient Mesopotamia; the great "sacred cities" of Southeast Asia (e.g., Angkor Wat); the massive temple complexes of the Maya and the great "city of the gods," Teotihuacán in Mexico; the Vatican complex in Rome; the Mall and adjacent Federal Triangle in Washington, D.C., are well-known examples.

But much smaller scale historic landscapes, for example gardens or indi-vidual streetscapes, may reflect ideologies as well. Mark Leone (1984: 26), in his study of eighteenth-century gardens in colonial Annapolis, observes that

> Ideology takes social relations and makes them appear to be resident in nature or history, which makes them apparently inevitable. So that the way space is divided and described, including the way architecture, alignments, and street plans are made to abide by astronomical rules, or the way gardens, paths, rows of trees, and vistas make a part of the earth's surface appear to be trained and under the man-agement of individuals or classes with certainability or learning, is ideology.

Other microscale examples include mining landscapes in the nineteenth- and early twentieth-century American West. Stone cairns and other markers of mining claims represent not only miners' knowledge of where ore bodies should occur but also legal concepts in mining law. The geographical distri-bution of settlements, buildings, and structures on mining landscapes reflects some combination of "ideal" concepts of settlement and community and "real" determinants, such as topography, water availability, transportation routes, and mine locations. Thus, miners coming from the eastern United States typically carried with them cultural concepts of settlements laid out in a grid pattern. Miners coming from China carried the cultural concept of feng shui as the key determinant of settlement pattern. Both sets of idealized concepts resulted in a wide variety of actual settlement patterns on mining landscapes.

Ideology, Meaning, and Sans Document Archaeology

The issue of whether searches for what might be called "*paleo-meanings*" is an appropriate archaeological activity in sans documents situations was a matter of intense debate over a number of years between processual and "post-processual" archaeologists. The current (2000) consensus seems to be that it is an appropriate activity, but difficult of achievement. There presently are several "interpretive" archaeologies, each with its own theoretical framework within which archaeologists attempt to "get from artifacts, ecofacts," and other sources to what she or he regards as valid statements about human behavior, including paleo-meaning (Preucel and Hodder 1996).

Having declared that an expanded environmental archaeology should search for meanings associated with past landscapes, we are faced with the question of how to go about it. Gallay (1986: 197–200, 281) "has argued that no way can be found to demonstrate an isometric relation between our ideas about the past and ideas that were actually held in the past"—except through document-aided archaeology—and "that the relationship between material culture and its symbolic meaning may be essentially arbitrary" (Trigger 1989: 351). Butzer (1990: 95–102) makes the same point, noting that without documents he would not have understood human–environment interactions in Pharaonic Egypt nor in Medieval Spain in any but the most general terms—and, indeed, would have misinterpreted much of his data:

> Without contemporaneous written records, and working with configurations well removed from the ethnographic "present," archaeologists can only postulate how economic structures functioned, and they have little prospect of grasping the values and goals of a society by whatever leap of ethnographically-based optimism. (Butzer 1990: 95)

Some of the new interpretive archaeologists are more sanguine, asserting that extracting paleo-meanings from sans document archaeological records is indeed possible (Hodder et al. 1995; Tilley 1994). But there are formidable methodological, epistemological, semiotic, and analogical obstacles (Hesse 1992). It would seem difficult enough to extract paleo-meanings relating to social forms or even technologies from the archaeological record. To seek the meanings of historical landscapes adds another level of difficulty. Can we understand what and how historical landscapes meant to those who created and used them except in the most general way? Yes, perhaps, through ethnographic analogy and careful historic or ethnohistoric retrodiction for "late" periods—some few decades prior to the advent of written documents. But, as the recession toward "deep time" increases, the possibility seemingly diminishes, perhaps exponentially.

Risk Assessment and "Paleo-Decisions"

Among the by-products of the Cold War were "think tanks," such as the RAND Corporation, devoted to formalizing and "objectifying" an age-old human activity: assessing risk. By the 1970s, risk assessment had moved beyond war room game theory and insurance company actuarial tables to more general social sciences applications.

This brings us to "paleo-attitudes" and "paleo-decisions" as subsets of paleo-meanings. According to Crumley (1994), human attitudes toward the environment can be determined through inference, permitting the study of their effects. The conscious (and unconscious) decisions that are made affect human lives and, ultimately, the earth itself. Most such attitudes and decisions toward environments and landscapes involved risk assessments of various sorts. Whether or not such attitudes and decisions can be extracted from sans document archaeological records remains to be demonstrated, but should be attempted. In most instances, for example in the pre-Spanish American Southwest, inferences about changing human attitudes toward risk are based on ethnographic analogy, backed by the extremely fine-grained archaeological and paleoenvironmental records (in some cases, year by year) available for portions of the region. In other contexts and further back in time, Gallay's and Butzer's warnings should be heeded, but innovative ways to get at paleo-meanings should continue to be sought, presented, and evaluated.

An Expanded Environmental Archaeology

Fact making (data production) in archaeology, as in all other fields of scholarship, is a sociocultural process. Facts, and hypotheses to account for them, are sociocultural constructs, or "situated knowledges," to use Donna Haraway's (1991) term. Data and hypotheses emerge from careful investigation and ongoing evaluation and debate. Data and hypotheses are, indeed, theory-laden, but they provide the only means archaeologists and other researchers have to seek answers to questions of general importance.

The various environmental sciences, such as climatology, ecology, hydrology, geology, and epidemiology, have made great strides in redefining and understanding the processes and regularities that form the "environments," the historical landscapes, upon which humans exist and with which they interact (Blumler 1996: 25–39; Soones 1999). Environmental archaeologists build upon these data and understandings in their search for the physical and biological factors relating to culture change. We suggest that environmental archaeology as a field of study should also be concerned with questions of human agency and meaning, thus combining historical science and humanistic history.

That environmental archaeology can make such a contribution is more than a pious hope; it already does so. For example, at the Center for Environmental Studies at Arizona State University in Tempe, environmental archaeology provides needed time depth to a great variety of studies of contemporary environmental problems in the American West and other world areas. A book by the center's founding director, Charles Redman (1999), *Human Impacts on Ancient Environments*, provides examples of how archaeological data may be used in contemporary environmental analyses and management of current ecosystems.

Many current ecological projects in the United States aim to "restore" environments to some "pristine" level assumed to have existed before Euroamerican settlement. But Native Americans actively modified their ecosystems and environments by fire, farming practices, and other means for at least twelve thousand years before the arrival of Euroamericans. As Shepard Krech (1999: 122) says:

> By the time Europeans arrived, North America was a manipulated continent. Indians had long since altered the landscape by burning or clearing woodland for farming and fuel. Despite European images of an untouched Eden, this nature was cultural not virgin, anthropogenic not primeval.

Archaeological research has verified that the environments of North America were the direct result, over a period of many centuries, of the processes Krech describes. For example, the mixed grasslands and woodlands characteristic of the prairies of the central United States are the result of environmental manipulation over many centuries, and not the "pristine" environment the early Euroamericans thought they were entering.

The key point is that environmental archaeologists and their partners, paleoenvironmental specialists, can provide sophisticated pictures of past landscapes through time and describe the natural processes and human actions that created them. Knowing those historical dynamics hopefully will help environmental managers and planners better understand the consequences of their decisions when they set out to "develop" areas by radically modifying them or "returning" them to some imagined past ecology. The benefits can only be positive.

References

Beaudry, M. C. 1986. "The Archaeology of Historical Land Use in Massachusetts." *Historical Archaeology* 20(2): 38–46.

———, ed. 1988. *Documentary Archaeology in the New World*. Cambridge: Cambridge University Press.

Bender, Barbara. 1978. "Gatherer-Hunter to Farmer: A Social Perspective." *World Archaeology* 10: 204–22.

Blumler, M. A. 1996. "Ecology, Evolutionary Theory and Agricultural Origins." In D. R. Harris, ed., *The Origins and Spread of Agriculture and Pastoralism in Eurasia*, 25–50. Washington, D.C.: Smithsonian Institution Press.

Brooks, A. 1995. "Anticipating Mobility: How Cognitive Processes Influenced the Historic Mining Landscape in White Pine, Nevada and the Black Hills of South Dakota." Ph.D. dissertation, University of Nevada, Reno.

Brumfiel, E. 1992. "Distinguished Lecture in Archaeology: Breaking and Entering the Ecosystem—Gender, Class, and Faction Steal the Show." *American Anthropologist* 94(3): 551–68.

Butzer, K. W. 1971. *Environment and Archaeology: An Ecological Approach to Prehistory.* 2nd ed. Chicago: Aldine-Atherton.

———. 1976. *Early Hydraulic Civilization in Egypt: A Study in Cultural Ecology.* Chicago: University of Chicago Press.

———. 1990. "A Human Ecosystem Framework for Archaeology." In E. F. Moran, ed., *The Ecosystem Approach in Anthropology: From Concept to Practice*, 91–130. Ann Arbor: University of Michigan Press.

———. 1996. "Ecology in the Long View: Settlement Histories, Agrosystemic Strategies, and Ecological Performance." *Journal of Field Archaeology* 23(2): 141–51.

Cameron, Catherine M., ed. 1995. *Special Issue: Migration and the Movement of Southwestern Peoples. Journal of Anthropological Archaeology* 14(2).

Carver, T. 1991. "Reading Marx: Life and Works." In T. Carver, ed., *The Cambridge Companion to Marx*, 2–25. Cambridge: Cambridge University Press.

Clark, J. D. 1960. "Human Ecology during the Pleistocene and Later Times in Africa South of the Sahara." *Current Anthropology* 1: 307–24.

Clarke, D. L. 1979. *Analytical Archaeologist: Collected Papers of David L. Clarke.* Edited by his colleagues. New York: Academic.

Cordell, L. 1997. *Archaeology of the Southwest.* Orlando, Fla.: Academic.

Crosby, A. W. 1986. *Ecological Imperialism: The Biological Expansion of Europe, 900–1900.* Cambridge: Cambridge University Press.

Crumley, C. L. 1994. "Historical Ecology: A Multidimensional Ecological Orientation." In C. L. Crumley, ed., *Historical Ecology: Cultural Knowledge and Changing Landscapes*, 1–16. Santa Fe, N.Mex.: School of American Research Press.

———. 1996. Abstract: Anthropology and Environment Symposium. AAA Annual Meeting, San Francisco.

———, ed. 1994. *Historical Ecology: Cultural Knowledge and Changing Landscapes.* Santa Fe, N.Mex.: School of American Research Press.

Deagan, K. A. 1996. "Environmental Archaeology and Historical Archaeology." In E. J. Reitz, L. A. Newsom, and S. J. Scudder, eds., *Case Studies in Environmental Archaeology*, 359–76. New York: Plenum.

Deetz, J. 1977. *In Small Things Forgotten: The Archaeology of Early American Life.* Garden City, N.Y.: Anchor Press/Doubleday.

Falk, L., ed. 1991. *Historical Archaeology in Global Perspective.* Washington, D.C.: Smithsonian Institution Press.

Flannery, K. V. 1968. "Archaeological Systems Theory and Early Mesoamerica." In B. J. Meggers, *Anthropological Archaeology in the Americas*, 67–87. Washington, D.C.: Anthropological Society of Washington.

Fowler, D. D. 1987. "Uses of the Past: Archaeology in the Service of the State." *American Antiquity* 52(2): 229–48.

———. 1993. "Hermes Trismegustus in Eden: Praxis, Process and Postmodern Archaeology." *Society for California Archaeology Proceedings* 6: 1–14.

———. 1996. "Digging Museums: An Appreciation." *Museum Anthropology* 19(3): 69–71.

Gallay, A. 1986. *L'Archéologie demain.* Paris: Belfond.

Gunn, J. D. 1994. "Global Climate and Regional Biocultural Diversity." In C. L. Crumley, ed., *Historical Ecology: Cultural Knowledge and Changing Landscapes,* 67–97. Santa Fe, N. Mex.: School of American Research Press.

Haraway, D. J. 1991. *Simians, Cyborgs, and Women: The Reinvention of Nature.* New York: Routledge.

Hardesty, D. L. 1977. *Ecological Anthropology.* New York: Wiley.

———. 1995. "The Cultural Resources Legacy of Mining." Paper presented at the 1995 Annual Conference of the American Society for Environmental History, Las Vegas, Nev.

Hattori, E. M., and M. Thompson. 1987. "Using Dendrochronology for Historical Reconstruction in the Cortez Mining District, North Central Nevada." *Historical Archaeology* 21(2): 60–73.

Heider, K. G. 1972. "Environment, Subsistence and Society." *Annual Review of Anthropology* 1: 207–26.

Hesse, M. 1992. "Archaeology and the Science of the Concrete." In T. Shay and J. Clottes, eds., *The Limitations of Archaeological Knowledge.* Etudes et Recherches Archéologiques de l'Université de Liège no. 49, 107–13.

Hodder, I., et al. 1995. *Interpreting Archaeology: Finding Meaning in the Past.* London: Routledge.

Kelly, R. L. 1995. *The Foraging Spectrum: Diversity in Hunter-Gatherer Lifeways.* Washington, D.C.: Smithsonian Institution Press.

King, R. E. 1993. "Mining on 'The Last Frontier': The Case of John Babel (1882–1979) in the Valdez Drainage of Central Alaska, 1920s–1950s." Paper Presented at the Twenty-Sixth Conference of the Society for Historical Archaeology, Kansas City, Mo.

Kirch, P. V. 1992. *The Archaeology of History.* Vol. 2 of *Anahulu: The Anthropology of History in the Kingdom of Hawaii,* by P. V. Kirch and M. Sahlins. Chicago: University of Chicago Press.

Krech, Shepard, III. 1999. *The Ecological Indian: Myth and History.* New York: Norton.

Leone, M. 1984. "Interpreting Ideology in Historical Archaeology." In D. Miller and C. Tilley, eds., *Ideology, Power, and Prehistory,* 25–35. Cambridge: Cambridge University Press.

McGuire, R. H. 1992. *A Marxist Archaeology.* San Diego: Academic Press.

O'Brien, Michael J., Robert E. Warren, and Dennis E. Lewarch. 1982. *The Cannon Reservoir Human Ecology Project: An Archaeological Study of Cultural Adaptation in the Southern Prairie Peninsula.* New York: Academic.

O'Neill, R. V., D. L. DeAngelis, J. B. Waide, and T. F. H. Allen. 1986. *A Hierarchical Concept of Ecosystems.* Monographs in Population Biology 23. Princeton, N.J.: Princeton University Press.

Orser, C. E., Jr. 1996. *A Historical Archaeology of the Modern World.* New York: Plenum.

Preucel, R. W., and I. Hodder, eds. 1996. *Contemporary Archaeology in Theory: A Reader.* Cambridge: Blackwell.

Pyne, S. J. 1995. *World Fire: The Culture of Fire on Earth.* New York: Holt.

Redman, Charles L. 1999. *Human Impacts on Ancient Environments.* Tucson: University of Arizona Press.

Reno, Ronald L. 1996. "Fuel for the Frontier: Industrial Archaeology of Charcoal Production in the Eureka Mining District, Nevada, 1869–1891." Ph.D. dissertation, University of Nevada, Reno.

Sanderson, S. K., ed. 1995. *Civilizations and World Systems: Studying World-Historical Change.* Walnut Creek, Calif.: AltaMira.

Smith, E. A. 1991. *Inujjuamiut Foraging Strategies: Evolutionary Ecology of an Arctic Hunting Economy.* New York: Aldine de Gruyter.

Soones, I. 1999. "New Ecology and the Social Sciences: What Prospects for a Fruitful Engagement?" *Annual Review of Anthropology* 28: 479–507.

Steward, J. H. 1955. *Theory of Culture Change.* Urbana: University of Illinois Press.

Sullivan, A. P., and C. E. Downum. 1991. "Aridity, Activity, and Volcanic Ash Agriculture: A Study of Short-Term Prehistoric Cultural–Ecological Dynamics." *World Archaeology* 22(3): 271–88.

Teltser, P. A., ed. 1995. *Evolutionary Archaeology, Methodological Issues.* Tucson: University of Arizona Press.

Tilley, C. 1994. *Interpretive Archaeology.* Oxford: Berg.

Trigger, B. G. 1971. "Archaeology and Ecology." *World Archaeology* 2: 321–26.

———. 1989. *A History of Archaeological Thought.* Cambridge: Cambridge University Press.

Tringham, R. E. 1991. "Households with Faces: The Challenge of Gender in Prehistoric Architectural Remains." In J. M. Gero and M. W. Conkey, eds., *Engendering Archaeology: Women and Prehistory,* 93–131. Oxford: Blackwell.

Wallerstein, I. 1976–89. *The Modern World System.* 3 vols. San Diego: Academic Press.

Webster's New World Dictionary of the American Language. 1960. New York: World Publishing.

Yoffee, N., and A. Sherratt, eds. 1993. *Archaeological Theory: Who Sets the Agenda?* Cambridge: Cambridge University Press.

5

Interdisciplinary Borrowing in Environmental Anthropology and the Critique of Modern Science

Michael R. Dove

The lily is beautiful, the cabbage is provender, the poppy is maddening—but the weed is rank growth . . . it points a moral.—Henry Miller

No man is a prophet in his own country.—Henrik Ibsen[1]

The early years of ecological anthropology involved the adoption and use of a number of influential concepts from ecology and other natural sciences. All of these concepts came from a common paradigm, one of whose defining characteristics was the assumption of stability and homogeneity in the physical environment. When ecological anthropologists started using these conceptions of stability, something noteworthy happened: as the concepts were being used to interpret local human ecologies, the human actors in these ecologies—our informants—contradicted them. That is, as the concepts were being applied to novel ethnographic contexts in novel ways, they were transformed. This experience caused us to rethink these concepts, which eventually contributed to a wider critique of the modern scientific understanding of the environment.

This past interaction between ecological anthropology and the natural sciences can be compared with the current interaction between postmodern critics and modern science. The subject matter of the postmodern critique of science overlaps with that of ecological anthropology: it has been strongly influenced by theories of environmental homogeneity versus heterogeneity, determinacy versus indeterminacy, and stability versus chaos—all of which it draws on to support a critique of the validity of scientific representation. The two cases, the postmodern critique and ecological anthropology, also resemble one another in first reaching across disciplines and then in critically transforming what they bring back to their own fields. Comparative analysis of the two cases can help us to better understand the nature of interdisciplinary relations and, in consequence, offers insights into what anthropology has to contribute to our understanding of the environment as well as the scientific enterprise itself.

I will draw here on my own as well as others' studies of anthropogenic grasslands, whose liminality and volatility have made them a rich arena of debate. Whereas grasslands were once thought of as models of ecological stability, now they are thought of as models of instability—a change in view that accurately reflects larger transformations in the scientific understanding of the world. Anthropologists have been heavily involved in this debate, as both consumers and critics of modern views of grassland ecology. In my own work, I carried a "modern," static view of grasslands into the field some twenty years ago, and ever since I have been coming to terms with its inadequacies.

I use the term *modern science* to refer to the analytic paradigm that presumes a static, stable, homogeneous, and readily knowable reality. I use the term *late-modern science*, in contrast, to refer to a paradigm that assumes a dynamic, unstable, and heterogeneous reality that is knowable with difficulty.[2] Finally, I use the term *postmodern* to refer to that paradigm self-characterized by "incredulity toward metanarratives" (Lyotard 1984: xxiv)—referring here to conceptual paradigms that are so hegemonic as to leave little space for critique—with my particular concern here being the postmodern incredulity toward the metanarrative that I have referred to here as modern science.

I will begin with a comparison of modern and late-modern concepts in ecological anthropology concerning the environment in general and grasslands in particular. I will then discuss the general significance of interdisciplinary borrowing, its use in the development of views of the environment in anthropology, and then its use in the development of the postmodern critique of science. I will conclude by discussing the implications of this analysis for anthropological contributions to environmental studies.

Modern versus Late-Modern Views of the Environment

The critique of modern science began long before its popularization in the 1980s by literary critics, who were followed by anthropologists and other social scientists. Modern science, including the way that it views the environment, has undergone a radical, internal critique over the past half-century.

The modern view of the environment is characterized, according to its critics, by a "unifying logic" that "marginalized heterogeneity, spontaneity, and difference" (Zimmerman 1994: 103). This is challenged by a revisionist (viz., late-modern) view in which nature has no direction, no progression, only change (Zimmerman 1994: 102). This shift in views has temporal, spatial, and conceptual dimensions.

With regard to the temporal dimension, the former emphasis on stability and homeostasis has become an emphasis on instability and chaos. The former emphasis was reflected in the study of, search for, and valorization of so-called "climax" ecological communities, epitomized by "primeval tropical rainforest."[3] The new emphasis is reflected, in contrast, in studies of ecological "perturbation." The classic anthropological studies of swidden cultivation in the 1950s and 1960s, with their focus on recurring perturbation of the forest by fire, are perhaps an early example of this. Ecological scientists now believe that perturbations like fire, flood, and storm—and perhaps even some human impacts—play an integral and necessary role in the functioning of ecosystems. This shift in thinking has been reflected in anthropology, at the most specific level, in increased interest in the study of disasters (Oliver-Smith 1986). At a more abstract level, this shift is reflected, albeit less immediately, in some reorientation of the ethnographic gaze from stability to instability. Abrahams (1990) notes that an anthropologist, Edmund Leach, was one of the earliest scholars in any field to challenge—as he did in his 1954 study of highland Burma—the then-reigning notion of stability of social systems.[4] Today, many ethnographers believe that the "comfortable" anthropology that studies working social institutions must be coupled with an "uncomfortable" anthropology that studies social breakdown, the "anthropology of suffering" (Davis 1992). This interest in temporal perturbation falls within a wider interest that has developed in looking at *change*, in placing ecology (Crumley 1994), as well as society, within its historical context (Wolf 1982).

The spatial dimension of the modern/late-modern shift is reflected in essentialist views of the environment and in the current anti-essentialist critique (cf., Vayda 1990). Categories of vegetation or examples of ecotypes that were formerly regarded as "real," fixed, and meaningful—like "forest versus grassland"—are now problematized. As some of the pioneering research is summarized by Worster (1990: 8): the forest (e.g.) is now seen as just "an erratic, shifting mosaic of trees and other plants." The essentialist view of the environment was associated in the social as well as natural sciences with a broader valorization of the "untouched other"—*terra incognita*, the virgin forest or the uncontacted tribe—that has today been completely discredited. The essentialist view of the environment also was associated with an essentialist view of human systems for exploiting natural resources, which also has been giving way, albeit more slowly. Whereas rural communities were formerly characterized by anthropologists and others as "swidden cultivators" or "wet rice cultivators" or "collectors of forest products" (etc.), today it is believed that most rural communities have "composite" economies based on the simultaneous and constantly evolving exploitation of many different resources and environmental niches, at different levels of intensity, with market as well as subsistence orientations (Dove 1983; Netting 1993).[5] Greater appreciation of the complexity of local social and ecological systems has developed alongside a new interest in interpreting the dynamics of ecological systems in terms of the dynamics of larger political systems (Bryant 1992; Greenberg and Park 1994).

As these examples show, the modern/late-modern shift has an important conceptual dimension, which is perhaps best reflected in views of nature versus culture. The modern view of the environment dichotomized nature and culture, such that if culture was present, then nature was not. This romantic vision of nature was epitomized by Thoreau's (1906/1962)[6] mid-nineteenth-century lament that the human impact on New England left him only a "partial poem" of nature to read:

> I take infinite pains to know all the phenomena of the spring, for instance, thinking that I have here the entire poem, and then, to my chagrin, I hear that it is but an imperfect copy that I possess and have read, that my ancestors have torn out many of the first leaves and grandest passages, and mutilated it in many places. I should not like to think that some demigod had come before me and picked out some of the best of the stars. I wish to know an entire heaven and an entire earth.

Cronon (1983: chapter 1) has criticized this idealized "complete poem" of nature as a fiction based on a problematic dichotomy. One of the problems with this dichotomization of nature and culture is that it abstracts people from their physical environment (Williams 1980: 75) and thereby provides the conceptual "distancing" necessary for the idea of human "intervention in nature." The possibility of such intervention is matter-of-factly implied in the titles of past prominent publications like *Man's Role in Changing the Face of the Earth* (Thomas 1956) or "Managing Planet Earth" (Clark 1989). A number of scholars are now problematizing the distancing that is thought to make such "management" possible (Williams 1980; Sachs 1992).[7] As Ingold (1993: 39) writes, "To intervene in the world . . . implies the possibility of our choosing not to do so. It implies that human beings can launch their interventions from a platform above the world, as though they could live *on* or *off* the environment, but are not destined to live *within* it." The growing belief that we need to collapse the dichotomy of nature and culture is perhaps reflected in the fact that some ecologists now speak, albeit metaphorically, of the possibility of an ethnographic-like knowledge of the one by the other, as in Janzen's (1979) famous article "How to Be a Fig," which hearkens back to the suggestion by the pioneering environmentalist Aldo Leopold (1949/1987) that we should try to "think like a mountain."[8]

One of the most salient expressions of the dichotomization of nature and culture by modern science involves the contemporary notion of "forests." The concept of "virgin forest" is seen increasingly today as an egregious result of this dichotomy. Formerly not just the focus of research but also the end point on the ecological scale of values, this concept is today criticized for disregarding tens of thousands of years of interaction between people and environment, in addition to privileging an unreal concept of stability, as noted earlier (Balée 1994; Denevan 1992). The artificial segregation of nature and culture may also be seen in such things as the rallying cry of international environmentalism, "Save the rain forests." The heavy focus of national and international conservation efforts on tropical rain forests, although continuing in many quarters (and certainly of great merit in its own right), is now critiqued by some observers as "rain forest fundamentalism" (Buttel 1992: 19), which overlooks the nonforest landscapes on which most rural peoples live and privileges the northern industrialized nations at the expense of rural peoples in southern nations. The empirical basis for this "degradation narrative" has also been questioned (Fairhead and Leach 1996; McCann 1997).

Modern versus Late-Modern Views of Grasslands

The differences between modern and late-modern views of the environment are associated with dramatically different visions of grasslands. Based on diametrically opposed evaluations of the value of tropical grasslands for agriculture and animal husbandry, grasslands are characterized in the modern scientific view as a sign of resource degradation and inutility, whereas they are characterized in the late-modern view as a sign of resource modification and (possible) productivity.[9] As this distinction implies, grasslands tend to be seen as something that is unmanaged in the modern view but managed in the late-modern view. The former sees them as an *un*intentional outcome of environmental relations, whereas the latter sees them as an intentional outcome. In an important corollary to this, in the modern view grasslands need outside intervention (e.g., to be managed and made productive), whereas in the late-modern view they do not. There is also an important rhetorical dimension here: whereas the modern view acknowledges only differences in "understanding" of a shared landscape, the late-modern view portrays conflicts over grasslands as contested differences between an official landscape and a "vernacular" landscape (cf., Jackson 1984: 148). Anthropologists have contributed to the recognition of this vernacular landscape through studies of local views of the environment, including local views of grasslands (Conklin 1959; Dove 1986a, 1986b; Netting 1968; Sherman 1981).

A key distinction between modern and late-modern views of grasslands pertains to their imputed stability versus instability: according to the modern view, grasslands are stagnant and a sign of the resistance of the environment to change, whereas according to the late-modern view they are dynamic and a sign of the propensity of the environment for change. Thus, whereas grassland was for modern scientists an exemplar of stability, it has become for late-modern scientists an exemplar of *in*stability (Worster 1990: 10).[10] The view of grasslands as stable versus unstable has important development implications: those who see grasslands as stable classify them as a developmental "dead end"; in contrast, those who see grasslands as unstable classify them as a potential stage in the transition to intensive agriculture (Dove 1986a, 1986b; Sherman 1980). According to modern science's view of grasslands, the events leading to and from grassland successions are linear and predictable: overuse or abuse of resources lead in, and massive external technological inputs (with luck) lead out. In contrast, the late-modern view of grassland development is multilinear: grassland succession can be precipitated by a number of different social and ecological factors (Conklin 1959), operating singly or collectively and with or without human intention. Similarly, grassland development can be terminated by a number of different factors, including more intensive land-use (from intensive agriculture and grazing [Conklin 1959: 61–62; Wharton 1968]) as well as less intensive land-use (leading to natural afforestation). There is an implicit difference here with regard to directionality: whereas both modern and late-modern views recognize that forest can become grassland and grassland can become forest, the former is characterized in the modern view as a much easier and therefore more threatening shift and the latter is characterized as much more difficult and thus challenging. Typical of the modern view is this statement: "*Imperata cylindrica* grasslands are a fire-climax vegetation type *derived from* [emphasis added] cleared forest lands" (Vandenbeldt 1993: 3). It would be equally ecologically valid, yet it is unheard-of in modern science, to describe such grasslands as "a fire-climax vegetation type *terminating in* closed forest." The modern emphasis is on the forest>grassland direction of change to the exclusion of the grassland>forest direction.

The most critical variable in precipitating or terminating grasslands is the attitude of the local human population toward them: anthropologists have made a unique contribution to our understanding of grasslands in this regard by demonstrating how these attitudes vary among communities and even within the same community, according to a complex interplay of social, economic, political, and ecological variables.[11] This interplay also has a historical dimension. Grassland succession—like other environmental phenomena—is increasingly viewed as something that takes place within, as opposed to without, human history.[12] An important contribution of the late-modern critique has been to show that this history is not a given (as implied in the modern view) but is contested: for example, Fairhead and Leach (1996) show how an actual historic progression from savanna to forest in Guinea is "read backwards" (viz., as forest succeeding to grassland) by government officials anxious to portray their country as needing funding for forest conservation. This misreading is supported by the tenacious modern myths of grassland that makes a single stage of vegetative succession appear to be eternal.

Williams (1980: 70–71) insightfully suggests that debates like this about "the idea of nature" are often really debates about "the idea of society." Indeed, it seems clear in looking at debates about the temporal and spatial dimensions of grassland dynamics that their real subject is not grasslands or society but the relationship between the two. A major difference in modern and late-modern views of grasslands is the belief that grasslands can be understood apart from society or not, respectively. The late-modern view insists that grasslands (indeed, any ecotype) cannot be dealt with apart from society, because society and environment in effect "coevolve" (cf., Norgaard 1984). Recognition of a pattern

of reciprocal interaction between society and environment has material implications: if this relationship is denied, then any labor that is invested in height-
ening the productive capacity of grasslands (or forests, etc.) also is denied,[13]
which can mean the disenfranchisement of local landholders.[14]

A final distinction between modern and late-modern views of grasslands
pertains to the conventions of research and their role in helping to reveal
versus *obscure* grassland dynamics. One of the most obvious places these
conventions manifest themselves is in the questions that are asked or not
asked. For example, I suggest that questions that are persistently raised in development circles—such as "How can we *reclaim* the grasslands of Southeast
Asia?"—must be rejected because of the political assumptions contained in
them (e.g., about why the grasslands need to be reclaimed, what reclamation means, who will control this process, and who will benefit from it). Late-
modern scholars have not just studied the grasslands themselves, therefore,
they have also problematized grassland studies. They have rejected the "modern" assumption that research is neutral and instead asked of all research *Cui
bono?* (Who benefits?). More generally, they have rejected the premise that the
development process in which such research is embedded is neutral, and again
they have asked who is truly served by this process (cf., Escobar 1995).

Interdisciplinary Relations

Williams (1980: 80) notes that one of the "strengths" of the modern view of
nature is that it makes other ideas of nature so difficult to imagine. The foregoing review of grassland studies in particular, and environmental thinking in
general, suggests that somehow it became possible to imagine something
other than the modern view. I suggest that this possibility began with interdisciplinary borrowing, referring here to the taking of concepts, models, and
metaphors from one field for use in another, a subject of increasing interest to
scholars of science (e.g., Fujimura 1992).

Interdisciplinary Borrowing

Interdisciplinary borrowing is an old and important source of scholarly advancement and authority in nearly all disciplines, with early attempts by the
social sciences to borrow models and metaphors from mathematics, biology,
and physics extending back to the beginning of the era of modern science. For
example, one of the founders of modern anthropology, Emile Durkheim
(1933/1964), drew heavily on organic metaphors in writing his classic work,
Division of Labor in Society. As Cohen (1994: 35, 40) writes:

> Analogy has always functioned as a tool of discovery, reducing a problem to an-
> other that has already been solved or introducing some element or elements that

have proved their worth in a quite different area of knowledge. Jeremy Bentham once said that hints from analogies constitute one of the most important tools available for scientific discovery.

The power of such analogy derives, in part, from allowing us to think about the "unthinkable." This principle was articulated within our own discipline by Bateson (1958: 302, 299):

> It is not, in the nature of the case, possible to predict from a description having complexity C what the system would look like if it had complexity C + 1. When the scientist is at a loss to find an appropriate language for the description of change in some system which he is studying, he will do well to imagine a system one degree more complex and to borrow from the more complex system a language appropriate for his description of change in the simpler.

One way to obtain "complexity C + 1" is to borrow it from another discipline.

The borrowing of a concept from one discipline to another inevitably entails *some* transformation of the concept involved.[15] Counterintuitively, such borrowing tends to entail an emphasis not of the similarities but *differences* between the disciplines involved. Indeed, the success of the borrowing may even vary directly with the magnitude of these differences.

> The history of the natural sciences . . . shows that many of the greatest advances have come not so much from a cloning transfer of ideas from one branch of science to another as from a transformation, from a significant alteration of the original. (Cohen 1994: 63)

The act of borrowing thus results in some severing of ties between the concept in its new discipline and the concept in its original discipline. As the economist Claude Ménard writes, in every such transplanting, "these concepts take on a life of their own in the reorganized science" (cited in Cohen 1994: 62–63). Most dramatically—and problematically, in terms of interdisciplinary relations—a concept may retain validity in its adopted discipline even after it has been abandoned in the discipline in which it was originally developed.[16]

Given that the most powerful concepts may be those that undergo the most change when borrowed, there is some benefit to looking for a donor discipline that is *least* similar to one's own. The benefits of "borrowing far" are supported by the fact that the ability to generalize about others—whether disciplines or cultures—is heightened by the *lack* of knowledge. Cohen (1994: 65) even suggests that misunderstanding of the borrowed concept, and hence of the donor discipline, may be not an impediment but an aid to the success of the borrowing:

> There are, however, many examples of fruitful advances in social thought resulting from transfers in which the original concept or principle may not be

fully understood. . . . Indeed, it is generally known among social scientists that misinterpretations often lead to fruitful results. . . .

In short, the psychodynamics of cross-disciplinary analogy and borrowing seem to be those of preaching to the unfamiliar.

The explanatory value of the analogy depends upon the way that it is constructed and used. Cohen (1994: 28) suggests that explanatory value suffers if what is borrowed is treated as an homology, if it is interpreted not abstractly but literally. He suggests that the "organicist" sociologists of the nineteenth century (like Johann Caspar Bluntschli, Paul von Lilienfeld, and Herbert Spencer) committed this error in trying to draw overly literal and insufficiently abstract parallels between social systems and living organisms (Cohen 1994: 27–28). Cohen (42) suggests that it is also an error to use a borrowed concept to try to "prove a proposition," as opposed to using it for "the elucidation of the sense of a given proposition" or "to clarify the meaning of propositions." According to Cohen, thus, the power of borrowed concepts lies in their creative value as general symbols, not in any value as specific and precise statements.

Anthropology and Environmental Science

Ecological anthropology is an apt field to illustrate the dynamics of interdisciplinary borrowing because of the number of key concepts it has borrowed from other fields. In the past two decades alone, these include patch theory, optimal foraging, vernacular landscapes, complex systems, and global change. Earlier on in the development of ecological anthropology, the field borrowed a general natural science paradigm that idealized localized, in-human, climax communities. This was reflected in the appearance in anthropology of analytic concepts like ecosystem, carrying capacity, and homeostasis. Of most relevance to the current analysis, it also was reflected in an understanding of vegetative cover predicated on the notion that virgin forest would cover most lands wherever natural dynamics were not prevented from operating.

The anthropologists who borrowed these conceptual tools used them to critique then-prevailing understanding of human–environment relations, including the assumption that indigenous tropical land-use was inferior to modern scientific models. Instead, anthropologists argued that manipulation by local communities of ecological perturbation (viz., by clearing and fire) and the dynamics of vegetative succession often represented a superior system of resource management. One example of this is the practice of "integral" swidden agriculture in tropical rain forests (Conklin 1957; Freeman 1970; cf., Dove 1983, 1985); another is the practice of semi-intensive agriculture and animal husbandry in anthropogenic grasslands (Dove 1986a, 1986b; Sherman 1981). The insights obtained into these indigenous systems of resource use contributed, in time, to undermining orthodoxy in the natural sciences.

Anthropology's contribution to this process was based on submitting the modern scientific model to an indigenous critique. To take an example from my own work: I initially journeyed to Southeast Kalimantan in 1980 to study the "breakdown" in the system of Banjarese swidden agriculture thought to be responsible for grassland succession and to assess the prospects for a government afforestation program. What I found was local Banjarese intensively exploiting and actively maintaining the grasslands and telling me that "We could not live without them" (Dove 1986a). To return to the earlier reference to Bateson: this submission to an indigenous critique literally provided "complexity C + 1." It provided an opportunity to think the unthinkable, via the standard ethnographic experience of conversing with those whose thinking is *not* framed by our own conceptions.

Numerous research experiences of this sort by ecological anthropologists demonstrated the intimate associations that often exist between local communities and their physical environments and the great knowledge of the environment that many local peoples acquire through this association. Of great importance, ecological anthropologists showed that these associations are not always destructive for the physical environment, information that was critical to the late-modern move away from a dichotomized conception of nature and culture. Of equal importance, their studies showed that local environments have social histories and that most (indeed, perhaps all) of what we consider to be "nature" actually represents the historical interaction of both society and environment.[17] Finally, their studies showed that local ecological systems were often poorly represented by modern scientific concepts compared with the concepts of local peoples.

The Postmodern Critique and Environmental Science

The postmodern critique of science similarly relies on the cross-disciplinary borrowing of concepts, models, and metaphors (Franklin 1995: 172–73)—much of it from rather distant disciplines.[18] One of the acclaimed pioneers of postmodern thought, Michel Foucault, actually argued for the study and denaturalization of not the exotic but the everyday (cf., Barthes's [1972] analyses of everyday phenomena). In explaining why he tackled such subjects as mental and physical health, Foucault (1977: 109) wrote:

> If, concerning a science like theoretical physics or organic chemistry, one poses the problem of its relations with the political and economic structures of society, isn't one posing an excessively complicated question. . . . But on the other hand, if one takes a form of knowledge like psychiatry, won't the question be much easier to resolve, since . . . psychiatric practice is linked with a whole range of institutions, economic requirements and political issues of social regulation?

But the postmodern critique of science has been characterized more by the scrutiny of distant and different rather than near and familiar fields. Practices

Figure 5.1: "Scratch Plough" used by Banjarese to till lands covered by *Imperata cylindrica.*

Figure 5.2: Banjarese grazing water buffalo in a field of *Imperata cylindrica.*

and fields more embedded in everyday life, like Foucault's mental and physical health, have received less attention from postmodern critics of science than more exotic aspects of nuclear physics, molecular chemistry, artificial intelligence, etc. Indeed, some years ago Best (1991: 189) could characterize postmodern scholarship's "three main branches of influence" as "thermodynamics . . . quantum mechanics . . . and chaos theory." This stretch to distant disciplines has seemed to "work"; however, the creativity and influence of the postmodern critique often has seemed to vary directly with the very foreignness of the scientific field being scrutinized.

The creativity of this critique has also seemed to vary directly with the degree to which the concepts acquired in distant disciplines have been reinterpreted and transformed. Some of the most prominent postmodern scholars have argued that they should concentrate on revealing indigenous critiques instead of imposing external and alien ones (see Marcus and Fischer 1986: 132, 133). But, again, the postmodern critique of modern science has been often (although not always) an external one, based on idealizing and essentializing scientific models such as that of indeterminacy (cf., Cohen 1994: 158) and literal (mis)reading of scientific tropes such as "The universe is chaotic."[19] The resultant transformations can be diametric. As Argyros (1992, cited in Zimmerman [1994: 350]) writes regarding chaos: "For deconstructionists, chaos repudiates order; for scientists, chaos makes order possible." The magnitude of these transformations is reflected in a strong countercritique from the disciplines that first developed these concepts, as in the widely publicized volume by Gross and Levitt (1994) or the case of the New York University physicist (Sokal 1996) who published in a leading postmodern journal (*Social Text*) what he subsequently revealed to be an intentional parody of postmodern science critiques. This sort of response is neither new nor atypical, however. For example, Roy Rappaport's (1968) stimulating borrowing of models from cybernetics and biology, to explain ritual and agricultural cycles in the New Guinea highlands, provoked an extended debate about the validity of his use of these unorthodox (within anthropology) models.

Whereas the postmodern critique has provoked some hostile responses, it also has helped to stimulate the development of a critique—outside of postmodern circles—of some of the same subjects. The attention focused by postmodern scholars on environmental indeterminacy, for example, has stimulated other observers to ask: Why are we paying so much attention to indeterminacy now and not before? Thus, Kellert (1993: 154) suggests that chaos theory could have been developed fifty years before it was, and he suggests that one of the main reasons this did not happen was past "social interest in the quantitative prediction and dominating control of natural phenomena." Addressing this same question, Worster (1990: 11–12; 1995: 77) explains the shift in the dominant scientific paradigm, from an assumption of order to an assumption of chaos, in terms of political disinterest in social planning, as dictated by the "logic of late capitalism" (following Jameson 1984).[20] An assumption of competition and disturbance is compatible, he suggests, with the likelihood that "global capitalism will continue to promote unchecked economic and population growth, will continue to stoke the rising aspirations of the poor, and will intensify its currently intense demands on nature" (Worster 1995: 77; cf., Zimmerman 1994: 8).[21] Worster's suggestion, that is, is that the logics of science and markets in the contemporary era have co-evolved to be mutually supportive, which, if true, may have implications for the ability of the former to adequately explain the latter.

Discussion

The manner in which both postmodern scholars and ecological anthropologists have drawn from and critiqued the modern, biophysical sciences offers insights into how scientists relate to those who precede them in time and also to those who work in other disciplines.

Scientific Denial

Two dimensions of the current, postmodern critique of science have important historical precedents. First, the critique of the modern premise of a static, homogeneous, and knowable world is just the latest addition to an antimodern critique of science that has been going on within science itself for decades. Second, the current reworking of concepts from the biophysical sciences like chaos and indeterminacy by social scientists and humanists is just the latest instance of a long history of creative, interdisciplinary relating and borrowing, which extends back, indeed, to the beginnings of modern science.

It is noteworthy that these precedents are denied by *both* sides in the science debates. Both sides seem to be resorting to Wittgenstein's trick of the "magic drawer," wherein one puts something in a drawer and closes it and then turns around and reopens the drawer and removes the same object with an exclamation of surprise (Kellert 1993: ix). On the one hand, the postmodern critics of science are guilty of this when they reach into the magic drawer and pull out their critique with an expression of delight, accompanied by declarations that this critique represents a unique historical "moment," which we now know to be not true. On the other hand, the scientists who are the object of this critique are engaged in something similar when they attack the use and abuse of their concepts by scholars from other fields. When they reach into the magic drawer and pull out this fact with an expression of dismay, implying that this runs counter to the norms of science, we know that this too is incorrect.

The tendency for scholars to deny their intellectual antecedents has long been noted. Mary Douglas (1986), for example, has drawn on the work of the sociologist Robert Merton (1963), who found that scientific "discoverers" routinely deny the existence of prior discoveries that contributed to their work. As a result, the same scientific question may remain "in a static condition, as though it were permanently condemned to repetition without extension" (Merton, cited in Douglas 1986: 74). Both Merton and Douglas believe that scientific denial is not "accidental" but is, rather, sociologically meaningful.[22] Their analyses suggest that the denial that characterizes both sides of the science critique—postmodern critics ignoring a preexisting critique of modern science, and scientists ignoring a tradition of interdisciplinary borrowing—is integral to contemporary academic relations of production.

Both scientists and their postmodern critics seem to be reluctant to place their views in wider context, which is reflected in the curiously nonsociological stances that both sides adopt in this debate. On the one hand, postmodern critics regard the emergence of indeterminacy and chaos theory, for example, as something qualitatively different from the emergence of any other, past scientific paradigm. They regard the development of chaos theory as the *end* of science as opposed to just another episode *in* science. On the other hand, scientists have responded to the postmodern critique by attributing it to "laziness" (Fox 1992: 51) or "muddleheadedness" (Gross and Levitt 1994: 1). If such terms were used in a state critique of peasants, I would suspect that the purpose was to obfuscate underlying political–economic conflicts—which also may be the case here.

Interdisciplinary Relations

The pattern of interdisciplinary borrowing that has been discussed here is characterized by persistent asymmetries. I have already suggested that borrowing tends to be skewed toward conceptually distant sources; but distance is not the only factor involved. There are also strategic considerations of power: there is a tendency to borrow up, from ascendant fields. The oft-mentioned "physics envy" (cf., Lenoir 1997), for example, reflects the desire of many other fields—in the natural as well as social sciences—to emulate the models, and perceived stature in society, of theoretical physics (Ludwig, Hilborn, and Walters 1993). The opposite situation is reflected in American anthropology, which, as Fredrik Barth (1997) observed, tends more often to borrow from other disciplines than to impress its arguments upon them.

Concepts are borrowed from ascendant fields because some of this ascendancy attaches to them and has an empowering effect on the recipient field. This explains why we have, as Worster (1993a) writes, "deep ecology" but no "deep entomology" or "deep Polish literature." The recently ascendant value of community studies, for example, helps to explain the development of such new and hybrid fields as community-based resource management, conservation and development, environmental justice, common property, and community forestry. Borrowing from ascendant fields is empowering even if the stance taken by the borrowers toward the donor field is a critical one; thus, extension of the postmodern critique from literature—a nonascendant field with minimal impact on the wider society—to science—an ascendant field

that has enormous impact on society—catapulted this critique into a prominent place on the academic stage.

Conclusions

This analysis has a number of implications for the way that we read postmodern scholarship, the history of anthropological engagement with environmental studies over the past generation, and the potential within anthropology to contribute to the next generation of environmental studies.

Postmodern Studies

First, the analysis of the relationship between the biophysical sciences and
their postmodern critics helps us to place in relief the intellectual history of
anthropological engagement with ecological studies. At the same time it
makes clear how important it is to comprehend this history in order to understand current theoretical developments. The postmodern claim to transcend modernism—which would in fact be impossible to make unless modernism had already been transcended[23]—helps us to see the earlier role that
ecological anthropology played in this transcendence. Postmodern discourse has in this sense (among others) played a necessary and salutary role.
Being labeled "modern," in short, helps ecological anthropologists to begin
to understand how, when, and why we in fact became something more than
modern.

Second, analysis of postmodern practices of interdisciplinary study, borrowing, and critique help us to denaturalize our own practices of crossing disciplinary boundaries in studying the environment. This prompts us to think
more explicitly about where we get our concepts from, and how we transform
them as we use them, and why we do this. Given anthropology's typical position as recipient rather than donor discipline, this gives us a special advantage
in thinking about the receipt of concepts from others and the occasional return of critical feedback to these same others. The resulting self-reflexivity can
only be salutary for the further development of studies of the environment
within as well as beyond anthropology.

Anthropological Studies of the Environment

Anthropology's greatest contribution to environmental studies is the ability to submit scientific models of human–environment interactions to indigenous critiques. In studies of the environment and in other areas as well,
ethnographic study will continue to have value and continue to be an important aspect of what anthropology can bring to the table. These indigenous
critiques promise to offer one of the most important points from which to

interrogate and problematize modern, Western notions of the nature–culture divide and to offer ways of perceiving the world that are not based on this divide. Since many scholars and activists alike regard this Cartesian divide as the source of most of the world's environmental ills, anthropology's unique ability to contribute to the continued evolution of thinking about this divide is a vitally important contribution.

Finally, anthropological access to indigenous critiques offers one of the few avenues, within reigning paradigms for understanding the environment, for thinking "outside the box." As a result, anthropology is likely to continue to play an important role in critiquing, and presenting alternatives to, orthodox thinking about human environmental relations. Anthropology's capacity to play this role is strengthened by its own reflexivity. For a number of reasons— anthropology's conceptual tools for studying institutions and ideational systems, its marginal and hence self-conscious status as a discipline, and the way that its own concepts are directly interrogated through the study of the ethnographic "other"—anthropologists have a greater than usual capacity to reflect on their own theory, method, and intellectual underpinnings. Human– environment relations have already proven to be a fast-evolving and heavily politicized field, and the ability to reflect upon what happens in this field as it is happening may turn out to be one of anthropology's most important contributions to it.

Acknowledgments

I carried out research on the grasslands of Kalimantan while based in Java between 1979 and 1985, making periodic field trips to Kalimantan, with support from the Rockefeller and Ford Foundations and the East-West Center. A recent series of field trips to Kalimantan, beginning in 1992, have been supported by the Ford Foundation, the United Nations Development Programme, and the John D. and Catherine T. MacArthur Foundation. I gratefully acknowledge comments on earlier versions by Carol Carpenter, Laura Nader, and David H. Maybury-Lewis, in addition to Carole Crumley and several anonymous reviewers. I alone am responsible for the analysis presented here.

Notes

1. I am grateful to Daniel M. Kammen for this reference.
2. Cf., Escobar's (1993: 383) characterization of modernity in terms of belief in linear progress, absolute truth, theories of universal application, and rational forms of social organization and planning versus postmodernism's belief in heterogeneity and difference versus homogeneity, in fragmentation versus totalization, in decenteredness

versus centeredness, and in scientific indeterminacy versus certainty and universal laws.

3. Cf. Anderson's (1952/1971: 45–46) pioneering critique of this focus:

> Follow in the taxonomist's footsteps when he leads an expedition into the tropics or establishes a field station in Central America. There one meets with wide areas of thorn scrub and savanna used as range and pasture, considerable land in field crops and in gardens, and at higher elevations, wide expanses of pinewood, more or less pastured and more or less cut over. Very rarely a remote ridge rises to a peak and is clothed around the summit with a cloud forest. From the moment a taxonomist arrives in the area these tiny patches of cloud forest are the center of his interest; from his behavior one would suppose they were his main reason for being in Central America. Admittedly they are beautiful and biologically interesting in more ways than one. Scientifically they offer no more fundamental problems than do dump heaps or dooryards or maize fields or village gardens, all of which will be ignored by your true taxonomist.

4. Abrahams (1990: 16) notes that another anthropologist who early on pointed out some of the problems with equilibrium theory was Bateson.

5. In addition to one part of the composite agricultural system being valorized, certain parts tended to be valorized over others, in particular intensive irrigated systems (Dove 1983, 1985).

6. The passage cited is from the *Journal's* volume VIII, page 221 (March 23, 1856).

7. Criticism of the nature–culture dichotomy, and of the environmental "management" that is produced by this distancing, has been called the "central intuition" of the "deep ecology" movement (Fox 1984: 196).

8. The title of one of the most famous essays in Leopold's book *A Sand County Almanac* (1949/1987: 129–33) is "Thinking Like a Mountain." Cf., Worster's "Thinking Like a River" (chapter 10 in Worster 1993b).

9. This opposition is diametrical: for example, whereas scholars long insisted that the soils under the sword grass *Imperata cylindrica* were barren and useless for cultivation, some scholars now support the counterinsistence by farmers that this grass may actually be a sign of arability in soils (Dove 1986a: 124). There are similar, complete differences of opinion regarding the palatability of this grass for cattle: some observers say that it is as nutritious as so-called "improved grasses," while others say that it will kill cattle (Dove 1986b: 176)!

10. My attention was drawn to this point by Williams (1995).

11. For example, Conklin (1959: 60) has pointed out that the Hanuno'o of Mindanao may encourage grassland succession in one part of their territory while discouraging it in another; and Dove (1986b) has demonstrated how attitudes toward grasslands vary in different regions of Indonesia, according to how closely grassland resembles the local preferred fallow land vegetative cover.

12. Cf. Robbins's (1963) study linking the contemporary occurrence of grasslands in New Guinea to historic population movements and the studies that link contemporary grasslands in Southeast Asia to historic centers of pepper cultivation (Potter 1988: 129).

13. Cf. Williams (1980: 78): "Some forms of this popular modern idea of nature seem to me to depend on a suppression of the history of human labour."

14. Indigenous conceptions of tenure in systems of grassland exploitation are typically based on the expenditure of labor on the land to make it arable (Dove 1986a).

15. Cohen (1994: 64) writes, "Whether the transfer occurs on the level of analogue, homologue, or metaphor, there is commonly some kind of distortion or transformation that arises from the differences between disparate realms of knowledge."

16. Cohen notes (1994: 74–75) that "Historians cannot fail to be impressed when finding that the validity of concepts, principles, laws, and theories in the social sciences transcends the corresponding present validity of the counterparts in the natural sciences that served as the original sources of inspiration or of generation of ideas."

17. That which fell into this category of combined nature and culture formerly was simply ignored, as Anderson (1952/1971: 45) points out:

> Once he is in the field, the average taxonomist is an incurable romantic. Watch him take a group of students on a field trip. The nearest fragments of the original flora may be miles away and difficult of access but that is no barrier. With truck, bus, train, jeep, or car, on foot if need be, the class is rushed past the domesticated and semidomesticated flora among which they spend their lives to the cliff side or peat bog or woodland which most nearly reflects nature in prehuman times.

18. Best (1991: 217, 218) notes: "Interestingly, the postmodern critique against science and technology often draws freely from scientific findings and scientific metaphors." Gross and Levitt, in their polemical 1994 work, carry out one of the more sustained, critical analyses of the cross-disciplinary use of metaphor in the antiscience literature, which they refer to in one place (p.116) as "metaphor mongering."

19. This sort of error has become a subject of anthropological study: see (e.g.) Obeyeskere's (1992: 175) critique of literal interpretation of native statements such as "Captain Cook is a god."

20. Some observers argue that the contemporary conservation movement also fits well into this logic (Buttel 1992: 20).

21. Radical ecologists also have concluded as much, as Zimmerman (1994: 12–13) suggests:

> For radical ecology, the potential implications of this shift in ecological theory [from an assumption of ecological balance to an assumption of chaos] are important. If in fact there is no such balance and if natural processes are constantly in flux, why should anyone take seriously radical ecology's warning that the practices of advanced technological societies are throwing nature "out of balance"?

22. This process is exemplified in the fact that understandings of grassland ecology are periodically obtained, and published, but ignored. Thus, Gerlach (1938) published one-half century earlier an accurate account of the same system of Banjarese grassland agriculture described in Dove (1986a) but with no noticeable impact on development scientists' "understanding" of this system.

23. I am indebted to Carol Carpenter for this insight.

References

Abrahams, Ray. 1990. "Chaos and Kachin." *Anthropology Today* 6(3): 15–17.
Anderson, Edgar. 1952/1971. *Plants, Man and Life.* Berkeley: University of California Press.

Argyros, Alexander J. 1992. *A Blessed Rage for Disorder: Deconstruction, Evolution, and Chaos.* Ann Arbor: University of Michigan Press.

Balée, William. 1994. *Footprints of the Forest: Ka'apor Ethnobotany—The Historical Ecology of Plant Utilization by an Amazonian People.* New York: Columbia University Press.

Barth, Fredrik. 1997. "How Others See Us: An Interview with Fredrik Barth." *Anthropology Newsletter* 38(2): 58, 60.

Barthes, Roland. 1972. *Mythologies.* Translated by Annette Lavers [From *Mythologies.* 1957. Paris: Editions du Seuil.]. New York: Hill and Wang.

Bateson, Gregory. 1958. *Naven.* Stanford, Calif.: Stanford University Press.

Best, Steven. 1991. "Chaos and Entropy: Metaphors in Postmodern Science and Social Theory." *Science as Culture* 2, 2(11): 188–226.

Bryant, R. L. 1992. "Political Ecology: An Emerging Research Agenda in Third-World Studies." *Political Geography* 11(1): 12–36.

Buttel, Frederick H. 1992. "Environmentalization: Origins, Processes, and Implications for Rural Social Change." *Rural Sociology* 57(1): 1–27.

Chambers, Robert. 1983. "Whose Knowledge?" In *Rural Development: Putting the Last First,* chap. 4. London: Longman Scientific and Technical.

Clark, William C. 1989. "Managing Planet Earth." *Scientific American* 261(3): 47–54.

Cohen, I. Bernard. 1994. *Interactions: Some Contacts between the Natural Sciences and the Social Sciences.* Cambridge, Mass.: MIT Press.

Conklin, Harold C. 1957. *Hanunó'o Agriculture: A Report on an Integral System of Shifting Agriculture in the Philippines.* FAO Forestry Development Paper No. 12. Rome: FAO.

———. 1959. "Shifting Cultivation and Succession to Grassland Climax." *Proceedings of the Ninth Pacific Science Congress* 7: 60–62.

Cronon, William. 1983. *Changes in the Land: Indians, Colonists, and the Ecology of New England.* New York: Hill and Wang.

Crumley, Carole L., ed. 1994. *Historical Ecology: Cultural Knowledge and Changing Landscapes.* Santa Fe, N.Mex.: School of American Research.

Davis, J. 1992. "The Anthropology of Suffering." *Journal of Refugee Studies* 5: 149–61.

Denevan, William M. 1992. "The Pristine Myth: The Landscape of the Americas in 1492." *Annals of the Association of American Geographers* 82(3): 369–85.

Douglas, Mary. 1986. *How Institutions Think.* Syracuse, N.Y.: Syracuse University Press.

Dove, Michael R. 1981. "Symbiotic Relationships between Human Populations and *Imperata cylindrica.*" In M. Nordin et al., eds., *Conservation Inputs from Life Sciences,* 187–200. Bangi: Universiti Kebangsaan Malaysia.

———. 1983. "Theories of Swidden Agriculture and the Political Economy of Ignorance." *Agroforestry Systems* 1: 85–99.

———. 1985. "The Agroecological Mythology of the Javanese, and the Political-Economy of Indonesia." *Indonesia* 39: 1–36.

———. 1986a. "Peasant versus Government Perception and Use of the Environment: A Case Study of Banjarese Ecology and River Basin Development in South Kalimantan." *Journal of Southeast Asian Studies* 17(1): 113–36.

———. 1986b. "The Practical Reason of Weeds in Indonesia: Peasant versus State Views of *Imperata* and *Chromolaena.*" *Human Ecology* 14(2): 163–90.

Durkheim, Emile. 1933/1964. *The Division of Labor in Society.* Translated by George Simpson [Original *De la division du travail social.* Paris: Félix Alcan, Editeur]. New York: Free Press.

Escobar, Arturo. 1993. "The Limits of Reflexivity: Politics in Anthropology's Post-Writing Culture Era." *Journal of Anthropological Research* 49: 377–91.

———. 1995. *Encountering Development: The Making and Unmaking of the Third World.* Princeton, N.J.: Princeton University Press.

Fairhead, James, and Melissa Leach. 1996. *Misreading the African Landscape: Society and Ecology in Forest-Savanna Mosaic.* Cambridge: Cambridge University Press.

Foucault, Michel. 1977. "Truth and Power." In *Power/Knowledge: Selected Interviews and Other Writings 1972–77 by Michel Foucault,* edited by Colin Gordon. New York: Random House.

Fox, Robin. 1992. "Anthropology and the 'Teddy Bear' Picnic." *Society* November/December: 47–55.

Fox, Warwick. 1984. "Deep Ecology: A New Philosophy of Our Time?" *The Ecologist* 14(5/6): 194–200.

Franklin, Sarah. 1995. "Science as Culture, Cultures of Science." *Annual Review of Anthropology* 24: 163–84.

Freeman, Derek. 1970. *Report on the Iban.* London School of Economics Monographs on Social Anthropology No. 41. London: Athlone Press.

Fujimura, Joan. 1992. "Crafting Science: Standardized Packages, Boundary Objects, and 'Translation.'" In Andrew Pickering, ed., *Science as Practice and Culture,* 168–211. Chicago: University of Chicago Press.

Gerlach, J. C. 1938. "Bevolkings methoden van ontginning van alang-alang-terreinen in de Zuider en Ossterafdeeling van Borneo" (Methods used by the local population for reclamation of *Imperata* fields in the South and East residencies of Kalimantan). *Landbouw* 14: 446–50.

Greenberg, J. B., and T. K. Park. 1994. "Political Ecology." *Political Ecology* 1: 1–12.

Gross, Paul R., and Norman Levitt. 1994. *Higher Superstition: The Academic Left and Its Quarrels with Science.* Baltimore: Johns Hopkins University Press.

Ibsen, Henrik 1987. *Plays: Six. Peer Gynt, The Pretenders.* Translated by Michael Myer. London: Methuen.

Ingold, Tim. 1993. "Globes and Spheres: The Topology of Environmentalism." In Kay Milton, ed., *Environmentalism: The View from Anthropology,* 31–42. ASA Monograph 33. London: Routledge.

Jackson, John B. 1984. *Discovering the Vernacular Landscape.* New Haven, Conn.: Yale University Press.

Jameson, Frederick. 1984. "Postmodernism, or the Cultural Logic of Late Capitalism." *New Left Review* 146: 53–92.

Janzen, Daniel H. 1979. "How to Be a Fig." *Annual Review of Ecology and Systematics* 10: 13– 51.

Kellert, Stephen H. 1993. *In the Wake of Chaos: Unpredictable Order in Dynamical Systems.* Chicago: University of Chicago Press.

Leach, Edmund R. 1954. *Political Systems of Highland Burma: A Study of Kachin Social Structure.* Boston: Beacon.

Lenoir, Timothy. 1997. *Instituting Science: The Cultural Production of Scientific Disciplines.* Stanford, Calif.: Stanford University Press.

Leopold, Aldo. 1949/1987. *A Sand County Almanac, and Sketches Here and There.* New York: Oxford University Press.

Ludwig, D., R. Hilborn, and C. Walters. 1993. "Uncertainty, Resource Exploitation, and Conservation: Lessons from History." *Science* 260: 17, 36.

Lyotard, J. F. 1984 (1979). *The Postmodern Condition: A Report on Knowledge.* Minneapolis: University of Minnesota Press.

McCann, James C. 1997. "The Plow and the Forest: Narratives of Deforestation in Ethiopia." *Environmental History* 2(1): 138–59.

Marcus, George E., and Michael M. J. Fischer. 1986. *Anthropology as Cultural Critique: An Experimental Moment in the Human Sciences.* Chicago: University of Chicago Press.

Merton, Robert K. 1963. "Resistance to the Systematic Study of Multiple Discoveries in Science." *Archives of European Sociology* 4: 237–82.

Netting, Robert McC. 1968. *Hill Farmers of Nigeria: Cultural Ecology of the Kofyar of the Jos Plateau.* Seattle: University of Washington Press.

———. 1993. *Smallholder, Householders: Farm Families and the Ecology of Intensive, Sustainable Agriculture.* Stanford, Calif.: Stanford University Press.

Norgaard, Richard A. 1984. "Coevolutionary Agricultural Development." *Economic Development and Culture Change* 32(3): 525–46.

Obeyesekere, Gananath. 1992. *The Apotheosis of Captain Cook: European Mythmaking in the Pacific.* Princeton, N.J.: Princeton University Press; Honolulu: Bishop Museum Press.

Oliver-Smith, Anthony, ed. 1986. Natural Disasters and Cultural Responses. *Studies in Third World Societies,* Special Issue 36.

Potter, Lesley. 1988. "Indigenes and Colonisers: Dutch Forest Policy in South and East Borneo (Kalimantan) 1900 to 1950." In John Dargavel, Kay Dixon, and Noel Semple, eds., *Changing Tropical Forests: Historical Perspectives on Today's Challenges in Asia, Australasia and Oceania,* 127–49. Canberra, Australia: Centre for Resource and Environmental Studies.

Rappaport, Roy A. 1968. *Pigs for the Ancestors: Ritual in the Ecology of a New Guinea People.* New Haven, Conn.: Yale University Press.

Robbins, R. G. 1963. "Correlation of Plant Patterns and Population Migration into the Australian New Guinea Highlands." In Jacques Barrau, ed., *Plants and Migrations of Pacific Peoples,* 45–59. Honolulu: Bishop Museum Press.

Sachs, Wolfgang. 1992. "One World." In Wolfgang Sachs, ed., *The Development Dictionary: A Guide to Knowledge as Power,* 102–15. London: Zed Books.

Sherman, George. 1981. "What 'Green Desert'? The Ecology of Batak Grassland Farming." *Indonesia* 29: 113–148.

Sokal, Alan. 1996. "Transgressing the Boundaries: Toward a Transformative Hermeneutics of Quantum Gravity." *Social Text* 46–47: 217–52.

Thomas, William L., ed. 1956. *Man's Role in Changing the Face of the Earth.* Chicago: University of Chicago Press.

Thoreau, Henry David. 1906/1962. *The Journal of Henry David Thoreau.* Edited by Bradford Torrey and Francis H. Allen. 2 vols. New York: Dover.

Vandenbeldt, R. J. 1993. "Imperata Grasslands in Southeast Asia: Executive Summary." In R. J. Vandenbeldt, ed., *Imperata Grasslands in Southeast Asia: Summary Reports from the Philippines, Malaysia, and Indonesia,* 1–5. The Forestry/Fuelwood Research and Development Project, Report #18. Washington, D.C.: Winrock International.

Vayda, Andrew P. 1990. "Actions, Variations, and Change: The Emerging Anti-Essentialist View in Anthropology." *Canberra Anthropology* 13(2): 29–45.

Wharton, Charles H. 1968. "Man, Fire and Wild Cattle in Southeast Asia." *Annual Proceedings of the Tall Timbers Fire Ecology Conference* 8: 107–67. Tallahassee: Tall Timbers Research Station.

Williams, Dee Mack. 1995. "Subjective Landscapes and Resources Management on the Chinese Grasslands of Inner Mongolia." Ph.D. dissertation, Columbia University.

Williams, Raymond. 1980. "Ideas of Nature." In *Problems in Materialism and Culture: Selected Essays,* 67–85. London: NLB.

Wolf, Eric R. 1982. *Europe and the People without History.* Berkeley: University of California Press.

Worster, Donald. 1990. "The Ecology of Order and Chaos." *Environmental History Review* 14(1/2): 1–18.

———. 1993a. "The Shaky Ground of Sustainability." In Wolfgang Sachs, ed., *Global Ecology: A New Arena of Political Conflict,* 132–45. London: Zed Books.

———. 1993b. *The Wealth of Nature: Environmental History and the Ecological Imagination.* New York: Oxford University Press.

———. 1995. "Nature and the Disorder of History." In Michael E. Soule and Gary Lease, eds., *Reinventing Nature: Responses to Postmodern Deconstruction,* 65–85. Washington, D.C.: Island Press.

Zimmerman, Michael E. 1994. *Contesting Earth's Future: Radical Ecology and Postmodernity.* Berkeley: University of California Press.

2

Beliefs, Values, and Environmental Justice

Political Ecology and Constructions of Environment in Biological Anthropology

Thomas L. Leatherman and R. Brooke Thomas

This chapter addresses the ways in which biological anthropology has conceptualized human–environment interactions and what insights and perspectives it offers for addressing the human dimensions of contemporary environmental issues. Not only can biological anthropology contribute much to our basic understandings of human adaptation to a diversity of environments, but it offers considerable potential for addressing the biocultural impacts of environmental changes that will dominate our concerns in the twenty-first century. A concern with global environmental issues, however, will demand a far broader view of environmental and social relations than the current emphasis on local constraints and proximate indicators of stress. Thus, we argue for an expanded view of environmental context in our analyses and for developing a political ecological approach that integrates political economy with human adaptability perspectives in biological anthropology.

First, we present a brief overview of the historical development of human adaptability perspectives that have shaped notions of human–environment interaction. This review highlights tendencies within human adaptability research to focus on the natural environment as the source of stressors or constraints and to naturalize the social environment, thereby trivializing the social contexts and history that shape so much of human biology. Drawing on recent efforts in biological anthropology to incorporate political–economic issues and perspectives into research on human biology we suggest new directions for human adaptability approaches (see Goodman and Leatherman 1998). Here, we see a host of environmental problems posing important challenges for human societies and biologies in the next century and suggest that by incorporating political–economic perspectives into human biology research, biological anthropology can contribute greatly to our understandings of the human dimensions of environmental change. The potential for a political ecology of human biology to address a range of environmental issues is outlined in discussions of environmental toxicity, new and resurgent infectious diseases, the biological and social impacts of tourism, and the biology of poverty.

Historical Background

Biological anthropology came of age in the 1960s with a merging of ecological and evolutionary perspectives, in which the concept of adaptation provided a powerful means of understanding human biological diversity and change. The application of this new evolutionary paradigm was rapidly taken up by physical anthropologists. As opposed to a focus on races as "ideal types," the human population became the focal unit of evolutionary analysis, and the environment the principal organizing feature of human adaptation. An emerging human ecology was defined not only to include adaptations to the natural environment, but to sociocultural conditions as well. Livingstone's (1958) work on the adaptiveness of the sickle-cell trait to malaria in the context of agricultural change demonstrated the utility of a human biocultural and ecological approach. Furthermore, it convinced biological anthropologists of the power of the evolutionary perspective in finding genetic adaptations in contemporary human populations. It is interesting that what is remembered and reproduced in Livingstone's work is how the sickle-cell trait provided a case of natural selection. Less emphasized is that the environmental context for endemic malaria to serve as a selective agent was largely a product of a host of social and economic factors (e.g., Bantu migration, forest clearing, root crop agriculture, displacement of animal hosts by a population of human hosts). That is, in the case of sickle cell we see a genetically based adaptive response to a problem of human making; what Singer (1996) and Santos and Coimbra (1998) have called "un-natural selection." In retrospect, we may have been misguided in so readily accepting this sort of identifiable genetic adaptation as typical of human populations (Smith 1993), for it set the agenda for much subsequent research on human adaptation. Most of this work failed to produce similar findings of demonstrable genetic adaptation to environmental stress.

Throughout the 1960s and 1970s, studies in human adaptation focused on human–environment interactions that emphasized biocultural responses to relatively harsh and extreme physical environments such as the arctic, desert, tropical, and high-altitude mountainous regions (Baker and Weiner 1966). Results of this work concluded, for example, that individuals were stockier in cold climates, more slender in hot dry climates, and short but with large chests and delayed growth in some high-altitude environments. These studies generally operated with "single-stress" models, in which a significant aspect of the physical environment was the determining or causal/independent variable and biological response the affected/dependent variable (see Frisancho 1993). The key process linking the two in a cause–effect relationship was initially assumed to be natural selection.

At the same time that anthropologists were concentrating on climatic adaptation through body morphology and composition, environmental physiologists were defining variations in climatic tolerance among native peoples resident in extreme environments (Frisancho 1993). Interests in morphological and physiological adaptations broadened to include mechanisms of adaptability, placing emphasis on phenotypic adjustments that might complement genetic adaptation. A focus on climatic stress therefore expanded to include multiple aspects of the physical environment as well as aspects of the biotic environment such as nutrition and disease. This led to a consideration of how these factors affected morphology, particularly their role in shaping growth and development processes. A concurrent emphasis on demographic characteristics of populations provided a linkage between individual phenotypic responses and household and population outcomes in morbidity and mortality (see Little 1982, 1995; Ulijaszek and Huss-Ashmore 1997).

What two decades of research showed was that human populations exhibited relatively few genetic adaptations and rather a large degree of biological plasticity. Evolutionary history apparently had not produced a species fine tuned to any particular environment, but one adept at rapid adjustments to a range of environmental conditions (Harrison 1993; Thomas et al. 1979). It was also clear that there were limits to plasticity (Baker 1984). As the effects of modernization on the resilience of many populations to cope with rapid change became increasingly apparent, much of the biological variation measured was attributable to states of undernutrition and disease (Boyden 1987; Huss-Ashmore and Johnston 1985).

Because undernutrition and disease are such quintessential social issues, the human adaptability paradigm was increasingly drawn into the social arena, and conceptions of environment broadened to include the social and economic as well as the physical. Factors such as socioeconomic status, land holdings, and occupation were studied as important correlates of food intake and nutritional status, as well as living conditions that might increase exposure to insults (Greene 1977; Gross and Underwood 1971). The way in which psychosocial stress as a response to real and perceived environmental stressors could lead to a variety of functional disorders including cardiovascular disease, hypertension, and immune suppression was an important avenue for linking the social and the biological in adaptability research (Goodman et al. 1988; James and Brown 1997).

Human adaptability research in the 1980s increasingly became oriented toward documenting biological compromise or dysfunction in impoverished environments and the biological impacts of ubiquitous social change (Boyden

1987). The refutation of the "small but healthy hypothesis" (Seckler 1980) in a special collection in *Human Organization* edited by Pelto and Pelto (1989) provided an effective corrective to notions of "cost-free" adaptations. Relying heavily on epidemiological approaches, biological anthropologists were successful at relating a range of proximate social indicators to nutrition and disease: indicators such as socioeconomic status, household demographics, education, and occupation. Such work also provided rich detail on the costs of development to factors such as diet, working capacity, and physiological stress (see Ulijaszek and Huss-Ashmore 1997).

The historical development of perspectives on human–environment interactions in biological anthropology clearly illustrates a movement toward a much broader view of environment that includes both social and economic conditions. However, people were often treated as rather passive agents in the adaptive process, adjusting and accommodating to environmental variations rather than having a role in constructing the environments in which they operated. There has also been less emphasis on variation in how human agents perceive and experience their environments and respond to problems they confront. Culture was portrayed as equally shared by all, and environmental changes—as natural constructions—were seen as uniformly affecting all members of a population. The population approach, while far superior to old racial typologies, nonetheless had a strong homogenizing effect on conceptions of human variation. In particular, the field has not problematized the roots of social and economic variation or the underlying dynamics of change and, rather, has assumed social conditions as natural or given in much the same way as it analyzed arctic, desert, and high-altitude environments. For example, poverty as expressed through low incomes, little education, limited food intake, and unhygienic conditions is frequently studied as an independent variable to disease (dependent variable). In many analyses, it is taken as a given that some will be rich and some poor—with little thought as to what processes create and sustain these inequities. In addressing impacts of social change, many biological anthropologists began to draw on "modernization" approaches, comparing groups who have remained more traditional to those that have become increasingly modern. Interesting results regarding the biological cost of "modern" life have been produced in analyses of diet, working capacity, obesity, and physiological stress, which have often altered for the worse with the social, economic, and environmental changes that accompany modernization. But what are we to make of these biological findings and the social contexts they are associated with? In these studies we know virtually nothing about the historical and political–economic forces behind such transitions. We fail to ask why some people have embraced change, while others have been dragged along, and still others have been more insulated or have resisted. We know little of how the people studied articulate into new, more diversified, and asymmetrical economies. In short, we learn almost nothing about the rich contexts that shape their everyday lives. In these examples, poverty and change are conceptualized as *natural and even inevitable* components of ecological systems in an evolving world, rather than a product of the intersection of global–local histories of human social and economic relations.

Toward a Political Ecology of Human Biology

These conceptual shortcomings in ecological and adaptability approaches have led a number of biological anthropologists to attempt to integrate perspectives from anthropological political economy and human adaptability in order to build versions of a political ecology analysis of human biology and behavior (see Goodman and Leatherman 1998; Leatherman and Goodman 1997). Common to these efforts is a greater attention to the social relations that structure (and are structured by) human–environment interactions, an expanded view of environmental and historical contexts, and a stronger sense of human agency in coping with and structuring environmental and social relations.

(1) *Social relations.* First is a shift toward framing the social contexts of human biology not simply in terms of proximal indicators of socioeconomic status, but in the social relations through which people access and control basic resources (and labor), as well as the poverty, inequality, and exploitation resulting from differential control over these resources. These relations of power are key to what individuals eat; how many crops they grow; their exposure to pathogens, toxins, and warfare; their ability to cope with everyday as well as extraordinary events (floods, famine, revolution); and the ultimate consequences of these events on their lives and biology. In short, a political–ecological approach calls for the analysis of social processes shaping human biology; these processes are full of complexity and contradiction and are in constant change.

(2) *Environmental and historical contexts.* Second is expanding the scope of environmental and historical contexts to recognize the role of extra-local, regional, and global processes in shaping local environments and social relations. Contingencies of history are critical to understanding the intersection of the global and the local and the direction of social, political, and economic transformations that can lead to profound consequences on human biology. For example, the poverty, malnutrition, and consequent effects on human growth and working capacity in sugarcane workers in Haiti and the Dominican Republic are linked to changing tastes for sugar in England, the development of colonialism in the eighteenth-century Caribbean, and more recent human rights and migration policies (Mintz 1985; Martinez 1995).

(3) *Human agency.* Third is to provide human subjects with a stronger sense of agency. This includes explicit recognition that environments are socially constructed and that the range of appropriate behaviors in studies of human–environment interactions can be expanded from adjustments to

environmental problems to social activism, resistance and rebellion that seek to radically transform the environment. When applied to the arena of coping and adaptation, it is clear that all agents do not experience environments the same, nor have equal goals and opportunities for response. What is beneficial to one individual or group often conflicts with the goals and actions of another. Thus coping carries costs, creates conflicts, and sets the context for future action. This allows us to follow the consequences of coping actions through to the production and reproduction of environmental contexts of stress and response. When human agents find that the combination of local and extra-local constraints are great, and the resources and options for coping are diminished, they sometimes conclude that whatever adjustments they might engage in are likely to carry added costs and serve to reproduce the conditions of their vulnerability. In such instances, it may be quite rational to seek to change the system, not adjust to it. Yet this sort of response has been out of the realm of appropriate action in ecological frameworks that saw the goals of human action as maintaining some form of social equilibrium (Starn 1991).

While perspectives from political ecology are being incorporated into biocultural models in biological anthropology, nutrition, and medical ecology, it is still the case that much work continues to examine human biology within closed systems, emphasizing autoregulation and homeostasis in the interaction of system components. Even in this work, biological anthropologists are contributing useful detail on microenvironmental stress and biosocial response within human–environment interactions. For example, they might provide analyses of energy flows within local environments and identify proximate correlates to disease and malnutrition, as well as household demography and reproduction. Nevertheless, as a subdiscipline, we are not poised to address the larger environmental issues likely to dominate the social, political, and environmental landscape in the twenty-first century. It is important to the relevance of anthropology, and biological anthropology in particular, that we build approaches that can address these human dimensions of environmental change.

Environmental Issues

An example of processes that we expect to impact human populations and environments with increased urgency in this century might include the following: further degradation of environmental resources and biodiversity accompanied by substantial population growth; increased penetration of world capitalism, resulting in higher rates of resource extraction, consumption, and waste; iatrogenic effects of modern technologies, including increased levels of toxins in the environment and new and resurgent infectious diseases; political and ethnic conflicts that produce environmental destruction, human displacement, and refugee populations; and the increased dislocation of peoples from their homelands and the loss of local systems of knowledge.

As environmental degradation spreads and intensifies, this will deny growing segments of local populations access to basic needs, forcing them to further abuse homelands and/or migrate from them. Along with environmental degradation, we can expect an increase in pollution following from expanding consumption patterns. New types and quantities of toxins will severely threaten environmental quality and human resilience. Similarly, we are seeing the emergence of new diseases and the resurgence of infectious disease thought to be controlled several decades ago. Increasing population growth and the concentration of migrants (especially in refugee camps), coupled with inequities in access to and distribution of resources, will exacerbate these conditions. Human health will be put at greater risk, and social, cultural and psychological measures of well-being will decline in a growing number of groups. Further expansion of world capitalism into local economies will further erode the capacity of self-production and local systems of knowledge and exaggerate present inequities between rich and poor, north and south. Any of these changes can increase the vulnerability of the poor to the consequences of stress in their ordinary lives and to the devastation of extraordinary events such as floods, famines, and wars (Watts and Bohle 1993). These processes, which are linked to climate change, will have a profound effect on public health at a global level.

As people find their own efforts insufficient to make ends meet, and even to preserve their own health and that of their children, they will search for ways to circumvent or change the social systems that constrain them. Here we can expect a diversity of creative adaptive strategies, which range from systemic adjustment to transformation, from resistance to revolution. It is out of these trends that a new set of anthropological problems will be formed. Our ability to understand the social, biological, and environmental dimensions of these problems will test the imagination and relevance of biocultural anthropology.

Case Studies in the Political Ecology of Human Biology

To illustrate how more political–ecological notions of human–environment interaction might aid biocultural research in addressing these and other similar issues, we briefly review four examples in which biological and biocultural anthropologists are currently engaged. These include studies of environmental risk in urban settings, problems of new and resurgent infectious diseases, the social and biological effects of tourism, and the biology of poverty and social conflicts. These cases illustrate the costs of modernization perspectives and policies, the unequal distribution of environmental risk in human populations, and how consequences of stress help reproduce the environmental contexts of this inequality.

Toxins in Urban Environments

A growing concern and research interest among many environmental anthropologists and political ecologists is in issues of environmental racism and
environmental justice. Biological anthropologists have recently entered this
arena by examining the distribution of risk and consequences to pollution in
urban environments. While a growing body of research in environmental epidemiology examines toxin–disease interactions, most research from biological anthropologists has examined the effects of various contaminants on
human growth and reproduction. The pollutants studied include PCBs (poly-
chlorinated biphenyls) at Love Canal, air and noise pollution (e.g., around air-
ports), and lead and other inorganic metals (Schell 1991).

Larry Schell (1997) recently modeled the social determinants and biological consequences of exposure to lead in urban environments. Chronic exposure to ambient lead in air, food, and water produces detrimental effects on
growth, cognition, reproduction, and other physiological parameters (e.g.,
disruption to hematological, neurological, and kidney functions). Lead is dispersed at trace-level concentrations in the environment, but a variety of
human activities concentrate it so that acute exposures can also occur with
similar biological effects. Children are at greater risk from lead toxicity, compared to adults, because they are exposed to more contaminated dust and dirt
through play activities; once exposed they absorb a far greater percentage of
ingested lead from both the gastrointestinal tract and in respiration. Lead is
stored in bone and has a biological half-life that may exceed twenty years, and
thus its potentially toxic effects are not removed easily (Hughes 1996).

In the United States, exposure varies considerably by race, class, and place of
residence. The highest exposures are found in inner-city environments of large
urban centers, where populations are overwhelmingly poor and nonwhite. For
example, African American children in the United States are eight times more
likely to have elevated blood lead levels than white children. Data from the
NHANES II survey conducted from 1976 to 1980 show that among children living in central areas of large cities, one in six African American children had elevated lead levels, while only one in fifty white children had similar levels above
30 mg/dL—a standard three times higher that what the Centers for Disease Control and Prevention presently designate as a detrimental level (Schell 1997).

The distribution of lead burden in children is not simply the result of recent exposure but of a multigenerational experience since lead is transferred
from mother to fetus during gestation. In Schell's model, residence in poor
neighborhoods increases exposure to lead from a variety of sources. Lead dust
from dilapidated, lead-painted homes, demolished buildings, and automobile
exhaust are present in the air and concentrated in the soil. Parental residence
in these urban environments increases the risk of lead exposure in children
from fetal through childhood development. High lead levels can affect growth
and, importantly, cognitive development. Thus it plays a role in poor school

performance and job preparation, and increases the chances that people will continue to live and raise families in similar environments, thus reproducing the exposure. Obviously, larger economic forces are at play in structuring exposure to toxic environments and ensuring unequal access to economic and educational resources. What this example shows is that the biological consequences of living in marginal environments can play a role in reproducing the contexts of exposure and, in this case, reinforcing existing inequalities of environmental injustice found in inner-city America. This, then, is an example of social relations leading to impaired biological function, in turn perpetuating a set of social conditions.

New and Resurgent Infectious Diseases

George Armelagos, a biological anthropologist with interest in the evolution of human–disease interactions, speaks about a third epidemiological transition (Armelagos and Barnes 1995). The first was associated with shifts in food production, population growth, and eventual urbanization, which radically altered human–environment relationships and was accompanied by the emergence of infectious diseases in epidemic proportions. The second transition marked the dominance in the West of what are called "diseases of civilization": the ascendancy of cardiovascular disease, cancer, hypertension, and other noninfectious diseases often associated with changes in diet and lifestyle, social stress, and exposure to new human-made environmental risks. The third transition is the emergence of new infectious agents and the resurgence of diseases previously considered all but eradicated. "Once expected to be eliminated as a significant public health problem, infectious diseases remain the leading cause of death worldwide and a leading cause of illness and death in the United States" (Bryan et al. 1994: 346). Several recent publications have identified a number of new and resurgent infectious diseases linked to environmental change. New diseases are ones that may have been present in the environment but had not previously been detected in significant numbers or had a human impact. Resurgent diseases are those with substantial history that are presently on the rise despite public health efforts that previously diminished and controlled levels of infection. Examples of new diseases include HIV-1, Ebola, hepatitis C and E viruses, Legionnaire's disease, Lyme disease, toxic shock syndrome, new variants of cholera, and the Hantaan virus pulmonary syndrome (Levins et al. 1994). Reemerging or resurgent diseases on the rise include tuberculosis, malaria, cholera, dengue fever, schistosomiasis and leishmaniasis, and a variety of sexually transmitted diseases.

What is particularly relevant from a political–ecological perspective is the recognition that these new and resurgent diseases are attributable, at least in part, to anthropogenic environmental disruption. The problem is summarized by Mary Wilson in an introduction to a volume on *Disease in Evolution: Global Changes and Emergence of Infectious Diseases*.

Profound changes in the world increase the likelihood that some of the known infectious diseases will increase, and that additional currently unknown infections will be recognized. This new reality challenges our confidence in the power of science and technology to control nature. (Wilson et al. 1994: 1)

Ironically, many of the forces that contribute to the appearance of new diseases and emergence of old ones are created by human activity—in many instances by what we consider extraordinary achievements. We have underestimated the complexity of our environment and the capacity of other species to adapt and evolve. Also, we have overestimated the power of tools such as antimicrobials, pesticides, and vaccines to free us of disease. We have failed to recognize that events in plants and animals can teach us and affect our health, while having paid little attention to the geoclimatic influences on health. (1994: 3–4)

Anthropogenic environmental disruptions that increase vulnerability include any changes that increase exposure and susceptibility, reduce coping capacities, and lower resilience to the consequences (biological, social, and economic) of disease. Environmental, demographic, and social conditions that have been linked to infectious disease emergence include deforestation; construction of roads, dams, and irrigation canals; poor sanitation and hygiene; climate change; urbanization; migration; inadequate health services; war and civil disorder; increased sexual activity and intravenous drug use; the overuse of antibiotics; air-conditioning; ultra-absorbent tampons; and others (Platt 1996: 22). Wilson et al. (1994) cites several additional reasons for vulnerability to disease, including aging, immunosuppression from AIDS or medical treatment (e.g., chemotherapy), medical devices and treatments that have prolonged the lives of many with disease and disability, crowding, pollution, social upheaval, and movement into new habitats where populations have not yet adapted.

The impact of new infectious agents is nowhere more apparent than in sub-Saharan Africa where two-thirds of the thirty-three million individuals infected with HIV reside (Sachs 1999). With rates between 20 and 25 percent of the adult population infected in some countries, this pandemic undermines the capacity of communities and governments to maintain basic economic and social infrastructures and production activities. As Brown and Halweil (1999: 22) state, "Like a powerful storm or war that lays waste to a nation's physical infrastructure, a growing HIV epidemic damages a nation's social infrastructure, with lingering demographic and economic effects. A viral epidemic that grows out of control is likely to reinforce many of the very conditions—poverty, illiteracy, malnutrition—that gave it an opening in the first place."

Another example of a new infectious agent is Lyme disease. Unknown prior to 1975, it has become the most common vector-borne disease in the United States, infecting approximately thirteen thousand Americans a year (Platt 1996). Its spread is related to the deforestation and more recent reforestation and restrictions on burning in the northeast United States, and a rapid rise since the 1960s in the deer (without significant predators) and mouse populations that serve as hosts for deer ticks. The deer tick, which carries the disease, has been able to spread unimpeded through the deer and mouse populations and to human populations as human settlement encroaches on wooded areas (Spielman 1994).

Infrastructure development, poverty, and pollution have also combined to create new niches for diseases. Sewage and fertilizers pouring nitrogen and phosphorus into marine ecosystems, loss of wetlands, overharvesting of fish and shellfish, and climatic change have all conspired to cause massive algal blooms—providing a rich environment for diverse communities of microorganisms (Epstein et al. 1994). Pathogens can lay dormant in algae for long periods, awaiting conditions of major blooms in which it can grow and spread. It is suspected that the *V. cholerae* 01 (El Tor biotype) virus that infected thousands in the Latin American cholera epidemic of 1991–92 was brought to Peru by an Asian freighter and dumped with bilge water. It lay dormant and resurfaced in massive algal blooms infecting fish and shellfish and eventually humans. It then entered a relatively unhygienic water system and spread rapidly, with highest rates of infection in poorer settlements surrounding coastal cities. From this base cholera spread to nineteen Latin American nations, where in fifteen months half a million people became sick and five thousand died (Mata 1994).

Multiple-drug resistant strains of *V. cholerae* 01 (El Tor) are increasingly widespread in Asia (Epstein et al. 1994). New cholera variants have been discovered, most likely due to algal blooms and high sea surface temperatures that can encourage a shift toward more toxic forms of pathogens. Among the new species identified is *V. cholerae* 0139, which human antibodies and vaccines for other variants of cholera do not recognize (Levins et al. 1994; Platt 1996). This new variant, first identified in 1992, has caused a South Asian epidemic that has infected over one million and killed ten thousand people. These forms of cholera still exist in the environment, and it appears likely that still newer strains will crop up under environmental pressures that increase mutation rates and pathogenicity (Platt 1996).

An example of a resurgent disease is tuberculosis (TB) (Platt 1996). The combined effects of antibiotic overuse and people's inability to use antibiotics in their intended way have led to the evolution of new resistant strains of TB and a number of other infectious agents such as malaria and diphtheria. Between 1985 and 1989, TB cases rose by almost one million—from 2.95 to 3.8 million cases. Just four years later the number of cases had more than doubled to 8.8 million. During the 1990s, at least thirty million were expected to die from TB as the number of cases complicated by drug-resistant strains and co-infection with HIV grew.

"The public health crisis of new and resurgent diseases can in large part be traced to a failure in understanding the interactions between the human population and the environment" (Epstein et al. 1994: 20). An understanding of the coevolution of disease agents and human hosts in the contexts of cultural iatrogenesis, and especially the social and economic relations of risk populations, are critical in addressing this phenomenon. Human biologists using a political–ecological perspective should be well positioned to focus on these issues.

Biology of Tourism

The third example addresses issues of capitalist penetration, resource degradation, loss of local systems of knowledge, and dislocation of human populations. Ongoing work on the biological and social effects of tourism in the Yucatan Peninsula (Mexico) is being carried out by a number of researchers, including ourselves, Magali Daltabuit, Alan Goodman, and Oriol Pi-Sunyer.

> In the last two and a half decades, the recently formed state of Quintana Roo on the eastern portion of the Yucatan Peninsula, has been experiencing massive penetration of tourism, transforming it from one of the most isolated areas of Mexico into a tourist bonanza. This development has been an unqualified success for the Mexican government and international investors, but less clear is how this change has affected the Maya: their environment, their diet and health, and cultural identity. (Pi-Sunyer and Thomas 1997)

The highly capital-intensive development of Cancun and the Caribbean coast has created a labor market based largely on construction and service industries for tourists. Several service communities have grown up around resorts comprised of migrants from elsewhere in the Yucatan. Here, they have insufficient access to land for agricultural fields or kitchen gardens. In communities from the interior, 75 percent or more of the men, as well as adolescent males and females, seek work on the coast, returning home on weekends. In established families this places an added burden on women, who must maintain home and family in their husbands' absence (Leatherman 1998; Daltabuit and Leatherman 1998). It has also led to an increase in consumption norms and expectations among younger generations of Maya, who are less interested in farming (making milpa) and tending kitchen gardens. Thus, their families are denied the time and labor needed to farm and harvest forest resources at a time when the cost of living is significantly increasing. This is making it impossible for many families to continue traditional subsistence farming, since the milpa provides little cash to cover medical expenses, bus rides, and school uniforms and books. The tourist industries' demand for natural building materials in order to simulate Mayan design has led to their scarcity. One informant estimated that to build a single pole and thatch house now takes as many as fifty round-trips into the forest—approximately 400 kilometers—to secure the hardwood upright posts and palm thatch needed in construction (Pi-Sunyer and Thomas 1997).

One of the most visible shifts in many of the Mayan communities in which we worked is in food consumption patterns. As households in the service communities are removed from home food production, the vast majority of their diet becomes store bought, processed foods imported from other parts of Mexico and the United States. Even in more rural farming communities, households regularly purchase beans, maize, tortillas, and other staples and have only limited access to expensive fruits and vegetables unless produced locally (Leatherman et al. 1998).

Most dramatic among dietary shifts is the high consumption of soft drinks and snack foods high in sugar, salt, and fat. For example, during a morning school break in the communities in which we work, it is typical for children to buy a Coke and cookies or chips. A typical drink and snack comes to about 350 calories, about one-quarter of an elementary school child's daily requirement (McGarty 1995). Mexico has one of the highest Coca-Cola consumption rates in the world—somewhere near one Coke per person per day (Coca-Cola Company 1993: 35), a rate confirmed in the four communities we studied.

Anthropometric studies carried out in three communities show that children are stunted or short for their age but relatively stocky, and some show signs of extreme fatness (Leatherman et al. 1998). Many adults are becoming overweight, and a number of women are obese (Daltabuit 1988). As Federico Dickinson and co-workers have noted, Maya in the Yucatan are beginning to experience the double-edged nutritional problems of obesity coupled with undernutrition; "when they are young malnutrition is highly prevalent (i.e., stunting), when they are older, obesity is quite common" (Dickinson et al. 1993: 315). While calorie deficits and protein–calorie malnutrition were common in the 1960s, present nutritional deficits are more closely linked to protein and potentially micronutrient deficiency (Gurri and Balam 1992). For example, the high levels of phosphoric acid in Coke can compromise the bioavailability of calcium and other positively charged elements such as zinc and iron (Calloway et al. 1993). These are also the kinds of diet shifts that are accompanied by obesity, diabetes, hypertension, and a host of diseases now occurring with relatively high frequencies among Native Americans experiencing rapid dietary change. While dietary delocalization and obesity have been observed in other development contexts, the intriguing aspect of the biology of tourism is the interplay between rapidly changing cultural perceptions, social and economic relations, environmental use, and human biology. This is an area of investigation where biological and cultural anthropologists will find rich potential in collaboration and a research problem that rests on a synthesis of adaptive and political–economic perspectives for interpretation.

Biology of Poverty

Each of the previous examples illustrates areas in which biological anthropologists using a political–ecological perspective have recently begun to work and/or in which they can make significant contributions to issues of social and environmental change. One area in which biological anthropologists have been more visible in an emerging political–ecological perspective is an approach that has been termed by Thomas (1998) the "biology of poverty." Human adaptability research has documented the consequences of social and economic marginality on growth, nutritional status, disease profiles, cognitive abilities, social functioning, etc. Yet, much of this work remains microfocused, relating biological parameters to proximate indicators of well-being such as socioeconomic status. More recently, biological anthropologists have attempted to go beyond these proximate correlations to uncover underlying vulnerability of human populations by examining the social relations structuring access to basic resources that shape peoples' ability to cope with problems, and their resilience to recover from assaults on their livelihood and biology (see Goodman and Leatherman 1998; Leatherman and Goodman 1997).

These perspectives have been developed in part through fieldwork in the Andes examining consequences and responses to illness among small-scale farming households (Leatherman 1998). The Andes provide an interesting location to develop and examine the utility of a political–ecological perspective because so much has been written about Andean biological and cultural adaptation from an ecological and evolutionary perspective. Early expectations in Andean research were that broad adaptive patterns would be discerned through cross-population and cross-cultural comparisons in high mountain systems in the Andes, Himalayas, and Ethiopian highlands. Yet most of these comparisons showed less similarity than expected. One reason for this lack of convergence was that each region and each population had distinctly different histories. For example, while the Andes were repeatedly described as a harsh marginal habitat, the region had provided ample resources for earlier Andean cultures operating in a different historical context with a different set of economic and social relations. It was clear that much of the marginality of the environment and populations was historical and political–economic in nature.

In the political–ecological perspective developed to address relationships between health and household economies, we attempted to play off both perspectives: a rich history of Andean biocultural adaptive systems and an equally destructive history of oppression and attempts by outside forces to control local resources and peoples. Our takeoff point in more recent history was the combined effects of a failed agrarian reform and increased capitalization of the rural economy beginning in the 1970s. Both of these combined to limit access to land and labor for rural farmers, the two most critical resources in agropastoral production. When illness impacted household labor, availability of cash and extensive networks of support were key resources for obtaining treatments and extra household help to replace lost labor power and meet critical production tasks in a timely manner. Help was hard to find for poorer households, and they were disproportionately impacted, suffering greater losses in production than middle-income households. As might be expected, it was poorer households that experienced the most illness and were the least able to cope with its effects, thus suffering greater disruption to their household economy. This reinforced and reproduced the conditions of poverty and hence greater degrees of undernutrition and illness. Over time, this led to an adaptive disintegration where some households were unable to reproduce the land, labor, and material resources necessary to maintain themselves in farming (Leatherman 1996).

Cynthia McClintock (1984) has argued that just this sort of perpetual poverty among Andean rural producers led to the spread and success of the *Sendero Luminoso* (Shining Path) revolution, which came to dominate the political landscape of Peru in the late 1980s and early 1990s. Indeed, it would have been hard to miss the poverty, vulnerability, and social unrest that increased throughout our research in the 1980s. Yet, as Orin Starn (1991) has pointed out, many Andean ethnographic and biocultural studies from the 1970s did "miss the revolution." He argues that the ecologically oriented community studies in the 1970s tended to erect analytical boundaries around the populations and cultures being researched to the neglect of interregional and national processes. The prevailing picture of Andean society then was one of stable adaptations, resistant and resilient to change and underlain by persistent cultural traditions. Thus, while it was also Andean to resist and revolt, this tendency was downplayed in part because adaptation theory has never been well equipped to handle resistance and revolution as adaptive behavior.

A political–ecological perspective that frames human adaptability within a political economy certainly increases the likelihood of capturing the kind of social, economic, and environmental disruptions precipitating conflicts. It is therefore critical to address many of the environmental issues and social conflicts that have shaped the past as well as those that have emerged in this decade and are likely to dominate sociopolitical landscapes in the future. Examples include the biological consequences of colonization and development in the Amazon (Santos and Coimbra 1998) and the human impacts of the *Sendero* revolt, particularly among the *desplazados* (displaced persons) forced to leave communities and now returning. More devastating examples of social dislocation and trauma have been seen in recent years in Rwanda, Burundi, Zaire, and the former Yugoslavia, where long-held ethnic conflicts have repeatedly flared up in response to international manipulations and strategies of control that dominated Cold War politics. Worldwide estimates of internal refugees are about twenty-five to thirty million, many of them in Africa south of the Sahara, where three-quarters of the countries are donors or receivers of significant refugee movements. The effects include disruption of livelihoods, agricultural production, and food security, leading to widespread malnutrition, and forced residence in overcrowded refugee camps where poor sanitation and contaminated food and water breeds disease along with human suffering (Kalipeni and Oppong 1998). The call is *not* for taking advantage of a "natural laboratory" but for using our expertise in human biology to advocate for and attempt to ameliorate the conditions faced by refugees and *desplazados*. This begins with a recognition that environments of social and political conflict are just as legitimate objects of inquiry as extremes of altitude or temperatures, that environments are as much a product as a cause of human actions, that social responses to environmental stressors can carry tremendous costs for the actor and other agents, and that actively seeking to break or otherwise transform systems of poverty and inequality may be a more logical response than ineffective adjustments and perseverance.

Conclusions

These selected examples cover a range of cases where biological anthropology has the potential to contribute to critical environmental issues that confront us now and that we are likely to encounter in the future. There are certainly many others, but the larger point we wish to make is that unless we develop biocultural approaches that broaden a conceptualization of environment to see how people are enmeshed in webs of social relations at the local level, and how the local is intricately tied to the global, it will be difficult to build a science that is capable of articulating with the rest of anthropology and contributing insights into future environmental issues.

We see at least two paths developing in biological anthropology. One continues to look inward, far inward toward our genes, as a way to further our evolutionary understanding of human–environment interactions. A second path, that we argue for here, is to adopt a more socially relevant and informed perspective that looks outward toward the social constructions of environment and biology and forward toward the sorts of issues that we will all confront in this century. A political–ecological approach provides biological anthropology with a way to link a long-term interest and expertise in analyzing environments as prime movers in human evolution with a politically, historically, and socially rich contextualization of human–environment interactions. Moreover, it provides an opportunity of making relevant one of the most relevant aspects of the human condition, peoples' biology.

References

Armelagos, George, and Kathleen Barnes. 1995. "The Evolution of Emerging Diseases in Human Populations." Paper presented at the Ninety-Fourth Annual Meeting of the American Anthropological Association, Washington, D.C.
Baker, Paul T. 1984. "The Adaptive Limits of Human Populations." *Man* 19: 1–14.
———, and Joseph Weiner, eds. 1966. *The Biology of Human Adaptability*. Oxford: Clarendon.
Boyden, S. V. 1987. *Western Civilization in Biological Perspective*. Oxford: Clarendon.

Brown, Lester, and Bryan Halweil. 1999. "Breaking Out or Breaking Down." *World Watch* 12(5): 20–29.

Bryan, Ralph T., Robert W. Pinner, and Ruth L. Berkelman. 1994. "Emerging Infectious Diseases in the United States." In Wilson et al., *Disease in Evolution*.

Calloway, D., S. P. Murphy, G. H. Beaton, and D. Lein. 1993. "Estimated Vitamin Intakes of Toddlers: Predicted Prevalence of Inadequacy in Village Populations in Egypt, Kenya, and Mexico." *American Journal of Clinical Nutrition* 58: 376–84.

Coca-Cola Company. 1993. *Annual Report of the Coca-Cola Company for 1993.* Atlanta, Ga.

Daltabuit, Magali. 1988. "Mayan Women: Work, Nutrition and Child Care." Ph.D. dissertation, University of Massachusetts, Amherst.

———, and Thomas Leatherman. 1998. "The Biocultural Impact of Tourism on Mayan Communities." In Goodman and Leatherman, eds., *Building a New Biocultural Synthesis*, 317–38.

Dickinson, Federico, M. T. Castillo, L. Vales, and L. Uc. 1993. "Obesity and Women's Health in Two Socioeconomic Areas of Yucatán, Mexico." *Coll. Antropol.* 2: 309–17.

Epstein, Paul R., Timothy Ford, Charles Puccia, and Cristina de A. Possas. 1994. "Marine Ecosystem Health: Implications for Public Health." In Wilson et al., *Disease in Evolution*, 13–23.

Frisancho, A. Roberto. 1993. *Human Adaptation and Accommodation.* Ann Arbor: University of Michigan Press.

Goodman, Alan, and Thomas Leatherman, eds. 1998. *Building a New Biocultural Synthesis: Political Economic Perspectives on Biological Anthropology.* Ann Arbor: University of Michigan Press.

———, R. Brooke Thomas, Alan Swedlund, and George J. Armelagos. 1988. "Biocultural Perspectives on Stress in Prehistoric, Historical and Contemporary Population Research." *Yearbook of Physical Anthropology* 31: 169–202.

Greene, L. 1977. "Hyperendemic Goiter, Cretinism and Social Organization in Highland Ecuador." In L. Greene, ed., *Malnutrition, Behavior and Social Organization*, 55–91. New York: Academic.

Gross, D., and B. Underwood. 1971. "Technological Change and Caloric Costs: Sisal Agriculture in Northeastern Brazil." *American Anthropologist* 73: 725–40.

Gurri, F. D., and G. Balam. 1992. "Regional Integration and Changes in Nutritional Status in the Central Region of Yucatan, Mexico: A Study of Dental Enamel Hypoplasia and Anthropometry." *Journal of Human Ecology* 3(2): 417–32.

Harrison, G. A. 1993. "Physiological Adaptation." In G. A. Harrison, ed., *Human Adaptation.* New York: Oxford University Press.

Hughes, W. William. 1996. *Essentials of Environmental Toxicology: The Effects of Environmentally Hazardous Substances on Human Health.* Washington, D.C.: Taylor and Francis.

Huss-Ashmore, Rebecca, and Francis Johnston. 1985. "Bioanthropological Research in Developing Countries." *Annual Review of Anthropology* 14: 475–528.

James, G. D., and D. E. Brown. 1997. "The Biological Stress Response and Lifestyle: Catecholamines and Blood Pressure." *Annual Review of Anthropology* 26: 313–35.

Kalipeni, Ezekiel, and Joseph Oppong. 1998. "The Refugee Crisis in Africa and Implications for Health and Disease: A Political Ecology Approach." *Social Science and Medicine* 46(12): 1637–53.

Leatherman, T. L., A. Goodman, A. Lebner, J. Martinez, T. Stillman, J. Jones, E. Seeber, C. Hudak. 1998. "Coca-colonization: The Political Ecology of Dietary Change in the Yucatan." Fourteenth ICAES, Williamsburg, Va.

Leatherman, Thomas. 1996. "A Biocultural Perspective on Health and Household Economy in Southern Peru." *Medical Anthropology Quarterly* 10(4): 476–95.

———. 1998. "Illness, Social Relations and Household Production and Reproduction in the Andes of Southern Peru." In Goodman and Leatherman, *Building a New Biocultural Synthesis.*

———, and Alan Goodman, eds. 1997. "Social and Economic Perspectives in Biological Anthropology." *American Journal of Physical Anthropology* 102(1): 1–78.

Levins, Richard, Tamara Awerbuch, Uwe Brinkman, Irina Eckardt, Paul Epstein, Najwa Makhoul, Cristina Albuquerque de Possas, Charles Puccia, Andrew Spielman, and Mary Wilson. 1994. "The Emergence of New Diseases." *American Scientist* 82: 52–60.

Little, M. A. 1982. "The Development of Ideas on Human Ecology and Adaptation." In F. Spencer, ed., *A History of American Physical Anthropology 1930–1980*, 405–33. New York: Academic.

———. 1995. "Adaptation, Adaptability and Multidisciplinary Research." In N. Boaz and L. Wolfe, eds., *Biological Anthropology: The State of the Science*, 1–23. International Institute of Human Evolutionary Research. Corvalis: Oregon State University Press.

Livingstone, Frank. 1958. "Anthropological Implications of the Sickle Cell Gene Distribution in West Africa." *American Anthropologist* 60: 533–62.

McClintock Cynthia. 1984. "Why Peasants Rebel: The Case of Peru's Sendero Luminoso." *World Politics* 27(1): 48–84.

McGarty, Catherine A. 1995. "Dietary Delocalization in a Yucatecan Resort Community in Quintana Roo, Mexico: Junk Food in Paradise." Honors thesis, School of Nursing, University of Massachusetts, Amherst.

Martinez, Samuel. 1995. *Peripheral Migrants: Haitians and Dominican Republic Sugar Plantations.* Knoxville: University of Tennessee Press.

Mata, Leonarda. 1994. "Cholera El Tor in Latin America." In Wilson et al., *Disease in Evolution.*

Mintz, Sydney. 1985. *Sweetness and Power: The Place of Sugar in Modern History.* New York: Viking.

Pelto, Gretel H., and Pertti J. Pelto. 1989. "Small But Healthy? An Anthropological Perspective." *Human Organization* 48(1): 11–15.

Pi-Sunyer, Oriol, and Brooke R. Thomas. 1997. "Tourism, Environmentalism and Cultural Survival in Quintana Roo, Mexico." In Barbara Johnston, ed., *Life and Death Matters: Human Rights and the Environment at the End of the Millennium.* Walnut Creek, Calif.: AltaMira.

Platt, Anne E. 1996. *Infecting Ourselves: How Environmental and Social Disruptions Trigger Disease.* Worldwatch Paper 129.Washington, D.C.: Worldwatch Institute.

Sachs, Jeffrey. 1999. "Helping the World's Poorest." *The Economist*, August 14, 1999, 17–20.

Santos, Ricardo, and Carlos Coimbra. 1998. "On the (Un)natural History of the Tupi-Monde Indians: Bioanthropology and Change in the Brazilian Amazon." In Goodman and Leatherman, *Building a New Biocultural Synthesis.*

Schell, Lawrence. 1991. "Pollution and Human Growth: Lead, Noise, Polychloro-biphenyl Compounds and Toxic Wastes. In C. G. N. Mascie-Taylor and G. W. Lasker, eds., *Applications of Biological Anthropology to Human Affairs*. Cambridge Studies in Biological Anthropology. Cambridge: Cambridge University Press.

———. 1997. "Culture as a Stressor: A Revised Model of Biocultural Interaction." *American Journal of Physical Anthropology* 102(1): 67–78.

Seckler, David. 1980. "'Malnutrition': An Intellectual Odyssey." *Western Journal of Agricultural Economics* 5(2): 219–27.

Singer, Merrill. 1996. "Farewell to Adaptationism: Unnatural Selection and the Politics of Biology." *Medical Anthropology Quarterly* 10(4): 496–515.

Smith, Malcolm. 1993. "Genetic Adaptation." In G. A. Harrison, ed., *Human Adaptation*. New York: Oxford University Press.

Spielman, Andrew. 1994. "The Emergence of Lyme Disease and Human Babesiosis in a Changing Environment." In Wilson et al., *Disease in Evolution*.

Starn, Orin. 1991. "Missing the Revolution: Anthropologists and the War in Peru." *Cultural Anthropology* 6(1): 63–91.

Thomas, Brooke. 1998. "The Biology of Poverty." In Goodman and Leatherman, *Building a New Biocultural Synthesis*.

Thomas, R. B., B. Winterhalder, and S. D. McRae. 1979. "An Anthropological Approach to Human Ecology and Adaptive Dynamics." *Yearbook of Physical Anthropology* 22: 1–46.

Ulijaszek, S. J., and Rebecca Huss-Ashmore, eds. 1997. *Human Adaptability Past, Present and Future*. Oxford: Oxford University Press.

Watts, Michael, and Hans Bohle. 1993. "The Space of Vulnerability: The Causal Structure of Hunger and Famine." *Progress in Human Geography* 17(1): 43–67.

Wilson, Mary E., Richard Levins, and Andrew Spielman, eds. 1994. *Disease in Evolution: Global Changes and Emergence of Infectious Diseases. Annals of the New York Academy of Sciences, Volume 740*, 13–23. New York: New York Academy of Sciences.

7

Anthropology and Environmental Justice: Analysts, Advocates, Mediators, and Troublemakers

Barbara Rose Johnston

Anthropologists engaged in the struggle for environmental justice use their training in medical, sociocultural, political, economic, ecological, archaeological, and other aspects of our discipline to study, challenge, and (ideally) transform human environmental relationships. They seek to illuminate the ties between social conditions and environmental quality; to challenge the inequities that structure the human environmental equation; and, through the production, dissemination, and use of information, to affect substantive change. Other chapters in this volume review some of the environmental issues tackled by anthropologists. This chapter reviews the praxis dimensions and sociopolitical implications of doing environmental anthropology—briefly outlining the emergence of the term *environmental justice*; mapping out where and how anthropologists are doing this work; summarizing some of the areas of success in local, national, and international arenas; and discussing some of the inhibiting factors to success. I conclude with a look toward the future— describing emerging opportunities for the discipline to provide baseline information, shape public policy, and work to resolve the biophysical consequences of environmental injustice.

Environmental Justice

Environmental justice is a relatively recent construct. The term emerges in large part from the work of scholars like sociologist Robert Bullard and activists like Charles Lee (principal author of the 1987 Christ Church report), who documented the disproportionate siting of hazardous activities and waste disposal in U.S. minority communities. Lee, Bullard, and others documented a pattern of environmental racism, where histories, socioeconomic conditions and relationships, and governmental policies played significant roles in structuring inequitable experiences. African American and minority communities bore a disproportionate share of the health hazards and risks associated with environmentally polluting industries and activities. Efforts to transform these inequitable conditions often involved coalitions of civil rights groups, religious and interfaith councils, environmental organizations, and labor unions, and their combined effort to link environmental quality issues with the struggle for social justice came to be called the movement for environmental justice.

The focus on the links between toxins and race in the social sciences was in part a response to the problems exposed and exacerbated by Reagan-era policies. The "New Federalism" of the 1980s included deregulating industrial practices and stripping the funds from domestic programs that monitored the environment and protected occupational safety and public health. Economic activity intensified and, with the removal of environmental and public health safeguards, conditions deteriorated to the point that not only were poor people of color experiencing harm, so too were affluent suburban consumers (as illustrated by rising cancer rates, growing awareness of problems like the circle of poison, and the rapidly growing environmental book market). Environmental social scientists and community activists documenting the links between toxins and cancer could no longer fail to ignore the links between toxins and race in the United States. While several coalitions of social scientists, environmental groups, and civil rights groups worked throughout the 1980s to educate and organize the community and lobby the government, it was not until the Clinton administration came into power in 1992 that we saw political acknowledgment of the existence of environmental racism and a growing use of the term *environmental justice.*

President Clinton's election in 1992 brought about sweeping reorganization in the executive branch with, in some areas, radically different sets of priorities. In regard to the environment, the Clinton administration instituted changes in funding, policy, and priorities that placed higher emphasis on the human dimensions of environmental crisis, in effect acknowledging that continued dismissal of problems like environmental racism posed significant political as well as long-term economic threats to national security. Environmental justice activism in the early days of the Clinton administration culminated in the February 11, 1994, presidential executive order on environmental justice (Executive Order 12898, *Federal Actions to Address Environmental Justice in Minority Populations and Low-Income Populations*). This set of regulations, policies, and procedure is meant to ensure that no group of people, including any racial, ethnic, or socioeconomic group, bears a disproportionate share of the negative environmental consequences resulting from industrial, municipal, and commercial operations or the execution of federal, state, local, and tribal programs and policies.

Anthropology and Environmental Justice: Expanding the Framework

While the term *environmental justice* is derived from an analysis of the links between toxins and waste in U.S. communities and has distinct political meaning, over the past few years the environmental justice framework has been expanded to include diverse peoples and problems from around the world and used to explore the links between environmental crisis and human rights abuse. In a global context, environmental justice refers to the movement to build social, cultural, economic, political, and environmental sustainability. In a disciplinary context, environmental justice as a field of study or work suggests problem-focused, action-oriented anthropology involving the relationship between environmental quality and social justice.

In articulating and illustrating the synergistic ties between culture, power, and the environment, anthropologists are playing a central role in expanding the environmental justice framework from a race/class analysis of environmental inequity to a broader consideration of the historical conditions, relationships, and beliefs that give rise to patterns of selective victimization and the human rights/environmental crisis intersect. Their work is typically structured in interdisciplinary arenas and weaves together historical data, sociocultural analyses, and ethnographic voice to map out the culture/power dimensions of human environmental crises—identifying explanatory factors that more quantified analyses might miss. Some of the environmental issues explored by anthropologists involve the biodegenerative aspects of industrialism (mining, manufacturing, use and disposal—especially problems of toxins, hazardous waste, and environmental hazards). A number of anthropologists have been involved in disaster-related work, examining, for example, the sociocultural context of oil spills, floods, and hurricanes. A growing number of researchers have been exploring the environmental justice contexts of war, looking at problems faced by refugees, repatriation, and postwar reconstruction, as well as the social justice dimensions of the nuclear age, including the mining, manufacturing, and processing of uranium ore; the production and testing of nuclear weapons; and the use and abuse of nuclear energy. As Bonnie McCay has outlined in this volume, a large number of anthropologists work in natural resource management, especially with common properties such as fisheries, forests, agrosystems, open space, and protected lands. Much of this work examines the inequities and ensuing conflicts associated with resource value, access, use, and control. Perhaps the greatest number of anthropological contributions to the environmental justice literature falls under the "Victims of Progress" rubric, where various economic development schemes contribute toward ethnocide, ecocide, and, at times, genocide.

Considering the Environmental Justice Segment
of the Anthropology Labor Force

In 1996 I cross-listed entries of U.S.-based currently active anthropologists with interests and expertise in environmental justice issues from four sources—the 1996 National Association of Practicing Anthropologists (NAPA), the Society for Applied Anthropology (SfAA) Directory, the Human Rights and Environment (HRE) Scholars Network, and the Committee on Anthropologists in Environmental Planning (CAEP)—and came up with a total of 764 anthropologists. This figure does not include anthropologists living and working in other countries. It does not include anthropologists who have worked on environmental justice issues in the past but are not presently active. Also, it does not include anthropologists who did not participate in SfAA, NAPA, HRE, or CAEP directory projects. Furthermore, it does not include anthropologists who work on environmental issues but are not members of the SfAA, American Association of Anthropologists, or CAEP. And it does not include some 250 anthropologists who have since contacted me in reference to their interests in working on environmental planning or problem-solving projects in U.S. communities. The point being, that given the broad definition of environmental justice (action-oriented work involving the relationship between environmental quality and social justice), the list of anthropologists who have or are doing environmental justice work is quite long and rapidly expanding.

In reviewing the published work and practitioner directory entries, it is apparent that anthropologists engage environmental justice issues from four institutional sites: positions within political structures, economic institutions, civic organizations (NGOs), and research/educational institutions. And they do this at three levels: community, state, and international. Some anthropologists work for tribal governments, helping define the nature and extent of natural and cultural resources and facilitating tribal government efforts to develop culturally appropriate management strategies. Others work in similar capacities but as independent consultants hired by tribal nations, local governments, or other state and federal entities. A growing number of anthropologists work on environmental quality/social justice issues as employees or consultants for the U.S. federal government (including, e.g., the National Oceanic and Atmospheric Administration/Sea Grant and the Marine Fisheries Service, Environmental Protection Agency [EPA], National Parks Service, Department of Energy, U.S. Forest Service, State Department Human Rights Office, and Federal Emergency Management Agency). A few anthropologists are directly employed by the United Nations, and a much larger number of anthropologists work as consultants for UN agencies and offices (including, e.g., FAO, the Human Rights Commission, UNDP, UNHCR, UNEP, UNESCO, and WHO).

A number of anthropologists engage environmental justice issues within economic institutions, attempting to minimize and soften the blows felt by people in the way of World Bank, International Monetary Fund, and other large development bank–funded projects and to direct funds in ways that may enhance opportunities to build sustainable communities. A small, but growing, number of anthropologists are employed by private foundations (e.g., Ford Foundation, Rockefeller Brothers, Wenner Gren, and Conservation International).

Perhaps the most visible area of anthropological involvement with environmental justice issues is the fourth institutional category—that work which is done in education and research settings. Anthropologists work on environmental justice issues within university, college, K–12, research institute, and professional organizational settings. Their work is highly visible because they teach and train students and publish and disseminate findings in varied arenas.

Ironically, it is the least visible category of work that produces the greatest evidence of sociopolitical change. It is hard to estimate the number of anthropologists working on environmental justice issues with grassroots and nongovernmental organizations (NGOs). A great deal of this work occurs in a temporary, and often unpaid, capacity. Most of us at one point or another work as advisers, consultants, participants, organizers, or supporters. We do this work in our hometowns and in our research "homes," with community, national, and international organizations. We are often the sole anthropologist, occasionally the sole intellectual, and frequently involved for personal reasons and at times do not define our engagements as "anthropological work." In terms of impact, paid and voluntary interaction with local, state, and international NGOs may represent the area with the greatest capacity for influencing peoples' lives and futures. In terms of numbers, this area of work is arguably the largest portion of the environmental anthropology "workforce." Yet, for professional, economic, and simply personal reasons, this work is barely visible in the published literature and rarely valued in the ways that more traditional anthropological work is valued.

Doing Environmental Justice Work

The role of the anthropologist in environmental justice work is often varied, with any or all "hats" worn at different times. The spectrum of roles includes researcher, educator, analyst, planner, policy adviser, policymaker, organizer, facilitator, culture-broker, mediator, advocate, and activist. A few examples here illustrate.

Case 1. This anthropologist is a member of the Anthropology and Environmental Studies faculty at a Ph.D.-granting university. Engagement with environmental justice issues includes curriculum development, teaching, and organizing and supervising an environmental education student internship program where undergraduate students research local environmental problems and host "environmental justice" workshops for teachers and students in area grade schools. This anthropologist also works with international NGOs on social justice and environmental health issues. She has woven these issues into summer fieldwork projects in Central America, identifying the incidence of environmental health problems by class and ethnicity and tying these problems to water quality and tourism development. And she has applied her research in support of nascent efforts to build a global coalition of artisanal fishers whose lifestyles are threatened by mangrove deforestation for shrimp mariculture farms. Her research findings have been published and are regularly cited.

Case 2. This anthropologist holds an M.A. in applied anthropology and works as a policy analyst for the EPA. She was initially hired to develop strategies that strengthen the community role in environmental protection and support efforts to assert social science in the environmental planning and problem-solving process. Part of her job is to explain the advantages of anthropology to other EPA offices and to the communities they serve. She helped shape a five-year cooperative agreement with the Society for Applied Anthropology (1996–2001) and serves as EPA project officer. Her efforts are creating a growing demand for anthropological input at the earliest phases of the planning process within the agency and within the many different communities that the agency serves.

Case 3. After receiving her B.A., this anthropologist spent two years working as a Peace Corps volunteer teaching English to schoolchildren on Mili, an atoll in the Marshall Islands. Two years on the remote atoll left her with a growing command of the language, skills that landed her a position in the Republic of the Marshall Islands (RMI) Foreign Office and a staff position at the RMI Embassy in Washington, D.C. As the RMI has only one ambassador, her duties not only included advising on foreign policy issues pertaining to the United States (largely involving the health and environmental consequences of U.S. nuclear weapons testing), but also providing information and input on matters pertaining to the United Nations and the other nations of the world. To assist her efforts in meeting these responsibilities, she enrolled in an American University Ph.D. program and completed her Ph.D. while serving as the senior adviser to the ambassador. As part of an effort to lobby the U.S. government for additional funds to cover the human environmental damages from nuclear testing, she conducted a number of ethnographic surveys, recording the testimony of radiation survivors and preparing these materials for presentation to the U.S. Congress and other bodies. She continues to serve in a part-time capacity as the senior adviser to the ambassador, assisting efforts to renegotiate the Compact of Free Association between the RMI and the U.S. government.

Case 4. This anthropologist is "retired" and is keenly aware of both the blessings and the burden of time (freed up from teaching and university service work, yet constrained by age and health). Because much of his life had been spent in the Arctic documenting the impacts of development on indigenous peoples, retirement could easily have been spent writing the definitive book (which, as he puts it, might have been read by some two thousand people, "if I am lucky"). Instead, after attending a February 1995 university-sponsored workshop on the World Wide Web, he redefined his notion of audience, subject, and voice. He created a Web site for Arctic peoples with information on natural resources, history, culture, social equity, and environmental justice. The Web page includes a virtual museum, where Arctic residents can view, modify, and challenge representations of their history, and a virtual classroom, where high schools and colleges across the Arctic log on, use the syllabus, add new information, and interact with each other in cyberspace. In November 1996, when I first visited his site, I was visitor number 64,748. In February 2000, I was visitor number 581,430.

Case 5. My final example is an organizer who holds an M.A. in anthropology. We met over coffee at the AAA meetings in 1988 and with another colleague brainstormed strategies for developing environmental action–oriented anthropology. One wanted to develop culturally appropriate responses to human environmental crises via the market, another argued for a textbook that moved human ecology into the realm of political economy, and the third suggested the need for alternative information flows. We went our separate ways, and I have not seen the "organizer" since. But I greet the evidence of her ideas daily. She went back to San Francisco and with a small group of computer types started the Institute for Global Communications (IGC), an Internet provider run through the nonprofit Tides Foundation, which hosts econet, peacenet, human rights net, women's net, and conflict net. Millions of people communicate via these systems. The IGC has helped create networks and coalitions and regularly provides cyberspace training for environmental justice groups. I know that none of the work I have done over the past five years could have been accomplished without the information and exchanges that occur via the IGC. In some ways this work, of all the cases briefly described, is the most far-reaching contribution to environmental justice. Information access and control is key to any system of power and key to any effort to restructure systems of power.

Difficulties: Personal, Professional, and Political Risk

Obviously, these descriptions illustrate just a few of the varied ways anthropology engages environmental justice. A common feature in these examples is that each anthropologist engages problem-focused, action-oriented, public service anthropology. This engagement requires commitment and carries certain personal, professional, and political risks. Coming to terms with risk requires compromise, and this involves struggles with objectivity, ethics, and voice.

At the personal level, environmental justice work rarely translates into a dependable wage with health benefits and retirement. Environmental justice work involves Big Issues, life and death matters that are rarely resolved in short periods of time, if at all. Like all activism, sustained engagement with environmental justice issues can absorb huge chunks of time and severely strain personal and family finances. Dissertations get pushed aside. Articles and books are begun and never finished. Faculty evaluations trivialize the importance of this work. Time conflicts intensify, and relationships grow stale or deteriorate. Burnout happens, and it is easy to succumb to depression and feelings of futility. Because environmental justice work occurs most often in isolated, marginal contexts, the psychosocial impacts are real. Furthermore, when environmental justice work involves advocacy and action—confrontational politics—a number of professional bridges are burned. "Cause-oriented" anthropology suggests people who make trouble. Troublemakers are celebrated in this discipline when their cause succeeds and justice prevails. But often "justice" is elusive, success is hard to gauge, and action results in unforeseen adverse consequences. One of the risks of action anthropology is the disasters you failed to prevent or the messes you helped create. At the professional level, engaging environmental justice issues requires confronting questions of power, voice, praxis, ethics, and goals: As Peter Brosius notes elsewhere in this volume, though perhaps articulated in different terms, these questions include: Working for whom? Whose definition of problem? Whose interpretation of justice? Who controls activist agendas? Is the anthropologist an insider or outsider? An observer or participant? An objective researcher, neutral facilitator, informed advocate, or impassioned activist? Each of these roles offers advantages and poses certain risks. Structuring engagements in ways that emphasize objective research and impartial participation allows the anthropologist to act as an authoritative voice and neutral facilitator in problem resolution. The danger of this approach is that involvement can reinforce the status quo. On the other hand, the perceived bias that accompanies advocacy or activist roles significantly erodes the authoritative voice, as illustrated in British Columbia in 1996, when Supreme Court Chief Justice Allan McEachern ruled against a land claim by the Gitksan-West'suwet'en tribal councils. The justice dismissed testimony given by an anthropologist in support of Native communities, ruling that the anthropologist's evidence was biased, given the researcher's primary ethical responsibility to his subjects.

And then there are the political implications of doing action anthropology in the environmental justice arena. By studying the origins, structure, and sociocultural consequence of environmental injustice (by mapping out the timelines and documenting the way problems are created and resolved) are we providing power structures with the means to maintain and reinforce the status quo? Conversely, what happens when movements "succeed"? The struggle to achieve transformations in decision-making systems requires confronting, challenging, and changing power structures. Backlash is inevitable.

Oftentimes, political response to environmental justice movements involves providing services or meeting demands in ways that serve, intentionally
or not, to co-opt the goals of the movement and deflate the power of movement leadership. Disinformation campaigns, publicly acknowledging culpa-
bility but responding to problems and victims in relatively minor ways, and
creating regulatory and decision-making frameworks that give the image of
addressing the concern but are implemented in limited and restrictive fashion
are all actions that neutralize a potential threat to the status quo. In other cases
backlash is more overtly violent, with actions that terrorize communities and
result in the loss of liberty and life. Movement leadership receive threats, have
their offices ransacked and records confiscated, are arrested and imprisoned,
or killed. Community supporters—including anthropologists—are threatened, beaten, banished, or killed. Government may be directly responsible, or,
through their approval or "blind eye," indirectly responsible.

The May 4, 1999, execution of Colombian anthropologist and University of
Antioquia professor Hernán Henao all too sadly illustrates these points. Professor Henao was the director of the Instituto de Estudios Regionales (INER),
a university research center coordinating studies of conflict, community development, environmental policy, and cultural diversity in the region surrounding Antioquia. At the time of his death, Professor Henao was conducting research on the social impact of proposed energy development and the
living conditions of the displaced populations of nearby Uraba, some 1.3 million peasants who had been forced off their lands by paramilitary organizations. On May 4, 1999, three unknown gunmen forced entry into a faculty
meeting and shot and killed Henao.

In this case, it is important to note that the paramilitary organizations were
originally set up by the Colombian military to fight leftist guerrillas and are
supported by local landlords who, according to news accounts, are active in the
drug trade and involved in a concerted effort to depopulate the countryside in
order to expand large cattle ranching enterprises and implement other development plans. Recent massacres of whole village populations have been reported, with no government response to such abuses. As a result, by May 1999
there were twice as many internal refugees in Colombia as there were at that
time in Kosovo. Colombian scholars who study this phenomenon have increasingly come under paramilitary threat and attack. Hernán Henao is the
seventh professor at the University of Antioquia to be murdered in the past ten
years, and the university has received violent threats from numerous armed
groups, both on the right and the left, unhappy with its research agenda.

Needs

As exploitation of the world's resources and degradation of the biosphere intensify, movements to reshape priorities and ways of life will play an increas-

ingly significant role. Anthropologists will engage environmental justice issues in increasing ways and will be continually confronting these personal, professional, and political risks. Which brings me to the final section of my chapter—a discussion of needs and a consideration of possible futures for disciplinary actors in the environmental quality/social justice arena.

Action-oriented anthropology can be anthropology at both its finest and its worst. To be a player in the political arena requires a balance of heady idealism and pragmatic cynicism. Effective engagement requires a continual awareness of what needs to be done; what the limitations and constraints might be; the ability to persevere in the face of all odds because the moral imperative drives you on; and the ability to compromise and move quickly as events, priorities, and people's needs change. As outlined in this chapter, some of the difficulties encountered in doing this work include the psychosocial, economic, and political impacts of working in typically isolated and marginalized settings—difficulties that contribute to the personal, professional, and political risks outlined above. Strengthening the role of anthropology in the environmental justice arena requires strategies that reinforce the value of this work and structures and arenas that improve information flow.

There is evidence of response to these needs. Doctoral programs in ecological and environmental anthropology have been created in a number of places, including the University of Hawaii, University of California at Santa Barbara, University of Washington, and University of Georgia. American University and Northern Arizona University offer applied master's degrees with an environmental anthropology emphasis. A growing number of undergraduate programs require internships and senior theses from their students, track post-B.A. employment, and host job fairs for graduating seniors. These actions significantly enhance employability. Professional organizations have sponsored environmental anthropology sessions, symposiums and meetings at conferences, and environmental anthropology newsletters, Web sites, and email list serves—all of which contribute to the growing sense of environmental anthropology community, improve information flow, provide opportunities for structured reflections on the efficacy and ethics of praxis, and suggest where the jobs are or might be.

In regards to employment and employability, opportunities for anthropologists in government, foundations, and NGOs will continue to grow, especially in the United States, but also in international organizations and institutions. Foreign aid is declining, while NGO activities have increased. There is a growing demand for people with anthropological training to work inside the NGO and private foundation community. In the United States, one effect of government downsizing has been a growing reliance on outside consultants to provide technical expertise to the government and the communities it serves. This fact, coupled with environmental justice regulations, means that the role of anthropology in the public arena will continue to expand.

To elaborate: As noted earlier in this chapter, U.S. environmental justice regulations articulated in Executive Order 12898 (*Federal Actions to Address Environmental Justice in Minority Populations and Low-Income Populations*) instruct all federal agencies to analyze environmental effects, including human health, economic, and social effects, of federal actions—including effects on minority communities and low-income communities—when such analysis is required by the National Environmental Policy Act (NEPA). The Departments of Defense, Energy, Transportation, Health, Education, Commerce, Housing and Urban Development, and all other agencies and departments of government, whenever they are required to prepare an environmental assessment or impact analysis, must consider the ways in which their actions create or perpetuate injustice, as well as the ways in which actions move communities toward justice.

While the environmental justice mandate originates from a presidential executive order rather than legislated act, and thus represents policy rather than law, the EPA, in its April 1999 implementation guidelines, has linked environmental justice goals to existing legislation (*National Environmental Policy Act of 1969*, 42 U.S.C. §4321 et seq.). EPA guidelines direct all federal agencies to include environmental justice assessments as a regular category of concern in all NEPA-mandated environmental impact statements (EISs) and environmental assessments (EAs). Any and all action involving the use of federal funds requires determination of whether an EA or EIS is needed—and thus requires consideration of sociocultural and other human environmental impacts. This linkage of environmental justice issues to existing legal mandates suggests potential research and technical assistance opportunities for anthropologists and other applied social scientists to not only document environmental injustices, but to develop the tools, data sets, and methodological strategies that serve to minimize or prevent future inequities.

Environmental Justice Assessments

Procedural methods for conducting the environmental justice assessments outlined in the EPA's guidance document include (1) determining whether an environmental justice assessment should be undertaken by characterizing the population affected by the proposed action in terms of racial and ethnic composition and in terms of relative income distribution to identify the presence of minority and/or low-income communities; (2) determining whether environmental impacts are likely to fall disproportionately on minority and/or low-income members of the community; and (3) assessing the degree to which proposed actions will have disproportionately high and adverse direct, indirect, or cumulative effects. Once a determination is made that there exists a potential for disproportionate risk, key questions become whether communities have been sufficiently involved in the decision-making process and whether communities currently suffer, or have historically suffered, from environmental and health risks or hazards.

This analysis requires the review of baseline demographic, socioeconomic, and environmental conditions; an assessment of the types of impacts that may be imposed upon all human and natural resources (e.g., air, water, soils, wildlife); and a determination of how these impacts may translate into human health concerns. Executive Order 12898 clearly stipulates that environmental human health analyses shall include diverse segments of the population in epidemiological and clinical studies, including groups at high risk from environmental hazards, such as minority and low-income populations and workers who may be exposed to substantial environmental hazards, and that environmental human health analyses, whenever practicable and appropriate, shall identify multiple and cumulative exposures.

Important considerations include:

1. The number and concentration of point and nonpoint release sources;
2. The presence of listed or highly ranked toxic pollutants with high exposure;
3. Multiple exposure sources and/or paths for the same pollutant and historical exposure sources and/or pathways;
4. The potential for aggravated susceptibility due to existing air pollution (in urban areas), lead poisoning, the existence of abandoned toxic sites;
5. The frequency of impacts; and
6. Cultural, health, and occupation-related variables such as health data reflective of the community (e.g., abnormal cancer rates, infant and childhood mortality, low birthweight rate, blood-lead levels); occupational exposures to environmental stresses that may exceed those experienced by the general population; and diets or differential patterns of consumption of natural resources that may suggest increased exposures to environmental pathways presenting potential health risk.

In considering direct, indirect, and cumulative impacts on natural resources, analysts must identify and assess the patterns and degrees to which the affected communities depend on natural resources for their economic bases (e.g., tourism and cash crops), as well as the cultural values that the community and/or native tribe may place on a natural resource at risk.

Once a determination has been made that an environmental justice assessment is needed, the key questions become whether or not there exists a potential for disproportionate risk; whether or not communities have been sufficiently involved in the decision-making process; and whether or not communities currently suffer, or have historically suffered, from environmental and health risks or hazards. Addressing these questions requires consideration of demographic, geographic, economic, and human health and risk factors.

Demographic factors include race, ethnicity, low-income status, population age, population density, population literacy, population/economic growth (including changes in low-income or minority populations in an area (e.g., migration), high birth rates, and cumulative impacts due to multiple sources of population increases.

Geographic factors include climate/weather patterns, geomorphic features, and hydrophilic features (presence of surface water and/or aquifers that may provide drinking water, subsistence fisheries, culturally significant water sources and use patterns, and recreational use).

Economic factors include:

1. Individual conditions (whether affordable or free quality health care is available and whether any cultural barriers exist to seeking health care);
2. Infrastructure conditions (whether historic allocation of resources has resulted in inadequate infrastructure development and maintenance);
3. Life-support resources (whether subsistence living situations such as fishing, hunting, gathering, farming, and other differential patterns of consumption of natural resources result in an additional risk exposure pathway or whether dietary practices within a community or ethnic group, such as a diet low in certain vitamins and minerals, may increase risk factors for that group);
4. Distribution of costs (whether proposed action will result in user fees for goods and services that impose a disproportionate distribution of costs on low-income families);
5. Community economic base (the degree to which a community is reliant on polluting industries for jobs and economic development may inhibit ability or will to take actions that would avoid risk to health and the environment at a cost to the industry, and the degree to which minority or low-income communities share the benefits in proportion to the risks or impacts they bear);
6. "Brownfields" (whether community revenue is sufficient enough to finance economic rehabilitation efforts that would improve the physical environment of a community);
7. Natural resources (the degree to which the community relies on natural resources for its economic base—tourism, crops, use of resources to create salable items, subsistence and commercial fisheries; and
8. Other indirect effects that a low-income or minority population, due to economic disadvantage, may not be able to avoid and that will have a synergistic effect with other risk factors (for example, vehicle pollution, lead-based paint poisoning, existence of abandoned toxic sites, dilapidated housing stock).

Human health and risk factors include emissions, toxins (presence or exposure to), exposures and exposure pathways, pollutants, pesticides (exposure and misuses), exposure through multiple locations, and exposure to emissions from concentrated locations of the same type of industry (or industries). Health data for the population in question is critical (e.g., abnormal levels of cancers, asthma, emphysema, birth defects, low birthweight, infant and childhood mortality, blood lead levels, asbestosis). This data could indicate historical hazards and health risks that, in concert with the effects of the proposed action, could cumulatively or indirectly raise environmental justice issues. Also important are identified research gaps (e.g., subsistence consumption, demographics, dietary effects, synergistic effects of chemicals).

Factors relating to cultural and ethnic difference and communications concerns include:

1. Community access to the decision-making process;
2. Cultural expectations and understanding of the decision-making process;
3. Meaningful information;
4. Job security (potential for fear within the community that participating in the process may jeopardize job security);
5. Literacy rate (should presentations to the community involve nonwritten materials, such as videos?);
6. Primary language and the need for translations of written and oral material;
7. Community representation;
8. Community identification (did identification of minority and/or low-income communities take into account all potentially impacted communities? If communities were geographically defined rather than culturally defined, certain communities that are impacted, given other cultural factors, may be unfairly excluded); and
9. Indigenous populations.

When projects or activities may affect tribal lands or resources or Native American communities, the EPA advises all federal agencies to include analysts familiar with Native American issues and culture, and the agencies are directed to formally request that the affected native tribe(s) seek participation as a cooperating agency. Factors to consider in such situations include, but are not limited to, (1) the trust responsibility to, and treaties, statutes, and executive orders with, federally recognized tribes and (2) the effect of insufficient financial and technical resources for the development and implementation of tribal environmental programs. Projects or activities that may affect Native American treaty–protected resources and natural and cultural resources considered sacred due to religious beliefs and/or social/ceremonial ties must also be taken into account.

Environmental justice assessments also require looking at historical conditions, existing conditions, and the impact of future actions. For example, the

concentration of industries may create a high risk of exposure to environmental hazards for the community's economic base. There may have been an
inconsistent application of standards. There maybe research gaps and questions about the validity of past data collection practices (data relevant to low-
income communities may not be adequately collected and analyzed given the
potential for inadequate resources within the community to collect and analyze data). Program gaps between tribal, state, and federal programs may have
subjected communities to risk of exposure to environmental hazards. Nonin-
clusive processes of decision making, documentation, and resource allocation
may result in "community representation" that reflects the potentially affected
industry and socioeconomic elite rather than the actually affected broader
community.

The environmental justice guidance document outlines a wide range of
methods and tools that can be used to conduct environmental justice assessments and emphasizes the need for methodological flexibility, noting that the
application of any tool is dependent upon the type of study, the particular attributes of the area under study, and the data available to undertake the study.
Tools described include locational and distributional implements (maps, aerial photographs, and interactive geographical information systems) and risk
assessment and risk management. Characterizing the likelihood for a chemical or substance to cause adverse health effects to humans and assessing the
possible impacts on a population require considering the differential patterns
of subsistence consumption of natural resources (rates of consumption for
fish, vegetation, water, and wildlife among ethnic groups and among cultures)
and differential land and water resource use patterns (consumption, economy,
cultural use, and/or recreation).

As you can see in the above summary, the EPA's guidelines for implementing environmental justice regulations present multiple avenues for anthropological input. Anthropological research can generate baseline information
useful in the analysis of a wide variety of environmental health and socioeconomic variable factors. We can develop databases that identify and describe
sources of information, data, and knowledge pertaining to historical conditions and sociocultural groups in a given region. We can use applied ethnographic methods to develop sociocultural profiles of current communities in
ways that constitute a "baseline" database—documenting different cultural
and social group behavior, conditions, and consequential concerns that might
affect cumulative and indirect impacts. We can document and articulate subsistence patterns and lifeways that might contribute to increased vulnerability.
We can work with vulnerable communities to understand environmental
threats, recognize "high-risk" behavior, and generate culturally appropriate
strategies for reducing risk. By using applied ethnographic techniques to conduct baseline surveys we can facilitate educational outreach and informed
participatory involvement in environmental planning and decision-making
processes. I believe we can do all this and more in response to (and sustained

by) federally funded mandates for considering the sociocultural dimensions of environmental impact analysis. And, in doing so, we will not only be contributing to efforts to shape and reshape public policy and the meaning and power of community in the environmental planning and problem-solving process, this public interest work may indeed prevent, at one level or another, future inequities.

If the above discussion infers that anthropology's future in environmental justice work is simply that of technocrat, then I urge the reader to consider the many ways that U.S. legislation, policies, and implementing mechanisms are reproduced in multilateral, international, and national entities around the world. Environmental impact analysis has become the central decision-making tool used at all levels of governance and, increasingly, in financial and corporate organizations. Environmental justice assessments provide the opportunity to resituate the focus of impact analysis studies, from their current emphasis on the costs and benefits of decisions at a given point in time, to one that considers historical and projects future conditions and inequities and places these concerns in a decision-making framework where sociocultural consequences are deemed significant categories of concern.

Conclusion

Anthropology engages environmental justice in crucial ways: in the production and distribution of information and in the creation and facilitation of arenas where information is disseminated, ideas exchanged, problems defined, decisions made, and solutions achieved. At one point or another in our lives we are all analysts, advocates, activists, and troublemakers. We influence change in subtle and sometimes surprising ways. The EcoJustice home page (November 1996) is a new site summarizing the content of the EcoJustice World Wide Web training sessions hosted by the IGC. Their cyberspace training guide, used by minority activist participants and accessed by anyone who logs on, uses a quote from Margaret Mead as an introductory theme: "Never doubt that a small group of thoughtful citizens can change the world. Indeed, it's the only thing that ever has" (http://www.igc.org/envjustice/training).

References

Key Federal "Environmental Justice" Legislation

Council on Environmental Quality. January 1997. *Considering Cumulative Effects under the National Environmental Policy Act.*
———. March 1998. *Guidance for Addressing Environmental Justice under the National Environmental Policy Act (NEPA).*

Executive Order 12898. February 11, 1994. *Federal Actions to Address Environmental Justice in Minority Populations and Low-Income Populations with Accompanying Memorandum.*
Executive Order 13007. May 24, 1996. *Indian Sacred Sites.*
The National Environmental Policy Act of 1969 as Amended. 42 U.S.C. 4321-4347. January 1, 1970.
U.S. Environmental Protection Agency, Office of Federal Activities. April 1999. *Final Guidance for Incorporating Environmental Justice Concerns in EPA's NEPA Compliance Analyses.*
U.S. General Accounting Office. June 1, 1983. *Siting of Hazardous Waste Landfills and Their Correlation with Racial and Economic Status of Surrounding Communities.*

Published Literature

Bodley, John. 1990. *Victims of Progress.* 3rd ed. Palo Alto, Calif.: Middlefield.
Bryant, Bunyan, ed. 1995. *Environmental Justice: Issues, Policies, Solutions.* Washington, D.C.: Island Press.
Bullard, Robert. 1990. *Dumping in Dixie: Race, Class and Environmental Quality.* Boulder, Colo.: Westview.
———. 1993. *Confronting Environmental Racism: Voices from the Grassroots.* Boston: South End Press.
Davis, Shelton H. 1977. *Victims of the Miracle: Development and the Indians of Brazil.* Cambridge: Cambridge University Press.
Donahue, John, and Barbara Rose Johnston, eds. 1998. *Water, Culture and Power: Local Struggles in a Global Context.* Washington, D.C.: Island Press.
Johnston, Barbara Rose, ed. 1994. *Who Pays the Price? The Sociocultural Context of Environmental Crisis.* Washington, D.C.: Island Press.
———. 1997. *Life and Death Matters.* Walnut Creek, Calif.: AltaMira.
Lee, Charles. 1993. "Beyond Toxins and Race." In Bullard, ed., *Confronting Environmental Racism,* 41–52.
Oliver-Smith, Anthony. 1996. "Anthropological Research on Hazards and Disasters." *Annual Review of Anthropology* 25: 303–28.
Rappaport, Roy. 1993. "The Anthropology of Trouble." *American Anthropologist* 95: 295–303.
———. 1994. "Human Environment and the Notion of Impact." In Johnson, ed., *Who Pays the Price?* 157–69.
Sachs, Aaron. 1995. *Eco-Justice: Linking Human Rights and the Environment.* Worldwatch Paper #27. Washington, D.C.: Worldwatch Institute.
Szasz, Andrew. 1994. *Ecopopulism: Toxic Waste and the Movement for Environmental Justice.* Minneapolis: University of Minnesota Press.
United Church of Christ Commission for Racial Justice. 1987. *Toxic Wastes and Race in the United States, A National Report on the Racial and Socioeconomic Characteristics of Communities with Hazardous Waste Sites.* New York: United Church of Christ.
Wolfe, Amy K., David P. Vogt, Ho-Ling Hwang. 1995. "Incorporating Environmental Justice into Environmental Decision Making." In *Environmental Challenges: The Next Twenty Years: National Association of Environmental Professionals 20th Annual Proceedings* (1995), 277– 85.

Internet References

ArcticCircle Web site
(http://www.lib.uconn.edu/arcticcircle)
EcoJustice Training Session
(http://www.igc.org/envjustice/training)
Institute for Global Communications
(http://www.igc.org)
Society for Applied Anthropology, Environmental Anthropology project
(http://www.sfaanet/eap/abouteap.html)

8

The Politics of Ethnographic Presence: Sites and Topologies in the Study of Transnational Environmental Movements

J. Peter Brosius

On March 31, 1987, Penan hunter-gatherers in the Baram and Limbang Districts of Sarawak, East Malaysia, erected a series of blockades against logging companies that were encroaching on their lands. It was not long before photographic images of these blockades, accompanied by transcripts of Penan statements, made their way to Japan, Australia, Europe, and North America. Though the struggle for indigenous rights in Sarawak had been developing for several years through the efforts of Malaysian environmental activists, the circulation of images of Penan facing down police at blockades resulted in a dramatic upsurge in interest in the issue of logging in Sarawak among Northern environmental and indigenous rights activists.[1] Within a very short time, the Penan became the focus of a broad-based transnational environmental and indigenous rights campaign involving organizations in Europe, North America, Japan, and Australia. The momentum of the campaign to stop logging in Sarawak grew continually through the late 1980s and early 1990s. In a manner analogous to the case of the Kayapó of Brazil, the Penan, singled out among other involved indigenous groups in Sarawak, acquired a very high international media profile and were supported by numerous prominent political figures and celebrities. For a while at least, the spotlight of global environmental activism was focused directly on Sarawak.

This campaign is of considerable historical significance. Reaching its apogee at precisely the time that Malaysia was giving shape to its highly visible role at the 1992 Rio Summit, it profoundly influenced how Northern environmental nongovernmental organizations (NGOs) approach issues affecting the South. Furthermore, Malaysia's response provided a blueprint for other Southern nations to respond to Northern environmental campaigns. The Malaysian government responded vigorously to the criticisms of Northern environmentalists, denouncing what they portrayed as Northern "eco-colonialism" and making compelling arguments about Northern consumption. They attempted to delegitimize Penan resistance to logging by attributing it to the influence of foreign "instigators" and undertook a broad-based effort to discredit both local and international environmental NGOs. The International Tropical Timber Organization (ITTO), the International Hardwood Products Association (IHPA), and large transnational public relations firms eventually became involved as well, all with the intent of countering the campaign against logging in Sarawak.

For the last several years my ethnographic research has focused not merely on Penan resistance to logging, but on the dynamics of the campaign itself. I am interested in examining its discursive and institutional contours in order to understand how various agents—the Penan, the Malaysian government,[2] Malaysian NGOs, Northern mainstream NGOs, and Northern grassroots NGOs—have each constructed and contested the terms of the debate. More than this, however, I want to learn more about how environmental discourses configure (or are in turn configured by) emerging forms of political agency. A campaign such as this is not merely the sum total of a series of points of contestation among a range of actors with a diversity of fixed perspectives. Rather, it is a campaign that has been transformed from a singular focus on the imperative to stop the progress of bulldozers, to one forced to contend with the Uruguay Round of the General Agreement on Tariffs and Trade, i.e., post-UNCED (the 1992 United Nations Conference on Environment and Development, the Rio Earth Summit) conventions, ITTO criteria indicators of sustainability, and the North–South debate. In the process, certain actors have been marginalized, while others have been privileged. If anthropologists are concerned with understanding the processes by which emerging forms of political agency are constituted and configured, it defeats our purpose to regard these debates in terms of mere polyvocality. In fact, certain voices are able to edge others out, certain voices may be co-opted, certain voices may be dismissed as disruptive, and certain voices may be taken to be irrelevant. How does the process of forcing open spaces for newly emerging political agents occur? How or why do such spaces close on others? These are the types of questions that are central to my current project.

This research is an example of a much broader trend: recent years have witnessed a dramatic upsurge in interest among anthropologists in analyzing subaltern social movements, particularly those mobilizing around environmental and indigenous rights issues. Anthropological interest in these movements is in part a product of the fact that they have become such highly visible players in a terrain that anthropologists once thought they could claim as their own—the rural/remote field site, most likely occupied by indigenous communities of one sort or another (Turner 1991). It is also a product of recent theoretical trends within (and beyond) the discipline. One such trend is the way anthropologists have come to define our work as an exercise in cultural critique (Marcus and Fischer 1986). If there is a single, recognizable trend in contemporary work on social movements among anthropologists, it is that we have linked them to transnational discourses. Because the line between what is "theirs" (subaltern, especially Southern or indigenous, social movements) and what is "ours" (metropolitan, especially Northern, forms of representation) is thereby blurred, these discourses become suitable subjects for critique. An equally important source for anthropological interest in subaltern social movements has been our embrace of post-Foucauldian insights into the intersections of discourse/power/knowledge, which have likewise intersected with a series of critiques of, or challenges to, traditional anthropological conceptions of culture.[3]

Sites of Ethnographic Inquiry

These trends have important implications for theorizing the practice of ethnographic writing and have produced studies that are qualitatively different from traditional ethnographic research projects. Most significantly perhaps, they raise the question of what constitutes an ethnographic research site. Gupta and Ferguson (1992) have made the influential argument that "an anthropology whose objects are no longer conceived as automatically and naturally anchored in space will need to pay particular attention to the way spaces and places are made, imagined, contested, and enforced" (17–18). Indeed, research on a campaign such as I have described cannot presume the existence of a single, coherent research site nor be conducted in any single location, because the events that constitute its history have occurred in so many places. This campaign consists not merely of a set of blockades in a remote part of Borneo but is also manifested in environmentalists' direct actions in Los Angeles and Sydney, decisions by the Austrian Parliament, U.S. congressional resolutions condemning the use of Sarawak timber, high-profile Malaysian government delegations to Europe, strategizing meetings, press conferences, benefit concerts, letter-writing campaigns, newspaper articles, faxes, e-mail messages, and more. In my attempts to try to give coherence to all of this, I have carried out "field" research at a diverse number of sites: at encampments of nomadic Penan; at the Ministry of Primary Industries in Kuala Lumpur; at Rainforest Action Network headquarters in San Francisco; at World Wildlife Fund international headquarters near Geneva; at the Parliament building in Vienna; at the offices of the ITTO in Yokohama; and in London, Copenhagen, Munich, Basel, Sydney, Penang, and elsewhere.

Ethnographic "sites" are both physical and discursive. Marcus (1995) has identified "multi-sited ethnography" as distinct from the traditional anthropological practice of conducting intensive, intimate ethnographic studies of a particular site, whether it be a remote village in the New Guinea highlands, a peasant community in Mexico, or an urban neighborhood in the United States. According to Marcus, multi-sited ethnography moves out from the single sites and local situations of conventional ethnographic research designs to examine the circulation of cultural meanings, objects, and identities in diffuse time-space. This mode defines for itself an object of study that cannot be accounted for ethnographically by remaining focused on a single site of intensive investigation. This mobile ethnography takes unexpected trajectories in tracing a cultural formation across and within multiple sites of activity. . . . Just as this mode investigates and ethnographically constructs the lifeworlds of variously situated subjects, it also ethnographically constructs aspects of the system itself through the associations and connections it suggests among sites. (Marcus 1995: 96)

To be sure, the idea that an ethnographic research project might be carried out at more than a single research site is, by itself, nothing new. Most notable here have been studies of immigrant or diasporic communities. What differentiates multi-sited ethnography, as it is articulated by Marcus, is that it takes as its focus not some community or category of people, however dispersed or mobile they may be, but rather some cultural formation or discourse, following it as it moves through, across, among, and between sites of cultural production, institutions, communities, and categories of actors, often in unpredictable ways and with unpredictable results.

There is yet another dimension of multi-sitedness that Marcus does not consider: the phenomenon of multi-sitedness describes not only an explicit research design, but also a state of affairs that increasingly impinges on anthropological field sites, existing whether researchers make it central to their analyses or not. That is to say, it is critical that we distinguish between multi-sitedness as a form of *analysis*, and multi-sitedness as a *condition*. The growing effectiveness of various forms of capitalist penetration, the increasing ubiquity and effectiveness of technologies of state power, and continually globalizing processes of cultural production all contribute to the proliferation of "chains, paths, threads, conjunctions, or juxtapositions of locations" (1995: 105) that characterizes the *condition* of multi-sitedness.[4]

Acknowledging these two dimensions of multi-sitedness has important implications for how anthropologists think about the consequences of the research projects in which they engage. It suggests to me that anthropologists have a great deal more work to do examining the extent of their own accountability as they engage in attempts to represent multi-sited contexts, particularly when such projects focus on subaltern social movements. Responsible anthropological engagement with environmental and indigenous rights movements (and other types of movements as well) demands that the matter of our accountability be placed at the forefront of our efforts—at the level of epistemology—rather than contained as an afterthought in a code of ethics.

In the following I take up this challenge with reference to my own work on the Sarawak campaign. I do so as a way of elucidating the argument that taking seriously the multi-sitedness of research projects such as this demands that we rethink the implications of our ethnographic presence and our efforts at representation. This in turn might have a transformative effect in our thinking about the possibility for alternative forms of ethnographic practice.

Situating the Sarawak Campaign

Penan and the State: The Project of Development

In interior central Borneo there exist two broad classes of people: long-house-dwelling swidden agriculturalists and hunting and gathering forest nomads such as the Penan. While agriculturalists live along the main rivers, Penan and other hunter-gatherers are found in interior headwaters. The Penan of Sarawak are divided into two distinct populations, Eastern and Western Penan (Needham 1972: 177), together numbering some seven thousand individuals. The Eastern Penan inhabit the Baram and Limbang watersheds, while the Western Penan are mostly found in the Balui watershed. Though in broad outline the forest adaptations of Eastern and Western Penan are very similar, and though they speak mutually intelligible subdialects of the same language, there are significant differences between these two groups with regard to subsistence technology, settlement patterns, and social organization.[5]

Sarawak has a rather notable colonial history, in that for a century it was controlled by three so-called "White Rajahs": James Brooke (1841–1868), his nephew Charles Brooke (1868–1917), and Charles's son Vyner Brooke (1917–1941). Sarawak was ceded to the British crown in 1946 and joined Malaysia in 1963. Through much of their reign, the Brookes remained resolutely opposed to the establishment of large-scale commercial enterprises, particularly European-run plantations (Reece 1988). This conservative attitude was perpetuated both by a self-interested concern that a European commercial class in Sarawak might challenge Brooke authority and by a belief that such enterprises were antithetical to the interests of indigenous communities (Reece 1988: 32). As such, the Brookes maintained a system in which native "welfare" was defined by the preservation of traditional lifeways. It was only in the 1930s that one begins to discern a shift from an ideology of preservation to one of transformation. Government commitment to the idea of transforming indigenous communities increased during the British colonial period and intensified even more after 1963. In the postcolonial period the concept of development became an increasingly central point of articulation between the government and local populations: in upriver areas the government undertook an accelerated effort to establish schools and dispensaries, eradicate malaria, and promote agricultural development.

With respect to Penan, the government focused its efforts on persuading nomadic bands to settle and take up agriculture. In both the Baram and Belaga Districts Penan communities were provided with goods intended to help them make the transition to a settled life: chainsaws, outboard motors, corrugated zinc roofing, plywood, piped water systems, and the like. Such efforts have had a transformative effect on the lives of Penan. In the late 1950s perhaps 70 to 80 percent of Eastern and Western Penan were still nomadic. During the 1960s, they began to settle in increasing numbers, such that by 1970 only a handful continued their nomadic way of life. Today fewer than four hundred Eastern Penan remain fully nomadic, approximately 5 percent of the total. Though most Penan are settled, they remain on ancestral lands.

The Penan Response to Logging

Even more consequential than settlement for the lives of Penan has been the advent of logging. In the 1980s Sarawak became a major supplier of tropical hardwoods on the international market and experienced one of the highest rates of deforestation in the world. Today the pace of logging has diminished, as timber stands are much depleted, and companies from Sarawak have moved to Papua New Guinea, Suriname, Guyana, and elsewhere.[6]

Logging has a dramatic effect on the lives of Penan. Sago palms (*Eugeissona utilis*), which form the basis of traditional subsistence, are uprooted by bulldozers; fruit trees and rattan are destroyed; game disappears; severe river siltation occurs; and graves are obliterated. Logging not only undermines the basis of Penan subsistence but, by transforming sites with biographical, social, and historical significance, also destroys those things that are iconic of their existence as a society. Moreover, though Sarawak is notable within Malaysia for the degree to which it has historically recognized the land rights of indigenous communities, Sarawak state law does not recognize Penan principles of land tenure. According to Sarawak land law, communities can only claim land that they cultivated before 1958. Because the majority of Penan settled after that, their claims to land are without legal basis, and they are effectively unable to resist the incursions of timber companies through legal means.

Whether they are actively engaged in resistance or appear to acquiesce, Eastern and Western Penan everywhere are, with but a few notable exceptions, opposed to logging. Penan narratives tell of confrontations between themselves and company representatives or state authorities and recount the arguments that they put forth: why a particular watershed belongs to them, why bulldozers have no place in the forest, and why surveyors should not mark trees. Logging is, for Penan, an all-consuming topic.

Their response to logging is a product not only of the tangible effects of environmental degradation, but also of the way they perceive themselves to have been treated by those with an interest in its continuation: camp managers, police, politicians, and others. Penan feel that they are looked down upon, ignored, and treated unjustly, and that this indicates an utter disregard for their humanity. They characterize government officials as people who "don't know how to pity." As one woman stated, "When they [the government or company people] look into our eyes, they see the eyes of a monkey, the eyes of a dog."

The Penan express overwhelming frustration at the apparent inability of government officials to hear them. Indeed, state officials most often attribute Penan disaffection either to the fact that they have been instigated by foreign environmentalists or that they have been "neglected": if only the government had done more to help Penan develop, one hears officials say, they would not be so "confused" and unruly.

Consistently the response of Penan has been to try to explicate their situation and their point of view to those representing timber interests, to environmentalists, and to anyone else who will listen. Most often, they do so in the form of analogies, which they feel will express their feelings in a way intelligible to outsiders. They compare the forest to a warehouse, shop, or bank and compare the act of felling the forest to driving a bulldozer through the middle of someone's house. They contrast their way of life with that of civil servants who must merely go to their offices to make a living.

Eastern Penan have also responded to the injustices they perceive by actively espousing a desire for a return of colonialism, manifested in the person of the Queen. Contemporary Eastern Penan seem intent on insisting on the illegitimacy of contemporary Malay rule[7] and on the legitimacy of colonial rule, based on precedence and historical depth. It was *orang putih* (white people), they state, who governed them in ancestral times, whereas Malays are mere newcomers. In the Eastern Penan view, during the colonial period, government authorities behaved in a manner that was appropriate to their role: they interceded for Penan in trade meetings, brought about an end to headhunting, and respected the integrity of the lands they occupied. Not only did they not transgress Eastern Penan boundaries, they maintained those boundaries so that others would not violate them. The current government, by contrast, is transgressing those boundaries on a massive scale.

While Western Penan have been conspicuously acquiescent to the activities of logging companies, Eastern Penan have responded with grievances and, when those proved ineffective, with the erection of blockades in the late 1980s and early 1990s. Eastern Penan from distant groups flocked to blockade sites to lend support, and these sites were sometimes occupied by several hundred people at a time. Inevitably these blockades were broken up, and those at the site were arrested; however, what is most striking about these blockades is the degree to which they have been characterized by a sense of unity among bands of people who have no history of unified political action. They blockaded because they believed this was their only recourse, a matter of last resort, and they stress that they were not blocking anyone else's land but their own. From their perspective, because they patiently made numerous good faith attempts at dialogue, they were entirely without fault when they at last took action: they were driven to it by the inaction of the government.

The Sarawak Campaign

The portion of the campaign that interests me here began in 1987 when images of Penan blockades began to circulate transnationally. The result—at a time when concern about rain forest destruction was increasing among the Euroamerican public at large—was a dramatic upsurge in interest in the Penan among numerous Northern environmental organizations. For a while at least, the Penan became icons of resistance for environmentalists worldwide. This was not to last.

The early part of the campaign focused on the civil disobedience of the Penan—blockades, arrests, and trials—as well as on the local efforts of the Malaysian environmental organization Sahabat Alam Malaysia (SAM, Friends of the Earth–Malaysia) to support the Penan struggle on local and worldwide levels. SAM representatives helped Penan draft letters in an attempt to establish land claims, provided lawyers, helped Penan with material support at blockade sites, and played a prominent role in educating local peoples about their rights under the law. Eventually, other organizations became involved in the Penan cause. SAM was instrumental in the formation of the Sarawak Penan Association. Indigenous activist Anderson Mutang formed the Sarawak Indigenous People's Alliance (SIPA), which provided a conduit for information and support to Penan involved in civil disobedience.[8]

The early part of the campaign also focused on the charismatic figure of Swiss environmentalist Bruno Manser. In 1984, breaking off from a cave-exploring expedition to which he was attached, Manser disappeared into the forest and took up residence with a band of nomadic Eastern Penan in the upper Tutoh River area. He remained among various nomadic groups for six and a half years. More than any other single actor, it is Manser who is most responsible for bringing the situation of the Penan to world attention. Beginning in 1985, Manser began writing to a number of environmental organizations describing in vivid terms the plight of the Penan. In a very short time reporters, filmmakers, and environmentalists began to seek him out in the forest. At the same time that Manser was working to make their situation known outside of Sarawak, he was simultaneously engaged in organizing the normally retiring Eastern Penan to resist. Manser traveled extensively throughout the Baram and Limbang Districts, organizing large meetings that were attended by representatives from numerous communities. At these meetings Penan representatives discussed cases of harassment by timber company employees, the desirability of blockading, what they should do if arrests occurred, and other such issues. The overall purpose of these meetings was to gauge the degree to which Penan were of a common mind and to persuade them to act in concert. Along with SAM, Manser provided Penan the opportunity to internationalize their cause, and he spelled out to them both the benefits and costs of blockading and being arrested.

As the international Sarawak campaign accelerated, numerous individual environmentalists attempted to visit Eastern Penan in order to document their plight for international distribution. In their visits to Penan communities, these individuals frequently told Penan of efforts made on their behalf in Europe, Australia, North America, and Japan. In speaking with Eastern Penan today it is evident that the stories told to them about outside efforts to support them, and indeed the very fact of visits by foreign environmentalists, provided them with a strong sense of the legitimacy of their own efforts.

Much of the rhetoric of the Sarawak campaign at this time, from Northern NGOs in particular, centered around the imperative to "save" the Penan. The threat facing the Penan and the rain forest was constructed by environmentalists according to what might be termed the *Fern Gully* allegory, after the animated film. The image presented was of pristine indigenous innocents living a timeless existence in the depths of the rain forest, as bulldozers churned toward them, devouring everything in their path. Such an image had the effect of producing a sense of great urgency, as did statements to the effect that the Penan had only a few months left or that the forests of Sarawak would be gone in just a few years.

An explosion in media coverage served to raise the profile of the Penan even further. The Sarawak situation received coverage on *NBC Evening News, National Public Radio*, CNN, and *Primetime Live*, as well as in *Newsweek, Time, The New Yorker, The Wall Street Journal*, and *Rolling Stone*.[9] BBC and *National Geographic* both produced documentaries on the Penan. The Australian film *Blowpipes and Bulldozers* and the Swedish film *Tong Tana* both reached large audiences and received wide acclaim. Meanwhile, Penan were awarded the Reebok Human Rights Award and the Sierra Club–sponsored Chico Mendez Award, and SAM activist Harrison Ngau was awarded the Goldman Prize for his work against logging in Sarawak. As the campaign became increasingly internationalized in the late 1980s, there was a sustained series of direct actions and other campaign activities in the United States, the United Kingdom, Japan, Australia, and Europe that served to keep a focus on the situation in Sarawak. Numerous public figures supported the cause of indigenous rights in Sarawak. In 1989 members of the Grateful Dead testified before the U.S. Congress on behalf of the Penan. Al Gore held two press conferences with Bruno Manser and supported the Penan cause in his book *Earth in the Balance* (1992).

As noted, the Malaysian government responded vigorously to this campaign. At the local level, there was (and continues to be) outright repression: the arrest of several hundred Penan at blockade sites, the employment of gangsters to provide extralegal "security" on timber concession lands, and the harassment or arrest of members of Malaysian environmental organizations. Along with such explicitly repressive measures, government officials dismissed Penan blockades as the product of foreign "instigators." Through the rhetoric of instigation, Penan were portrayed as "confused": deluded objects of pity to whom only sympathy was due.

Malaysia also initiated an extremely effective rhetorical offensive against Northern environmentalists. Initially, when they took up the Sarawak campaign, Northern NGOs were convinced that they had the moral high ground and never expected that their actions would be met with such a sustained, aggressive response from Malaysia. The line between good and bad seemed evident: a group of corrupt politicians were devouring Sarawak's forests for short-term profit at the expense of indigenous communities. With time, however, as Malaysia began to refine its response, it became less easy for Northern environmentalists to dismiss.

One of the most effective elements of the Malaysian response was the linking of Northern environmental activism to the legacy of colonialism. This was used to delegitimize Penan civil disobedience, Malaysian NGO activism, and Northern NGO involvement in Malaysian affairs. Further, in responding to criticisms from Northern environmentalists, Malaysian officials insisted that Penan should be given the opportunity to enter the "mainstream" of Malaysian society by bringing them the "fruits of development." Advocates of rain forest conservation and indigenous rights were accused of wishing to relegate indigenous communities to the status of museum specimens.

Malaysian officials also began to make compelling counterarguments about the linkages between North and South. They raised questions about the place of temperate forests in the global forest equation, asking why the North should impose standards of sustainability for logging in tropical forests when no such efforts are made in their own countries. Linked to this were arguments tying forest destruction in the South to Northern consumption. At the same time, Malaysia began increasingly to adopt the rhetoric of sustainable forestry. One manifestation of this was its greater visibility in the activities of the ITTO, particularly following the 1990 visit of an ITTO delegation to Sarawak.[10]

Such arguments were highly effective in blunting much of the moral/ political force of Northern environmentalist rhetoric. These efforts proved particularly useful to Malaysia as environmentalist efforts in Europe began to have an effect on the market for Malaysian timber. Malaysia hired the public relations firms Burson-Marsteller and Hill & Knowlton to counter environmentalist rhetoric about the use of tropical timber. At the same time, it developed its own public relations apparatus—the Malaysian Timber Council and the Sarawak Timber Association. High-profile trade delegations visited Northern countries in an effort to put a softer face on the Malaysian timber industry and to foreground its efforts to promote sustainable forestry.

In time, Northern environmentalists realized that this had ceased to be a simple morality play. No longer was it merely an issue of stopping bulldozers and saving endangered forest-dwellers. Given Malaysia's sustained critique of "eco-colonialism," no longer did urgent demands for action have much salience. Northern NGOs responded in part by placing greater emphasis on the Northern role in tropical deforestation, turning their efforts toward reducing tropical timber consumption in their own countries.

The overall effect of these developments was that the debate over logging in Sarawak shifted from a focus on forest destruction and the rights of indigenous communities to an issue of sustainable forest management. At the center of the early Sarawak campaign were arresting images (in the most literal sense) of Penan and charismatic figures such as Bruno Manser. However, as some Northern NGOs began participating in ITTO meetings and other efforts aimed at achieving sustainable forest management, the role that such images and individuals could play was diminished. At an ITTO meeting in which criteria indicators of sustainability are on the agenda, images of blockades and arrests are not merely irrelevant but disruptive, and there is no place whatever for committed activists such as Bruno Manser. The critical dynamic here is the shifting pattern of marginalizations and privilegings that occurred as the discursive contours of the debate were shifted—not innocently—away from the moral/political domain toward the domain of governmentality, management, bureaucratization, and institutionalization. Little wonder that by the early 1990s the passion that maintained the momentum around this issue began to dissipate.

Old Contexts, Old Concerns: The Problem of Appropriation

The prospect of writing about the Sarawak campaign is one that makes me very nervous. For the most part, concern about the "unintended consequences" of ethnographic research has centered around the worry that it will somehow be appropriated by those in positions of power and used to the disadvantage of those who are the object of study. Such concerns are by no means trivial. This is something that has profoundly concerned me in my own work on the Sarawak campaign. Indeed, I have already seen my own work used in ways that I find very troubling.

In 1992 the Sarawak Museum organized a special exhibition on the Penan. Though ostensibly ethnographic, it was much more an effort to demonstrate the government's interest in the welfare of the Penan. The structure of this exhibition reproduced in form the rhetoric of bringing Penan into the mainstream. It was constituted as a passage from "tradition" to the "modern world": from such traditional Penan pursuits as sago making and blowpipe construction to agriculture, modern medicine, and education.

I was asked by the Sarawak Museum for advice on what should be included in the exhibition, particularly with respect to the "traditional" elements of Penan life. Recognizing that I had a responsibility to the institution that had sponsored my research, and wanting to convey to the Malaysian public what I knew of Penan conceptions of the landscape (in the perhaps naive hope that this would contribute to an unsympathetic public's rethinking of what lay behind the Penan struggle), I obliged.

While I was concerned to provide what I felt to be accurate information on the Penan, I had no say in the design of the exhibition itself (nor did I ever see the final product). Clearly the intent of the exhibition was political, what with its unabashedly progressivist narrative structure. I expected this to be the case and intended my contribution to be a subtle subversion of that message. What I did not anticipate was that my own personage would be used to give legitimacy to the government's message. As I learned only later, the exhibition featured a large glossy picture of myself, along with text implying that my research on Penan could be taken to be an indication of the government's concern to improve the welfare of the Penan. Drawing on my status as an "expert," it also served as a kind of validation of the interpretations provided in the exhibition.

More disquieting has been the way in which my work has been taken out of context and meanings attached to it that were never intended. One focus of my research has been an attempt to understand the Penan perception of the campaign that is being carried out on their behalf, in particular what they make of the visits of numerous foreign environmentalists since 1987. Among other things I found, as noted, that many Penan keenly desire the "return" of the Queen. More than simple colonial nostalgia, many believe that this is indeed a possibility and that foreign environmentalists are a vanguard for her return. I have written about this belief in a series of pieces (Brosius 1993a, 1997b, 1999b) and spoke about it at a government-sponsored conference in Malaysia. In describing this my concern was to suggest that it is a lack of acknowledgment of the legitimacy of Penan land claims that has compelled them to embrace the colonial legacy rather than to define themselves as Malaysian citizens. To my surprise, this argument surfaced in 1994—in completely distorted form—in an address by a government official to a group of indigenous leaders. This was reported in the local press—which is tightly controlled by the government—under the headline "White men will return, Penan told" and "'European governments will colonise Sarawak to stop logging' goes the lie."[11] The article went on to report how a number of foreign environmentalists had been spreading such rumors in an effort to persuade Penan not to cooperate with the government.

I can only assume that appropriations of both my work and my status as an "expert" are likely to continue as long as Penan land rights are a contentious issue. To be sure, those cases that I have described are relatively innocuous in their direct effects on Penan. Certainly one could imagine any number of more damaging ways in which my work could be used. That such a thing has not yet occurred does not detract from the possibility that it might, particularly given Malaysia's ever more widespread employment of public relations firms that carefully monitor whatever is written about indigenous and rain forest issues in Sarawak and quickly formulate media strategies designed to limit the damage to Malaysia's timber industry. As I write about Penan civil disobedience I can and do, of course, take steps to protect particular individuals and communities. The problem arises when I believe that these steps can actually address concerns about the impact of my work or exonerate me from further responsibility.

New Contexts, New Concerns: Subaltern Social Movements and Multi-Sited Ethnography

Traditional conceptions of ethnographic practice are premised on what might be termed a *topology of simple locality:* a topology that defines the task of the ethnographer as one of inscribing and representing for an anthropological audience some actually existing place or set of places. The convenience of such a topology lies in the fact that the intended or unintended consequences of the act of representation can be measured by the degree of actual or potential impact *on a particular place* (or places) and on those who live there. If we are fortunate, we can rely on the probability that the ethnographic material we present is irrelevant to the concerns of the state or other dominant agents. Where that is not the case, and where we are concerned about those who have what we consider to be an inappropriate interest in our material, our tendency has been to avoid negative consequences through disguise: change the name of the community (usually rather ineffectual), change the names of informants, or perhaps delete any mention of what we might know about the occurrence of illegal activities. All such efforts are premised on a topology of simple locality.

Such consideration of the possible consequences of our work has been premised on a simplistic sort of risk assessment shaped by the topology of simple locality: we try to imagine who might see our work and what they might do with it *in a particular place.* Such assessments are too often little more than cursory thought experiments and tend to be limited to consideration of a narrow field of explicit forms of surveillance and repression on a narrow field of individuals. They tend to ignore less obvious but potentially more consequential effects.

The topology of simple locality has also allowed us to exonerate ourselves from worrying too much about the consequences of representation by engaging in actions that can have positive consequences for the communities in which we work. Indeed most of us have probably participated in advocacy on behalf of our host communities in some way or another. Certainly the more politically engaged among us might be deeply involved in local political struggles. The question is whether such efforts on our part, no matter how strenuous, outweigh the possible consequences that follow from our attempts to represent those places.

The topology of simple locality, then, is a kind of focalizing strategy. In that sense, it is something quite different than strategies for constituting "otherness" (Fabian 1983; Said 1978; Trouillot 1991) or "thereness" (Geertz 1988). It is a strategy for discursively constituting a *focalized* "there," a move made specifically in contexts where we are compelled to think about the consequences of our work.

In many respects the topology of simple locality suffers from some of the same shortcomings as that other convention of anthropological writing, the "ethnographic present." Though anthropologists today are much more alert to the politics and histories that have shaped the communities they study,[12] the "ethnographic present" is a still-extant convention of ethnographic writing wherein an anthropologist, describing a particular set of cultural practices, writes about them in the present tense, even though his or her research may have occurred many years in the past and though much of what is described may no longer exist in the same form it did when it was observed. As Fabian has so persuasively argued, writing in the ethnographic present is an act of discursive distancing (1983: 26), one element in "*a persistent and systematic tendency to place the referent(s) of anthropology in a Time other than the present of the producer of anthropological discourse*" (1983: 31, emphasis in original). As Tsing observes, "The use of the 'ethnographic present' is tied to a conceptualization of culture as a coherent and persistent whole" (1993: xiv): one which is locatable in particular places.

Both of these conventions are relevant to the present discussion in that they shape how we think about the consequences of what we do. Both are nothing more than convenient fictions, our constructions of the political spaces in which and about which we write, rather than actually existing configurations of space or place. The *ethnographic present* acts as a distancing mechanism that relegates our research subjects to a timeless irrelevancy, immune, if not from history, then from the effects of *our ethnographic presence*. So too does the topology of simple locality create a coherent "there" that can be known and represented, in which the consequences of our presence in that place can presumably be anticipated and in which we can undertake ameliorative strategies that either prevent negative consequences or promote positive ones.

If our topologies for imagining the consequences of our work are problematic in traditional ethnographic research contexts, those problems multiply exponentially in the convergence between (1) our emerging interest in the study of subaltern social movements and (2) in the multi-sitedness of contemporary research contexts.

Studies of Subaltern Social Movements

Today anthropologists who study social movements are placed in a precarious position. In a world of online library databases and Internet search engines, where texts and images can be instantly circulated and received across global information networks, there is no longer any such thing as a distanced academic critique safely ensconced in an obscure academic journal. The production of meanings and identities is now occurring in a global political space in which claims to authenticity are a critical dimension of legitimacy. We are now participants—mostly uninvited—in the production of identities, or in the legitimation of identities being produced by others. To the degree that these movements represent an attempt to create new meanings and new identities—which in turn have the potential to produce new configurations of power—such a role cannot remain unacknowledged.

Can we reconcile the form and content of our accounts and critiques with their political consequences, however unintended? This is much more than a purely ethical matter: it presents a challenge to the epistemological grounds upon which transnational cultural critique is carried out. Theories of reflexivity have been much concerned with our presence in the frame of analysis, but not with the possibility of the exploitation of our presence by others. Likewise, discussions of ethnographic authority have not examined the possibility that, while we ourselves have become self-conscious about our strategies for establishing authority, the extent to which our opinions are cited as authoritative may have nothing to do with how we write, but merely with the fact that we have written. I am not advocating that anthropologists should necessarily retreat from critique altogether or that the answer lies in a return to a supposed objectivity. Yet if the critical stance is to retain its vitality and the emancipatory promise that inspired it in the first place, then commentators in these zones of contestation must take this challenge seriously.

Addressing this issue is particularly urgent today because of what Anna Tsing, Charles Zerner, and I have identified elsewhere as "a growing divergence in advocate and scholarly projects for understanding the situation of marginalized communities" (Brosius, Tsing, and Zerner 1998: 159). As we describe in the context of a discussion of community-based natural resource management:

> advocates have found concepts of *indigenous, community, custom, tradition,* and *rights* useful in promoting possibilities for local empowerment in national and transnational policy discussions, while scholars have become increasingly aware of the fragility, mutability, hybridity, and political variability of these concepts. While some advocates are concerned about the political consequences of deconstructionist scholarly agendas, some scholars are concerned about the potential political and legal consequences of community-based advocacy programs in which rights to territory, resources, and governance are linked to concepts of ethnicity, space, and indigenous identities. (1998: 159)

It is precisely this divergence of scholarly and advocate agendas that has given rise in recent years to the vigorous debate over what Lattas (1993) has termed the "politics of authenticity" in assertions of indigenous identity.[13]

Anthropological interest in the study of social movements is problematic for other reasons as well. At its most basic level, ethnographic writing is concerned with bringing coherence—broadly defined—to some set of observations about the world. In that sense, whether it be a rural village or a subaltern social movement, the task of the ethnographer is to give shape to (indeed, to constitute) a particular ethnographic context. Ethnographic texts, as Marcus suggests (1995: 96), are maps of a sort. Therein lies the problem. With but a few exceptions, anthropologists have yet to seriously address the political implications of the difference between mapping the life of a village (or an urban community, or wherever it is that field research is conducted) and mapping the contours of a social movement.

To the extent that subaltern social movements are engaged in struggles against dominant interests—whether the state, transnational capitalism, or local elites—the oppositional stance that defines them makes them targets to those they oppose. Anthropologists and other scholars need to consider what happens when they explicitly set out to describe these terrains of resistance, providing maps for those who would wish to subvert subaltern struggles.

To be sure, anthropologists working in politically oppressive contexts— peasant communities, company towns, and the like—have long recognized that the ethnographic accounts they produce may provide those who wield power with maps by which they may perpetuate systems of domination. They have gone beyond the more immediate, agonizing questions over how much they should reveal and how much they should disguise or omit in their published accounts: they have posed serious questions about the ultimate value of a discipline—forged in the context of colonialism and come of age in the Cold War—that derives its narrative power in proportion to the intimacy of the portraits it can provide of those who are subject to study.

What is different about the study of subaltern social movements lies in the convergence of a series of novel factors that impinge on how sites of struggle today progressively extend beyond local contexts, how well they are able to project their message into a broadening transnational domain, and how new technologies of power and institutions dedicated to "managing perceptions" are ever more able to manipulate the outcomes of these struggles and thereby counter them.[14] The success of social movements is at least in part predicated on their ability to effectively strategize, both among themselves and in coalition with others. In doing so, they have a face they reveal to the world and a face shown only to themselves; they engage in the active deployment of "public transcripts" as well as in the closed circulation of "hidden transcripts" (Scott 1990). Their struggles to convey a set of compelling moral/political imperatives to local, national, or transnational audiences are cultural productions that are met by a series of competing productions—the outcomes depend upon who is able to deploy the most compelling images.[15]

The presence of an anthropologist can affect this outcome. Again, items we disclose in the act of reporting our findings—in-house conversations, strategy meetings, anxieties expressed—provide a map for dominant interests to counter or suppress these movements. We provide the raw material for opponents to construct counterimages, thereby increasing the likelihood that they will be unable to effect change. In short, we undercut resistance when we show how it works (Said 1989: 220). To the extent that we do so, are we not, as Fabian asks, "the ultimate *collaborateur*" (1991: 246)?

The strategy of disguise that was perhaps effective in the context of traditional ethnographic research is utterly ineffectual in the study of subaltern social movements. While we can perhaps change the names of particular activists, and therefore possibly insulate them from arrest or other explicit forms of repression, we lay the groundwork for forms of counterresistance that may be much more consequential in frustrating the aims of these movements.

The problem lies in our lack of understanding of what constitutes a negative outcome and of the connection between such outcomes and our literal or representational presence. The threat to subaltern social movements is not simply that they may face repression—that they are not allowed to publish, that their offices are closed down, or that their members are arrested—but that *their efforts may prove ineffective because of the effectiveness of efforts to counter them*. It is an uncomfortable truth that our ethnographic presence in these sites of struggle may contribute to that.

This is precisely the situation confronting me as I anticipate writing about the Sarawak campaign. The public relations apparatus put in place by the Malaysian government (Hill & Knowlton, Burson-Marsteller, Malaysian Timber Council, Sarawak Timber Association) was designed precisely to counter environmentalist rhetoric, both by launching vituperative, *ad hominem* attacks on local and Northern environmentalists and by its efforts to put a softer face on the Malaysian timber industry. Strategically admitting that they had made mistakes in the past, Malaysian officials stressed the sincerity of their efforts to put in place an effective forest management regime. The end result, as noted, was that they effectively shifted and displaced the issue. Instead of stopping bulldozers and saving endangered forest-dwellers, the issue became one of developing scientifically based guidelines for sustainable forest management. That was all that was necessary to dissipate the momentum of the Sarawak campaign. No matter how carefully I edit my account, providing any sort of portrait of those behind the movement against logging in the face of such a sophisticated image-making apparatus is a perilous enterprise indeed.

Multi-sited Ethnography

The multi-sitedness of contemporary ethnographic research projects focusing on subaltern social movements is of equally great consequence with respect to our ability (or inability) to imagine the consequences of our work. Acknowledging this multi-sitedness, whether as an explicit part of our research design or not, makes the topology of simple locality ever less defensible as a way of conceptualizing the contexts in which we conduct research. Several implications follow from this.

Acknowledging the condition of multi-sitedness suggests that we must also acknowledge that our topologies for describing any situation, and hence the threats that arise from our attempts at representation, are always incomplete. Not only are we increasingly scripted into the events we are attempting to study, but we (and others) are scripted in ways we perhaps cannot even imagine. The problem, for us at least, is knowing where we (and they) are actually situated and how we ourselves are implicated in events. When we carried on with our work under the assumption of simple locality, we at least thought we could discern who might subject us or our research subjects to surveillance. This is no longer the case (if it ever was). The agents that may impinge on the sites we are studying may be completely outside our field of vision, either by virtue of the inherent complexity of contemporary multi-sitedness or by conscious design. In the study of subaltern social movements, it is therefore imperative that we be alert to the possible covert presence of those beyond our field of vision, whose very effectiveness in countering such movements may depend on their strategic invisibility. The delegitimizing mission of public relations firms such as Burson-Marsteller comes particularly to mind in this regard. These are powerful actors who are vitally interested in what we are doing, precisely because they are charged with countering the efforts of the kinds of movements we study.[16]

To the extent that we are engaged in multi-sited studies of subaltern social movements, our research is inherently transgressive. Such studies demand that we devote attention not only to understanding the struggles of subalterns, but also to the perspectives of actors that would subvert or suppress the emancipatory projects in which these movements are engaged. A fact central to ethnographic research is that it cannot be done in an atmosphere of hostility. Hence our concern always to establish "rapport" (a term that speaks more to the superficial presentation of self than to any sort of moral/political commitment) with our research subjects, whether they be rural villagers, members of a local NGO, or the executives of a timber company. Largely unexamined is the question of what is involved in our efforts to establish rapport as we move among and between sites. How many different stories do we tell those from whom we have an interest in learning something, and to what extent are those stories contradictory? In telling such stories, to what extent do we shade or color our own political sympathies?

In short, our engagement in multi-sited ethnographic projects is inevitably linked to questions about the positionality of the observer in a field of relations of power/knowledge. Marcus recognized this when he stated that

> In contemporary multi-sited research projects moving between public and private spheres of activity, from official to subaltern contexts, the ethnographer is bound to encounter discourses that overlap with his or her own. In any contemporary field of work, there are always others within who know (or want to know) what the ethnographer knows, albeit from a different subject position, or who want to know what the ethnographer wants to know. Such ambivalent identifications, or perceived identifications, immediately locate the ethnographer within the terrain being mapped and reconfigure any kind of methodological discussion that presumes a perspective from above or "nowhere." (1995: 112)

Conclusions

Central to contemporary ethnographic practice is a thorough self-consciousness about the practice of ethnographic writing: about how we place ourselves within the frame of analysis and about the conventions that we use to establish ethnographic authority. Anthropologists today are as much concerned about how they write as about what they write. And yet, we have largely failed to examine the consequences of turning our attention from the traditional subject of anthropological interest—whether it be an isolated village or an urban community—conceived in terms of the topology of simple locality to multi-sited studies of contemporary subaltern social movements. To assume that the topology of simple locality has salience any longer is not merely naive, but irresponsible.

As our notion of what constitutes a research site changes, so too must the way we think about the consequences—intended or unintended—of our writing. To be sure, all those risks that exist in traditional research contexts remain. But a newer set of risks emerges both from the multi-sitedness of contemporary projects and from the fact that we have shifted our focus to newly emerging forms of political agency dedicated to challenging traditional configurations of power. These risks are as much about the possibility that our attempts at representation may contribute to efforts at disempowering counter-representation as they are about explicit forms of repression. If our conventional habits for thinking about the risk to our informants were ill-conceived in the past—most especially what I have termed the topology of simple locality—they are all the more so today. The multi-sitedness of contemporary research contexts makes it virtually impossible for any researcher today to think through, in any comprehensive way, the risks of the projects in which he or she is involved.

What is of particular concern to me at present, as I undertake the writing of my book on the Sarawak campaign, is the degree to which such concerns should influence the form of my analysis and the content of my disclosures. What might be the impact of an analysis that explores the similarities between Northern environmentalist representations of the Penan and colonial travel narratives? To what degree are the former similar to what Pratt has termed *anti-conquest narratives:* "the strategies of representation whereby European bourgeois subjects seek to secure their innocence in the same moment as they assert European hegemony" (1992: 7)? At a time when the Malaysian government is attempting to articulate a distinct set of "Asian values," do I compromise the efforts of Malaysian NGOs when I examine how their pronouncements partake of a larger transnational discourse of social justice and indigenous rights? To what degree are the efforts of the Penan undermined when I discuss environmentalist efforts to organize them? As I attempt a critical analysis of the ways in which institutionalization has served to marginalize certain actors—Penan and grassroots environmentalists in particular—to what extent might my commentaries undermine efforts to establish forestry practices that are even marginally less destructive than those currently in place? Should I respond to my own misgivings with a kind of ethnographic cleansing? Is it even possible to write an ethnography of this campaign without compromising someone? If this isn't possible, then according to what measures should one decide whom one cares the most about the prospect of compromising?

In her essay "Situated Knowledges: The Science Question in Feminism and the Privilege of Partial Perspective," Haraway makes "an argument for situated and embodied knowledges and an argument against various forms of unlocatable, and so irresponsible, knowledge claims" (1988: 583). In the present discussion I have attempted to open up a line of questioning with regard to the consequences of our location, indeed our very presence, within multi-sited research contexts. Having recognized this, the task becomes one of considering the possibility for alternative forms of ethnographic practice. What such alternatives might look like are difficult to discern at present. Certainly it is not enough just to address our strategies of representation and retreat to a "politics of textuality" (Said 1989: 209). As Fabian argues, "Hanging the walls full with reflexive mirrors may brighten the place but offers no way out" (1991: 260). Nor, as some have suggested, should we simply cease all efforts at representation. Rather, we need first to clearly locate ourselves (both to ourselves and to our research subjects) within the "concrete contexts of power" (Fabian 1991: 256) we are attempting to represent. Such a task, I have argued here, is far from simple, given the multi-sitedness of contemporary research contexts. But making a conscious and determined effort to do so is perhaps one of the most critical tasks for an anthropology aware of its past and present complicity in structures of domination and alert to the power of its visualizing practices.

Notes

This discussion is based on research among nomadic and settled Eastern Penan in 1992 and 1993; interviews with rain forest activists in the United States, Canada, Europe, the United Kingdom, Australia, Japan, and Malaysia from 1993 to the present; and interviews with numerous Malaysian officials and timber industry representatives over the same period. Support for the research on which this discussion is based was provided by the Social Science Research Council, the University of Georgia Research Foundation, and the Body Shop Foundation (special thanks to Shane Kennedy for his efforts to help me secure the latter). I am grateful to each for their support. I also wish to thank the participants in the 1995 "Unintended Consequences" panel at the American Anthropological Association meetings, most of whom have contributed to the present volume. Listening to their original papers and reading their subsequent revised versions helped me clarify my own thinking about the consequences of ethnographic writing. I am also grateful for the perceptive comments of the anonymous reviewers who read an earlier draft of this article. Finally, I must thank Nina Glick Schiller, who gave this paper such a thorough and perceptive reading and provided numerous valuable suggestions for strengthening the argument. Responsibility for all statements herein is exclusively mine.

This essay has been adapted from two essays that appeared in a 1999 special issue of *Identities: Global Studies in Culture and Power* 6(2–3) entitled *Ethnographic Presence: Environmentalism, Indigenous Rights and Transnational Cultural Critique*, J. Peter Brosius, special guest editor. Most of this essay is adapted from "Locations and Representations: Writing in the Political Present in Sarawak, East Malaysia" (179–200), with minor portions included from "On the Practice of Transnational Cultural Critique" (345–86).

1. In speaking of "Northern" activists, I am following current usage, wherein the "North" refers to the industrialized countries of Europe, North America, Japan, and Australia. Likewise, in speaking of the "South," I am referring to the so-called "Third World."

2. In referring to the "government," it is important to keep in mind the distinction between the Sarawak state government and the Malaysian federal government. Sarawak agreed to join Malaysia in 1963, some six years after Malaysia's independence in 1957. It was able to negotiate the terms of its entry into Malaysia and therefore has a considerable amount of control over its internal affairs. The policies of the state and federal governments are often at odds. This is a matter of considerable frustration to the federal government, which has consistently attempted to establish greater control over Sarawak.

3. Appadurai 1991; Bhabha 1994; Brightman 1995; Clifford 1988; Featherstone 1990; Gupta and Ferguson 1992; Rosaldo 1989; Strathern 1995; Tsing 1993. See Brosius 1999a for a more complete discussion of the sources of anthropological interest in the study of environmental social movements.

4. An interesting precursor to this argument is Radway 1988. The recent volume edited by Gupta and Ferguson (1997) also provides an important intervention into traditional anthropological understandings of "the field" and the practice of "fieldwork."

5. In Sarawak there are also several small, scattered groups of long-settled Penan with close linguistic affinities to Eastern and Western Penan. For more information on Penan in Sarawak, see Brosius 1986, 1988, 1991, 1992, 1993a, 1993b, 1995a, 1995b, 1995–96, 1997a, 1997b, 1999b; Harrisson 1949; Kedit 1982; Langub 1972a, 1972b, 1975, 1984, 1989, 1990; Needham 1954a, 1954b, 1954c, 1965, 1972; Nicolaisen 1976a, 1976b, 1978.

6. For information on the effects of logging in Sarawak see Bevis 1995; Colchester 1989; Hong 1987; Hurst 1990; INSAN 1989; World Rainforest Movement and Sahabat Alam Malaysia 1990. For a detailed account of the movement of Malaysian timber companies into Africa, Mainland Southeast Asia, Oceania, and South America, see World Rainforest Movement and Forests Monitor, Ltd. 1998.

7. In speaking of "Malay rule" I am referring to the Penan conception of political authority. Though Malays (or Malay/Melanau) are politically dominant in Sarawak, both state politics and the civil service are conspicuously multiethnic, to a much greater degree than in peninsular Malaysia.

8. Mutang was arrested in February 1992, after bringing a Canadian MP to a blockade site. The SIPA office was ransacked by police, and the organization was disbanded.

9. For example, see Linden 1991 and Sesser 1991.

10. See International Tropical Timber Council 1990.

11. Ritchie 1994b.

12. Particularly influential in this respect have been individuals such as Eric Wolf (1982), Sidney Mintz (1986), William Roseberry (1989), and Immanuel Wallerstein (1974). See also Schneider and Rapp 1995 and Dirks, Eley, and Ortner 1993.

13. See Beckett and Mato 1996; Conklin 1997; Friedman 1992a, 1992b, 1996, 1998; Hanson 1989, 1991; Jackson 1989, 1995; Jolly 1992; Keesing 1989; Keesing and Tonkinson 1982; Linnekin 1991, 1992; Ramos 1994; Rogers 1996; and Sahlins 1993. This divergence of agendas in the domain of environmentalism and indigenous rights is, of course, but one manifestation of a larger series of encounters between those who take their theoretical inspiration from a set of propositions loosely referred to as postmodernist or poststructuralist and advocates of an engaged progressive politics. See Reyna and Schiller 1998; Scheper-Hughes 1995.

14. This phrase is taken from the masthead of the Burson-Marsteller Web site (www.bm.com/MN01.html).

15. See DeLuca 1999.

16. See Herman and Chomsky 1988 and Stauber and Rampton 1995. An example of the power, and strategic invisibility, of these firms can be seen in the central role that Hill & Knowlton played in shaping American public opinion during the Gulf War (Stauber and Rampton 1995: 167–75).

References

Appadurai, Arjun. 1990. "Disjuncture and Difference in the Global Cultural Economy." *Public Culture* 2(2): 1–24.

———. 1991. "Global Ethnoscapes: Notes and Queries for a Transnational Anthropology." In Richard G. Fox, ed., *Recapturing Anthropology: Working in the Present*, 191–210. Santa Fe, N.Mex.: School of American Research Press.

Asad, Talal, ed. 1973. *Anthropology and the Colonial Encounter*. Atlantic Highlands, N.J.: Humanities Press.

Beckett, Jeremy, and Daniel Mato, eds. 1996. "Indigenous Peoples/Global Terrains." *Identities: Global Studies in Culture and Power* Special Issue 3(1–2).

Berreman, Gerald. 1968. "Is Anthropology Alive? Social Responsibility in Social Anthropology." *Current Anthropology* 9(5): 391–96.

Bevis, William. 1995. *Borneo Log: The Struggle for Sarawak's Forests*. Seattle: University of Washington Press.

Bhabha, Homi. 1994. *The Location of Culture*. New York: Routledge.

Brightman, Robert. 1995. "Forget Culture: Replacement, Transcendence, Relexification." *Cultural Anthropology* 10(4): 509–46.

Brosius, J. Peter. 1986. "River, Forest and Mountain: The Penan Geng Landscape." *Sarawak Museum Journal* 36(57) (New Series): 173–84.

———. 1988. "A Separate Reality: Comments on Hoffman's The Punan: Hunters and Gatherers of Borneo." *Borneo Research Bulletin* 20(2): 81–106.

———. 1991. "Foraging in Tropical Rainforests: The Case of the Penan of Sarawak, East Malaysia (Borneo)." *Human Ecology* 19(2): 123–50.

——. 1992. "The Axiological Presence of Death: Penan Geng Death-Names." Ph.D. dissertation, University of Michigan, Ann Arbor.

——. 1993a. "Contrasting Subsistence Ecologies of Eastern and Western Penan For-agers (Sarawak, East Malaysia)." In C. M. Hladik, et al., eds., *Food and Nutrition in the Tropical Forest: Biocultural Interactions and Applications to Development*, 515–22. Paris: UNESCO–Parthenon Man and the Biosphere Series.

——. 1993b. "Penan of Sarawak." In Marc S. Miller, ed., *State of the Peoples: A Global Human Rights Report on Societies in Danger*, 142–43. Boston: Beacon Press (for Cul-tural Survival, Inc.).

——. 1995a. "Bornean Forest Trade in Historical and Regional Perspective: The Case of Penan Hunter-Gatherers of Sarawak." In Jefferson Fox, ed., *Society and Non-Timber Products in Tropical Asia*, 13–26. East-West Center Occasional Papers: Envi-ronmental Series No. 19.

——. 1995b. "Signifying Bereavement: Form and Context in the Analysis of Penan Death-Names." *Oceania* 66(2): 119–46.

——. 1995–96. "Father Dead, Mother Dead: Bereavement and Fictive Death in Penan Geng Society." *Omega: Journal of Death and Dying* 32(3): 197–226.

——. 1997a. "Endangered People, Endangered Forest: Environmentalist Representa-tions of Indigenous Knowledge." *Human Ecology* 25(1): 47–69.

——. 1997b. "Prior Transcripts, Divergent Paths: Resistance and Acquiescence to Logging in Sarawak, East Malaysia." *Comparative Studies in Society and History* 39(3): 468–510.

——. 1999a. "Analyses and Interventions: Anthropological Engagements with Envi-ronmentalism." *Current Anthropology* 40(3): 277–309.

——1999b. "Green Dots, Pink Hearts: Displacing Politics from the Malaysian Rain-forest." *Ecologies for Tomorrow: Reading Rappaport Today. American Anthropologist* Special issue, 101(1): 36–57. Aletta Biersack, Guest Editor.

——, ed. 1999. "Ethnographic Presence: Environmentalism, Indigenous Rights and Transnational Cultural Critique." *Identities: Global Studies in Culture and Power* Special issue 6(2–3).

Brosius, J. Peter, Anna Tsing, and Charles Zerner. 1998. "Representing Communities: Histories and Politics of Community-Based Resource Management." *Society and Natural Resources* 11(2): 157–68.

Clifford, James. 1983. "On Ethnographic Authority." *Representations* 1(2): 118–45.

——. 1988. *The Predicament of Culture: Twentieth-Century Ethnography, Literature and Art*. Cambridge, Mass.: Harvard University Press.

——. 1994. "Diasporas." *Cultural Anthropology* 9(3): 302–38.

——, and George Marcus, eds. 1986. *Writing Culture: The Poetics and Politics of Ethnography*. Berkeley: University of California Press.

Colchester, Marcus. 1989. *Pirates, Squatters and Poachers: The Political Ecology of Dis-possession of the Native Peoples of Sarawak*. London and Petaling Jaya (Malaysia): Survival International and INSAN (Institute of Social Analysis).

Conklin, Beth. 1997. "Body Paint, Feathers, and VCRs: Aesthetics and Authenticity in Amazonian Activism." *American Ethnologist* 24(4): 711–37.

DeLuca, Kevin. 1999. *Image Politics: The New Rhetoric of Environmental Activism*. New York: Guilford.

Dirks, Nicholas, Geoff Eley, and Sherry Ortner, eds. 1993. *Culture/Power/History: A Reader in Contemporary Social Theory*. Princeton, N.J.: Princeton University Press.

Fabian, Johannes. 1983. *Time and the Other: How Anthropology Makes Its Object.* New York: Columbia University Press.

———. 1990. "Presence and Representation: The Other and Anthropological Writing." *Critical Inquiry* 16: 753–72.

———. 1991. "Dilemmas of Critical Anthropology." In Johannes Fabian, ed., *Time and the Work of Anthropology: Critical Essays 1971–1991,* 245–65. Chur, Switzerland: Harwood Academic Publishers.

Featherstone, M., ed. 1990. *Global Culture: Nationalism, Globalization, and Modernity.* London: Sage.

Friedman, Jonathan. 1992a. "Myth, History and Political Identity." *Cultural Anthropology* 7(2): 194–210.

———. 1992b. "The Past in the Future: History and the Politics of Identity." *American Anthropologist* 94(4): 837–59.

———. 1994. *Cultural Identity and Global Process.* London: Sage.

———. 1996. "The Politics of De-Authentification: Escaping from Identity, a Commentary on 'Beyond Authenticity' by Mark Rogers." *Identities* 3(1–2): 127–36.

———. 1998. "The Heart of the Matter." *Identities* 4(3–4): 561–69.

Geertz, Clifford. 1988. *Works and Lives: The Anthropologist as Author.* Stanford, Calif.: Stanford University Press.

Gore, Al. 1992. *Earth in the Balance: Ecology and the Human Spirit.* New York: Plume/Penguin.

Gough, Kathleen. 1968a. "Anthropology and Imperialism." *Monthly Review* 19(11): 12–27.

———. 1968b. "New Proposals for Anthropologists." *Current Anthropology* 9(5): 403–7.

Gupta, Akhil, and James Ferguson. 1992. "Beyond 'Culture': Space, Identity, and the Politics of Difference." *Cultural Anthropology* 7(1): 6–23.

———, eds. 1997. *Anthropological Locations: Boundaries and Grounds of a Field Science.* Berkeley: University of California Press.

Hanson, Allan. 1989. "The Making of the Maori: Culture Invention and Its Logic." *American Anthropologist* 91(4): 890–902.

———. 1991. "Reply to Langdon, Levine, and Linnekin." *American Anthropologist* 93(2): 449–50.

Haraway, Donna. 1988. "Situated Knowledges: The Science Question in Feminism and the Privilege of Partial Perspective." *Feminist Studies* 14(3): 575–99.

Harrisson, Tom. 1949. "Notes on Some Nomadic Punans." *Sarawak Museum Journal,* n.s., 5(1): 130–46.

Herman, Edward, and Noam Chomsky. 1988. *Manufacturing Consent: The Political Economy of the Mass Media.* New York: Pantheon.

Hong, Evelyne. 1987. *Natives of Sarawak: Survival in Borneo's Vanishing Forests.* Penang (Malaysia): Institute Masyarakat.

Huizer, Gerrit, and Bruce Mannheim, eds. 1979. *The Politics of Anthropology: From Colonialism and Sexism toward a View from Below.* The Hague: Mouton.

Hurst, Philip. 1990. *Rainforest Politics: Ecological Destruction in South-East Asia.* London: Zed Books.

Hymes, Dell, ed. 1969. *Reinventing Anthropology.* New York: Pantheon.

INSAN (Institute of Social Analysis). 1989. *Logging against the Natives of Sarawak.* Petaling Jaya (Malaysia): INSAN.

International Tropical Timber Council. 1990. "Report Submitted to the International Tropical Timber Council by Mission Established Pursuant to Resolution I (VI), 'The Promotion of Sustainable Forest Management: A Case Study in Sarawak, Malaysia.'" Unpublished document in possession of author.

Jackson, Jean. 1989. "Is There a Way to Talk about Culture Without Making Enemies?" *Dialectical Anthropology* 14: 127–43.

———. 1995. "Culture, Genuine and Spurious: The Politics of Indianness in the Vaupes, Colombia." *American Ethnologist* 22(1): 3–27.

Jolly, Margaret. 1992. "Specters of Inauthenticity." *The Contemporary Pacific* 4(1): 42–72.

Kedit, Peter M. 1982. *An Ecological Survey of the Penan. Sarawak Museum Journal*, n.s., Special Issue No. 2, 30(51): 225–79.

Keesing, Roger. 1989. "Creating the Past: Custom and Identity in the Contemporary Pacific." *The Contemporary Pacific* 1(1–2): 19–42.

———, and R. Tonkinson, eds. 1982. *Reinventing Traditional Culture: The Politics of Kastom in Island Melanesia. Mankind* Special Issue 13(4).

King, Anthony, ed. 1997. *Culture, Globalization and the World System: Contemporary Conditions for the Representation of Identity*. Minneapolis: University of Minnesota Press.

King, Victor. 1993. *The Peoples of Borneo*. Oxford: Blackwell.

Langub, Jayl. 1972a. "Adaptation to a Settled Life by the Punans of the Belaga Subdistrict." *Sarawak Gazette* 98(1371): 83–86.

———. 1972b. "Structure and Progress in the Punan Community of Belaga Subdistrict." *Sarawak Gazette* 98(1378): 219–21.

———. 1975. "Distribution of Penan and Punan in the Belaga District." *Borneo Research Bulletin* 7(2): 45–48.

———. 1984. "Tamu: Barter Trade between Penan and Their Neighbors." *Sarawak Gazette* 110(1485): 11–15.

———. 1989. *Some Aspects of Life of the Penan. Sarawak Museum Journal*, n.s., Special Issue No. 4, Part III, 40(61): 169–84.

———. 1990. "A Journey through the Nomadic Penan Country." *Sarawak Gazette* 117(1514): 5–27.

Lattas, Andrew. 1993. "Essentialism, Memory and Resistance: Aboriginality and the Politics of Authenticity." *Oceania* 63(3): 240–67.

Linden, Eugene. 1991. "Lost Tribes, Lost Knowledge." *Time* September 23, 46–56.

Linnekin, Jocelyn. 1991. "Cultural Invention and the Dilemma of Authenticity." *American Anthropologist* 93(2): 446–48.

———. 1992. "On the Theory and Politics of Cultural Construction in the Pacific." *Oceania* 62: 249–63.

Manser, Bruno. 1996. *Voices from the Rainforest: Testimonies of a Threatened People*. Basel and Petaling Jaya (Malaysia): Bruno Manser Foundation and INSAN (Institute of Social Analysis).

Marcus, George. 1995. "Ethnography in/of the World System: The Emergence of Multi-Sited Ethnography." *Annual Review of Anthropology* 24: 95–117.

———, and Michael M. J. Fischer. 1986. *Anthropology as Cultural Critique: An Experimental Moment in the Human Sciences*. Chicago: University of Chicago Press.

Mintz, Sidney. 1986. *Sweetness and Power: The Place of Sugar in Modern History*. New York: Penguin.

Needham, Rodney. 1954a. "A Penan Mourning Usage." *Bijdragen tot de Taal-, Land- en Volkenkunde* 110: 263–67.

———. 1954b. "Penan and Punan." *Journal of the Malayan Branch, Royal Asiatic Society* 27(1): 73–83.

———. 1954c. "The System of Teknonyms and Death-Names of the Penan." *Southwestern Journal of Anthropology* 10: 416–31.

———. 1965. "Death-Names and Solidarity in Penan Society." *Bijdragen tot de Taal-, Land- en Volkenkunde* 121: 58–76.

———. 1972. "Punan-Penan." In Frank M. Lebar, ed., *Ethnic Groups of Insular Southeast Asia, Vol. 1: Indonesia, Andaman Islands, and Madagascar*, 176–180. New Haven, Conn.: Human Relations Area Files Press.

Nicolaisen, Johannes. 1976a. "The Penan of Sarawak: Further Notes on the Neo-Evolutionary Concept of Hunters." *Folk* 18: 205–36.

———. 1976b. "The Penan of the Seventh Division of Sarawak: Past, Present and Future." *Sarawak Museum Journal*, n.s., 24(45): 35–61.

———. 1978. "Penan Death-Names." *Sarawak Museum Journal*, n.s., 26(47): 29–41.

Pratt, Mary Louise. 1992. *Imperial Eyes: Travel Writing and Transculturation*. New York: Routledge.

Radway, J. 1988. "Reception Study: Ethnography and the Problems of Dispersed Audiences and Nomadic Subjects." *Cultural Studies* 2(3): 359–76.

Ramos, Alcida. 1994. "The Hyperreal Indian." *Critique of Anthropology* 14(2): 153–71.

Reece, R. H. W. 1982. *The Name of Brooke: The End of White Rajah Rule in Sarawak*. Oxford: Oxford University Press.

———. 1988. "Economic Development under the Brookes." In R. A. Cramb and R. H. W. Reece, eds., *Development in Sarawak: Historical and Contemporary Perspectives*, 21–34. Melbourne: Centre for Southeast Asian Studies, Monash University.

Reyna, Stephen, and Nina Glick Schiller, eds. 1998. "Regimes of Truth." *Identities: Global Studies in Culture and Power* Special Issue 4(3–4).

Ritchie, James. 1994a. *Bruno Manser: The Inside Story*. Singapore: Summer Times.

———. 1994b. "White Men Will Return, Penan Told: 'European Governments Will Colonise Sarawak to Stop Logging' Goes the Lie." *New Straits Times*, August 15: 1–2.

Rogers, Mark. 1996. "Beyond Authenticity: Conservation, Tourism, and the Politics of Representation in the Ecuadorian Amazon." *Identities* 3(1–2): 73–125.

Rosaldo, R. 1989. *Culture and Truth: The Remaking of Social Analysis*. Boston: Beacon.

Roseberry, William. 1989. *Anthropologies and Histories: Essays in Culture, History, and Political Economy*. New Brunswick, N.J.: Rutgers University Press.

Rousseau, Jérôme. 1990. *Central Borneo: Ethnic Identity and Social Life in a Stratified Society*. Oxford: Clarendon.

Sahlins, Marshall. 1993. "Goodbye to Triste Tropes: Ethnography in the Context of Modern World History." In R. Borofsky, ed., *Assessing Cultural Anthropology*, 377–95. Oxford: Berg.

Said, Edward. 1978. *Orientalism*. New York: Pantheon.

———. 1989. "Representing the Colonized: Anthropology's Interlocutors." *Critical Inquiry* 15: 205–25.

Scheper-Hughes, Nancy. 1995. "The Primacy of the Ethical: Propositions for a Militant Anthropology." *Current Anthropology* 36(3): 409–40.

Schiller, Nina Glick, ed. 1997. *Transnational Processes/Situated Identities. Identities: Global Studies in Culture and Power* Special Issue, 4(2).

Schneider, Jane, and Rayna Rapp, eds. 1995. *Articulating Hidden Histories: Exploring the Influence of Eric R. Wolf.* Berkeley: University of California Press.

Scott, James. 1990. *Domination and the Arts of Resistance: Hidden Transcripts.* New Haven, Conn.: Yale University Press.

Sesser, Stan. 1991. "Logging the Rain Forest." *New Yorker,* May 27, 1991, 42–67.

Siva, Kumar G. 1991. *Taib: A Vision for Sarawak.* Kuching: Jacamar.

Strathern, Marilyn. 1995. *Shifting Contexts: Transformations in Anthropological Knowledge.* London: Routledge.

Stauber, John, and Sheldon Rampton. 1995. *Toxic Sludge Is Good for You: Lies, Damn Lies and the Public Relations Industry.* Monroe, Maine: Common Courage Press.

Sturgeon, Noel. 1999. "Ecofeminist Appropriations and Transnational Environmentalists." In *Ethnographic Presence: Environmentalism, Indigenous Rights and Transnational Cultural Critique. Identities: Global Studies in Culture and Power.* Special Issue, 6(2–3): 255–79.

Trouillot, Michel-Rolph. 1991. "Anthropology and the Savage Slot: The Poetics and Politics of Otherness." In R. G. Fox, ed., *Recapturing Anthropology: Working in the Present,* 17–44. Santa Fe, N.Mex.: School of American Research Press.

Tsing, Anna. 1993. *In the Realm of the Diamond Queen. Marginality in an Out-of-the-Way Place.* Princeton, N.J.: Princeton University Press.

Turner, Terence. 1991. "Representing, Resisting, Rethinking: Historical Transformations of Kayapó Culture and Anthropological Consciousness." In George Stocking, ed., *Colonial Situations: Essays on the Contextualization of Ethnographic Knowledge,* 285–313. Madison: University of Wisconsin Press.

Wallerstein, Immanuel. 1974. *The Modern World System: Capitalist Agriculture and the Origins of the World Economy in the Sixteenth Century.* Orlando, Fla.: Academic.

Wolf, Eric. 1982. *Europe and the People without History.* Berkeley: University of California Press.

Wolf, Margery. 1992. *A Thrice Told Tale: Feminism, Postmodernism, and Ethnographic Responsibility.* Stanford, Calif.: Stanford University Press.

World Rainforest Movement and Forests Monitor, Ltd. 1998. *High Stakes. The Need to Control Transnational Logging Companies: A Malaysian Case Study.* World Rainforest Movement and Forests Monitor, Ltd.

World Rainforest Movement and Sahabat Alam Malaysia. 1990. *The Battle for Sarawak's Forests.* Penang: World Rainforest Movement and Sahabat Alam Malaysia.

9

Do Anthropologists Need Religion, and Vice Versa? Adventures and Dangers in Spiritual Ecology

Leslie E. Sponsel

Read this chapter at your own risk: you might get hooked on religion! This is not an attempt to convert you to any particular religion. However, it is an attempt to attract your attention to an extraordinarily rich, rewarding, and flourishing new field—spiritual ecology. The second aim of this chapter is to sketch points of mutual relevance between ecological anthropology and spiritual ecology, including ways to become more involved with spiritual ecology through studying, teaching, research, and so on. So be forewarned of the intellectual adventures and dangers ahead if you continue reading. Proceed only if you have an open mind!

Apocalypse Now?

Many intelligent and informed people have speculated about impending global environmental disintegration and catastrophe, with similar consequences for human society. One scenario is something like what is supposed to have happened to the Ik of Uganda: a complete breakdown of their society resulting from environmental changes. There have been doomsday predictions at least since the time of Thomas Robert Malthus (1766–1834) to the present, including Ted Kaczynski's manifesto as the Unabomber. With the onset of the new century and millennium, some may believe the time is finally ripe for global catastrophes. Are such predictions simply alarmist? Is there ample room for even greater human impact on the environment with the accelerating growth of population and economic pressures? Will science and technology still rescue the biosphere from human abuse? Consider these facts: The human population of today is already six billion and will grow to ten billion by the year 2050; it already appropriates about 40 percent of the primary biological production of Earth (Sponsel 2000a).

Necessary, But Sufficient? Of course, some progress has been made toward reducing if not resolving environmental crises. Witness Earth Day 1970, the UN Stockholm Conference on the Human Environment in 1972, President Jimmy Carter's Global 2000 Report in 1980, and the Rio Summit in 1992. Are these and numerous other initiatives enough? We are still surprised by alarming discoveries of new environmental crises. Just a few years ago, who imagined, let alone worried, about a hole in the ozone layer, acid rain, widespread gross deformities in frogs, and so on? What new environmental crises are awaiting discovery?

Maybe science, technology, government, politics, economics, and education are necessary, but not sufficient, to effectively cope with environmental crises. What else could there be? When all else fails, try religion! Specifically, what about spiritual ecology? Before pursuing it, let us first consider religion in general to set the stage.

That Old Time Religion

The pivotal role of religion in human lives and societies has long been recognized by anthropologists, among others. However, the task of defining religion has also long been problematic. For example, Edward B. Tylor in 1871 established a minimal definition of religion as the belief in spiritual beings. This fits some religions, such as Shintoism in Japan, which encompasses some eight million different spirits. On the other hand, in principle, neither Buddhism, Confucianism, Daoism (Taoism), nor Jainism are concerned with spirits or a supreme deity; thus other criteria need to be used if they are to be included as religions. With such problems in arriving at a single definition to fit all religions, I will simply offer a list of attributes of religion as a set of propositions or hypotheses to be explored and tested in particular cases.

Religion is ancient, universal, integral, sacred, ultimate, and influential. Among some nearly seven thousand distinct cultures extant, anthropologists have yet to discover a single one without religion. In most societies, religion is a pivotal and integral component of the cultural system. Religion is usually focused on the sacred as a special domain often contrasted with the profane or ordinary. The *sacred* includes extraordinary ideas (myths, symbols), behaviors (rituals and ceremonies), and artifacts (material culture) in special contexts (place and time). The extraordinary may involve feelings of mystery, awe, power, transcendence, tranquility, unity, and/or healing.

Religion also deals with ultimate meanings, realities, concerns, and powers. Among the ultimate concerns are elemental questions of life and death as well as the place of humans in nature. Religion provides the primary source of guidelines for ideal and moral behavior, steering people in their relations with others, nature, and the supernatural. In addition, religion includes prohibitions (taboos) and proscriptions that are often related to ideas about purity and pollution. In short, religion can be a very powerful emotional, spiritual, and intellectual force in the lives of many individuals and for society as a whole.

If you think religion is not important, consider Jesus Christ; Muhammad; the Spanish Inquisition; Holy Crusades; Islamic Jihad; the Jonestown mass suicide; the Branch Davidians at Waco, Texas; the Heaven's Gate cult; Asahara Sahoko and the Aum Shinrikyo gassing of subways in Tokyo; the Buddha; the Dalai Lama and Tibetan exiles; the pope and the official position of the Catholic church on birth control; the bombings and assassinations of medical doctors at abortion clinics in the United States by people who profess to be "pro-life"; the school shooting of a girl in Littleton, Colorado, who confessed to being a Christian; the multitude of Serbian sacred sites in Kosovo; Albert Schweitzer; Mother Teresa; Gandhi and British colonialism in India; Ayatollah Khomeini and the Iranian revolution; the Chinese government and Falun Gong; Billy Graham; the Moral Majority and Christian Coalition in the United States; and on and on. These examples should suffice to convince even a nonbeliever of the potential and actual powers of religion to significantly influence some people's behavior, whether in positive or negative ways.

Religions and ecology relate to each other in a variety of fascinating and important ways. Here it must suffice to briefly give three examples: animism, neopaganism, and Jainism.

Spirits in Nature

Animism is a religion focused on a belief in multiple spiritual beings in nature. The spirits are thought to reside in "natural" phenomena such as rocks, trees, forests, animals, lakes, rivers, waterfalls, and mountains. Consequently, in animism, the natural and the supernatural are not always rigidly separated into discrete domains. The *unity* of the natural and supernatural is also one of the central tenets of spiritual ecology as well as a key attribute of sacred places in nature. Indeed, it can be argued that ecology and theology were isomorphic for most traditional indigenous societies. Given the great antiquity and former universality of animism, together with its obvious ecological relevance through special respect for spirits and sacred places in nature, the cumulative environmental impact of animism must have been significant and largely positive.

The spread of new religions into a region can precipitate profound changes in the trajectory of the historical ecology of local societies, because different religions can contribute to very different relationships between humans and nature with varying impacts on biodiversity, ecosystems, and ecological processes. As Christianity, Judaism, and Islam spread into many parts of the world, often they suppressed or even destroyed previous religions, most of which were animistic, including those of ancient Europe. Indeed, at least some Christians still advocate such destruction. While many people still devalue animism and paganism in principle, it is ethnocentric to disparage them or any religion. In some contexts it may be racist as well.

Not all animists have converted to another religion. Many indigenous peoples throughout the world remain essentially animists. Also, even after a new religion becomes dominant, in numerous cases some elements of previous religion persist. Sometimes elements of the prior religion are creatively mixed with the new one (syncretism). Thus, the religious system of many societies does not necessarily neatly fall into one category or another. A single individual may even follow more than one religion, as is commonplace in much of East Asia with a varied mixture of animism, Buddhism, Confucianism, and Daoism. Of course, multiethnic societies are likely to include multiple religions.

Neopaganism

Some contemporary Europeans and Euroamericans have rediscovered animism in the form of neopaganism. It is distinctive from mainstream Western religions in its central focus on nature. For example, the key to neopaganism in England is particular sacred places like ancient woods, Glastonbury, and Stonehenge and particular sacred times like the seasons, midwinter, summer solstice, autumn equinox, and other annual calendrical events. What appears to attract people most to neopaganism is its focus on honoring the beauty and power of nature. Rather than worshiping a spirit or deity, neopagans consider everything that lives to be holy.

The essence of neopaganism as a spirituality of nature is ecology, according to one authority, Graham Harvey. The sun is recognized as the source of all energy, plants as primary producers of energy and nutrients for other organisms, and everything is seen as interconnected. Neopaganism supposedly blends the lasting insights of ancient ancestors with the clearest understandings of modern science to create an ecologically sound religion (Harvey 1997).

Regardless of whether or not one accepts animism or neopaganism as having any validity and utility, the fact is that millions of people do, and that fact can have ecological consequences as a form of spiritual ecology. One needn't accept or believe in something to find it worthy of study, understanding, and respect.

Jainism

Jainism is probably the most extreme case of spiritual ecology, a universal belief in the sacredness of all beings. It integrates spirituality and ecology with respect and even reverence for biodiversity to a far greater extent than any other religion. The Jains of India consider every organism as an individual with basic needs, the capacity to feel pain, and even a soul. They extend the principle of *ahimsa* (nonviolence) beyond humans to aim at the protection of as many organisms as possible, or in other words, universal love.

Jains reduce violence and suffering by limiting their resource consumption to basic needs, as for example through eating only one meal each day, unless they are fasting. They avoid eating animal foods and using animal products. As vegetarians they consume only certain fruits, nuts, vegetables, and grains. Jains renounce all professions and trades that harm animals in any way. They visit markets to rescue animals destined to be slaughtered by others for food, and even maintain welfare centers for old, sick, and dying animals.

The most ardent Jains use a filter to drink water to minimize consuming organisms that might be in it, walk naked and barefooted using a small broom to push aside any organisms they might otherwise step on, and through numerous other practices try as much as possible to reduce violence and suffering for other organisms. In fact, strict Jains even practice celibacy to avoid killing sperm. In these and numerous other ways, individual Jains daily maximize empathy, compassion, and reverence for all beings, while they minimize their environmental impact, resource consumption, and violence.

Characterizing Spiritual Ecology

Having considered the above three examples we are now in a better position to appreciate the definition of spiritual ecology as *a complex and diverse arena of spiritual, emotional, intellectual, and practical activities at the interface of religions and environment.* Ultimately, spiritual ecology reflects philosophical, religious, and moral traditions, ancient and contemporary, which, at least in principle, view all beings and things in nature and thereby planet Earth as a whole as sacred. Ultimately, for spiritual ecology, a pivotal point is to comprehend that the natural and supernatural are not rigidly separate and antithetical domains, but interwoven into the very fabric of human experience and ultimate reality.

Since the 1990s, spiritual ecology has been rapidly developing into a focus of academic teaching and research as well as personal and institutional action. Among the best indicators of this progress are the first textbook on this subject, written by David Kinsley (1995); a monumental anthology edited by Roger Gottlieb (1996); and a new professional journal (*Worldviews: Environment, Culture and Religion* 1997–). Indeed, already there is sufficient material to allow a dedicated scholar to focus a whole career on teaching, research, and/or writing about spiritual ecology, a particular topic like sacred places, or a single religion such as Buddhism in relation to ecology and environmental concerns.

A convenient starting point for considering scholarship in spiritual ecology is the now classic article published in 1967 by Lynn White Jr. in the prestigious journal *Science*. White asserts: "What people do about their ecology depends on what they think about themselves in relation to things around them. Human ecology is deeply conditioned by beliefs about our nature and destiny—that is, by religion" (23). He continues: "More science and more technology are not going to get us out of the present ecological crisis until we find a new religion or rethink our old one" (28).

> Both our present science and our present technology are so tinctured with orthodox Christian arrogance toward nature that no solution for our ecological crisis can be expected from them alone. Since the roots of our trouble are so largely religious, the remedy must also be essentially religious, whether we call it that or not. We must rethink and refeel our nature and destiny. The profoundly religious, but heretical, sense of the primitive Franciscans for the spiritual autonomy of all parts of nature may point a direction. I propose Francis as a patron saint for ecologists. (30–31)

Unfortunately, White's essay is remembered only or mostly for his argument that most Christians tend to interpret the Creation account as giving humans free license to aggressively dominate and rapaciously exploit nature for their own selfish benefit. Christian apologists strongly attacked White, and the ensuing controversy persists to this day as what I would consider a subfield of spiritual ecology labeled *Christian ecotheology*. (We'll return to consider these critics and other such nonbelievers later.)

What is usually completely missed, or at least neglected, by superficial readers of White's essay, is the fact that he did not totally dismiss the possibility that religion could have some positive relevance for resolving the environmental crisis. Indeed, he proposes St. Francis of Assisi (1182–1226) in Italy as the patron saint of ecology. (There are some interesting parallels between St. Francis and the Jains.) Unfortunately, the revolutionary ideas of St. Francis about spiritual ecology did not generate a major movement within his religion of Catholicism. No doubt the world would be quite a different place had this happened. Maybe it isn't too late?

The relationships between religion and environment can be complex. A particular religion as a whole may be either relevant or irrelevant to the environment, or various specific aspects of it may be relevant while others aren't. If a particular religion is relevant to the environment, then it may be either part of the problem or else part of the solution. Alternatively, various specific aspects of it may be part of the problem, while others are part of the solution. Some religions, or aspects thereof, may be more positive or negative than others in these respects. White pursued one possibility in the 1960s when he pointed to one aspect of Christianity, the prevailing interpretation to multiply and subdue the Earth, as the cause of the environmental crisis, and another part, the ideas and practices of St. Francis, as a potential solution.

Even within religions that have been celebrated as environmentally friendly, there may be some specific practices that are harmful. For example, in Buddhism in Thailand, some individuals release animals in order to gain merit toward a better life in the next reincarnation, yet this also means that animals are first trapped commercially and held captive where they suffer and sometimes die. In such situations part of the solution is to educate more people about the consequences of their behavior in order to reduce or eliminate harmful aspects. In Thailand, some who sell birds for people to release for merit have another solution. They train the birds to return to them after release, so they can be resold many times. Is this a form of recycling?

Revelations from Wildlife and Harvard

In recent years, however, there has been a complete turnaround in two respects. First, now a *wholly positive* approach is pursued—religion is being explored as part of the solution to the crisis. No blame is being laid on any religion. Second, rather than singling out any particular religion, *every religion* is considered to be a potential source for its own adherents to derive or develop the principles for a more viable environmental ethic in dealing with the environmental problems they face as well as for constructing a more sustainable and greener (ecological) society. It remains to be seen to what extent such an optimistic and relativistic approach will be successful. Will nonbelievers, such as atheists and agnostics, have to discover and cultivate some alternative secular analog to spiritual ecology?

Since the late 1980s, this constructive, eclectic, relativistic, and holistic view has been advanced in various international conferences with a wide diversity of scholars, scientists, theologians, religious leaders, environmentalists, and others. Just two brief examples must suffice here—the World Wildlife Fund in Europe and Harvard University in the United States.

In 1986, the World Wide Fund for Nature (WWF), famous for hard-nosed environmental conservation, organized an interfaith dialogue among leaders in Buddhism, Christianity, Hinduism, Islam, and Judaism in Assisi, Italy. Each wrote a concise statement on the environmental ethics inherent in their own religion, and these were collectively published as the *Assisi Declarations*. In the early 1990s, the newly named World Wide Fund for Nature sponsored a series of edited books with one on each of these five major religions in relation to ecology. For several years the WWF published a newsletter on religions and environment called *The New Road*. Subsequently leaders from other religions joined the initiative: Baha'ism 1987, Sikhism 1989, Jainism 1991, and Daoism 1995. In 1995, the Summit on Religions and Conservation was held in Ohito, Japan, and also in Windsor Castle, England, with nine different religions represented. Another statement was issued (the *Ohito Declaration on Religion, Land, and Conservation*) and the Windsor conference generated further statements on Baha'i, Buddhism, Christianity, Hinduism, Islam, Jainism, Judaism,

Sikhism, and Daoism (see Edwards and Palmer 1997). These important initiatives in turn gave rise to the international Alliance for Religions and Conservation (ARC), which is based at the International Consultancy on Religion, Education, and Culture (ICOREC) in Manchester Metropolitan University, Manchester, England. By 1995, more than 120,000 environmental projects based on religion were operating, many supported by the WWF.

During 1996–98, a series of nine international and multidisciplinary conferences were developed on "Religions of the World and Ecology." The co-organizers were Mary Evelyn Tucker and John Grim of the Department of Religion at Bucknell University and Lawrence E. Sullivan of the Center for the Study of World Religions in the Divinity School at Harvard University. The religions covered were Buddhism, Christianity, Confucianism, Hinduism, Indigenous, Islam, Jainism, Judaism, Shintoism, and Daoism. General conclusions were presented in subsequent conferences at the American Academy of Arts and Sciences, the United Nations, and the American Museum of Natural History. Collectively, the conferences involved more than seven hundred scholars, scientists, religious leaders, environmental specialists, and activists. The first ten conferences will each yield a substantial edited book. This groundbreaking work still continues as the "Forum on Religion and Ecology" (FORE).

The Harvard conference series and FORE recognize that environmental crises continue to be grave and urgent, that previous approaches for resolution (mainly science, technology, government, and education) have proven inadequate, and that many more fundamental social changes are sorely needed in order to reestablish a sense of balance with nature grounded in worldviews that reflect a sense of mutually enhancing human–environment relations. Furthermore, *the primary goal of the conferences and FORE is to map the contours of a new field of study* in religion that also has implications for contemporary environmental ethics and public policy concerns. This new field I consider to be a component of spiritual ecology (for a summary of the Harvard conferences see *Earth Ethics* Fall 1998).

When considering religions, one is often reminded of tensions and conflicts between them that may even break out into violence and warfare. However, the initiatives of the WWF, the Harvard conferences, and FORE focus on interfaith dialogue and collaboration. Such ecumenism may be facilitated by the fact that environmental crises do not discriminate on the basis of religion or anything else. Each and every human being depends on the environment for survival and well-being, and, ultimately, all humans are threatened by global ecocide.

Spiritual Ecology Made Simple

From sources such as the above it is possible to extract various general principles of spiritual ecology that are inherent, to some degree and in various ways, in many animistic and other religions of the world.

Behind spiritual ecology is the erosion, if not complete loss, of confidence in the adequacy of secular approaches such as science, technology, and government to reduce if not resolve environmental crises. It is recognized that secular approaches have made progress and are necessary. However, they are not considered sufficient because they focus on superficial symptoms and proximate causes of environmental problems, rather than facing their ultimate causes and consequences.

Advocates of religion as part of the solution to environmental crises believe that the *ultimate* cause resides in morality, wherein religion can play a crucial role. They think that a more fundamental and powerful source is required to change, direct, and motivate human behavior, individually and collectively, to be more sustainable, green, and adaptive. Religion has the potential to provide a worldview, values, attitudes, practices, rituals, institutions, and sacred places for the effective development of a vibrant and adaptive spiritual ecology. Religions are alternative ways of representing nature; affording it spiritual, moral, and cultural meanings and values; and defining the place of humans in nature, including how they should and shouldn't act toward nonhuman beings and other natural phenomena.

Most spiritual ecologists tend to think that we already have the solution to environmental crises and know how to live in harmony with nature. We mainly need to more closely approximate the appropriate ideals and principles of our religion in practice. Religions are already in place, well established, and followed to varying degrees by billions of people. The pivotal task ahead is for more people to better understand the environmental as well as human and social consequences of their behaviors and institutions in the short and long term, explicitly construct and more closely follow a viable environmental ethic, and recognize and effectively practice the spiritual ecology in their own religion, including the sacredness of all life. As Huston Smith (1992) appreciates, the world's religions are the collective wisdom of humanity and can be channeled for enormous good.

Ideally, in spiritual ecology nature is considered to be an interwoven web of material and spiritual relationships among beings and things from the local to the global levels. Thus, spiritual ecologists view humans as an integral part of nature, rather than uniquely and absolutely separate, superior, and dominant. If effectively realized in practice, then such an ideal should make a positive difference in creating more adaptive human–environment interactions. Of course, that "if" is a big challenge, to say the least.

To the extent that nature is considered sacred, then the degradation and destruction of the environment, including species, habitats, landforms, and waters, is sacrilegious and morally irresponsible and reprehensible. Thus, spiritual ecology focuses on an *ecocentric environmental ethic,* instead of an anthropocentric and/or egocentric ethic. A common ingredient in an ecocentric ethic is restraint as well as efficiency in exploiting land and resources for satisfying basic needs, instead of blind pursuit of insatiable greed as if resources were infinite. Ideally, in interacting with the environment, spiritual and moral values are primary, while any utilitarian values are secondary.

The maintenance and restoration of the balance, harmony, or dynamic equilibrium of society in nature is a pivotal concern of spiritual ecology. As Eugene Anderson (1996) has convincingly argued, effective land and resource management and conservation have an emotional as well as rational component. Those indigenous and other societies that are adaptive necessarily bond with their homeland not only in historical, economic, cultural, and ecological ways, but also in intellectual, spiritual, moral, and emotional ways.

Spiritual ecology is a primary component of a much larger process, a growing convergence in rethinking the place of humans in nature and of our responsibilities to nature. No doubt science and religion differ on many points, but they can share a common concern with environmental problems. Potentially they can offer complementary approaches to the environment: science, material and utilitarian; and religion, spiritual and moral. The profound potential of this growing reconciliation between religion and science in the context of environmental crises should not be underestimated, considering the many centuries of attempts since the Renaissance by Western philosophers and scientists to demystify, objectify, and atomize nature through an exclusively materialistic and mechanistic worldview, as well as the long history of antagonisms between science and Christianity.

Obstacles and Limitations

Although spiritual ecology has developed impressive momentum and is already yielding some significant positive contributions, it also faces a variety of serious obstacles and limitations.

Materialism

One of the underlying assumptions of spiritual ecology in general is mentalistic—that ideas influence behavior, which in turn has environmental consequences. However, materialist critics question this by pointing out the frequent *discrepancies between ideals and actions*. Furthermore, in modern society they see money and greed as transcending all other interests, whether in business, government, community, or personal matters. The sheer power and momentum of such material forces supposedly automatically overwhelm everything, no matter what religious influences may remain.

It is a reduction to the point of absurdity, however, to consider all humans, regardless of culture and other factors, to be nothing more than economic animals, simply maximizing profit while minimizing effort and risk. There are numerous exceptions that invalidate such generalizations about the economic animal as some kind of invariant law of human nature. One counter-example is altruistic acts, even some in which individuals sacrifice their own lives to save others. Various monastic communities in which monks take vows of poverty and celibacy are another example (e.g., Sponsel and Natadecha-Sponsel 1997). Also consider Henry David Thoreau at Walden Pond and contemporary cases of voluntary simplicity by laypersons.

Within the history of spiritual ecology, an exception is the Bishnois of Rajasthan, India, in the fifteenth century. They believed that cutting a tree was sacrilegious. When a king sent soldiers to cut their forest to construct a new palace, Bishnois women hugged the trees with their bodies to protect them. Soldiers killed 363 villagers before the king heard of this massacre, stopped the operation, and provided state protection for their beliefs and forests. This Hindu-based ritual defense of nature was subsequently cultivated by the Chipko movement along the Himalayan foothills starting in 1973 (Gottlieb 1996: 159–60). Of course, any hard-core materialist would retort that the Bishnois were just protecting trees as part of their livelihood. In any case, ideas, even religious ones, were also involved in their actions.

Objectivity

It would be unscientific for any scientist to close his or her mind to any possibility, including religion, although many have. Obviously scientists can be just as hypocritical as anyone else. The objective thing for any scientist or scholar to do would be to formulate and test empirically falsifiable hypotheses about the natural or environmental consequences of religious behavior. A few ecological anthropologists have actually done this to some extent with varying degrees of success, as we shall discuss shortly.

Anachronism

Critics also thought religion would go out of style with the development of the modern rational world. As an ancient, cross-cultural universal, religion is unlikely to disappear from society, at least as long as people find it meaningful in dealing with ultimate questions, personal crises, and the unknown. In fact, religion not only persists, despite secular tendencies in society, but there is even a proliferation of new religions. In part this may reflect a growing disenchantment with seeking happiness solely through technology, materialism, and consumerism.

Negativity

Throughout history and to this day, many people have committed horrible evil in the name of their religion, such as the political manipulations of relations between Christian Serbs and Muslim ethnic Albanians in Kosovo in recent years. Still, the existence of negative episodes in religion is not sufficient grounds to summarily dismiss all of the positives, but only to be critical, cautious, and vigilant. Almost any human domain, including science, technology, medicine, government, and even education, can have some negative aspects, factions, and fanatics. Who or what is absolutely perfect? As previously indicated, there are a growing number of interfaith conferences and alliances on the environment that demonstrate that mutual understanding, appreciation, tolerance, and cooperation among religions is quite feasible and can be highly productive.

Resistance

Admittedly, resistance is likely to grow with the realization that spiritual ecology, like deep ecology and the green political movement, call for profound changes in lifestyles, society, and the status quo. It is important to seriously consider that some religious people view environmentalism and spiritual ecology as a serious threat, rather than as a healthy challenge for constructive rethinking, revision, and revitalization of their religion (e.g., Whelan et al., 1996).

Enter the Anthropologists

Many anthropologists have published research relevant to spiritual ecology, even if they and others do not necessarily identify it as such. Because most readers are likely to be familiar with such work and given space limitations, here only some of the highlights for a sample of pioneers will be presented.

Tsembaga

Until recent decades Roy Rappaport (1984) provided the most detailed, empirical, and elegant application of the systems approach in ecological anthropology to document and explain the natural functions of the supernatural. His fieldwork with the Tsembaga of Papua New Guinea is the first substantial ethnography in spiritual ecology. He analyzed Tsembaga ritual and warfare as mechanisms regulating the delicate balance between the human and pig populations to reduce competition between them. (Humans and pigs are surprisingly close in physiology, omnivorous diet, and body and group size.)

Sacred Cows

Marvin Harris developed cultural materialism as by far the most explicit and systematic research strategy within cultural anthropology. Materialism asserts that causal primacy most likely stems from the material conditions of existence, rather than ideas. Accordingly, materialism assigns research priority to the material over the mental (1979). Harris's analysis of the sacred cow in India is the classic application of cultural materialism. Harris (1966, 1985) argues that the cow is not sacred simply because of Hindu and other religious beliefs. Instead, the cow is primarily sacred because it is indispensable to the agricultural economy in the historical ecology of India, especially for plowing, fertilizer (dung), cooking fuel (dried dung), and milk (instead of meat). Few publications have stimulated so much opposition; rebuttals have occasionally been published in major anthropology journals, such as *Current Anthropology*, for over three decades now.

Tukano

Gerardo Reichel-Dolmatoff (1971, 1976, 1999) argued that the Desana, a Tukano group, in the Colombian portion of the northwest Amazon, are intimately tuned into their forest and river ecosystems, not only through their subsistence activities, but also through their social organization, myths, rituals, and symbols. The shaman even serves as a manager of natural resource exploitation by regulating a complex system of faunal and sexual prohibitions. In these and other ways, the Desana population maintains a balance with its environment below carrying capacity, and thus does not irreversibly deplete natural resources and degrade the ecosystems in its habitat. They are circumscribed by other groups and therefore cannot expand geographically, unless resorting to warfare and conquest. Reichel-Dolmatoff's elaborate and penetrating analysis comes closest to a holistic cultural and spiritual ecology, which integrates materialist and mentalist approaches to culture–environment relations.

Koyukon

Richard Nelson (1983) has for many years explored traditional environmental knowledge (TEK) and natural resource use, management, and conservation systems of indigenous peoples. In one study, he explores in rich detail the cultural and spiritual ecology of the Koyukon, northern Athapaskan Indians in Alaska and the Yukon. He convincingly illustrates how their deep respect and reverence for the animals they hunt and fish tempers their relationship with their forest, lake, and river ecosystems. In part, this worldview derives from not drawing discrete boundaries between humans, nature, and the supernatural, but viewing and treating animals as humanlike kin closely linked with the spirit world. Taboos and rituals are pivotal in these relationships. For instance, there are special protocols for treating an animal when it is butchered, distributing parts to different persons, and disposing of unusable parts. The Koyukon even perform funeral rituals for special animals like wolverines and bears. All beings and things are potentially spiritual and sacred.

Bali

Stephen Lansing (1991), with a multidisciplinary team of colleagues in applied systems ecology and computer simulation, constructed a model of how temple priests in Bali regulate irrigation waters for wet rice paddies through their religious beliefs and rituals (see the video *Goddess and the Computer* [Appendix 1]). More than any other anthropologist before or since, he demonstrates empirically and convincingly the efficacy of the natural functions of the supernatural. His team also considered the practical applications of their research findings for economic development and central government concerns.

Cree

Biologist Fikret Berkes (1999) analyzes how traditional environmental knowledge (TEK); natural resource use, management, and conservation; and religious beliefs and practices are all interrelated in the case of the Cree Indians of James Bay in subarctic Canada. Berkes views TEK as a challenge to the positivist–reductionist paradigm in Western science, and he concludes that TEK can potentially contribute a needed ethical dimension to the science of ecology and resource management.

Beliefs and Emotions

In a wide-ranging book with diverse examples, Eugene Anderson (1996) offers a compelling critique of and counterargument to the extremists among the evolutionary ecologists (optimal foraging theory), cultural materialists, and postmodern revisionists. The bottom line is that sustainable use, management, and conservation of natural resources depends not only on rationality and hard facts, but also on beliefs and emotions. Traditional indigenous and other societies that invest heart and soul as well as mind and body in caring for their environment usually do so successfully. Resource management strategies linked with religious beliefs and practices that may superficially appear to be irrational are actually grounded in intimate and daily observations of nature over many years and even generations of experience. Anderson comes closest to providing *a holistic and comparative anthropological synthesis of spiritual ecology.*

Functionalism

The earlier work of Rappaport, Harris, and others of a similar nature has been criticized on many points, but especially for conflating functions and origins and in assuming that almost anything that persists must be adaptive: the Dr. Pangloss syndrome (e.g., Edgerton 1992). However, it would be nonsense to assume or argue that no component of culture ever had or has any practical consequences in influencing the interactions between a human population and the ecosystems in its habitat. Undoubtedly functionalism has its limitations and pitfalls, but there is no point in entirely rejecting the practical consequences of culture. Too many anthropologists, sucked into the academic circus of career advancement, are quick to dismiss anyone and anything before their own time as no longer having any validity or utility, ignoring in their egocentric myopia the continuities as well as discontinuities in the historical development of the profession and the fact that someday even they too may be superseded. Cultural ecology, functionalism, and cultural materialism are not completely dead and buried, even for those who repeatedly delude themselves and others to the contrary. Fortunately, some scholarly visionaries can see the past as well as the present and possibilities for the future. Among the visionaries are the authors of the seven case studies just highlighted.

Hooked on Spiritual Ecology

Spiritual ecology has increasingly consumed my teaching, research, and publications in recent years. Actually there has been little choice; since 1986 field research in southern Thailand has inevitably drawn me into spiritual ecology. In the southernmost provinces near Malaysia, although the majority of people are Muslims it is common to find adjacent villages, one Muslim and the other Buddhist. Furthermore, Buddhists and Muslims usually get along quite well and even cooperate in many ways. When a Thai research team I directed compared the cultural ecology of Muslim and Buddhist villages, we discovered that they may use the same environment but do so differently, and their religion is the decisive factor (Sponsel and Natadecha-Sponsel 1992). Also, the phenomenon of Buddhist forest monks as environmental activists led us to explore the relationship between Buddhism, forests, and deforestation in Thailand (Sponsel and Natadecha-Sponsel 1993, 1995, 1997). We gradually realized that the landscape of Thailand is permeated with sacred places in nature: single trees, groves, forests, rocks, caves, and mountains, all considered sacred in various ways. Indeed, it can even be argued that sacred places in nature contribute to biodiversity conservation (Sponsel et al., 1998). In short, I'm a true believer in spiritual ecology, interested most in two components in particular—sacred places in nature plus Buddhist ecology.

So What's in It for You?

There are several cutting-edge research frontiers in ecological anthropology that may well be much more than just the usual temporary academic fads, fashions, and fantasies. Whether you are a believer or not, spiritual ecology is certainly one frontier. Indeed, the Harvard conferences and FORE mentioned earlier are explicit attempts to systematically ground spiritual ecology in academia and beyond. *What are some of the possibilities for anthropological research and teaching on spiritual ecology?*

Materialism and/or Mentalism

A pivotal issue in cultural anthropology has been the major rift between materialists and mentalists. Materialists give primacy to the material conditions of existence (e.g., food, water, shelter), mentalists to ideas (e.g., beliefs, values, myths, rituals, and symbols). Although this dichotomy has been repeatedly challenged and weakened, it remains problematic. Nevertheless, either a materialist or a mentalist approach may be pursued in spiritual ecology. Moreover, spiritual ecology offers a special opportunity to explore and develop a middle ground between these two approaches, a third approach that might be called integrative. Among the cases discussed earlier, Rappaport and Harris emphasize materialism; Nelson mentalism; and Reichel-Dolmatoff, Lansing, Berkes, and Anderson an integrative approach. However, in his later work Rappaport (1999) tends more toward an integrative approach. Materialist and mentalist approaches are not necessarily antithetical. After all, humans are simultaneously biological, cultural, mental, and spiritual beings. In short, spiritual ecology provides the special opportunity for pursuing in teaching and research materialist, mentalist, or integrative approaches.

Sacred Places and Communities

One needn't necessarily go to a foreign country to find possibilities for study, research, and participation in spiritual ecology. There are innumerable sacred places in the United States: the Black Hills, Cahokia, Chaco Canyon, Crater Lake, Devil's Tower, the Everglades, the Grand Canyon, Kilauea, Mesa Verde, Mount Rainier, Mount Shasta, Serpent Mound, Shiprock, White Sands, and Yellowstone. It is no coincidence that many of these places are associated with *indigenes, the original practitioners of spiritual ecology.* Sacred places are visited by others like naturalists, some even on a pilgrimage or vision quest of their own. Many sacred places are of concern to environmentalists as well. The link between all three categories—indigenes, naturalists, and environmentalists—is spiritual ecology. Indeed, many naturalists have been inspired to become environmentalists by sensing the sacredness of natural phenomena, such as Henry David Thoreau, John Muir, Gifford Pinchot, Aldo Leopold, William O. Douglas, and Rachel Carson (Swan 1990: 105–7).

There are numerous possibilities for research on spiritual ecology and sacred places associated with Euroamericans and other nonindigenous peoples in the United States. There are special religious communities or subgroups like the Amish, Buddhists, Franciscans, Hindus, and Jains. Beyond many national parks, there are also religious buildings and their surroundings (e.g.,

Chimayo in New Mexico); cemeteries and memorials (Arlington National Cemetery, the U.S.S. *Arizona* War Memorial at Pearl Harbor, the U.S. Holocaust Memorial Museum, the Vietnam War Memorial); and historic sites (Gettysburg, Williamsburg). Some of these are simply sacred sites; others may be relevant to spiritual ecology as well. Also *sacred places are still being created.* For example, a tree that survived the Oklahoma City bombing has been interpreted as a sign of the persistence and renewal of life, and is assuming the status of a sacred tree.

Movements

Spiritual ecology is a social, political, and intellectual movement as well as a religious one, not merely a transdisciplinary arena of academic research, scholarship, and teaching. For example, in the United States, several years ago Catholic, Jewish, and Protestant organizations established a coalition called the National Religious Partnership for the Environment. It is basically an educational initiative in applied spiritual ecology. Anthropologists have long documented religious movements, some called revitalization or millennial movements. Spiritual ecology also needs to be documented and understood as such, through library and field research (participant observation, interviews, etc.).

Changes and Dangers

Cultural and environmental change are interrelated, whether from the perspective of Julian Steward's cultural ecology, or a more recent emphasis, historical ecology (Balee 1998). For those concerned with biodiversity conservation, sacred places are just being recognized for their actual and potential roles. However, as new religions spread into an area, they may have a profound influence on local cultural, historical, and spiritual ecologies. Certainly Christian missionaries have declared pagans as evil and done their best to destroy indigenous spiritual ecology and sacred places throughout the world (Sponsel 2000). A comparative study of before and after cases of Christian missionization could be most revealing. It could also be considered heretical.

Preservation and Rights

This points to another possibility: protecting religious freedom and sacred places can help protect cultural diversity, biodiversity, and the environment (e.g., see the video *Mount Shasta*). Here there are numerous vital and urgent prospects for advocacy anthropology in collaboration with indigenous and other peoples who are battling to pursue their own religion and defend their sacred places and human rights against economic "development," government, religious fanatics, and other threats (see Sponsel 2000 and Swan 1990).

Conversion in Three Easy Steps

The first step in becoming engaged in spiritual ecology is to explore it for yourself. Test the waters yourself with an open mind. Convenient and safe places to begin are with the first textbook (Kinsley 1995) and the most comprehensive anthology (Gottlieb 1996). Subscribe to the first journal devoted to the subject, *Worldviews: Environment, Culture, Religion.* Check out Web sites such as the Forum on Religion and Ecology. (See Appendix II.) Read some of the book-length case studies cited in this chapter. View some videos, especially *Spirit and Nature*, based on an interdisciplinary and interfaith dialogue at Middlebury College in 1990, where participants addressed the question Why is the environment a religious issue? (See Rockefeller and Elder 1992.)

The second step is to pick a religion. Become a sensitive and sensible student of that religion, respectfully probing aspects of beliefs, rituals, symbols, myths, and sacred places that are especially relevant to ecology and environmental problems and issues. Again, do some library research on the subject. Then do fieldwork as a participant observer and interviewer. For you this may be no more than an exercise in intellectual curiosity, but be careful—you might even get emotionally and spiritually involved.

Career Development

The third step, if you really get hooked on spiritual ecology, is to cultivate additional background. If you are a student in anthropology, then perhaps take a minor in religion and focus in on the particular religion that interests you most. You might even consider taking a second degree in religious studies. If you have a Ph.D., then it is still not too late to be saved. You can attend professional meetings, conferences, or workshops on religious studies, a particular religion, spiritual ecology, or some aspect like sacred places. (The Harvard conferences, for example, continue occasionally under FORE.) If you are entitled to a sabbatical, you might spend your next one on further training or coursework to round out your background for spiritual ecology or develop a grant proposal and research project. You could develop a whole new course focused on spiritual ecology and sacred places. There is a whole new world of possibilities in spiritual ecology waiting for you to imagine and cultivate; heaven is the limit!

What If It Doesn't Work?

Religion is fascinating and important, whether you are a believer or not. Ecology is fascinating and important as well. Integrate the two in the form of spiritual ecology, and the result is something that is at least doubly fascinating and important, if not simply awesome. But what if it doesn't work? What if religion, in the form of spiritual ecology, is not the missing ingredient that will finally turn the environmental crises away from getting worse toward actually improving? Then what? In that case, there may be no solution left. Ecocide is assured suicide for Homo sapiens. Engage in spiritual ecology in whatever way suits your fancy, solely intellectually or with deep emotion and spirituality. The human species needs all the help it can get in returning to some modicum of ecosanity!

Appendix I. Videos on Spiritual Ecology and Sacred Places

An Ecology of Mind (Millennium series), *Biodiversity* (American Academy of Sciences), *Bhutan: The Last Shangri-La, Brother Sun, Sister Moon* (St. Francis), *Butterfly* (Julia "Butterfly" Hill), *Dragonquest, Ecopsychology: Restoring the Earth, Healing the Self, The Eleven Powers* (Bali), *From the Heart of the World* (Kogi, Colombia), *Goddess and the Computer* (Bali), *The Greening of Thailand, Heroes of the Earth, In the Light of Reverence* (Native American), *Keeping the Earth: Religious and Scientific Perspectives on the Environment, Ladakh: Kingdom in the Clouds, Kumao and Koya: In the Heart of Japan, The Last Wave* (Australian Aborigine), *Listen to the Forest* (Hawaii), *Miho Museum* (Japan), *Mount Shasta: Cathedral of Wilderness, Places of Peace and Power: The Sacred Site of Pilgrimage of Gary Martin, Primal Mind* (Native American), *The Rebirth of Nature* (Rupert Shelford), *Sacred Ground* (Native American), *Sacred Sites of Europe* (Cathedrals), *The Shaman's Journey, Shinto: Nature, Gods, and Man in Japan, The Shrine* (El Sanctuario de Chimayo), *Spirit and Nature* (Middlebury conference), *Thailand* (Mini-Dragons II series), and *The Web of Life.*

Appendix II. Selected Organizations

Alliance of Religions and Conservation (ARC)
9A Disdbury Park
Manchester M20 5LH, UK
www.salford.ac.uk/env-res/wwf/

Forum on Religion and Ecology (FORE)
c/o Department of Religion
Bucknell University
Lewisburg, PA 17837
http://divweb.harvard.edu/cswr/ecology
http://environment.harvard.edu/religion

Greenearth Foundation
P.O. Box 327
El Verano, CA 95433
www.rmetzner-greenearth.org/biblio.html

Honoring Sacred Sites/Indigenous Environmental Network
North American Indigenous Peoples Biodiversity Project
2105 First Avenue South
Minneapolis, MN 55404
www.alpacdc.com/ien

Martin Gray
The Geomancy Foundation
P.O. Box 4111
Sedona, AZ 86340
www.sacredsites.com

The Mountain Institute
Main and Dogwood Streets
Franklin, WV 26807
www.mtnforum.org

Sacred Land Film Project
P.O. Box C-151
La Honda, CA 94020
www.sacredland.org
(video *In the Light of Reverence*)

Sacred Sites International Foundation
1442A Walnut Street #330
Berkeley, CA 94709-1405
www.sitesaver.org
publishes newsletter *Site Saver*

References

Albanese, Catherine L. 1990. *Nature Religion in America: From the Algonkian Indians to the New Age.* Chicago: University of Chicago Press.

Anderson, E. N. 1996. *Ecologies of the Heart: Emotion, Belief, and the Environment.* New York: Oxford University Press.

Balee, William. 1998. *Advances in Historical Ecology.* New York: Columbia University Press.

Barney, Gerald O. 2000. *Threshold 2000: Critical Issues and Spiritual Values for a Global Age.* Ada, Mich.: CoNexus Press.

Beck, Peggy V., Anna Lee Walters, and Nia Francisco. 1996. *The Sacred: Ways of Knowledge, Sources of Life.* Tsaile, Ariz.: Navajo Community College Press.

Berkes, Fikret. 1999. *Sacred Ecology: Traditional Ecological Knowledge and Resource Management.* Philadelphia: Taylor & Francis.

Bernbaum, Edwin. 1990. *Sacred Mountains of the World.* San Francisco: Sierra Club Books.

Brockman, Norbert C., ed. 1997. *Encyclopedia of Sacred Places.* Santa Barbara, Calif.: ABC-CLIO.

Callicott, J. Baird. 1994. *Earth's Insights: A Multicultural Survey of Ecological Ethics from the Mediterranean Basin to the Australian Outback.* Berkeley: University of California Press.

Carmichael, David L., et al., eds. 1994. *Sacred Sites, Sacred Places.* New York: Routledge.

Carroll, John E., and Keith Warner, eds. 1998. *Ecology and Religion: Scientists Speak.* Quincy, Ill.: Franciscan Press.

Chidester, David, and Edward T. Linenthal, eds. 1995. *American Sacred Space.* Bloomington: Indiana University Press.

des Jardins, Joseph R. 1997. *Environmental Ethics: An Introduction to Environmental Philosophy.* Belmont, Calif.: Wadsworth.

Driver, B. L., Daniel Dustin, Tony Baltic, Gary Elsner, and George Peterson. 1996. *Nature and the Human Spirit: Toward an Expanded Land Management Ethic.* State College, Penn.: Venture.

Dwivedi, O. P., and B. N. Tiwari. 1987. *Environmental Crisis and Hindu Religion.* New Delhi, India: Gitanjali Publishing House.

Earth Ethics. Fall 1998. *Religions of the World and Ecology: Discovering Common Ground.* Earth Ethics Special issue 10(1): 1–32.

Edgerton, Robert. 1992. *Sick Societies: Challenging the Myth of Primitive Harmony.* Berkeley: University of California Press.

Edwards, Jo, and Martin Palmer. 1997. *Holy Ground: The Guide to Faith and Ecology.* Northamptonshire, UK: Pilkington Press.

Fagan, Brian. 1999. *From Black Land to Fifth Sun: The Science of Sacred Sites.* New York: Addison-Wesley.

Gottlieb, Roger S., ed. 1996. *This Sacred Earth: Religion, Nature, Environment.* New York: Routledge.

Grim, John. 2000. *Indigenous Traditions and Ecology.* Cambridge, Mass.: Harvard University Press/Center for the Study of World Religions.

Guthrie, Stewart. 1993. *Faces in the Clouds: A New Theory of Religion.* New York: Oxford University Press.

Hamilton, Lawrence S., ed. 1993. *Ethics, Religion and Biodiversity: Relations between Conservation and Cultural Values.* Cambridge, UK: White Horse Press.

Hargrove, Eugene C., ed. 1986. *Religion and Environmental Crisis.* Athens: University of Georgia Press.

Harpur, James. 1994. *The Atlas of Sacred Places: Meeting Points of Heaven and Earth.* New York: Henry Holt.

Harris, Marvin. 1966. "The Cultural Ecology of India's Sacred Cattle." *Current Anthropology* 7: 51–66.

———. 1979. *Cultural Materialism: The Struggle for a Science of Culture.* New York: Random House.

———. 1985. *Good to Eat: Riddles of Food and Culture.* New York: Simon and Schuster.

Harvey, Graham. 1997. *Contemporary Paganism: Listening People, Speaking Earth.* New York: New York University Press.

Hessel, Dieter T., and Rosemary Radford Reuther, eds. 2000. *Christianity and Ecology: Seeking the Well-Being of Earth and Humans.* Cambridge, Mass.: Harvard University Press.

Holm, Jean, and John Bowker, eds. 1994a. *Attitudes to Nature.* London: Pinter.

———. 1994b. *Sacred Place.* London: Pinter.

Hughes, Donald. 1983. *American Indian Ecology.* El Paso: Texas Western Press.

Kawagley, A. Oscar. 1995. *A Yupiaq Worldview: A Pathway to Ecology and Spirit.* Prospect Heights, Ill.: Waveland Press.

Kaza, Stephanie, and Kenneth Kraft, eds. 2000. *Dharma Rain: Sources of Buddhist Environmentalism.* Boston: Shambhala.

Khalid, Fazlun M., and Joanne O'Brien. 1992. *Islam and Ecology.* London: Cassell Ltd.

Kinsley, David. 1995. *Ecology and Religion: Ecological Spirituality in Cross-Cultural Perspective.* Englewood Cliffs, N.J.: Prentice-Hall.

Lansing, J. Stephen. 1991. *Priests and Programmers: Technologies of Power in the Endangered Landscape of Bali.* Princeton, N.J.: Princeton University Press.

McFadden, Steven. 1991. *Profiles in Wisdom: Native Leaders Speak about the Earth.* Santa Fe, N.Mex.: Bear.

McPherson, Robert S. 1992. *Sacred Land, Sacred View: Navajo Perception of the Four Corners Region.* Salt Lake City, Utah: Brigham Young University Press.

Metzner, Ralph. 1994. *The Well of Remembrance: Rediscovering the Earth Wisdom Myths of Northern Europe.* Boston: Shambhala.

———. 1999. *Green Psychology: Transforming Our Relationship to the Earth.* Rochester, Vt.: Park Street Press.

Milne, Courtney. 1995. *Sacred Places in North America.* New York: Stewart, Tabori, and Chang.

Molyneaux, Brian Leigh. 1995. *The Sacred Earth.* Boston: Little, Brown.

Nelson, John K. 1996. *A Year in the Life of a Shinto Shrine.* Seattle: University of Washington Press.

Nelson, Lance E., ed. 1998. *Purifying the Earthly Body of God: Religion and Ecology in Hindu India.* Albany: State University of New York Press.

Nelson, Richard K. 1983. *Make Prayers to the Raven: A Koyukon View of the Northern Forest.* Chicago: University of Chicago Press.

Norberg-Hodge, Helena. 1991. *Ancient Futures: Learning from Ladakh.* San Francisco, Calif.: Sierra Club Books.

Palmer, Martin. 1996. *Sacred Mountains of China.* San Francisco: HarperCollins.

Prime, Ranchor. 1992. *Hinduism and Ecology.* London: Cassell.

Ramakrishnan, P. S., K. G. Saxena, and U. M. Chandrashekara, eds. 1998. *Conserving the Sacred for Biodiversity Management.* Enfield, N.H.: Science Publishers.

Rappaport, Roy A. 1979. *Ecology, Meaning, and Religion.* Richmond, Calif.: North Atlantic Press.

———. 1984. *Pigs for the Ancestors: Ritual in the Ecology of a New Guinea People.* 2d ed. New Haven, Conn.: Yale University Press.

———. 1999. *Ritual and Religion in the Making of Humanity.* New York: Cambridge University Press.

Reichel-Dolmatoff, Gerardo. 1971. *Amazonian Cosmos: The Sexual and Religious Symbolism of the Tukano Indians.* Chicago: University of Chicago Press.

———. 1976. "Cosmology as Ecological Analysis: A View from the Rainforest." *Man* 11(3): 307–18.

———. 1999. "A View from the Headwaters." *The Ecologist* 29(4): 276–80.

Rockefeller, Steven C., and John C. Elder, eds. 1992. *Spirit and Nature: Why the Environment is a Religious Issue.* Boston: Beacon.

Rose, Aubrey. 1992. *Judaism and Ecology.* London: Cassell.

Sheldrake, Rupert. 1994. *The Rebirth of Nature: The Greening of Science and God.* Rochester, Vt.: Park Street Press.

Smith, Huston. 1992. *Forgotten Truth: The Common Vision of the World's Religions.* San Francisco: HarperCollins.

Sponsel, Leslie E. 1997. "Ecological Anthropology." In Thomas Barfield, ed., *Dictionary of Cultural Anthropology,* 137–40. London: Blackwell Scientific Publications.

———. 2000a. "Human Impact on Biodiversity: Overview." In Simon Levin, ed., *Encyclopedia of Biodiversity.* San Diego: Academic [forthcoming].

———, ed. 2000b. *Sanctuaries of Culture and Nature: Sacred Places and Biodiversity Conservation* [forthcoming].

———. 2000c. "Advocacy in Anthropology." In *International Encyclopedia of the Social and Behavioral Sciences.* New York: Pergamon [in press].

Sponsel, Leslie E., and Poranee Natadecha-Sponsel. 1992. "A Comparison of the Cultural Ecology of Adjacent Muslim and Buddhist Villages in Southern Thailand: A Preliminary Field Report." *Journal of the National Research Council of Thailand* 23(2): 31–42.

———. 1993. "The Relevance of Buddhism for the Development of an Environmental Ethic for the Conservation of Biodiversity." In Lawrence S. Hamilton, ed., *Ethics, Religion, and Biodiversity: Relations between Conservation and Cultural Values,* 75–97. Cambridge: White Horse Press.

———. 1995. "The Role of Buddhism in Creating a More Sustainable Society in Thailand." In Jonathan Rigg, ed., *Counting the Costs: Economic Growth and Environmental Change in Thailand,* 27–46. Singapore: Institute for Southeast Asian Studies.

———. 1997. "A Theoretical Analysis of the Potential Contribution of the Monastic Community in Promoting a Green Society in Thailand." In Mary Evelyn Tucker and Duncan Williams, eds., *Buddhism and Ecology: The Interconnection of Dharma and Deeds,* 45–68. Cambridge, Mass.: Harvard University Center for the Study of World Religions.

———, Nukul Ruttanadakul, and Somporn Juntadach. 1998. "Sacred and/or Secular Approaches to Biodiversity Conservation in Thailand." *Worldviews: Environment, Culture, Religion* 2(2): 155–67.

Spring, David, and Eileen Spring, eds. 1974. *Ecology and Religion in History.* New York: Harper and Row.

Swan, James A. 1990. *Sacred Places: How the Living Earth Seeks Our Friendship.* Santa Fe, N.Mex.: Bear.

Tobias, Michael. 1991. *Life Force: The World of Jainism.* Berkeley, Calif.: Asian Humanities Press.

Tucker, Mary Evelyn. 1997. "The Emerging Alliance of Religion and Ecology." *Worldviews: Environment, Culture and Religion* 1(1): 3–24.

———, and John Berthrong, eds. 1998. *Confucianism and Ecology: The Interrelation of Heaven, Earth, and Humans.* Cambridge, Mass.: Harvard University Press and Center for the Study of World Religions.

Tucker, Mary Evelyn, and John A. Grim, eds. 1993. *Worldviews and Ecology.* Lewisburg, Pa.: Bucknell University Press.

Tucker, Mary Evelyn, and Duncan Ryuken Williams, eds. 1997. *Buddhism and Ecology: The Interconnection of Dharma and Deeds.* Cambridge, Mass.: Harvard University Center for the Study of World Religions.

Westerwood, Jennifer. 1997. *Sacred Journeys: An Illustrated Guide to Pilgrimages around the World.* New York: Henry Holt.

Whelan, Robert, et al. 1996. *The Cross and the Rainforest: A Critique of Radical Green Spirituality*. Grand Rapids, Mich.: Eerdmans.

White, Lynn, Jr. 1967 (March 10). "The Historical Roots of Our Ecological Crisis." *Science* 155: 1203–7.

Whole Earth. 1997. *The Earth in Crisis: Religion's New Test of Faith*, Special issue no. 91.

Wilson, Colin. 1996. *The Atlas of Holy Places and Sacred Sites*. New York: DK Publishing.

3

Application and Engagement

10

Historical Ecology: Landscapes of Change in the Pacific Northwest

Kathryn R. Winthrop

The silver salmon came in such multitudes in the fall runs that they were easily taken at the falls of Cow Creek. . . . The Indians would work two . . . traps and when the river began to raise in the fall they would take several hundred in a night. When the fall rains came sufficient to raise the river two or three feet the great run of salmon would come day and night. Crowding up under the falls hundreds of them being in sight at one time. (Reference to Indian fishing practices in the 1850s)[1]

In addressing biological diversity you should . . . develop alternatives for long-term management that meet the following objectives . . . maintenance and/or restoration of spawning and rearing habitat on Forest Service, Bureau of Land Management, and National Park Service lands to support recovery and maintenance of viable populations of anadromous[2] fish species and stocks and other fish species and stocks considered "sensitive" or "at risk" by land management agencies, or listed under the Endangered Species Act. . . . (U.S. President 1993: iv)

This is not a story about fish. It is a story about environmental change in the heart of what is known locally as the State of Jefferson, a part of the Pacific Northwest that encompasses the interior mountains and valleys of southwest Oregon and northern California.[3] This chronicle traces the transformation of a landscape sporting plentiful natural resources, such as fish, to one in which people today find their activities severely constrained by considerations of species and habitat depletion, and even by the danger of local species extinction.

How did this happen? This history of environmental change takes a specifically anthropological approach to answer this question, using the methods and

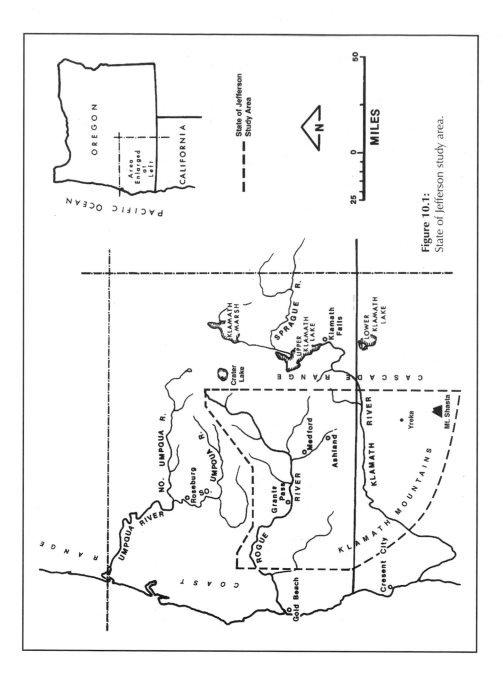

Figure 10.1:
State of Jefferson study area.

premises of historical ecology. It covers the land management practices of the region's American Indian inhabitants, who used a number of specific techniques to promote the abundance of those things—such as fish and acorns and deer—that supported their way of life. Native American land use contrasted strongly with the practices brought by nineteenth-century Euroamerican explorers and settlers. Nineteenth-century immigrants came with an extractive, market-driven economy and beliefs and values that promoted the rapid exploitation and transformation of the region's minerals, streams, grasslands, and forests.

Nineteenth-century patterns of thought and action carried through to the twentieth century, fueling the conflicts over natural resources that have characterized the politics of this region for decades. These conflicts often pit economic against ecological interests and values. By the end of the twentieth century environmental lawsuits had brought one of the region's major industries—logging—to a halt on federal land. Forced to reevaluate its land management practices, the federal government adopted ecosystem management (ESM) as a guiding policy for those agencies, especially the Forest Service and Bureau of Land Management, which manage much of this region's forests.

As part of ESM federal agencies must assess the current condition of the environment prior to making plans and decisions that affect it. These assessments must include an explanation of how environmental conditions came to be the way they are, and the history of human action is an important part of these explanations. This chapter synthesizes research from numerous government-sponsored studies done as part of ESM.[4]

The story told here is an important one. It informs land management policy on over 55 percent of the land in the State of Jefferson, which is managed by federal agencies, and influences practices on the rest. This history shows that humans are indeed part of the ecosystem and traces the links of that integration. This perspective has helped agency managers and scientists, as well as others involved in local economic and environmental issues, to look at the land differently and see the possibility of positive human action as well as the dangers of unmindful exploitation. In addition, demonstrating the human place within the ecosystem permits views that do not necessarily place economic and ecological values in opposition. In the State of Jefferson this view currently fosters ecological restoration work on public and private lands as one way to augment the local economy. Furthermore, a healthy environment is itself seen as contributing to "quality of life" values that attract new businesses and promote tourism, which in turn helps diversify and strengthen the economic base of the region.

Historical Ecology

Historical ecology provides a historic dimension to the study of anthropology and the environment and helps answer the question "How did we get where we are today?" Understanding environmental change over time is essential to assessing the current condition of the landscape and to understanding how and why healthy or damaged ecosystems have evolved to their current states. Such understandings form the basis for future decisions and actions, especially with regard to environmental policies.

Historical ecology is based on several premises. First, historical ecology recognizes that human beings are part of the ecosystem and that understanding the diverse and complex relationship of humans to the environment must proceed within a framework that integrates the natural and cultural realms. Second, historical ecology recognizes the dynamic interplay of natural and cultural processes over time and the fact that the effects of human–environment interactions during any period necessarily influence those interactions that follow. Finally, historical ecology is rooted in place. Human activity occurs in specific geographic locations but may have many links to larger and smaller spatial scales, reaching from the local to the global. Teasing out the connections to spatial and temporal dimensions is also a task for historical ecology.

Patterns of economy and belief are especially significant in guiding human action with regard to the environment. Human beings, like all other species on Earth, must obtain their material needs from the natural environment, and the economy of any society is the way it meets those material needs. Thus, the economy of any society *always* defines an important aspect of human relationships with the environment. Beliefs and values regarding the natural world and humanity's place within it also provide powerful motivations, both with regard to economic practices and other types of human action.

Economy and belief may differ tremendously among societies and thus account for significant differences in the ways in which people affect and are affected by the environments within which they live. Other factors, such as population and technology, may set parameters that influence other cultural practices and especially influence the way economic activities affect the environment. Furthermore, in large, complex societies such as ours, national politics and policies also mediate economic actions and social beliefs and values.

Historical Ecology in the State of Jefferson

The State of Jefferson is a regional term referring to portions of southwestern Oregon and northern California that share a common ecology and cultural history. The rugged Klamath and Cascade mountain ranges dominate the topography and constrain travel to and through the region. Two major rivers, the Rogue and the Klamath, flow west to the sea, and two major valleys, the Rogue and the Shasta, provide homes for most of the region's three hundred

Figure 10.2: Overview, State of Jefferson. Courtesy of the Bureau of Land Management, Medford District, Oregon.

thousand inhabitants today. The Klamath Mountains also contain mineral deposits, particularly gold, which have significantly influenced the local history.

The climate is seasonal and moderate with most of the precipitation falling in the winter and arriving as snow in the mountains. Rainfall varies with elevation; the valleys are dry, with average precipitation slightly less than 20 inches per year. Vegetation also follows an altitudinal gradient. Grasslands, oak woodlands, and oak/pine savannah once characterized valley and low-elevation hillsides, which today are primarily urban or agricultural. Mixed hardwood/conifer forests occur at intermediate elevations, and coniferous forests, punctuated by mountain meadows, cover high-elevation slopes. Floods and fires have shaped this landscape and continue to offer challenges to human inhabitants today.

Game animals such as deer and elk occur at all altitudes. Smaller mammals and large predators such as cougar and bear still range throughout the region, though grizzly bears and wolves disappeared a century ago. Though numbers are much reduced from times past, game birds still migrate through the area, and salmon still spawn in the streams.

Two major and contrasting ways of life have been part of this regional ecosystem, each with profoundly differing economies, technologies, and beliefs and effects upon the land. The first is the native pattern, encompassing the history of the American Indian peoples. The second arrived with Euroamerican explorers and settlers in the nineteenth century.

A Native Land

The environment encountered by the earliest Euroamerican explorers to this region reflected centuries of use and management by local American Indians. The land-use practices that characterized these native peoples at the time of contact with Euroamericans had been in place for centuries and were themselves an important component of the native ecosystem.

The Shasta and Takelma Indians occupied the major valleys and shared use of the uplands with other native groups. All these peoples pursued subsistence through a hunting–fishing–gathering economy. Regional population numbered in the thousands, with permanent winter villages occupied by groups of about twenty to one hundred people. Subsistence was rooted in key resources: salmon, deer and elk, camas and epos (edible bulbs and roots), and acorns. The climate and topography favored seasonal movement along an altitudinal gradient as plants ripened at higher elevations throughout the spring and summer and as game migrated between winter and summer pastures. Resources gathered during the warmer months of the year, and especially during the fall, were stored for winter use. Technology was based on tools crafted from stone, bone, vegetable products, hide, and sinew. This simple material technology was complemented by an intimate understanding of the natural world.

These local groups employed a variety of strategies to secure their subsistence. They carefully monitored the projected productivity of annual resources, such as camas roots or deer, and scheduled their seasonal travels to make the most of these resources where and when these necessities were most abundant. They also utilized a wide range of foods and materials that helped to buffer shortfalls in any of the staple crops. Fluctuating annual climatic cycles did occasionally result in shortages of staples, and such events were also countered through an elaborate regional redistribution system based on trade, intermarriage, and social stratification. Extensive kin networks, for example, meant that during hard times the people of one village had recourse to the resources of relatives elsewhere who might be in a better situation.

Biodiversity, exemplified by a variety of ecotones and vegetation communities, was extremely important to the survival of native peoples, as was the production of staple resources. They engaged in numerous activities to promote biodiversity and enhance resource abundance. They carefully managed root-gathering areas to ensure annual productivity by tilling, weeding, thinning, replanting, maintaining of reserve areas, and burning competing vegetation. Conservation measures, such as seasonal hunting of deer and elk, combined with regulated fish harvests, helped ensure continued abundance of those species. They pruned plants used for basketry or tools to create straight shoots. Among the most powerful of their technologies, however, was use of fire.

Interior southwest Oregon is comparatively dry, and natural fire cycles are frequent. Local Indians worked with this regime to suppress the encroachment of dense coniferous forests and to promote valued vegetation communities. Fires were set by specialists during the spring, summer, and fall for a variety of purposes and took into account the season, temperature, wind direction, humidity, and impacts upon specific plants.

This anthropogenic burning, together with natural fires, helped maintain an extensive oak woodland and oak/pine savannah in the lower elevations, prairies in the valleys, meadows in the uplands, and chaparral in the hills. These vegetation communities in turn provided an abundance of vegetable crops such as acorns and edible roots and useful materials such as bear grass for basketry. Burning also promoted habitat valuable for game species including deer, elk, small mammals, and birds such as grouse. Such purposeful burning was concentrated at lower elevations near villages and at higher elevations along meadows and ridgelines, where seasonal camps were frequently located.

This practical understanding of the environment was based on traditional knowledge: it was local, specific, and derived from centuries of experience in living closely with the land. The philosophical underpinnings of their way of life included a vision of the natural world as home—to be used, but also cared for. People saw themselves as existing within a web of relationships that included human as well as plant and animal kin. These views promoted notions of reciprocity with these "kin" and required appreciation, respect, and stewardship of them. Active management of the land and human relations to the land were part of a larger moral universe encoded in myth and upheld through rituals. These beliefs were as essential to their survival as the actions that they supported.

Contact and Cultural Transformation: 1827–1900

The earliest emissaries of Western civilization passed through this region in 1827–28. Others followed in the next two decades, though settlement did not occur until the discovery of gold in 1851, which brought this area rapidly into the fold of nineteenth-century American society.

Euroamerican exploration and settlement introduced a way of life that differed radically from that of the native peoples. It was (and still is) integrated into a global market economy and a political world transcending local influence and concern. It was also based on a very different vision of the human place in the natural world. Nineteenth-century Euroamericans saw humans as distinct from—rather than a part of—the natural world. They saw the land they entered as at once a natural paradise created by God and provided to them for use and profit and as a wilderness to be subdued and tamed, but never as a "home" that they cohabited with other species with whom they had mutual responsibilities of care. They brought with them as well increasingly powerful technologies to assist them in the transformation of this "wilderness."

By the end of the century an economy based on mining, ranching, farming, and logging was well established, and much of the native ecosystem had been transformed in significant ways. In addition, these industries supported a rural, town, and country society that was firmly connected to economic, political, and social networks that stretched across the continent.

Exploration and Settlement

Peter Skene Ogden was the first Euroamerican to enter the area. He came through in the late 1820s on an exploring and fur-trapping expedition for the British Hudson's Bay Company. The British and Americans were engaged in a contest for the Pacific Northwest; Odgen's purpose was to scout out and eliminate the beaver resources in order to discourage American competition. Global economic networks and politics fueled this first contact with the region, with the extraction of natural resources for outside political and economic purposes as the goal.

Entering the southern part of the study area in February of 1827, along the Klamath River, Ogden noted that "here we are surrounded by oaks, soft Maple and Grass six inches long and green as in the summer." Camped along a tributary to the Rogue River some few days later during an especially fine period of late winter weather, he noted:

> we encamped on a large Fork form'd by a number of small Streams which we crossed in our travels this day . . . and in many of them not long since there were Beaver. . . . [T]his is certainly a fine Country and probably no Climate in the Country equal to it . . . from the singing of Birds of all kinds, grass green and at its full growth Flowers in blossom . . . at present it is certainly fine weather and certainly a country well adapted from its Soil and timber (Oaks and Pine) for cultivation. The natives inform us that Deer are abundant in the hills and Mountains . . . from their being all well clad in Leather I can well believe them. . . . Arrow quivers made of Beaver Skins also their Caps. . . . Raccoons are certainly numerous in this Country. . . . The croaking of Frogs last night certainly surprised me . . . field mice are numerous all over the Plains.[5]

These statements, taken from various passages of Ogden's journal, describe a few warm days in February of 1827 and give a brief view of the landscape through which he passed. Many others followed Ogden, recording equally wondrous descriptions of the land and noting increasing hostilities between the newcomers and native inhabitants.

These early travelers through the region affected the environment in several ways. Trappers eliminated most of the beaver during these early decades and in so doing eliminated the beaver dams that contributed to the meandering, ponded courses of the local streams. Elimination of the dams led to greater channeling of some streams, increasing the propensity for damaging floods and reducing habitat for fish and waterfowl. In addition, all of the travelers lived off the land, especially through hunting. Some of these groups were comparatively large, with parties of up to a hundred people accompanied by their horses, mules, and dogs, all needing to be grazed and fed. Cattle drives through the area—with hundreds of head of cattle—trampled and grazed on native meadows and prairies. Foreign diseases brought by the explorers may have infected local groups. Native peoples must have viewed with considerable dismay these depredations upon themselves and their carefully maintained resources.

The deathblow to native culture came in the early 1850s. Congress passed the Donation Land Claim Act in 1850 to promote settlement in Oregon, and prospectors discovered gold in the Klamath Mountains in 1851 and 1852. Hoards of miners and settlers poured into the area, leading to brutal and bloody conflicts with the native peoples. Disease, starvation, and outright genocide perpetrated by self-proclaimed bands of "Exterminators" eliminated most of the Indian people in just a few years. The several hundred native survivors in the Rogue Valley were shipped to reservations in the northern part of Oregon in 1856, while Indians surviving along the Klamath River became part of the newly evolving rural culture, carrying what they could of their traditions and understanding into future years.

The passing of the indigenous way of life ended the careful maintenance of the land that provided the abundance so admired by the newcomers. Beginning perhaps as early as the 1830s disruptions affected the caretaking of the prairies, meadows, and woodlands. Absence of cool, low-burning, regular spring and fall fires contributed to a buildup of brush and fuels in some areas possibly as early as the 1840–50s. Meanwhile, the advent of new groups with an entirely different understanding of the human place in the natural world began to change the native landscape in powerful ways.

Mining

Mining in the State of Jefferson followed the boom and bust cycles typical of this industry in the American West, reflecting the interaction between national and global economic cycles, technological advances, and environmental constraints. The initial boom lasted for about a decade and attracted many individuals working singly or in small groups, generally with hand tools, assisted occasionally by animal labor. During this period most of the "easy" gold was mined from surface placers—deposits laid down by streams at some point in the past.

Once these sources were depleted, there was a slump in the industry until advances in mining technology in the 1870–80s permitted mining on a grander scale. Capital-intensive mining technologies, including hydraulic, dredge, and lode (hard-rock) mining, brought exploitation of the deeper mineral deposits. Urban investors well outside the region financed mining companies, which employed local men as hired wage-laborers. Global capital and modern technologies led to a boom lasting into the early decades of the twentieth century. Always responsive to major economic cycles, mining languished during the inflationary period of the 1920s, to recover in the Depression era of the 1930s when deflation and a rise in the price of gold made mining profitable again. The federal government ended gold mining during World War II, and the industry has never recovered the economic significance it had during the nineteenth and early twentieth centuries.

Mining affected portions of the landscape while contributing to the shape of the societies that developed in this region. Streams were muddied and their beds turned over; hillsides and terraces were washed into hydraulic flumes; ditches diverted water for many miles to service placer and lode mines; vegetation was burned or stripped from the land. Mining further channeled local streams and discouraged regrowth of vegetation along the stream banks, contributing to more devastating cycles of flood and loss of fish and other animal habitats.

Mining also contributed to the rapid Euroamerican settlement of this area and promoted the development of early rural societies in the region. Though many miners came and went in reflection of the boom and bust of the industry, many others stayed to settle in the new land and contribute some cash to local economies. During the Depression, mining contributed to a small-scale, rural, subsistence-oriented way of life, permitting some who would otherwise be on the dole in a city to eke out a living in the woods.

Agriculture: Farming and Ranching

Early settlers found a land ready for settlement once the contest with local Indians was won. The carefully tended landscape left by the native peoples provided meadows and grasslands for cattle, sheep, and hogs. There was ample game in the woodlands; abundant fish in the streams; and fine, tall timber in the forests.

Early settlers found local markets for their produce in the mining communities and then in the developing regional society. Transportation links to outside markets strongly affected the growth of local industry, and the advent of the railroad in the late 1880s gave a large boost to ranching, farming, and logging. The orchard industry especially boomed after the railroad came through, stimulating the local economy and society.

Farming and ranching transformed the land in many ways. Farmers cleared the land for crops, pastures, fuel, and timber. By 1900 most of the big trees of the valley and low-elevation woodlands were gone, while agricultural crops and animal pastures replaced the valley grasslands and meadows. Farmers diverted water from streams for irrigation, contributing to the depletion of local fisheries. Farmers and ranchers introduced a host of new species to the local ecology as crops such as wheat and various weedy grasses and as farm and ranch animals such as cattle, sheep, and hogs. A booming market in hides led to a severe drop in deer populations and eliminated elk. Local residents also rid the landscape of unwanted predators such as wolves

Figures 10.3 and 10.4: Nineteenth-century hydraulic mining. Courtesy of the Bureau of Land Management, Medford District, Oregon.

and grizzly bears and hunted other species—such as bighorn sheep and antelope—to local extinction.

Ranchers followed a pattern of seasonal movement reflecting the availability of cattle forage at different altitudes, driving sheep and cattle to lush upland meadows during the summer and wintering them at low-elevation pastures. By the end of the nineteenth century this unregulated grazing had damaged these meadows to such an extent that an early Forest Reserve (precursor to the National Forests) report was forced to note: "Here, as everywhere else in the region lying on the western plateau of the Cascades, cattle range through the forest. Every glade or grass patch is badly overgrazed, and the trampling by stock when the ground is wet in the spring or autumn prevents the small glades from becoming forested."[6]

Ranchers also burned the land to promote grazing land for their animals. Fires were also started out of disregard for their effects by others using the woods. In reference to a specific parcel of land, the Forest Reserve report notes that "Fires have ravaged much of the timbered sections, destroying 25 percent of the timber." The destructive character of these fires may also have derived from the demise of careful native burning, which kept many areas open and free of brush. Some twenty to thirty years after the removal of the Indians, this always fire-prone landscape must have been ready to burn indeed.

Timber

We found the finest cedar trees I ever saw, yellow and red, and the logs were thirty feet without a limb and could be slit with just an axe and wooden glut. You could strike in an axe and slit twelve feet as straight as a ribbon.... (Early settler quoted in Beckham 1986: 71)[7]

Early settlers to this land viewed the majesty of its forests through admiring and appraising eyes. Though miners and early farmers frequently saw the trees as obstacles for removal, timbermen saw their commercial value. Farmers cut trees for fences, houses, firewood, and to clear fields. Commercial exploitation of the timber resources of the region was initially hampered by difficulties in transportation and a technology dependent upon hand tools (axe and crosscut saw) and animal labor. Like gold, the most accessible resources were the first exploited, with the vast timber reserves of the high country awaiting the industrial technology of the twentieth century.

Large trees along the streams were the first to be cut for commercial purposes, since the streams themselves could be used to float the logs to local mills. The advent of the railroad in the 1880s created a demand for timber for ties, bridges, trestles, and fuel and also provided market access outside the region. Sugar pine disappeared from the valleys and foothills, with ponderosa pine and Douglas fir then falling to the axe. By the end of the century, the open forests and woodlands of the streams, valleys, and foothills were mostly gone.

The timber harvest fueled the local economy and provided settlers and miners with critical resources. At the same time, the loss of timber along waterways and the effects of using streams to transport logs damaged water quality and fish habitat. Slash and stumps left on the land contributed to fuel buildups, and open woodland areas became covered with brush and prone to fire.

A Wilderness for Them

Early settlers to this region effected these changes to the land with a strong sense of purpose, secure in the moral correctness of their actions. This attitude is captured well by a local historian, writing in the 1880s:

> To penetrate into the unexplored wilds and there subdue the earth, and lay the foundations of a state was to them a second nature—a desire transmitted from their parents, whose glorious characteristic was also to advance the bounds of progress and civilization, and make glad the waste places where man had never previously trod. Theirs was a mission to keep forever in the fore-front of the battle which man is ever waging with the forces of nature, and from the wildest region accessible to man to send back the glad news that freedom had found yet another breathing place.[8]

Nineteenth-century immigrants exploited the minerals, soils, water, meadows, and timber of their new land without a thought to the limits of these resources or to the immediate and long-term effects to the plants, animals, streams, and soils of their new home. Yet by the turn of the century environmental losses across the nation were contributing to a growing conservation ethic. Seen as both a frightful waste of commercial resources and a despoiling of the "pristine" wilderness, views of these excesses combined to bring about national programs aimed at preserving and sustaining the wilds and resources of the continent. In the State of Jefferson, new players were coming to the land.

A Century of Change: 1900–2000

The federal government manages over 55 percent of the land in the State of Jefferson today. The advent of the Forest Service in the early decades of the twentieth century and later of the Bureau of Land Management (BLM) focused national politics and policies on vast tracts of high- and mid-elevation lands. The twentieth century also saw the full application of industrial technologies to local businesses, leading especially to a boom in the timber industry in the years following World War II. With the advent of the environmental movement beginning in the 1960–70s, logging became the focus of political conflicts pitting economic and environmental interests against one another. Yet at the turn of the twenty-first century some areas of quiet consensus are emerging, where economic and ecological interests are finding common ground with the promise of significant effects on local environments.

Government and the Land

Overgrazing, overhunting, and reckless burning became the targets of the newly formed federal land management agencies before World War II. Federal policies emphasized the regulation of hunting and grazing and the regeneration of the range. State and federal regulations and the reintroduction of elk gradually led to an expansion of ungulates during the course of the twentieth century. Grazing regulations coupled with depressed markets for cattle and sheep products in the 1920s and 1930s also led to some recovery of upland meadows.

Yet the major long-term effect of government management from this period was the adoption of fire suppression as a mission. Despite lengthy protests by local ranchers, who strongly advocated continued burning for range management, the national policy to protect timber resources through the suppression of wild and human-caused fires became a defining feature of land management agencies. This perspective is eloquently expressed in this excerpt from a 1936 Klamath National Forest brochure:

> The fire-protection policy of the Forest Service seeks to prevent fires from starting and to suppress quickly those that may start. . . . Fire exclusion is the only practical principle on which our forests can be handled, if we are to protect what we have and to insure new and more fully stocked forests for the future. . . .

Today, we know that the policies of fire suppression have contributed to huge buildups of fuels in the forests and to actual and potential forest fires of terrible devastation. Fire suppression on public and private lands over the course of almost a century has also changed the character of plant communities on forested lands. Fire-resistant species such as oak and pine have been replaced by species such as Douglas fir and white fir, which are less tolerant of fire. The oak and oak/pine savannahs are mostly gone, upland meadows have shrunk perceptibly in size, and once open ridgelines now support dense forests of young trees.

Timber

Industrial technology brought better tools, roads, and transportation to the timber business, leading to the exploitation of the vast timber reserves of the high country in response to the market demand of the World War II and postwar years. Scientific methods of forestry guided the development, led by trained foresters in the public and private sectors of the industry. Clear-cutting became a dominant method by the last quarter of the century. Under this practice, a unit of land was cut of all trees, remaining slash was piled and burned, and nursery-raised and genetically improved seedlings were planted and frequently sprayed with herbicides to remove competing vegetation. On Forest Service and BLM-managed lands as well, congressionally mandated "targets" set timber production goals that land managers were obligated to meet.

Decades of intensive timber harvest affected the environment in many ways. The explosion of logging roads into the mountains contributed to erosion and sediment in the streams, causing problems for fish; soil compaction from tractor logging inhibited regrowth of plants; exotic plants and diseases were spread by vehicles moving through the forests; old-growth forests needed as habitat for certain species began disappearing at an alarming rate; and even-aged stands of single species trees effectively reduced biodiversity in the "tree-farm" portions of the landscape.

These years of logging also enhanced the way of life of small, timber-dependent communities. Several generations grew up working as loggers or in the timber mills, and timber companies made good profits working in the region. Roads into the uplands on public lands expanded the use of these areas by people seeking recreational or "wilderness" experiences, and—ironically—provided access to wilderness areas for the severest critics of modern logging.

Environmental Politics and Policies

In the 1960s and 1970s growing concern over widespread effects of the Industrial Age fueled an environmental movement that achieved sufficient political power to pass major federal legislation such as the National Environmental Policy Act (1969) and the Endangered Species Act (1979). Implementation of these emerging environmental values has had a rocky history, frequently pitting environmental interests against economic interests and characterized by natural resource conflicts involving national, regional, and local players operating through business interests, environmental organizations, government agencies, and the courts.

Changing values regarding the appropriate use of the land coincided, in the State of Jefferson, with the boom in modern logging. Not surprisingly, natural resource conflicts in the region have focused on logging and its effects on the remaining old-growth forests of the region. Environmental legislation provided tools for proponents to challenge logging on public lands, and environmentalists successfully brought such logging in the Pacific Northwest to a halt in the early 1990s. The Clinton administration sought resolution to the legal gridlock, resulting in a management plan incorporating the forested areas of western Washington, Oregon, and northern California. Known as the Northwest Forest Plan, these policies now guide land management practices on public lands and call for considerably reduced timber outputs from previous decades.

The Northwest Forest Plan directs federal agencies to use the principles of ecosystem management (ESM) to guide their actions. Ecosystem management calls for a more holistic view of the environment, which integrates the bio-physical realm with human society (the "human dimension"). Federal agencies must consider the condition of the landscape as a whole and scientifically analyze the long-term (both past and future) consequences of human action and environmental processes. Though driven by an explicitly scientific perspective, ESM also encourages the participation of local people, including those who live and work closely with the land and whose experience and specific knowledge of the environment may complement the dominant scientific perspective.

Ecosystem management has brought changes to commodity-based activities on public lands. There is an increasing emphasis on promoting practices that enhance and restore biodiversity. Changes in forestry practices, for example, include a decrease in road building and promote methods that minimize impacts to soils and erosion, such as helicopter logging. Timber harvests still occur, but with greater attention to taking trees from those areas most in need of thinning to maintain forest health and reduce the danger of catastrophic wildfire. There is greater recognition that fire itself is a part of the ecosystem and that fire is a necessary tool for restoration of some vegetation communities, such as meadows and oak savannahs.

The decrease in logging on federal lands brought about by changes in timber harvest policies has affected both the environment and local communities. The dislocation of timber workers has focused state, local, and federal policies on promoting a more diverse economic base in the region, which is helping develop a local economy that is less dependent on natural resources. Logging roads built during the timber boom have increased access to the mountains for hunters, hikers, bikers, and those utilizing the woods for small-scale commodity products such as mushrooms, decorative boughs, and firewood.

In addition to these alternative uses, the "amenity values" of the region's rivers, forests, mountains, lakes, wildlife, views, and recreational possibilities have themselves become an increasingly important commodity for the region. Local promoters and state economic plans foster recreation and tourism and attract businesses based on these environmental qualities. Newcomers to the area often bring environmental values and are part of local constituencies working to restore riparian areas and fish habitat, reduce fuel loads in local watersheds, maintain plant diversity in the woods and meadows, and monitor government actions to see that they conform to environmental policies.

Summary: A Dynamic Land

For centuries the Shasta, Takelma, and other American Indian groups in this region made their living as hunter–gatherer–fishers. This way of life depended upon a carefully maintained balance between their subsistence practices and those elements of the environment that were essential to their survival. Their way of life also required a sophisticated and intimate knowledge of the world in which they lived, and they used every tool—including fire—within their means to enhance the abundance of critical resources. They buttressed their actions with life-saving beliefs in reciprocity with and caretaking of the natural world of which they were part. Without these beliefs, which guided their actions, and without the careful stewardship and maintenance of critical resources, survival would not have been possible. Their actions left a legacy of prairies and meadows, open woodlands, productive streams, and fine stands of timber in the valleys and mountains of the region. Nineteenth-century Euroamerican immigrants entered a world of abundance richly suited to farming, ranching, hunting, fishing, and logging.

These new immigrants, beginning with the fur trappers in the 1820s and 1830s, simultaneously extolled and appropriated this abundance. They saw the resources of the region as God-given and virtually limitless and believed it was their right and duty to exploit them as they saw fit. They brought new cultural patterns, which fundamentally changed the human relationship with the environment from resource enhancement and production for local use to resource extraction and management based on external markets and national politics and policies. These new immigrants brought with them as well beliefs and values that guided these actions. They saw themselves as distinct from the natural world and placed a positive moral value on its transformation.

The transformations wrought over the past 150 years have disproved nineteenth-century assumptions about the limitless abundance of the land. The prairies, meadows, and open woodlands of the past are largely gone. Some of the once most common species—such as salmon—are approaching endangered status, and the vast stands of old-growth timber have shrunk to remnant patches in the mountains. Land-use activities today frequently pit ecological values against economic need and are fraught with issues concerning management and conservation to restore and maintain the biological diversity of this region.

Yet in the past several decades beliefs and values have changed significantly. There is an emerging consensus that humans are indeed a part of the natural world and that there is a value inherent in nature that exists outside of its utility to humans. These changing beliefs are reflected in land management policies such as ecosystem management, which attempts to provide a holistic view of those processes—natural and cultural—that shape the landscapes within which we live. In the State of Jefferson, furthermore, local groups and governments are seeking to bridge the gap between economic and environmental interests. The amenities of a healthy environment are themselves seen as valuable to the local economy. Perhaps, in the new millennium, new ideas and ideals will foster relationships to the land that will, again, leave possibilities rather than constraints to succeeding generations.

Notes

1. George W. Riddle, 1953, *Early Days in Oregon: A History of the Riddle Valley* (Riddle, Oreg.: Riddle Parent-Teachers' Association).

2. Salmon.

3. In this study the terms *environmental* and *natural* refer to the biological and physical components of the ecosystem, as well as to those processes such as changing climatic patterns or plant succession which are part of the biophysical realms. The geographic area considered here includes most of Jackson and Josephine Counties in Oregon and Siskiyou County in California.

4. I wish to acknowledge the contributions of other researchers in historical ecology or environmental history in the State of Jefferson (see references for selections from this literature). Any errors of fact or interpretation, however, remain my own. The views and opinions expressed in this paper are my own and do not represent those of any federal agency.

5. Jeff LaLande, 1987, *First over the Siskiyous: Peter Skene Ogden's 1826–1827 Journey through the Oregon–California Borderlands* (Portland: Oregon Historical Society Press).

6. John B. Leiberg, 1900, *The Cascade Range and Ashland Forest Reserves and Adjacent Regions* [Extract from the Twenty-First Annual Report of the U.S. Geological Survey, 1899–1900, Part V, Forest Reserves] (Washington, D.C.: Government Printing Office).

7. Stephen Dow Beckham, 1986, *Land of the Umpqua: A History of Douglas County, Oregon* (Roseburg, Oreg.: Commissioners of Douglas County).

8. A. G. Walling, 1884, *The History of Southern Oregon, Comprising Jackson, Josephine, Douglas, Curry and Coos Counties* (Portland, Oreg.).

References

Historical Ecology

Balee, William, ed. 1998. *Advances in Historical Ecology.* New York: Columbia University Press.

Biersack, Aletta. 1999. "Introduction: From the 'New Ecology' to the New Ecologies." *American Anthropologist* 101(1): 5–18.

Crumley, Carole L., ed. 1994. *Historical Ecology: Cultural Knowledge and Changing Landscapes.* Santa Fe, N.Mex.: School of American Research Press.

The State of Jefferson

Indian Land-Use Patterns

Karuk Tribe of California. 1996. *Karuk Tribal Module for the Main Stem Salmon River Watershed Analysis. Scoping of Tribal Issues for Karuk Aboriginal Territory.* Yreka, Calif.: USDA Forest Service, Klamath National Forest.

LaLande, Jeff, and Reg Pullen. 1999. "Burning for a 'Fine and Beautiful Country': Native Uses of Fire in Southwestern Oregon." In Robert Boyd, ed., *Indians, Fire and the Land in the Pacific Northwest,* 255–75. Corvallis: Oregon State University Press.

Pullen, Reg. 1996. *Overview of the Environment of Native Inhabitants of Southwestern Oregon, Late Prehistoric Era.* Report prepared for the DOI Bureau of Land Management, Medford District. Medford, Oreg.: USDA Forest Service; Rogue River National Forest, Medford Oregon; and Siskiyou National Forest, Grants Pass, Oreg.

Historic Period Land-Use Patterns

Atwood, Katherine C., and Frank A. Lang. 1995. *As Long as the World Goes On: Environmental History of Evans Creek Watershed.* Report prepared for the Bureau of Land Management, Medford District, Medford, Oreg.
LaLande, Jeff. 1995. *An Environmental History of the Little Applegate River Watershed.* Report prepared for the USDA Forest Service, Rogue River National Forest, Medford, Oreg.
McKinley, George, and Doug Frank. 1996. *Stories on the Land: An Environmental History of the Applegate and Upper Illinois Valleys.* Report prepared for the Bureau of Land Management, Medford District, Medford, Oreg.
U.S. Department of Interior. 1998. *Applegate–Star/Boaz Watershed Analysis.* Version 1.3. Medford District Bureau of Land Management, Medford, Oreg.
———. 1999. *Little Butte Creek Watershed Analysis.* Medford District Bureau of Land Management, Medford, Oreg.
———. 2000. *Klamath–Irongate Watershed Analysis.* Medford District Bureau of Land Management, Medford, Oreg.
Winthrop, Kathryn. 1995. *Glendale Environmental History.* Report prepared for the Medford District, Bureau of Land Management, Medford, Oreg.
———. 1997. *Grave Creek Watershed: Environmental History.* Report prepared for the Medford District, Bureau of Land Management, Medford, Oreg.

Current Economic and Social Trends

Kempton, Willett, James S. Boster, and Jennifer A. Hartley. 1995. *Environmental Values in American Culture.* Cambridge, Mass.: MIT Press.
Preister, Kevin. 1994. *Words into Action: A Community Assessment of the Applegate Valley.* Ashland, Oreg.: Rogue Institute for Ecology and Economy.
U.S. Department of Interior, and U.S. Department of Agriculture. 1998. *Applegate Adaptive Management Area Guide.* Report prepared by the Medford District Bureau of Land Management, Medford, Oreg.; the Rogue River National Forest, Medford, Oreg.; and the Siskiyou National Forest, Grants Pass, Oreg.

Ecosystem Management; Federal Land-Use Policies

Final Supplemental Environmental Impact Statement [FSEIS]. 1994. *FSEIS on Management of Habitat for Late-Successional and Old-Growth Forest Related Species within the Range of the Northern Spotted Owl.* Portland, Oreg.: U.S. Department of Agriculture; U.S. Department of the Interior [and others].
Forest Ecosystem Management Assessment Team [FEMAT]. 1993. *Forest Ecosystem Management: An Ecological, Economic, and Social Assessment.* Portland, Oreg.: U.S. Department of Agriculture; U.S. Department of the Interior [and others].

Record of Decision [ROD 1994]. 1994. *Record of Decision for Amendments to Forest Service and Bureau of Land Management Planning Documents within the Range of the Northern Spotted Owl.* Portland, Oreg.: U.S. Department of Agriculture; U.S. Department of the Interior.

Regional Ecosystem Office. 1995. *Ecosystem Analysis at the Watershed Scale: Federal Guide for Watershed Analysis.* Version 2.2. Portland, Oreg.: Regional Ecosystem Office.

Tuchmann, E. Thomas, Kent P. Cannaughton, Lisa E. Freedman, Clarence B. Moriwaki. 1996. *The Northwest Forest Plan: A Report to the President and Congress.* Portland, Oreg.: USDA Office of Forestry and Economic Assistance.

U.S. President (1993– : Clinton). 1993. *The Forest Plan: For a Sustainable Economy and a Sustainable Environment.* Washington, D.C.: Office of the President (LRS93-6864).

11

Getting the Dirt Out: The Culture and Political Economy of Urban Land in the United States

Alice E. Ingerson

This chapter was prompted by participant-observation from 1991 to 1997, among people who make and influence urban land-use policy in the United States. During that time, I directed the publications program of the Lincoln Institute of Land Policy, a nonprofit organization that worked on land-use planning; land conservation; and land taxation with elected officials, real estate developers, urban planners, economists, lawyers, and conservationists. A few urban anthropologists participated in the institute's international programs, particularly on housing issues in Latin America. However, no anthropologists participated directly in any of the institute's U.S.-based programs, nor was any anthropological work listed as recommended reading for such programs. As far as my observations extended, the same was true of most other U.S.-based organizations and agencies with which we worked, such as the American Planning Association, the National Trust for Historic Preservation, the Conservation Fund, the National League of Cities, the National Association of Counties, the Urban Land Institute, and the Brookings Institution.

All of this raised two questions: Why are anthropologists so nearly invisible in debates about urban land use in the United States? What kinds of anthropological research might help to clarify and reshape these debates?

Are Cities Part of "the Environment"?

Anthropologists' relative absence from public discussions of urban land use in the United States is not for lack of interest in public policy as such. Environmental anthropologists, for example, are increasingly visible in national policy debates about the management of public lands and rural development, and in a few cases about environmental justice—particularly the tendency to concentrate environmental "bads," such as sources of air or water pollution or seriously contaminated soils—in urban neighborhoods already suffering from high poverty and unemployment rates. Urban anthropologists have long had a very visible presence in national urban policy debates in the United States—most notably concerning crime, education, employment, poverty, and public health.

To some extent, the absence of anthropologists from debates about urban land use in the United States is a category problem. Most researchers, outside as well as within anthropology, have long seen urban land as more *urban* than *land*. Here are three examples:

1. An early review of this chapter noted that "most people are not used to thinking of urban space as a realm of the environment" and suggested "situating urban studies more thoroughly within environmental anthropology."

2. The hazardous materials plan for Harvard University contains a wonderful example. It defines "an incidental spill/release [in part as one that] DOES NOT reach the environment . . ." [emphasis *sic*]. The writer of that sentence probably thought of "the environment" as "the outdoors," forgetting that whatever is washed down a laboratory drain or mopped up with paper towels and thrown in a trash can eventually "reaches the environment," even in that narrow sense.

3. In a conversation with a university faculty member widely respected for both research and teaching about housing issues and urban redevelopment in the United States, I suggested that the relatively equal emphasis on land, labor, and capital in classical nineteenth-century political economy had some advantages over neoclassical economics for understanding urban land use. He responded:

   —But the political economists didn't mean by land what we mean by land.
   —You mean, they saw land as dirt, but we see it as location?
   —Right.

For the third researcher, rural land was a natural resource, but urban land was strictly "location, location, location," as realtors often say.

Community gardeners in New York and other cities recently learned that the third example is not merely academic, but has a powerful influence on public policy. During previous economic downturns, many northeastern U.S. cities allowed neighborhood groups to use vacant, often tax-foreclosed, lots for gardens. The lots usually remained in public (that is, local government) ownership, and the cities saw this land as inventory waiting for a market—for private real estate investors who would buy it, build, and begin paying taxes on it again. In the meantime, the gardeners invested considerable time and sometimes money (often with the help of environmental groups seeking to combat charges of suburban elitism) in removing debris, replacing or enriching the soil, and building raised beds or other garden structures. By 1999 a private market had reappeared for some of this land, and the city governments acted as good market participants to move the land out of inventory. In New York, this prompted storms of protest and intervention by entertainer Bette Midler, who contributed over $1 million to purchase some lots for permanent use as community gardens.

Legally, the cities had every right to sell this land for development. Politically, they were under pressure to do whatever they could to increase revenue after decades of cutbacks. But even if mayors and city councils were willing to give up these legal rights and ignore this political pressure, they faced the category problem illustrated above: on the tax rolls and planning maps, urban lots are pure locations. There is simply no way to recognize or value the gardeners' "improvements" to the soil, because this land is officially not "dirt."

Simply quoting such examples is usually enough to bring their working assumptions from the ideological background, where they powerfully shape both individual choices and public policy, into the research foreground, where they can be questioned. When did cities leave "the environment"? When, where, and why did land in cities stop being dirt and turn into location?

Many researchers are already exploring these questions. Historians of ideas have retraced the social construction of both "nature" and "the city." Environmental engineers and ecologists are developing new journals and major research programs in urban areas. The National Science Foundation recently funded long-term ecological research projects on the evolution of two cities: Baltimore, Maryland, and Phoenix, Arizona. Environmental anthropologists can make strong contributions to this research by the simple step of transferring research agendas and methods long used in rural areas to urban settings: for example, looking at everyday ideologies and practices about nature and cities.

Potential Research Topics

Beyond urban ecology, however, environmental anthropologists may want to explore several other topics often seen as linked to environmental issues in rural settings, but less likely to be seen as "environmental" in urban ones:

- settlement patterns
- land tenure
- land markets
- the state and civil society

In the urban and suburban United States, these issues implicate each other in complex ways (the same connections obviously exist but may take different forms in rural areas or developing countries). In the United States, real land slips easily across the conceptual divide between rural and urban, between being valued primarily as a productive resource and being valued primarily as a consumer good or a speculative investment. Local governments have the primary responsibility for land-use planning and are financed primarily by property taxes. This arrangement often leads to serious conflicts between local voters, not all of whom may own land, and landowners, not all of whom have formal voting rights where they pay property taxes. Anthropologists may be able to reveal the connections among these issues, and in the process show how both culture and political economy run through all of them.

Settlement Patterns

Policy

Relatively few policymakers or planners in the United States talk explicitly about either "settlement patterns" (as the overall way that the human population is distributed across a broad landscape) or "urban form" (as the way that the human population and activities are distributed within centers). However, there is a very lively policy debate in the United States about whether and how to manage changes in the spatial distribution of population and land uses in metropolitan areas. Many planners cite as "traditional" or "European" an ideal urban system of concentric rings, in which the most capital-intensive uses and highest land values occur at the center, and land-use intensity, population density, and land values all taper off gradually as distance from the center increases. This model lies behind the realtors' expression "the 100 percent corner," a street intersection where all the properties have the maximum possible land values (and office or other building rents) in the entire urban area.

This pattern has certainly been the exception rather than the rule in the United States since World War II. During that period, the area of land in urban uses has expanded at several times the rate of population growth in many metropolitan areas. In many places, the city center contains the lowest rather than (or as well as) the highest land values in the region as a whole. Some popular books, such as Joel Garreau's *Edge City: Life on the New Frontier*, suggest that the booming suburbs are now functionally almost independent of the old urban cores. Some observers argue that the growth of the Internet and telecommuting will further disperse jobs and residents, reducing average population densities even further, in a third round of the dispersion caused or allowed first by railroads and streetcars in the second half of the nineteenth century, and again by interstate and other high-speed highways in the mid-twentieth century.

An expanding national coalition of conservationists, preservationists, and urban advocates is arguing that public policy should aim to create, or restore, a "traditional" concentric pattern of urban land use in the United States. This coalition includes both "new urbanists" and "new regionalists." New urbanists hope to encourage pedestrian travel and reduce automobile traffic, and hence the spatial expansion of metropolitan areas, by redesigning individual homes, the spatial relationships between houses and their lots, and the layouts of streets and commercial or public spaces. New regionalists favor a range of options for metropolitan governance to help overcome the mismatch between land and labor markets, which grow and move incrementally, like regional amoebas, and fragmented local governments, which have fixed boundaries and compete against one another for both taxpayers and taxable land uses. Regionalist solutions range from creating regional or metropolitan governments that would function on the same scale as regional land and labor markets, midway between cities or towns and state governments; through "smart growth" policies, which permit the conversion of rural land to urban uses but provide state-government infrastructure subsidies, for everything from sewer lines to schools, only in previously developed areas; to legally binding urban growth boundaries, which prohibit urban land uses in areas that are classified as rural or resource zones.

Advocates of urban redevelopment have long supported regional policies such as tax-base sharing between economically stressed core cities and prosperous suburbs. But suburban advocates of open space preservation have recently found common ground with urbanists in recognizing that booming regional populations and economies must take up space somewhere, and that previous waves of white flight and suburbanization have left a relatively ample supply of vacant land ready for recycling in urban cores. Such policies are not necessarily swimming upstream. In contrast to decades-old trends in the United States, some eastern U.S. central cities have recently begun to gain residents, largely childless young workers and empty nesters.

In contrast to both the new urbanists and the new regionalists, many urban and regional economists in the United States argue that changing settlement patterns simply reflect underlying social preferences, which cannot be dictated by public policy. From their standpoint, metropolitan governance and regional land-use controls or incentives simply raise the cost of housing by restricting its supply, and will not counteract the market forces that encourage the location of most new jobs outside central cities. Some economists argue that the critical "spatial mismatch" is not between regional economies and local governments, but between the concentration of new jobs in the suburbs and the concentration of potential workers in the urban core. Rather than land-use regulation or incentives to pull jobs inward, some of these researchers recommend pulling urban workers outward by subsidizing their reverse commute to the suburbs, or by providing more affordable housing near new suburban jobs.

Anthropology

Anthropologists know a lot about settlement patterns, at least about the structural and spatial evolution of urban systems. Archaeologists, economic anthropologists, geographers, and other social scientists have long seen cities less as strictly bounded, distinct units than as nodes in flexible, evolving networks, concentrating some resources and people and dispersing others, from and to broad landscapes. Anthropologists recognize that the number of levels and degree of concentration, of both population and political power, in such networks varies widely from place to place and over time. Recent anthropological work has focused more explicitly on how settlement patterns shape, or are shaped by, political systems—in a sense, by culture and consciousness. Carole Crumley's exploration of heterarchy and hierarchy, for example, suggests that dispersed settlement can provide more egalitarian access to both natural and political resources than strict urban hierarchies.

However, anthropologists and archaeologists have seldom compared or measured the relative importance of structural change and conscious public policy in shaping settlement patterns. Without explicit attention to culture, consciousness, and politics, for example, the association between spatial heterarchy and political decentralization may suggest to policymakers that suburban sprawl and fragmented land-use governance are more democratic than urban growth boundaries and regional planning—in short, that public policy cannot and should not attempt to restrain sprawl.

To support new policy initiatives rather than market fatalism, anthropologists may have to invent new research methods or tap new data sources. Maps, aerial photographs, and other physical evidence are not necessarily adequate evidence for choosing between public policy and markets as competing explanations for the same settlement pattern. Making that choice may require adding new methods to the traditional research tool kit of archaeologists and geographers, including participant-observation, oral history, and archival research with real estate development firms, zoning boards, and banks.

Land Tenure

Policy

Since the early 1960s, the Land Tenure Center at the University of Wisconsin, Madison, has been conducting research on property rights and land use in developing countries. In the early 1990s, program staff of the center's new North American Program posted an announcement on a hallway bulletin board, and overheard this remark by one undergraduate who stopped to read it:

Gee, do we have land tenure in North America?

Yes, Virginia, there is land tenure in North America, but it goes more often under the name of "property rights." In the image used most often to teach property law in the United States, real property rights are a "bundle of sticks" associated with land. With few exceptions, such as use for criminal purposes or to create an obvious public nuisance, land tenure in the United States consists of the entire bundle, including the right to develop or subdivide the land, as well as the right to mine it to the center of the planet or, at least for some purposes, to use the air space above it. In many European countries, to draw a minimal but critical contrast, land tenure includes the right to keep the land in its current use, or sell it for that same use, but the right to convert land to another use—for example, to convert rural land to urban uses, or to subdivide it—is held by the state and granted to landowners only upon explicit request, often for an additional payment, and then only if the request conforms to some wider land-use plan.

Recent property rights controversies in the United States have focused on whether land-use regulation violates the federal Constitution. The Fifth Amendment to the U.S. Constitution, which prohibits the "taking" of private property for public use without "just compensation," was designed to prevent the state from using property seizure, or the threat of seizure, as a tool of political control. In rural areas in the 1970s, holders of grazing leases, water rights, and timber rights on federal lands rose up under the banner of the Fifth Amendment as the "Sagebrush Rebellion," arguing that their claims to these resources were private property rights, protected by the Constitution and requiring compensation if the government changed their terms or criteria.

In the 1990s, this movement expanded to urban and suburban areas, and rural resort regions, under the label of "Wise Use." Property owners invoked the Fifth Amendment to claim financial compensation for any public decision that reduced the market value of their land. The U.S. Supreme Court raised the stakes in these disputes by suggesting that many changes in land policy might require compensating any landowner with "distinct investment-backed expectations" based on the previous policy, even if the new policy was prompted by new scientific research or changing public preferences. In effect, this interpretation of the Constitution encouraged private landowners to treat land-use regulations as permanent guidelines, rather than temporary expressions of evolving social values or knowledge.

Although this view of property rights has a long history in the United States, so do some alternative views. In the last quarter of the nineteenth century, for example, the quintessentially American (i.e., amateur) political economist Henry George ran for mayor of New York on the basis of proposals for what was essentially an alternative form of land tenure. He did not propose public ownership of the land itself, but only of the "social increment" in land values, or the land "rent"—that portion of its value (in George's view by far the bulk) due to the land's natural qualities, its urban location, or any other factor not directly and exclusively created by the individual landowner or user.

The social increment may be defined roughly as the difference between the exchange and the use values of a given land parcel—the difference between what it is worth for speculation and what a buyer would pay if expecting to recover only enough income to justify putting the land into production, whether for resource extraction or as an industrial, commercial, or residential site.

Henry George's analysis was never taken up on any significant scale, though it inspired some local experiments in use value taxation and community ownership of land, or at least of land rents. But since the 1970s, some public agencies and nonprofit organizations have also looked to alternative forms of land tenure to influence land use, in part to avoid having to compensate landowners for "taking" the value of their property through regulation. Sometimes government or nonprofits purchase development rights, in which case the holder of those rights may retain the right to use or sell them in the future, and sometimes they purchase conservation or other easements, which prohibit certain future uses of the land. This kind of split land tenure has been applied most often to agricultural or forestland at the urban fringe, usually to prevent urban development and subdivision.

A few community land trusts, as distinguished from the conservation land trusts that often hold conservation easements, have used land tenure innovations to reduce land costs for urban housing as well as for farmers. As Henry George observed, land costs often rise far faster than either farm operating or housing construction costs, because the market price and location value of land may be relatively independent of the use to which the land is currently put. Community land trusts purchase and hold the land itself, then sell the use rights for farming or sell houses built on the land. This gives the land trust the lion's share of potential future gains (or losses) in value and reduces the price of access to the land for farming access or of the homes built on the land. Split tenure is also used in urban or suburban co-ops, condominiums, and gated communities, where ownership of private real estate also involves financial responsibility for shared amenities. In most gated or condominium communities, those shared amenities include only pathways, playgrounds, or swimming pools (or even schools, in some cases). In community land trusts, all land is owned in common, including the land under and around private homes.

The homeowners in urban community land trusts are not tenants; they are still considered owners. They may lease or sell their houses. Yet ownership does not have exactly the same meaning for them that it has for most property owners in the United States. They have given up the right to capture the portion of capital gains in the value of their property that is due to rising land values or to the difference between the land's value for its current use and its speculative value for some other use. In short, they have voluntarily given up the right to the exchange value of land and retained only a particular use value.

In contrast, most landowners in the United States make little or no distinction between the use value and the exchange value of land. These owners believe that the U.S. Constitution protects their rights to the land's maximum market value, and not merely to its "quiet enjoyment" or use. For much of U.S. history, as land economist Daniel Bromley puts it, "any old fool could, by sheer accident, have gotten quite rich indeed through owning land—and of course many did and continue to do so. Small wonder that so many celebrate this particular lottery and seek refuge in the Constitution to preserve their odds of winning." The old saying, "scratch a farmer, find a speculator" also applies to most homeowners. As a result, land trusts that try to split the role of owner-resident from the role of speculator seem, in the words of some critics, like "second-class ownership for the poor."

Anthropology

Anthropologists know a great deal about common property in rural areas and about property rights in informal urban settlements. Property rights and land tenure in these settings are often far more complex and subtle than the new tenure arrangements described above for the United States. Where most U.S. real estate economists, if not land-use lawyers, see all-encompassing private rights, extending from one property line to the next, and from the core of the earth into space, anthropologists are used to seeing overlapping, socially defined, periodically reallocated rights and responsibilities.

Yet the study of urban land tenure in the United States poses methodological challenges for anthropologists. The economic and social significance of rural land tenure depends largely on the amount and quality of the land owned, information that may be relatively accessible to direct observation or field surveys. The significance of urban land ownership depends less on topography or parcel size than on location in a complex urban system; on rights specified in (often deliberately) complex or opaque legal documents; and, as the U.S. landowners who "seek refuge in the Constitution to preserve their odds of winning" the real estate lottery know well, on markets.

Anthropologists can mine a wide range of sources to explain how, when, and why Americans have or have not recognized social or community as well as individual property rights, and the distinction between use and exchange value of land. Because land tenure in the United States is anything but "customary," it has been negotiated and renegotiated very much in the light of day, both in legal documents and in political rhetoric. For example, historians and policy analysts have conducted muckraking research on the reverse of public "takings" of private property—rural and resource "givings," in which land values due largely or wholly to public investments, in everything from land surveys to irrigation projects, were appropriated largely by private owners or investors. In many cases this was seen as entirely proper. How did both public officials and private landowners in these cases understand, and explain or justify, the relationship between public and private sectors (or as discussed below, between the state and civil society) embedded in land tenure?

Land Markets

Policy

For all the property rights issues raised above, physical possession and use of land is often only a small part of the story—the rest is about land values. In the United States, certainly in cities, land is a commodity. There is no sharp boundary between land tenure and land markets. Few urban Americans care about land-related rights or responsibilities that have no cash value. This poses a challenge for anthropologists who are used to studying land tenure issues—from inheritance to boundary disputes—shaped mostly by nonmarket forces or institutions.

When dealing with land, Americans implicitly put aesthetics, community, history, and ecology all on one side, and economics on the other. Yet real landscapes are simultaneously aesthetic, physical environments and economic commodities. Land markets are the invisible, silent infrastructure that creates visible urban landscapes. A recent Arnold Arboretum/National Park Service curriculum project about "the collective role that people play in shaping and caring for landscapes" asked elementary-school students to play the roles of Artist, Naturalist, or Historian. I asked one of the project managers whether anyone had considered adding Real Estate Developer to this list, since developers probably have more influence on most urban landscapes than artists, naturalists, or historians, but the idea had never been suggested. In fact, the author thought it probably would have been rejected. Most urban and real estate economics research reverses this choice, studying community aesthetics or amenities only through the proxy of real estate prices, and never directly.

Land markets themselves are usually at least regional, and for some specialized land-use markets are national or global. Yet land policy in the United States is essentially local. Local policymakers usually see land markets as something they must respond to, or anxiously monitor, not as something they can fundamentally influence. Still, they try. In recent years, the U.S. federal government has made redevelopment funds available within concentrated, local enterprise or empowerment zones, in an attempt to restore or jump start a private land market in depressed urban (and some rural) areas. Local governments have authorized "business improvement districts" (BIDs), which support improved amenities and services in a restricted neighborhood through property tax surcharges imposed on the owners of all property within the district's boundaries. In a BID, the private owners gamble that these shared improvements will generate new business, or increase property values, within the district enough to more than cover the additional taxes. In another approach, called "tax increment financing" (TIF), the local government itself takes the same gamble, floating bonds to pay for improvements that, it hopes, will increase property values. Any subsequent increase (a positive increment) in property tax revenues is then legally earmarked to pay off the bonds, before it can be applied to any other public services or investments.

All of these policy tools make local government, or neighborhood property owners, direct, collective players in urban land markets. Because local governments in the United States still rely heavily, though less than they once did, on property taxes, and because the bulk of the value of urban property is in land rather than buildings, even local governments that do not need or can resist the lure of enterprise zones, business improvement districts, and tax increment financing are nevertheless deeply affected by land markets. Unlike private investors, or even local residents, however, local governments cannot walk away from their losses in the real estate market. In that sense, they play the urban land game with a serious handicap.

Anthropology

Most anthropologists know far more about markets in general than about land markets. Many anthropologists may have a personal conviction that land in particular should not be treated strictly as a commodity and allocated through markets alone, and may even be lucky enough to work primarily in places where they can realistically hope to keep land itself "off the market."

But in U.S. urban areas, land is already a full-fledged commodity. Formal markets for urban, developed land should therefore be an acute test of whatever anthropologists believe they already have demonstrated about other kinds of markets. In particular, urban land markets challenge anthropologists to unpack the social, cultural, and political relations behind what appear to be "purely economic" land transactions.

Urban land markets should also attract the attention of anthropologists interested in the evolving relationship between nature and capitalism—markets literally transform land from an encompassing, unique, four-dimensional environment into a substitutable, two-dimensional commodity. Analyzing that transformation critically requires revealing the persistence and perhaps the active suppression of land as environment within or behind land as commodity.

Standard real estate economics defines the value of land as the intersection between what a "perfectly informed, uncoerced" buyer is willing to pay and what a similarly carefree seller is willing to accept. Yet cultural or social preferences, and personal or collective circumstances, obviously influence both parties' expectations, not only of the price at which the land will change hands but of the time it will take to convert land into cash or vice versa. Some economists readily admit that there is no such thing as "perfect information" in real estate markets, and that fully "uncoerced" buyers or sellers are the exception rather than the rule. But economists have generally not studied these market imperfections because they are not amenable to formal, statistical modeling.

Two books published in the 1970s suggest some fruitful avenues for research on the culture and political economy of urban land markets: *Rubbish Theory: The Creation and Destruction of Value* (1979), by Michael Thompson, and *Everything in Its Place: Social Order and Land Use in America* (1977), by Constance Perin. Thompson's major point is that supply and demand are culturally defined. Thus over the long term, goods—including some urban real estate—are first transient, then rubbish, then durable. Transient goods are those economists understand best—goods valued for their current use, for which supply increases to meet demand. In contrast, conventional economics is of less help in understanding either rubbish or durable goods—goods valued by something other than their direct use. By definition, the supply of rubbish always exceeds demand. For what Thompson calls durable goods (such as original artwork by deceased artists, or antiques, or historic homes in prestigious neighborhoods), demand, by definition, always exceeds supply.

Land is in a sense the classic "durable" good—as the saying goes, "buy land—they ain't makin' any more." Thompson explores the cultural component of urban land or location values in a chapter called "Rat-Infested Slum or Glorious Heritage?" Though he focuses on buildings, his analyses clearly applies to land/location:

> The fact that buildings last for generations is dependent upon their receiving "reasonable maintenance. . . ." The level of maintenance that is deemed reasonable . . . is a function of its expected life-span, and its expected life-span is a function of the cultural category to which that building at any moment is assigned. . . . Obsolescence derives from the interrelation of the form of the building, which is largely fixed at the time of construction, and two influences which do change through time. One of these is technology and the other fashion. . . . The role of technological innovation features in every textbook on economics, but what of fashion. . . . Fashion, being seen as frivolous, ephemeral, transient, and irrational, is not seen as a fit subject for scholarly attention where what is prized is the serious, the persistent, the durable, and the rational. (37–39)

Thompson illustrates this point with a story about a Regency house that he and a friend restored for sale, in the process "convincing [the buyer] that a mid-Victorian fireplace" for which the two friends deliberately overcharged the owner "was really a Regency one." A few weeks later a friend of the new owner complimented him on the fireplace, and "at that moment," relates Thompson, "I realized that we were the exploited ones. The fact that we knew the fireplace . . . was of the wrong period was irrelevant, for all that matters is that those who exert the widest overall control over time and place believe it to be original. . . . Credibility, not truth, is the name of this game" (53).

Realtors and developers understand that game well, as a combination of culture and political economy. It is hard to sell houses in a decaying, high-crime neighborhood even to affluent urban pioneers (who Thompson calls the "knockers-through"), but it is not impossible. The art of "infill"—redeveloping urban neighborhoods—is about cultural credibility, convincing buyers that a particular place will soon move from the "rubbish" category to the "durable" one. The more an investor anticipates this shift, before it is absolutely certain, the higher the investor's profits.

Constance Perin uses as cultural data both interviews with realtors and home buyers and published writing by real estate lawyers, economists, and planners. She focused on suburban sprawl in the United States rather than on urban gentrification in England. Yet her findings anticipated Thompson's in interesting ways. Where he found transient, rubbish, and durable real estate, she found distinct markets for new, used, and old houses and neighborhoods:

> The differing social and economic meanings of zoning or other forms of land-use control in each [of these three markets] have not been acknowledged. . . . All kinds of land uses belong in each of these markets . . . but each market operates on the basis of different amounts and availabilities of land and capital, each has a different set of actors, incentives, and outcomes, and each works from a different view of time and risk. (145)

As Thompson explored what moved certain neighborhoods from the "rubbish" into the "durable" category, Perin defined the "old- or obsolescent-property market" as places "where developed land occupied by buildings or by uses no longer viable is ripe for development, and thereupon reenters the new-property market" (145).

Perin's work provides a particularly useful model for anthropologists interested in public policy because she focuses, as do most U.S. local officials and citizens, on how local public decisions, especially zoning, interact with land markets. After quoting property law scholar Richard Ellickson's observation that "special influence problems have plagued zoning from its inception," she notes that

> Special influences initiated [zoning], and they will keep it going. . . . Even to its most convinced champions, zoning has never been a reliable mechanism for . . . limiting and channeling growth. In fact, just the opposite is true: it is a major piece of industrial equipment, quickly retooled . . . to produce the latest models favored by the capital market, national and regional. . . . Bankers and investors have . . . lost in the bargain the freedom to develop with the fewest restrictions on their project as possible, which as poor losers they keep trying to regain. (147, 153–54)

As Perin points out, most public policy and private real estate research focuses on new property markets, on managing or profiting from the initial conversion of land from rural resource (a factor of production) to urban location (consumer good). Similar if not equal profits can be made by reconverting abandoned or blighted urban neighborhoods into newly fashionable historic districts.

The third market, for used real estate, is less profitable and, Perin notes, "consistently understudied." It presents an important research opportunity for anthropologists, because it crosses conventional categories: "The consumer [is also] the producer of used housing" (133).

> Homebuyers are [not] free of producers' conceptions of social organization and social order. [Homebuyers and residents] are no less investors. The difference is that they live amid those arenas where social order is acted out. (162)

Owners and residents in this land market struggle constantly to keep their neighborhoods from becoming either rubbish (Thompson's "rat-infested slum") or fashionable and ultimately unaffordable (Thompson's "glorious heritage"). They receive little support in that struggle from most developers, planners, or environmentalists—yet their success is critical to any urban form of "sustainable development."

For anthropologists, studying formal urban land markets requires the same kind of methodological ingenuity required to study formal urban land tenure. Urban land markets also operate too slowly and require too much capital to be studied through traditional participant observation (imagine trying to participate as an active "player" in a Manhattan commercial real estate deal!). Yet this obstacle can be overcome by the same techniques of ethnohistory, community reconstruction, and record linkage that have been used to study other large-scale, long-term processes of social change, such as industrialization and labor migration. Formal land records, interpreted in context, can help to retrace the cumulative effects of both market forces and government interventions over time. Both formal hearings and informal conversations about property valuation and development can provide rich data about the "ethnoeconomics" of land—where people think land values come from, and who they think receives, or has a right to, those values.

Urban Land, the State, and Civil Society

Policy

U.S. policymakers are not much interested in "the State" with a capital "S." In contrast, they are consciously worried about "civic engagement" and "civil society." Policymakers and philanthropists are sensitive to indisputably low voter turnout, and to accusations by both conservative and communitarian scholars that citizens are less engaged than they once were with public or community issues. Whether from this concern, or in the hope of preventing potential lawsuits, local governments in the United States now seek out much more direct public participation in land-use decisions than in the 1960s and 1970s.

Approaches to direct public participation in urban land-use decisions vary. For example, at a recent conservation conference, a former state official from

Virginia reported that his state's Department of Transportation had invested heavily in a system of interactive, individual computer kiosks and one-to-one meetings with voters to plan new highway projects. The official also reported, however, that voters disliked the new system and expressed a strong preference for more traditional public hearings. He criticized Virginia's transportation planners for not responding to these reactions sooner, though he sympathized with their efforts to foster more inclusive participation, in response to past criticism that only certain well-organized or well-financed interests participate in formal hearings. He did not mention that the same planners could hardly have devised a more effective political technology for dividing and conquering citizens than easily accessible, individual "feedback stations." This approach to participation clearly assumed that public preferences were equal to the sum of individual opinions.

Property taxation deserves far more scrutiny than it usually receives from researchers interested in this issue, or in the intersection of culture and political economy. Property values—land markets—are often treated as purely economic institutions. Yet property values also embody relations between the state and civil society. Landowners—some of them nonresident—pay for local services. Local residents—not all of them landowners—have voting rights. It is no longer legal to impose a property qualification for voting. Yet in practice, local governments must pay at least as much attention to the interests of local property owners as to the interests of local voters. The relatively heavy reliance of local governments in the United States on the property tax creates a roughly circular relationship between land markets and the quality of local public goods and services. The better the local services, the higher local property values. The higher local property values, the more revenue can be raised for local services.

Economist Charles Tiebout and many other public finance and real estate economists since his original 1956 article have argued that this nexus simply guarantees the efficiency of local governments, which are essentially firms competing for customers/residents by offering different packages of prices/taxes and services. Over time, consumers should sort themselves out in their own best interests, congregating spatially with others who share their preferences. Many U.S. metropolitan areas now appear to approximate this model—with voters who prefer large yards and strong public schools living in some places, and voters who prefer smaller yards and parochial schools living in other places.

Gated communities may represent the Tiebout strategy taken to its logical extreme. Defenders of such developments portray them as direct democracy at its best, like old-fashioned town meetings or neighborhood associations—consumers banding together to increase their purchasing power in markets for both land and local services such as swimming pools, security guards, tennis courts, clubhouses, and in some cases even schools. Critics see these developments as reintroducing property qualifications for voting. By operating strictly through markets rather than through legislation, private communities can legally exclude economic diversity—and thus indirectly social, cultural, and racial diversity. They can directly exclude groups not covered by civil rights legislation, such as children. Sometimes they even award voting rights in community governance in proportion to the value of each owner's private property, which determines that owner's dues. If such dues become, in effect, a substitute for the taxes that underwrite public governments, then these communities are in fact governments, run on the principle of "one dollar, one vote" rather than "one person, one vote."

U.S. land-use planners and local governments complain bitterly that this "state as market" system forces them into "fiscal" or "exclusionary" zoning—making land-use decisions based on the need to maximize local revenue and minimize local expenditures. Local jurisdictions compete for businesses that need neither schools nor clinics nor libraries; wealthy residents who will send their children to private schools, use private health care, and buy books rather than borrow them; or, third best, less-affluent retirees who need clinics and libraries but at least do not need schools. The same jurisdictions race to exclude, by any legal means or by illegal means that are difficult to detect, families with school-age children and low incomes, because they need inexpensive housing (which pays lower taxes) but make heavy demands on schools, health care, and libraries. Yet "winning" this fiscal competition creates new problems. Because land costs are usually the bulk of housing costs, governments in areas of high or rising land values confront gentrification or displacement; often their own staffs cannot afford to live in the jurisdiction that employs them.

Also, competing local states serve niche markets. Tiebout's analysis assumes, implicitly, that choosing a place to live is like choosing a breakfast cereal or a television program. Competition should produce a wider range of choices, at lower cost, than planning. Yet land-use or locational choices, unlike most consumer choices, are complex, interdependent, and relatively both irreversible and exclusive rather than cumulative. Markets can easily meet the needs of households that like several breakfast cereals. The state as market may force those with complex land-use preferences to live in only one of several niches that fit them equally. For example, grandparents willing or economically motivated to care for young children may live in places largely devoid of children who need care.

Understanding the implications of the "state as market," and of alternatives to it, is becoming more, rather than less, urgent. This system is the exception rather than the rule internationally. Yet many developing countries or countries in transition from central planning are being counseled (often though not exclusively by American advisers) to adopt the U.S. model of local authorities as membership organizations dependent on "own-source" (usually meaning land-based) revenue. Land is the ultimately local—that is, immobile—resource, so it is easier to tax than many forms of highly mobile capital or labor. The American model of public finance is finding a ready audience among fiscally pressured policymakers elsewhere.

As both capital and jobs globalize, however, their relationships to real, landed places become more and more contingent and temporary, both in and outside the United States. Advocates of free trade argue that governments' only realistic choice under these conditions is to market their fixed assets—their land-use patterns and associated "quality of life"—in a global competition for both labor and capital. In contrast, protectionists argue that capital still needs the places if not the people represented by governments, which can therefore bargain hard over the conditions of access to land and local services. Local policymakers need all the help they can get in choosing between these two strategies.

Anthropology

As experts in "local community and culture," anthropologists are often already involved in managing public participation in planning. Much urban ethnography and political economy deals explicitly with the power relations revealed by land-use and planning conflicts. Anthropologists working in rural areas also know a lot about common property systems as bases for resistance to nation-states. Anthropologists who work in or around national parks, or on indigenous land uses and land claims, in developing countries have made significant contributions to inventing new institutions, or reviving old ones, for managing overlapping local and national or international interests in rural lands. It might be possible to build on this work in urban areas.

Anthropologists' first contribution to understanding the relationship of state and civil society to urban land may therefore be demystifying the ideas of "community" and "local." In the United States, policymakers often use these words to elicit public participation in both urban and environmental planning without looking too closely at class, ethnic, gender, or other divisions. Everyone, no matter what their politics, claims to support community-based conservation in rural areas and community preservation in urban ones. Anthropologists, along with social historians, know that what may serve one segment of "the community" well—for example, property owners—may only deepen the misery or cut off options for another segment—for example, tenants. Anthropologists have excelled at this kind of social deconstruction, in both urban and rural places.

Environmental anthropologists have only begun to pursue this kind of research recently, perhaps with good reason. Making social or other divisions within neighborhoods or communities more visible can be a two-edged sword. If requirements for public participation in planning become too onerous—because an anthropologist reveals that what planners saw as a single, unified community contains dozens of overlapping and conflicting interest groups—those requirements may be repealed or ignored.

Perhaps the more serious threat is that government will respond to the internal complexity of local "civil society" by deciding to consult or sample individuals or households. In essence, this treats collective choices or preferences as the simple sum of individual ones, as in the example above from transportation planning. This amounts, in essence, to another version of the "state as market."

Anthropologists could make another important contribution by looking more closely at exactly this model of relations between state and civil society. Anthropologists have seldom focused on the intersection of local government, democracy, and urban land use in the United States. In international settings, local government may seem a trivial topic because its relationship to national government is much like the relationship of a local post office to the U.S. Postal Service, or a local fast-food restaurant to its parent corporation—an outpost for example, but not a distinct institution. In the United States, however, local government is more than a field representative or branch office of the nation-state. As suggested by Tiebout, in some ways U.S. local governments function as small businesses. But partially and potentially, U.S. local governments also function as common property regimes—in which the commons consists of shared land uses such as schools, sewers, and roads, and the less visible but still essentially social goods called "the tax base" and "local property values." Land-based collective institutions in U.S. urban areas, including local governments themselves, may combine aspects of, or alternate between, "market" and "commons" models. As the market model is exported from the United States by development consultants and aid agencies, however, it becomes more important to understand which forces favor "state as market" and which favor "state as commons," and how and when local government shifts from one model to the other.

Anthropologists interested in the history and possibility of managing urban land as a commons must balance research on class, gender, and ethnic divisions within local, spatially defined communities with research on institutions and mechanisms that have been or can be used to make, enforce, and revise truly collective choices about land. Some community development corporations or land trusts may be such institutions. Others may be hard to find or hard to recognize starting from rural definitions. For example, the high level of geographic mobility among individuals and households in U.S. cities means that successful urban "commons" must have relatively fast, efficient ways of replacing lost participants and inducting new ones.

Translating the Culture and Political Economy of Urban Land into Public Policy

To get anthropological research on the culture and political economy of urban land applied to public policy in the United States, anthropologists will have to learn and to some extent adopt the language already used by local elected officials, land-use planners, real estate economists, and citizen advocates for conservation and community development. Rough translations of anthropology into land policy may be adequate for making initial connections:

- settlement patterns = managing growth, preserving open space
- land tenure = property rights
- land markets = property values, tax base, affordable housing
- state and civil society = community character, sense of place

Getting from first contact to improved understanding may be difficult, however. The everyday language of land policy, on the right in the equations above, expresses contradictory goals: growth should be managed, and open space, community character, and a sense of place should all be preserved, yet private property rights must be respected; property values should be maintained or enhanced, yet housing should be affordable. One increasingly popular response to these contradictions is to smother them in soothing rhetoric about "win–win solutions," "public–private partnerships," and "smart growth." Most of the coalitions that assemble behind these slogans focus on the visible landscape or leap quickly from the physical environment to culture, from visible landscapes to emotional "community."

In contrast, advocates tend to leap over the critical, intervening institutions— land tenure and land markets—which they find at best unaesthetic and at worst baffling. In contrast to "landscape" and "community," land tenure and land markets are difficult subjects for posters and television documentaries. In addition, most state and local officials in the United States see property rights as ahistorical, created once and for all by the U.S. Constitution, and real estate markets as "natural" systems rather than cultural or social institutions. In policy debates, property rights and real estate markets more often appear as fixed features, around which public policy must navigate, than as domains about which people can make conscious, collective choices.

Anthropologists who want to write about urban land tenure and land markets in the United States therefore have their work cut out for them. It will take far more than relabeling to transform inalienable, individual "property rights" and mysterious "real estate cycles" into socially contingent, evolving land tenure and land markets. It will take both cultural analysis and political economy.

In addition, contradictory public goals for urban land are often managed by assigning them to competing professions or public agencies: planners and designers manage growth, open space, and community character; real estate developers, lawyers, and tax assessors manage property rights and values; and community organizers demand or construct affordable housing. As a result, anthropologists who reveal and confront these contradictions may well find their most sympathetic audience not among land-use professionals but among amateurs—the elected officials and citizens who must live with the way that competing or merely rhetorical solutions self-destruct on the land, in real places.

Changing Anthropological Approaches to Urban and Environmental Policy

Most policymakers, if they think about consulting anthropologists at all, see them as experts on culture and cultural differences. Both urban and environmental anthropologists have influenced public policy in the past mostly by first creating, then responding to, this perception, and thus by focusing on culture and cultural differences as partial causes of policy problems or sources of policy solutions.

This is a useful strategic response when nation-states attempt to remake local land-use patterns in the interests of outside groups, from regional or national elites to transnational corporations and development agencies. Urban anthropologists have done this kind of work when revealing what is functional or valued about informal or squatter settlements in urban areas, and when lobbying national governments to improve public infrastructure for or legalize these settlements rather than clear them away or transform them into standard public housing. Environmental anthropologists have used the same approach when lobbying national governments to recognize and reinforce rural common property systems and indigenous environmental knowledge, rather than introduce standard (often meaning United States) property law or resource management practices.

In recent decades, however, urban anthropologists have shifted away from a focus on culture, for several important reasons. Urban anthropologists who focused on economically marginal ethnic, occupational, or neighborhood cultures were often dismayed to find their work used to justify "bootstrapping"—policies requiring the urban poor to lift themselves out of poverty by changing their values and attitudes. To head off such cultural determinism, urban anthropologists have focused more on the structural evolution of urban systems. When they address culture now, they are far less likely to present it as a direct cause of economic behavior, including land-use choices, than as an evolving strategic tool, fractured in both its making and its daily use by differences of class, ethnicity, and gender. They are less likely to write neighborhood or ethnic ethnographies than blow-by-blow accounts of particular conflicts between neighborhood activists and city or national policymakers and investors. One signal of this changed stance was changing the name of the Society for Urban Anthropology to the Society for Urban, Transnational, and Global Anthropology.

Environmental anthropologists may be following a trajectory similar to that of urban anthropologists but be at an early stage, because they began influencing public policy somewhat later. Following the model created by environmentalists' relatively successful defense of biodiversity and old-growth forests, environmental anthropologists have sometimes convinced policymakers to grant rural communities more formal rights to natural resources by idealizing the ecological traditions of these communities.

A few environmental anthropologists, particularly those interested in political and historical ecology, have begun to admit that, as happened with the focus on urban cultures or subcultures, a focus on rural "cultures of stewardship" may create new problems. Urban anthropologists' work on culture was used to justify forcing culture change. In contrast, environmental anthropologists are more likely to find their work on culture used to justify restraining or prohibiting change. The international environmental movement has often been persuaded to respect local traditions on the grounds that those traditions are good for the environment, regardless of whether they are equally good for all members of the local human community. In this situation, international organizations may make their support for local communities contingent on whether those communities live up to their anthropological advertising, requiring the people to give up the option of fundamentally changing their relationships with either the land or each other. At that point, environmental anthropologists may have to begin criticizing ideas about cultural preservation that they themselves implanted.

Can Political Economy Really Influence Public Policy?

A focus on political economy and national or global structures undoubtedly discourages policymakers from using anthropological research to justify trying to solve urban problems through local culture change, or environmental ones through a rigid approach to local cultural preservation. But there are also significant obstacles to moving ideas from political economy research into practical public policy.

These obstacles are less evident outside the United States, where both urban and environmental policies are often made in national ministries, staffed by people with critical attitudes toward "business as usual" in urban real estate and economic development. The university training of these government professionals often includes significant exposure to the language and approach of political economy. In the United States, however, few planners and lawyers, and very few economists, get such exposure as either undergraduates or graduate students. What they do hear about political economy is likely to be skeptical or critical or to present political economy as a fascinating but now-irrelevant historical episode rather than as a still-useful analytical tool. In addition, much U.S. land-use policy is ultimately made by local elected officials or volunteers serving on planning, zoning, historic district, or conservation commissions. Although many of these policymakers are highly educated in law, medicine, finance, engineering, or other fields, they often find the jargon of political economy opaque at best and politically offensive at worst.

All of these differences suggest that anthropologists interested in the political economy of land use must take different, and perhaps less direct, routes to influence urban land-use policy in the United States than in many other countries. At the same time, routes that now work primarily in the United States may soon be useful internationally. More international planning professionals are being trained in the United States, and international development agencies are actively exporting both technical expertise and a policy preference for decentralization or devolution from the United States to other countries.

The first obstacle between research in political economy and influence on land policy in the United States is politics. Many U.S. policymakers may reject this kind of research simply because it is highly critical of the political and economic status quo and hard to cite in support of any mainstream urban or environmental policies. It is hard to imagine any way to remove this obstacle without simply abandoning the criticism and joining the mainstream.

A second, perhaps more movable, obstacle between political economy and public policy for urban land in the United States is jargon. Political economists write in a language, often though not always Marxist, that is inaccessible to most nonacademics. (In fact, one good example is the paragraph above that uses "contingent" and "fractured," as well as a checklist of "class, ethnicity, gender.") Some of this linguistic ingenuity is necessary. More familiar terms would only reinforce the assumptions that political economists want to make visible and to challenge. But it should be possible to choose a few key assumptions and their associated language to challenge in any one piece of research or writing. This language could reach policy audiences who are willing to learn some new terms, or new meanings for some old terms, but who are not seeking a total conversion experience.

A third obstacle to effective communication between political economists and even radical policymakers and activists in the United States is the very choice to focus on transnational and global forces. This focus can make local initiatives—by definition most urban land policy in the United States—seem trivial or doomed. This is news few policymakers or activists want to hear, even if it is true. Removing this obstacle requires finding some role for culture in shaping urban land use, if culture can be defined as continuously evolving, collective aspirations and institutions rather than as fixed "traditions." Without visible local aspirations and initiatives, political economy can become a strictly academic exercise, useful primarily for explaining the "overdetermined," structural outcomes of urban land-use choices, but of little help in evaluating choices that are still "live," contingent, and conscious—in short, cultural.

Recombining Culture (Carefully) with Political Economy

Adding culture back into the methodological mix runs the risk of reintroducing either cultural determinism or preservationism. The first treats culture, paradoxically, as both a solution to policy problems (fix the culture and the problem will go away) and a passive reflection of noncultural factors (fixing the culture means adapting it to economic, i.e., noncultural, reality). Anthropologists may always have to be on the lookout for this use of culture as a concept. However, cultural determinism may be less of a risk now than it once was, thanks to the past success of anthropologists who have campaigned for public policies that would respect cultural differences without ignoring the distribution of economic opportunities and legal rights.

In contrast, preservationism may be a growing risk, also partly as a result of anthropologists' past successes. It is easy for the anthropological defense of a particular culture or landscape to imply that cultures and landscapes in general can either be saved or lost but cannot be consciously or responsibly changed, managed, or created. It is easy to drum up public and philanthropic support by arguing that, without such support, particular places or people will otherwise be "lost forever." It is much harder to galvanize support by arguing that without it a particular landscape or human group will have "different options for future evolution."

The second argument, however well supported by research, simply does not sound as urgent as the first. Perhaps urban and environmental anthropologists can collaborate to create more powerful and popular ways of expressing the second argument. Or perhaps, by using the existing language of "preservation" and "conservation" in new ways, they can stretch both concepts past what has always been their shared breaking point—the "right to change," for both nature and culture.

The Potential Rewards of Studying Urban Land Use

Despite the daunting list of obstacles above, there are several reasons for anthropologists to devote more attention to urban land use in the United States:

1. Urban land anywhere presents theoretically interesting challenges to the division of interests and labor between urban and environmental or ecological anthropology, as well as between other disciplines that separate the study of human action and ideas from the study of natural systems and resources. Reintegrating nature and culture requires finding ways to treat even intensely modified, densely occupied land as part of "the environment."

2. To paraphrase Marx, people consciously make and remake urban landscapes, starting from patterns of use and ownership not of their own choosing. Anthropologists may be able to use "culture" to capture the conscious choices involved in making land urban, and "political economy" to capture the unchosen circumstances of that making. If anthropologists interested in urban land can find positive ways to cross their own internal divide between studies of culture or consciousness and studies of political economy, they may find a ready audience outside anthropology. In the United States, some policymakers and citizens are

actively struggling to articulate and manage urban landscapes as simultaneously ecological, economic, and cultural. Although "cultural" in policy debates sometimes means formal landscape design and aesthetics, it often encompasses community history and identity as well. Anthropologists are well-positioned both to test and to reinforce that participatory meaning.

3. Despite a long tradition of acting as advocates for the people they study, and more recent arguments for "studying up," anthropologists are not always comfortable having the same people as informants and readers, let alone as neighbors. Yet the distinctions among these groups are rapidly breaking down, even for once-remote research sites, as their residents take an increasingly active role in commissioning, interpreting, and criticizing policy research. Anthropologists must learn to do work that they can literally live with, to apply the same ethical standards in the field and at home. Land in the metropolitan United States, where most anthropologists (and most Americans) live, is a good place to start.

References

Are Cities Part of "the Environment"?

The Harvard example comes from *Spill Prevention Control and Countermeasure Plan* (September 1997), prepared by the GZA/GeoEnvironmental Inc. and Harvard University Environmental Health and Safety Department.

For the controversy over community gardens in New York, see the *New York Times* ("Bette Midler Chips In To Rescue Gardens," 13 May 1999, A1; and Dan Barry, "Sudden Deal Saves Gardens Set for Auction," 13 May 1999, B1). On urban locations as "dirt," see: The Food Project in Lincoln and Boston, Massachusetts (http://www.thefoodproject.org/food/home.htm); "Philadelphia Green," a project of the Pennsylvania Horticultural Society (http://www.libertynet.org/phs/philagreen/pgintro.html); and CityFarmer, a clearinghouse run by Canada's Office of Urban Agriculture (http://www.cityfarmer.org/).

For research in urban ecology, see Nathaniel Lichfield, *Economics in Urban Conservation* (New York: Cambridge University Press, 1988); F. Stearns and T. Montag, eds. *The Urban Ecosystem: A Holistic Approach* (Stroudsberg, Penn.: Dowden, Hutchinson, & Ross, 1974); C. S. Holling & G. Orians, "Toward an Urban Ecology," *Bulletin of the Ecological Society of America* 52(2): 2–6 (1971); S. U. Boyden, "Integrated Ecological Studies of Human Settlements," *Impact of Science on Society* 27(2): 159–69 (1977); two new journals, *Urban Ecosystems* (founded 1997) and *Urban Ecology* (founded 1998); and the National Science Foundation's new urban Long-Term Ecological Research sites: for Phoenix and Central Arizona (http://caplter.asu.edu/) and Baltimore (http://baltimore.umbc.edu/lter/default.htm). The Arizona team includes several anthropologists, including project codirector Charles Redman.

Good starting points for urban environmental history are Joel Tarr's "The City and the Natural Environment," an online bibliographic essay, posted 14 January 1998 to the Urban History List Serve (http://www.h-net.msu.edu/~urban/); and William Cronon, *Nature's Metropolis: Chicago and the Great West* (New York: Norton, 1991).

Settlement Patterns

Policy

Daniel Kemmis's *Community and the Politics of Place* (Norman: University of Oklahoma Press, 1990) summarizes succinctly the contrast between those writers, including Thomas Jefferson and Frederick Jackson Turner, who believed that the health of American democracy depended on abundant land and a dispersed settlement pattern of self-reliant smallholdings, and those who thought urban density favored democracy (including Hegel, who believed that Americans could create a true civil society "only when, as in Europe, the direct increase of agriculturists is checked, and the members of the political body shall have begun to be pressed back on each other," as cited by Kemmis, p. 24).

U.S. policymakers are most likely to address this issue under the banner of "sprawl" (usually as a pejorative), and as alternatives to the sprawl, "smart growth" or "the new urbanism." Most active defenders of low-density settlement are economists, including Peter Gordon and Harry W. Richardson, "Are Compact Cities a Desirable Planning Goal?" *Journal of the American Planning Association* 63(1) (Winter 1997). For summaries of antisprawl positions, see the Web sites of the New England regional office of the Environmental Protection Agency (http://www.epa.gov/region01/ra/sprawl/); and the Vermont Forum on Sprawl (http://www.vtsprawl.org/index3.htm); as well as Dwight Young, *Alternatives to Sprawl* (Cambridge, Mass.: Lincoln Institute of Land Policy, 1995); Constance E. Beaumont, *Smart States, Better Communities, How State Governments Can Help Citizens Preserve Their Communities* (Washington, D.C.: National Trust for Historic Preservation, 1996); D. W. Miller, "Searching for Common Ground in the Debate over Urban Sprawl," *Chronicle of Higher Education* (21 May 1999), pp. A15 ff.; Rob Gurwitt, "The State vs. Sprawl," *Governing* (January 1999); Margaret Kriz, "The Politics of Sprawl," *The National Journal*, 6 February 1999; Greg Easterbrook, "Suburban Myth: The Case for Sprawl," *The New Republic*, 15 March 1999. Starting points for exploring the "new urbanism" include William Fulton, *The New Urbanism: Hope or Hype for American Communities?* (Cambridge, Mass.: Lincoln Institute of Land Policy, 1996); and the Congress for the New Urbanism (http://www.cnu.org/). On spatial equity in the metropolitan United States (addressed by the "new regionalists") see Neal R. Peirce, *Citistates: How Urban America Can Prosper in a Competitive World* (Washington, D.C.: Seven Locks Press, 1993); David Rusk, *Cities Without Suburbs* (Washington, D.C.: Woodrow Wilson Center Press and Johns Hopkins University Press, 1993); Myron Orfield, *Metropolitics: A Regional Agenda for Community Stability* (Washington, D.C.: Brookings Institution and Lincoln Institute of Land Policy, 1996); Thomas S. Moore and Aaron Laramore, "Industrial Change and Urban Joblessness: An Assessment of the Mismatch Hypothesis," *Urban Affairs Quarterly* 25 (June 1990): 640–58; Harry J. Holzer, "The Spatial Mismatch Hypothesis: What Has the Evidence Shown?" *Urban Studies* 28(1) (February 1991); Robert Cervero, "Jobs-Housing Balancing and Regional Mobility," *Journal of the American Planning Association* 55(2) (Spring 1989). Journalist Joel Garreau argues in *Edge City: Life on the New Frontier* (New York: Doubleday/Anchor, 1991) that new, de-centered settlement patterns and metropolitan economies more or less doom to failure any policy attempting to reduce these inequities.

Anthropology/Social Science

David Harvey has zeroed in on the connection between settlement patterns and land markets: "Thorsten Veblen has argued, and I think he was basically correct, that the whole settlement pattern of the United States should be understood as one vast venture in real estate speculation" (p. 6, in "From Space to Place and Back Again: Reflections on the Condition of Postmodernity," in Jon Bird, et al., eds., *Mapping the Futures: Local Cultures, Global Change* [New York: Routledge, 1993]).

The anthropological/archaeological literature on settlement patterns and urban form is large but seldom deals with contemporary policy choices. See the journal *Regional Science;* and Peter Hall, "The Urban Culture and the Suburban Culture," in John Agnew, et al., eds., *The City in Cultural Context* (Boston: Allen & Unwin, 1984); Carole Crumley, "Historical Ecology" and "The Ecology of Conquest," in Carole L. Crumley, ed., *Historical Ecology: Cultural Knowledge and Changing Landscapes* (Santa Fe, N.Mex.: School of American Research Press, 1994); T. R. Balakrishnan and George K. Jarvis, "Is the Burgess Concentric Zonal Theory of Spatial Differentiation Still Applicable to Urban Canada?" *Canadian Review of Sociology & Anthropology* 28(4): 526–39 (1991); Robert Paynter, *Models of Spatial Inequality: Settlement Patterns in Historical Archaeology* (New York: Academic, 1982); Peter W. Rees, "Railroads and the Development of the Urban Hierarchy in Nineteenth-Century Eastern Mexico," *Geoscience and Man* 21 (1980): 121–33; Peter Newman and Trevor Hogan, "A Review of Urban Density Models: Toward a Resolution of the Conflict between Populace and Planner," *Human Ecology* 9(3): 269–304 (1981); Anthony D. King, *Cultural Pluralism and Urban Form* (The Hague: Mouton, 1976); Peter J. Ucko, Ruth Tringham, and G. W. Dimbleby, eds., *Man, Settlement and Urbanism* (London: Duckworth, 1972.)

Land Tenure

The anecdote about the undergraduate at the University of Wisconsin was told at the June 1995 inaugural conference of the Land Tenure Center's North American Program *Who Owns America?* (http://ltcweb.ltc.wisc.edu/nap/).

Policy

On recent court cases and analyses of property rights and "takings" in the United States see Jerold S. Kayden, "Private Property Rights, Government Regulation, and the Constitution: Searching for Balance," in Henry L. Diamond and Patrick F. Noonan, eds., *Land Use in America: The Report of the Sustainable Use of Land Project*, ch. 11 (Washington, D.C.: Island Press and Lincoln Institute of Land Policy, 1996); Eric Freyfogle, "The Owning and Taking of Sensitive Lands," *UCLA Law Review* 43(1): 77–138 (October 1995); R. McGreggor Cawley, *Federal Land, Western Anger: The Sagebrush Rebellion and Environmental Politics* (Lawrence: University Press of Kansas, 1993); John Echeverria, *Let the People Judge: Wise Use and the Private Property Rights Movement* (Washington, D.C.: Island Press, 1995); Andrea Hungerford, "'Custom and Culture' Ordinances: Not a Wise Move for the Wise Use Movement," *Tulane Environmental Law Journal* 8(2): 457–503 (Summer 1995). The quotation about "any old fool" making money from land speculation throughout U.S. history is from Daniel W. Bromley, "Regulatory Takings: Coherent Concept or Logical Contradiction?" in *Vermont Law Review, Special Issue on Environmental Law: Papers from the Fourteenth Annual Environmental Law Conference* 17(3): 647–82 (Spring 1993).

On the distinction between the private and public, or social, creation of land values made by Henry George and most of the classical economists, see George's *Progress and Poverty: An Inquiry into the Cause of Industrial Depressions and of Increase of Want with Increase of Wealth . . . The Remedy* (New York: Robert Schalkenbach Foundation, 1990; orig. 1879); John L. Thomas, *Alternative America: Henry George, Edward Bellamy, Henry Demarest Lloyd and the Adversary Tradition* (Cambridge, Mass.: Belknap, 1983); Donald G. Hagman and Dean J. Misczynski, eds., *Windfalls for Wipeouts: Land Value Capture and Compensation* (Chicago: American Society of Planning Officials, 1978); H. James Brown, ed., *Land Use and Taxation* (Cambridge, Mass.: Lincoln Institute of Land Policy,1997); Chuck Matthei, "U.S. Land Reform Movements: The Theory behind the Practice," *Social Policy* 22(4) (Spring 1992); John Emmeus Davis, *Contested Ground: Collective Action and the Urban Neighborhood* (Ithaca, N.Y.: Cornell University Press, 1991); Charles Geisler and Gail Daneker, eds., *Property and Values: Alternatives to Public and Private Ownership* (Washington, D.C.: Island Press, 2000); and Boston's Dudley Street Neighborhood Initiative (http://www.dsni.org/).

On easements and other legal arrangements that separate development or exchange rights from current use rights for land see Eve Endicott, ed., *Land Conservation through Public/Private Partnerships* (Washington, D.C.: Island Press and Lincoln Institute of Land Policy, 1993); Alan A. Altshuler and José Gomez-Ibáñez, *Regulation for Revenue: The Political Economy of Land Use Exactions* (Washington, D.C.: Brookings Institution, 1993); Franklin J. James, *Zoning for Sale: A Critical Analysis of Transferable Development Rights Programs* (Washington, D.C.: Urban Institute, 1977); Norman Marcus, "A Comparative Look at TDR, Subdivision Exactions, and Zoning as Environmental Preservation Panaceas: The Search for Dr. Jekyll without Mr. Hyde," *Land Use and Environment Law Review Annual* 13 (1982): 231–301; as well as the New Jersey Pinelands Commission management plan (http://www.state.nj.us/pinelands/cmp.htm) and the New York City watershed agreement (http://www.state.ny.us/watershed/overview.html), both of which involve transferring developing rights from one parcel to others within a region or system.

Land Markets

The example of students who role-play as artists, naturalists, and historians—but not real estate developers—is from the curriculum package *Landscape Explorers: Uncovering the Power of Place* (Boston: National Park Service, Olmsted National Historic Site, and Harvard University, the Arnold Arboretum, March 1997).

Policy

For an overview of how local governments view land markets in the United States see Jonathan D. Cheney, *Local Governments and Boom/Bust Real Estate Markets* (Cambridge, Mass.: Lincoln Institute of Land Policy, 1995).

On business improvement districts see Bradley M. Segal, "Business Improvement Districts: Tools for Economic Development," *Management Information Service Report* 29(3): 1–21 (March 1997); Heather MacDonald, "BIDs Really Work," *City Journal* 6 (Spring 1996): 29–42; Janet Rothenberg Pack, "BIBs, DIDs, SIDs, SADs: Private Government in Urban America," *Brookings Review* 10 (Fall 1992): 18–21; and a New York City Council 1995 conference on Business Improvement Districts (http://tenant.net/Oversight/ BID/bidtitle.html). On tax increment financing see David Hitchcock, "CreaTIFity Helps Cities Find Development Dollars," *American City & County* 110 (May 1995); and Richard G. Mitchell, "Tax Increment Financing for Redevelopment: Is It as Bad as Its Critics Say? Is It as Good as Its Proponents Claim?" *Journal of Housing* 34: 226–29 (May 1997).

Anthropology/Social Science

The two studies quoted at length here are still the most in-depth work by anthropologists on the culture and political economy of developed-country urban land markets: Constance Perin, *Everything in Its Place: Social Order and Land Use in America* (Princeton, N.J.: Princeton University Press, 1977); and Michael Thompson, *Rubbish Theory: The Creation and Destruction of Value* (New York: Oxford University Press, 1979). In addition, see Leonard Plotnicov, "The Political Economy of Skyscrapers," *City and Society* 1 (1987): 35–51, and "Competition and Cooperation in Contemporary American Urban Development," *City and Society* 5(2): 103–17 (1991); Matthew Cooper and Margaret Rodman, "Conflicts over Use Values in an Urban Canadian Housing Cooperative," *City and Society* 4(1): 44–58 (1990); Susan D. Greenbaum, "Marketing Your City: Race, Ethnicity, and Historic Preservation in the Sunbelt," *City and Society* 4(1): 58–76 (1990); Katherine S. Newman, *Declining Fortunes: The Withering of the American Dream* (New York: Basic, 1993); Brett Williams, *Upscaling Downtown: Stalled Gentrification in Washington, D.C.* (Ithaca, N.Y.: Cornell University Press, 1988); Robert Verrey and Laura Henly, "Creation Myths and Zoning Boards: Local Uses of Historic Preservation," in Brett Williams, ed., *The Politics of Culture*, 75–107 (Washington, D.C.: Smithsonian Institution Press, 1991); Carol J. Greenhouse, Barbara Yngvesson, and David M. Engel, *Law and Community in Three American Towns* (Ithaca, N.Y.: Cornell University Press, 1994); and R. Timothy Sieber, "Waterfront Revitalization in Postindustrial Port Cities of North America," *City and Society* 5(2): 120–36 (1991). Nathaniel Lichfield's *Economics in Urban Conservation* (New York: Cambridge University Press, 1988) also discusses how urban land shifts "from resource to property and commodity."

Urban Land, the State, and Civil Society

The anecdote about the Virginia transportation planners was told by Albert C. Eisenberg, deputy assistant secretary for transportation policy in the federal Department of Transportation, at the *Keep America Growing: Balancing Working Lands and Development* conference held in Philadelphia in June 1999 (http://www.farmland.org/kag/work1.htm).

Policy

The ur-article for local "state as market" is Charles M. Tiebout's "A Pure Theory of Local Expenditures," *Journal of Political Economy* 64 (1956): 416–24. See also William A. Fischel, "Zoning, Capitalization, and the Efficiency of Local Government," in his *Regulatory Takings: Law, Economics, and Politics* (Cambridge, Mass.: Harvard University Press, 1995). Critiques of Tiebout include Gordon L. Clark, "Democracy and the Capitalist State: Towards a Critique of the Tiebout Hypothesis" (Cambridge, Mass.: Harvard University, Department of City and Regional Planning, Discussion Paper 79-8, 1979); and Konrad Stahl, "Local Collective Goods: A Critical Re-examination of the Tiebout Model" (Berkeley: Institute of Urban & Regional Development, University of California, Berkeley, Working Paper no. 347, 1981).

For economists' analyses of local perceptions and effects of the property tax in the United States see Helen Ladd and Dick Netzer, eds., *Local Government Tax and Land Use Policy* (London: Edward Elgar Publishers with Lincoln Institute of Land Policy, 1998); Timothy Bartik, "Effects of State and Local Taxes on Economic Development," *Economic Development Quarterly* (February 1992): 103–11; Joseph Gyourko, "Effects of Local Tax Structures on the Factor Intensity . . . of Manufacturing Activity across Cities," *Journal of Urban Economics* 22 (1987): 151–64. A sociologist's analysis is Clarence Lo's *Small Property versus Big Government: Social Origins of the Property Tax Revolt* (Berkeley: University of California Press, 1990).

On gated communities as private governments see Edward Blakely and Mary Gail Snyder, *Fortress America: Gated and Walled Communities in the United States* (Cambridge, Mass.: Lincoln Institute of Land Policy, 1995); Robert Jay Dilger, *Neighborhood Politics: Residential Community Associations in American Governance* (New York: New York University Press, 1992); Fred E. Foldvary, *Public Goods and Private Communities: The Market Provision of Social Services* (Brookfield, Vt.: Edward Elgar Publishing, 1994); Evan McKenzie, *Privatopia: Homeowner Associations and the Rise of Residential Private Government* (New Haven, Conn.: Yale University Press, 1994).

Anthropology/Social Science

It is difficult to find any anthropological research on property taxation; most of the scarce work done uses property tax records as sources for other kinds of analyses, especially historical community reconstruction or property relations. See Nancy Van Dolsen (Archaeological and Historical Consultants, Inc.), "Ethnography, Historic Landscapes, and Historic Preservation" (1995 annual meeting, American Anthropological Association), using eighteenth-century Pennsylvania tax records; and Dmitra Doukas (New York University), "The Landscape of Livelihood: Three Decades of Change in a Central New York Village" (1994 annual meeting, American Anthropological Association), analyzing property tax abatements that helped to attract outside investments but also "extract[ed] values from the local economy through measures that increase[d] residents' taxes." On urban land use and planning conflicts in general, see most recent issues of *City and Society* and an older article, D. Claire McAdams, "A Power-Conflict Approach to Urban Land Use: Toward a New Human Ecology," *Urban Anthropology* 9(3): 295–318 (1980).

Changing Anthropological Approaches to Urban and Environmental Policy

This account of work by urban anthropologists relies heavily on recent review articles: Setha M. Low, "The Anthropology of Cities: Imagining and Theorizing the City," *Annual Review of Anthropology* 25: 383–409 (1996); Owen M. Lynch, "Urban Anthropology, Postmodernist Cities, and Perspectives," *City and Society:* 35–52 (1994); Leonard Plotnikov, "Afterthoughts: Old and New Directions," *City and Society* 5(2): 169–71 (1991); Leo Howe, "Urban Anthropology: Trends in Its Development since 1920," *Cambridge Anthropology* 14 (1): 37–66 (1990); Andrew H. Maxwell, "The Anthropology of Poverty in Black Communities: A Critique and Systems Alternative," *Urban Anthropology* 17(2–3): 171–18 (1988); Jack R. Rollwagen, "Reconsidering Basic Assumptions: A Call for a Reassessment of the General Concept of Culture in Anthropology," *Urban Anthropology* 15(1–2): 97–133 (1986); and Irene Glasser and Lawrence B. Breitborde, eds., *Urban Anthropology in the 1990s: A Collection of Syllabi and an Extensive Bibliography*, revised & expanded edition (Arlington, Va.: American Anthropological Association/Society for Urban Anthropology, April 1996). The latter shows that urban anthropologists explore U.S. land use and ownership more often in their teaching than in their own published research, in part by using some of the nonanthropological work listed under "political economy" below. Examples include courses taught by Karen A. Curtis (University of Delaware); Robert Dannin, Owen Lynch, and Susan Slyomovics (all at New York University); George Gmelch (Union College); Stanley E. Hyland (University of Memphis); Kristin Koptiuch (Arizona State University West); Richard A. Lobban Jr. (Rhode Island College); Arthur D. Murphy (Baylor University); R. Timothy Sieber (University of Massachusetts at Boston); Costas Spirou (National-Louis University); and Brett Williams (The American University).

There has been more anthropological research, and *far* more anthropological influence on public policy for urban land, in developing countries than in the United States. See Lisa Peattie, *Rethinking Ciudad Guyana* (Ann Arbor: University of Michigan Press, 1987); Charles Reavis, "Global Trends, Urbanization, and (Urban) Anthropology," Society for Urban Anthropology, letter to the editor, in *Anthropology Newsletter* September 1996; Anthony Leeds (edited by Roger Sanjek), *Cities, Classes and Social Order* (Ithaca, N.Y.: Cornell University Press, 1984); and R. Timothy Sieber, "New Directions in Contemporary Urban Development," *City and Society* 5 (2): 99–102 (1991).

Can Political Economy Really Influence Public Policy?

The excellent work on the political economy of urban land by geographers, planners, political scientists, and historians is seldom cited by policymakers or journalists, though some has influenced academic policy analysts. See also Mark Gottdiener, *The Social Production of Urban Space* (Austin: University of Texas Press, 1985); John R. Logan and Harvey Molotch, *Urban Fortunes: The Political Economy of Place* (Berkeley: University of California Press, 1987); Manuel Castells, *The Urban Question* (Cambridge, Mass.: MIT Press, 1977); Joe Feagin, *The Urban Real Estate Game: Playing Monopoly with Real Money* (Englewood Cliffs, N.J.: Prentice-Hall, 1983); Ira Katznelson, *Marxism and the City* (Oxford: Clarendon, 1993); Saskia Sassen, *The Global City: New York, London, Tokyo* (Princeton, N.J.: Princeton University Press,

1991). David Harvey's earliest work, *Social Justice and the City* (New York: Blackwell, 1973), also fits this description, though it is written in a more accessible language than his later work such as *The Urban Experience* (Baltimore, Md.: Johns Hopkins University Press, 1989). See also Matthew Edel, Eliot Sklar, and Daniel Luria, *Shaky Palaces: Homeownership and Social Mobility in Boston Suburbs* (New York: Columbia University Press, 1984); Henry C. Binford, *The First Suburbs: Residential Communities on the Boston Periphery, 1815–1860* (Chicago: University of Chicago Press, 1985); Anthony M. Orum, *City Building in America* (Boulder, Colo.: Westview, 1995); Elizabeth Blackmar, *Manhattan for Rent, 1785–1850* (Ithaca, N.Y.: Cornell University Press, 1989); Sam Bass Warner, *Streetcar Suburbs: The Process of Growth in Boston, 1870–1900* (Cambridge, Mass.: Harvard University Press, 1978); Richard E. Foglesong, *Planning the Capitalist City: The Colonial Era to the 1920s* (Princeton, N.J.: Princeton University Press, 1986); Marc Weiss, *The Rise of the Community Builders: The American Real Estate Industry and Urban Land Planning* (New York: Columbia University Press, 1987).

12

Environmental Anthropology at Sea

Bonnie J. McCay

Paleoecologists, archaeologists, students of cultural diffusion, evolution and ecology, and sociocultural ethnographers have long studied communities of people who rely on fishing for subsistence and trade. The anthropology of fishing, or "maritime anthropology," is *environmental* anthropology in so far as the technical features of marine and coastal environments and the effects of human activities on those environments are included in that record. In recent decades, it has also become *applied* environmental anthropology in that anthropologists, and other social scientists, have had the opportunity to become involved in national and international efforts to improve the management of marine resources. This chapter provides an overview of this research tradition and some of its applications to marine science and resource management.

Cultures on the Fertile, Fragile, and Fickle Fringe

An intriguing question has been, "Under what conditions can people, without agriculture or domesticated animals, develop and sustain high population densities and complex social systems?" Many foraging groups rely significantly on fish, shellfish, and other marine and riverine fauna. Certain early historic and prehistoric groups living on the coast—particularly the tribes of the Pacific Northwest—were able to sustain population densities and sociological complexities, including class stratification and organized warfare, comparable to what is found among many agriculturalists. One answer for this accomplishment seems to have been the abundance and accessibility of valuable maritime sources of high-quality food and tradable goods. Maritime lifestyles were enhanced by runs of coastal and anadromous fishes; the year-round availability of shellfish; and occasional chances to capture sea lions, otters, whales, and other marine mammals. As Suttles (1987) has shown, however, the abundance of available sea life was not predictable, reliable, or trouble-free for Native Americans of the Pacific Northwest, and some features of social and cultural life, including kinship and marriage arrangements and ceremonial feasting, may be interpreted as ways to cope with erratic and unpredictable availability.

Fishing takes place in a multidimensional space, only a tiny proportion of which is easily visible to and knowable by human beings. Moreover, like all hunting–gathering activities, it depends on natural processes rather than managed ones, in contrast with agriculture, pastoralism, and industrial manufacturing. Natural processes are patently uncertain and often highly variable and irregular or stochastic. This is a major environmental condition for maritime groups: the risks and uncertainties of fishing have major implications for social organization, cultural representations, and other dimensions of fishing communities and societies. For example, the method of paying members of a fishing enterprise is typically through shares in the proceeds, rather than wages or salaries, even when many crew members own none of the technology used. This "share system" is widespread, cutting across ethnic, geographic, social class, and technological boundaries and may be interpreted as a good way to spread the risks and cope with the vagaries of fishing for a living.

The fact that their work involves trying to capture wild and migratory creatures sometimes leads to the claim that contemporary subsistence and commercial fishers are "hunter-gatherers" in some definitive way. Although tempting, it is a mistake to equate fishing with hunting when characterizing the sociology and culture of fishing communities. Fishing communities can be autonomous groups of foragers, but their work may be parts of the modes of production of tribal and peasant agrarian societies as well as kingdoms, empires, and industrialized nation-states. For example, a great deal of archaeological research in coastal Peru shows the significance of fishing to early stages of the development of the Incan empire (e.g., Marcus 1987). Fishers may be peasant producers, specialized producers in mercantile networks, members of marginal castes, or people fleeing forms of exploitation or repression. They may be in the backwater of industrial capitalist society or fully integrated into capitalist commodity production. The activity of fishing and social networks of those involved in it are likely to be embedded in distinctive sociopolitical and economic systems and webs of significance, calling for greater specificity.

Classics in the Ethnography of Fishing and Fishing Communities

The social anthropologist Bronislaw Malinowski (1935, 1948, 1984) was an early ethnographer of fishing in a tribal, non-Western setting, the Trobriand Islands of the western Pacific. Fishing was for local consumption, and trade, to some extent, was regulated by ritual beliefs and the power of local clans and chiefs. As such, his work was a precursor to the study of sea tenure (see below).

Another classic in the anthropology of fishing is Raymond Firth's ethnography *Malay Fishermen: Their Peasant Economy* (1966), which explores the social and economic relations of fishers who are linked to larger sociopolitical structures as peasants. They combine subsistence and commodity production with some autonomy from, but considerable dependence upon, those larger structures and the elites who control them. Here too, a rich body of work now exists, including studies of fish marketing and research on problems of underdevelopment of rural sectors. One theme of this work is the dependence of fishers on "middlemen" (or "middlewomen") for access to markets, information, and credit. This relationship is frequently asymmetrical, the fishers disadvantaged in the deal, hence great policy interest in marketing cooperatives as tools for rural development. Issues of rural development and cooperatives are thus part of the applied anthropology of fisheries.

If fishing is found among foragers, tribal groups, and peasants living within complex societies, then surely it exists in industrial nation-states as well. Indeed it does. The reality and the literature about it can be roughly divided into "inshore" and "offshore," a crude representation of social distinctions such as small-scale versus large-scale and "artisanal" versus "industrial." On the inshore side, a recent classic is *The Lobster Gangs of Maine* (Acheson 1988), which explores the social, economic, and cultural influences on important questions such as "Who does in fact end up being able to go fishing and how they are allowed to do it?" The book and Acheson's many articles about Maine fisheries contribute to the "sea tenure" tradition discussed below, showing the importance of territoriality as well as the ability of lobstermen to achieve it without the formal blessing of the government.

On the offshore side, a classic ethnography is *Hunters, Seamen, and Entrepreneurs: The Tuna Seinermen of San Diego,* by Michael Orbach (1977). It is about a highly industrialized fishery, using expensive vessels and gear to fish in distant waters for tuna, which are sold to canneries owned by multinational corporations that distribute their products worldwide. Similar ethnographic studies have been done of offshore fishing crews of Atlantic Canada.

The "inshore/offshore" distinction is relevant now to virtually every part of the world, because even the most remote islanders are likely competing for fish or fishing space with highly mobile, heavily capitalized fishing vessels from distant places. J. Russ McGoodwin's book *Crisis in the World's Fisheries* (1990) is an excellent anthropological approach to issues and problems in fisheries development and management. It is fundamentally an extended argument for acknowledging and doing something positive about the huge contribution and major problems of small-scale, inshore, and artisanal fishers and fishing communities confronted with fisheries depletion and competition from offshore operations as well as polluting activities.

"Maritime Anthropology" and Environmental Issues in North Atlantic Studies

The development of a conscious identity of "fisheries" or "maritime" anthropology began in the late 1960s and early 1970s through meetings, student and faculty exchanges, and publications. Several important collections of anthropological research in fisheries appeared in the 1970s, outcomes of the International Congress of Anthropology and Ethnology that was held in Chicago in 1973. Other edited collections followed as did arguments about whether a subfield of "maritime anthropology" could and should exist.

Regardless of one's opinion on that question, from the late 1960s through the 1980s, more specialized and regional work on the anthropology of fishing and fishing communities appeared in print. The North Atlantic became a major regional focus, stimulated by the creation of the Institute for Social and Economic Research at Memorial University, Newfoundland, Canada, and the idea of Robert Paine, who had studied Saami reindeer herders and fishers in northern Norway, to bring Norwegian social anthropologists Ottar Brox and Cato Wadel to Newfoundland to do fieldwork. They came from the social anthropology tradition of Fredrik Barth. Swedish, Norwegian, Canadian, Scottish, and other anthropologists soon interacted across the Atlantic (e.g., Andersen and Wadel 1972). In their work, relations with the environment and challenges in fisheries management were of less importance than questions about rural development, social structure, and culture. Environment was most important in the cultural ecology sense of generating particular relationships of work that in turn shaped social structure and marked culture.

The North Atlantic, particularly the early Norse settlements of Greenland and Iceland, has been the focus of work by ecological archaeologists intrigued by evidence of fragile adjustments to harsh environments and the effects of climate change (e.g., McGovern 1990). In Newfoundland, Andersen and Stiles (1973) were the first to examine how traditional practices intersected with resource management, and I brought a critical perspective on systems ecology to my early 1970s study of how islanders responded to decline in the fisheries, including their own unintended role in depleting certain fish stocks (McCay 1978). Subsequent work with Andrew P. Vayda led to delineation of an "actor-based" and processual approach to environmental anthropology (Vayda and McCay 1978; Vayda et al. 1991), which was strongly influenced by neo-Darwinism in ecology, natural hazards research in geography, and concerns about the requirements for explanation in anthropology.

In the late 1980s and early 1990s social science interest in environmental questions in the North Atlantic reemerged, prompted by crisis in the cod fisheries of both Canada and Norway. Sociologists and anthropologists examined causes and consequences of decline in cod stocks. They also focused on the issues of fishers' ecological knowledge and how it was or was not used in official science-based fish stock assessment, which is the basis of management decisions regarding how large a quota should be and on participation of fishers in the management process. This was in the context of rapid decline of cod stocks and the eventual collapse, and closure, of the Newfoundland fishery in 1992. *Fishing for Truth* (Finlayson 1994) critically examined the ideational and social bases for systematic errors and miscommunication within the scientific community, and Finlayson and McCay (1998) asked about potentials for and resistance to change in fisheries management institutions in the aftermath of ecological collapse.

The Canadian–Scandinavian network of scholars created in the early 1970s was reinstituted in the early 1990s, broadened to include sociologists, political scientists, and economists as well as an (American) anthropologist. One outcome is *Community, State, and Market in North Atlantic Fisheries* (Apostle et al. 1998), a coauthored book influenced by sociological theories of science and development as well as anthropological work on participatory processes and fishers' knowledge in fisheries management. A similarly transnational and interdisciplinary project addresses recent demographic, socioeconomic, and environmental change in the North Atlantic fringe (Hamilton and Otterstad 1998).

"Sea Tenure" Studies

A rich body of ethnographic research has developed based on studies of tribal, non-Western, and typically tropical and subtropical island communities, many in the western Pacific. One of the results with environmental implications is identification and appreciation of the sociocultural, political, and ecological ramifications of "sea tenure." Anthropologists, geographers, and others, including a few biologists, have contributed to appreciation of the ways that local communities and traditional societies conceptualize, allocate, regulate, and defend rights to marine resources. Distinctive and elaborate systems of property rights exist, contrary to the perceived wisdom that people who fish treat the sea as an open-access frontier. Or, they *have* existed in the past: colonial and "modernizing" experiences often impose the "freedom of the seas" institution on non-Western people.

Documentation of sea tenure and other territorial systems of allocating access to marine spaces and resources is one of the most important contributions of ethnography to the understanding of marine fisheries. It is clear that access to marine resources is often restricted by one or another local institution and that some of those institutions have salutary functions in mitigating conflict; spreading fishing effort over wider areas; and reducing the take of some species or, more likely, protecting fish in certain spaces or times of the year. These findings have contributed to the policy of the Food and Agricultural Organization (FAO) of the United Nations and other development agencies, through characterization of "Territorial Use Rights in Fisheries" (TURFs) as important fisheries management techniques.

Sea tenure studies have contributed directly and indirectly to the recent proliferation of projects in third world countries designed to protect, restore, or create anew TURF-like systems of controlled access to marine resources. They are now found under the rubrics of "community-based natural resource management" and "co-management." Community-based management emphasizes greater community control over resources. It is a sharp counterpoint to the "tragedy of the commons" way of understanding environmental problems, focusing on the capacities of some local communities, under some special circumstances, to develop effective systems of common resource management (McCay and Acheson 1987). Co-management refers to collaboration between local communities and other organizations, such as government agencies and nongovernmental assistance groups (Pinkerton 1989; Pinkerton and Weinstein 1995).

The focus on sea tenure and common property rights, while productive, also has tended toward "question-begging" research programs (Vayda and Walters 1999). The tendency is to claim that any and all sea tenure institutions are valuable because they promote marine conservation, despite evidence that many of them are intended to have very different functions, such as reducing conflict or maintaining the wealth and power of local elites, and that evidence for the ecological benefits of these and others is scant indeed. Clearly, there is danger in reading a "conservation" message into local systems of property rights or sea tenure without more information about their views of the world, the workings of the institutions, and their effects on natural systems.

Sea Tenure Institutions: Three Cases

Sea tenure studies show that people who use marine resources are not necessarily unfettered tragedians of an open-access commons. M. E. Smith (in McCay and Acheson 1987: 15–16) offers an encyclopedia definition of classical comedy: "The drama of humans as social rather than private beings, a drama of social actions having a frankly corrective purpose." People dependent on common resources can be comedians in this sense. Hence environmental anthropologists and others focus on institutions developed by fishers and other common resource users in their efforts to put things right. I offer three cases from my own research, two being cases of local-level regulation, the third a case of co-management and change to a system of privatized access rights.

Local-Level Fisheries Regulations of Fogo Island, Newfoundland

The history of fisheries for bay clams and oysters, highly sedentary species found close to shore, includes many instances of local regulation by the users or by local governments, such as the townships of Cape Cod, Massachusetts, or counties in New Jersey. In the United States, even where state governments claimed exclusive rights to manage fisheries on behalf of the "public trust," management rights and responsibilities are often delegated to the local level, such that the management systems become examples of co-management. Similarly, the successful cases of co-management as a vehicle toward sustainable use of small-scale fisheries in Chile concern benthic invertebrates such as conchs and sea urchins (Castilla and Fernandez 1998). Crabs and lobsters are more mobile but are often found within a well-enough defined area so that the fishers find it worth their while to defend exclusive territories and, in some cases, impose catch limits.

Fishers are also likely to manage sites of access to mobile resources in order to reduce the costly and dangerous effects of conflict and competition and achieve social norms such as fairness and equality. On Fogo Island, Newfoundland, access to inshore sites for placing large netted twine cod traps was regulated in locally distinct ways until the inshore fishery declined in the late 1980s. Along the rocky shores near the communities of Joe Batt's Arm and Tilting, on the northeast and eastern sides of the island, no one could set a trap in a "berth" until a certain day in June, and then only after a gun was fired, allowing all of the crews to leave for the berths they wished to use. If two or more crews converged on the same berth, the local fisheries officer drew straws to determine the proper claimant. On the other side of the island, particularly around the port of Seldom-Come-By, the regulatory system was different: the best trap berths were allocated according to inherited rights, the rest on a first-come-first-served basis. The system of Joe Batt's Arm and Tilting was devised around 1907 as a way of handling conflicts arising from increased demand on the trap berths, due to increased population and attempts by fish merchants to expand the use of traps. The situation had also become dangerous and costly: crews sometimes staked their claims early in the season, when high seas and ice were still likely. The new system addressed this with the opening gunshot.

Other rules in Fogo Island's fishery included restrictions on how close fishing gear could be placed to each other, particularly competing gears (i.e., gillnets versus cod traps) and whether or not baitless hooked fish lures called jiggers could be used on certain more distant fishing grounds. The jigger rule was partly *protectionist*: local fishers could more easily get bait for fishing on those grounds, so an anti-jigger rule kept others away. It was also *conservationist*: the hooks on jiggers strike the fish at any part of the body, ripping them open, but not always bringing them to the surface. This rule was particularly important at places and times when very large female cod were expected; these were referred to as "mother fish," fish to be protected for the future.

A supportive legal structure is often important to local-level systems of common pool resource management. The Newfoundland regulations described above were developed locally but written into the law of Newfoundland—as local rules—and enforced by the government's paid fisheries officer. When Newfoundland became part of Canada in 1949, and the fisheries became subject to federal management, the local rules were no longer legitimized at higher levels, but local observance of most of the rules continued, supported by the fishery officers (Matthews and Phyne 1988).

The scope and intent of the regulations described were, of course, inadequate to the task of conserving the fish stocks, which were migratory and covered huge areas, subject to predation by large offshore fishing fleets. Nonetheless, when the Canadian government abandoned the local rules, particularly after the 200-mile limit of 1977 allowed it to take a major role in managing the fish stocks, it also left behind social and ecological lessons about the local scale. Only today, and only in a very halting way, are fisheries scientists in Canada—and the United States—recognizing the importance of highly localized phenomena, such as breeding grounds and overwintering grounds, for the viability of fish stocks otherwise defined at large scale, and of locally derived knowledge about such phenomena.

New Jersey Cooperatives: Coping with Free Riders

Local-level regulation of how many fish are caught and landed is very rare, particularly for highly migratory species found over a large area. However, it was evident during the late 1970s and 1980s at two fish marketing cooperatives in New Jersey. The cooperatives not only regulated members' catches, but also found ways to handle heterogeneity. The cooperatives each had between eighteen and twenty-two vessel owners as members. Becoming a member was difficult. Making it worthwhile to try were attractions such as the cooperatives' control over a critical scarce resource: waterfront space for offloading and tying up boats. There were other benefits as well, including help in marketing catches and the possibility of annual "patronage refunds" of the profits.

Entry into the cooperative at "Gull Haven" (pseudonym, McCay 1980) was limited by the amount of dock space available and members' notions of who could be relied upon to be (a) "highliner" or very productive fishermen and (b) willing to go along with the informal and formal rules of the cooperative. This in effect imposed limits on entry into the fishery in the region because of the scarcity of dock space and fish packinghouses.

The fisheries are diverse and wide-ranging, but during the winter months most members specialized in fishing for a whiting species, this one also called silver hake. Although the cooperative sold to the large fish markets of the Atlantic seaboard, such as Fulton Market in New York City, demand for whiting was limited. Market gluts—when so many fish were offered for sale that the price plummeted—were very common and problematic because the price could vacillate by factors of ten or more (i.e., from 10 cents to $1.50).

The fishing cooperatives developed systems of imposing catch limits on members' boats when the market had the potential of being glutted. A sign was posted, for example, "40 boxes today." It made sense to do this even though the fresh-fish urban markets were served by fishing fleets around the globe, because the winter whiting fishery was virtually theirs alone. At this time, during the cold-weather months the fish were found fairly close to the New Jersey ports, in the warmer waters of deep submarine canyons emanating from the Hudson River system. The fish were less available to New England fishermen, who fished for them in the summer months instead. Accordingly, the New Jersey ports, as well as some in New York, had a near monopoly on the domestic part of this fishery during the winter months (far offshore foreign fishing boats targeted whiting as well, but rarely for the fresh-fish markets). This helped keep the prices reasonably high, but gluts were still a problem. It was to this problem that self-regulation was directed.

At "Gull Haven," the catch limits were implemented in ways that dealt with the problems of rewarding high performance while punishing those who violated the rules. During the early part of the fishing week, captains who came in over the limit were given credit for the catches, but later in the week, closer to the critical marketing period of Thursday and Friday, payment for anything they brought in over the limit was redistributed equally among the rest of the members. In these ways the cooperative was able to recognize the heterogeneity of its members while keeping free-riding to a manageable level. Too much free-riding and no one would be willing to keep to a collective agreement.

Free-riding was a far more serious problem at the regional level where other whiting fishers benefited from the market price effects of the catch limits imposed by the New Jersey cooperatives. From time to time, in the 1960s and 1970s, leaders of the cooperatives tried to persuade people in the New York ports to adopt a similar system. This did not work, but they were able to organize several regional "tie-ups" to protest low market prices. Even with free-riding the cooperatives persisted. Members were aware that their "sacrifices" benefited others but were convinced that without the catch limits, the price would plummet, hurting everyone.

This institutional arrangement was suspended throughout most of the 1990s. Free-riding was rampant, and the resource itself declined as many new boats entered the fishery in response to sharp declines in the total allowable catch (TAC) in the traditional groundfish fisheries of New England. Whiting were scarcer on the inshore grounds for which New Jersey boats had such an advantage. Accordingly, the limits on entry created by the cooperative's control over scarce dock space were inadequate to the task. It became an open access fishery, and self-regulation no longer made any sense. Members of the cooperatives had to find other fisheries, such as squid, and redirect their regulatory efforts to the workings of the regional fishery management councils, including attempts to use limited entry, to protect their positions.

The Surf Clam Fishery: Participatory Privatization

One of the constraints to self-regulation of common pool resources in the United States and other capitalist economies is that it can be interpreted as anticompetitive behavior, coming up against antitrust laws. The cooperatives noted above were absolved from this by a federal law protecting registered agricultural cooperatives from antitrust challenges. Participants in another important fishery of the Eastern seaboard, the fishery for surf clams, confronted this problem and turned their commons dilemma over to one of the regional management councils, showing yet another way that the embeddedness of locally devised systems can make a difference. By the 1960s and early 1970s participants in the relatively new surf clam fishery recognized that they had created an open-access monster, when more and more vessels, larger and more powerful all the time, entered the unregulated fishery. The clams, immobile and hence easily harvested once located, were quickly depleted. The fleets moved from patch to patch, from Long Island, New York, to Virginia.

There were discussions of industry-based regulation of catches or gear, but antitrust issues loomed large. Therefore nothing was done until the regional fishery management council system was created in 1977; the surf clam fishery was the very first to be regulated under the new U.S. system for managing fisheries from 3 to 200 nautical miles and was the very first to be put under limited entry. The council created a moratorium on new vessels, an overall TAC, and a system limiting how much time each vessel could fish for clams in order to spread the fishery out over the year on behalf of the processors.

The industry was ready and eager to use the management system to accomplish goals it could not legally accomplish by itself. The new council system provided the institutional solution to their second-order dilemma. It is probable that the industry could not have come to agreement anyway, given the large number of participants (over 180 boats at the peak) and their economic heterogeneity (a few very large vertically integrated firms; many "independents," some owner-operator vessels but others large fleets of vessels; plus of course geographic, personal, and ethnic differences).

The obstacle posed by sharp differences in wealth and power was plainly evident in the new system. Between 1978 and 1989, the surf clam industry had some co-management powers vis-à-vis the regional fishery management council, which at times asked the industry to come up with its own plans for adjusting the system. The very real differences in power and interest that existed made it extremely difficult for the industry to reach consensus on important issues, namely how to correct distortions created by the limited entry system. As fishing capacity increased, and certain year-classes of clams grew enough to be fished, the amount of time each vessel could fish had to be ratcheted back in order to spread the quota over the year. By 1986 surf clammers could fish only 6 hours every two or three weeks. From as early as 1980, there seemed to be agreement that some kind of allocation of the quota to individual vessels would be necessary, but agreement on exactly how that would be done was elusive. The power structure of the industry played a major role in causing an 11-year delay in the decision to make a major institutional change: *individual transferable quotas* (ITQs). This is a market-based system of management that has the potential of changing conditions that led to overcapitalization and dangers at sea (i.e., the race to fish against limited time or quotas).

ITQs went into effect in 1990, the first instance of this method of fisheries management in the United States and one of the few in the world. In this case, ITQs rapidly led to fleet downsizing and intensified existing patterns that concentrated ownership and control in relatively few firms. Nonetheless, the surf clam management regime remains a commons institution, because setting the annual TAC and other conditions of the fishery remain responsibilities of the regional fishery management council, on behalf of the public trust that remains in the clam resources themselves. The ITQ holders must continue to interact with each other, government regulators, and other members of the public as part of a management community. Interestingly, privatized fishing rights appear to have increased incentives for some forms of environmental stewardship in this case, because members of the industry have recently pooled resources with government and university researchers to improve knowledge about surf clam biology.

Social Impacts and Applied Anthropology

Much of my own recent research has concerned the social impacts of ITQs in the fisheries. Social impact analysis is the most evident form of applied environmental anthropology. It is not separate from other research, though. For example, Marian Binkley's work *Voices from the Offshore* (1994) focuses on the narratives of risk and danger elicited from interviews with Nova Scotia offshore fishermen and their wives and as such ties into the tradition of studying people's responses to risk and uncertainty, perceptions of luck and danger, and worldviews and ethos. In her second book, *Risk, Dangers, and Rewards in the Nova Scotia Offshore Fishery* (1995), she provides linkages to questions about the incentives to engage in dangerous, risky jobs and the consequences, in terms of health, lifestyles, and income opportunities.

Binkley's research reflects the applied anthropology tradition of examining the "impacts" of policy changes, major events, and longer-term processes upon communities, groups, families, and individuals. In industrialized nation-states of the "North," doing so is demanded by groups or communities affected by change or it is mandated by laws that include requirements for economic and social impact assessment.

In the United States, demand for social impact assessment of fisheries regulation accelerated with changes in the international Law of the Sea. In 1977 the United States claimed 200 nautical miles of adjacent sea as its zone of exclusive jurisdiction. This heralded the beginning of federal fisheries management, under the Magnuson Fishery Conservation and Management Act of

1976, which also created a new institutional structure for marine fisheries. Modern fisheries management, like other forms of natural resource and environmental management, is intended to be a rational, science-based system of control by the state, exercising its special claims over and responsibilities for common pool resources and ecological systems. The Magnuson Act created the institutional framework to realize this but in a novel way, where much of the decision making and planning would be done by regional councils made up of government officials, state and federal, and citizens, who are to use "the best available scientific data" and other sources of information to develop fishery management plans.

The Magnuson Act (now the Magnuson–Stevens Act) also contained language that highlighted the importance of social and cultural factors in fisheries management and called for social impact studies in a way still quite new in government. Accordingly, anthropologists and other social scientists are increasingly asked to provide expertise of the "social impact assessment" kind and produce reports that are published by government agencies and interest groups as "grey literature." Some do this as professional, full-time employees or owners of consulting firms; others as academics and independent scholars working through grants or providing advice to management organizations; a handful of others are employed by the federal fisheries agency or regional fishery management councils.

Sea Changes in Marine Policy

Anthropologists and the messages of their work have influenced marine fisheries policy in several ways (McCay 2000). One is the emphasis on democratization of policy processes, giving greater voice to fishers and members of fishery-dependent communities (McCay and Jentoft 1996), including a recent effort to provide a manual to help people participate in management policy (McCay and Creed 1999).

The second is a stronger emphasis on community-level impacts. In 1996 the Magnuson Act was amended to include a requirement that the needs of fishery-dependent communities be taken into account when devising management plans. This, combined with a wave of judicial activism, has given greater force to efforts by anthropologists and other social scientists to make social impact assessment a meaningful part of management planning. Signs of this sea change were evident in 1995 when the Atlantic States Marine Fisheries Commission, an interstate agency, created a committee that has worked toward improved collection of social and economic data, and in 1998 when the New England Fishery Management Council created a Social Science Advisory Committee to help improve its ability to provide social and economic impact assessments. Slower in coming, but within sight, is improved incorporation of related issues such as gender in impact assessment, given the often-slighted roles of women as fishers, fish-processors, marketers, and wives and kin left to worry as direct links to the community.

Farther from incorporation into policy and practice, but present in many policy fora as alternatives, are two other ideas promoted by social scientists involved in fisheries. One is the value of community-based alternatives to top-down management by government agencies, on the one hand, and market-driven management through individual transferable quotas on the other. The second is a critique of scientific paradigms and the use of science in fisheries management. M. E. Smith (1990) argued that New England fishermen perceive marine ecological systems as chaotic, and the economist James Wilson (Wilson and Kleban 1992) used chaotic processes in models to simulate the behavior of fish stocks. They challenge the dominant scientific paradigm of a predictable and determinate relationship between fish catches and the abundance of fish populations. This critique also has added force to the challenge of incorporating the observations and knowledge of fishers into the scientific framework for management.

Anthropologists are engaged in practice as well as theory. For example, John Kearney is trying to make community-based management a reality in the Bay of Fundy region of Canada. Michael Orbach, Jeffrey Johnson and others have used their craft to help fishers and managers develop acceptable limited-access fisheries systems in the South Atlantic, particularly a transferable, individual trap quota system for spiny lobsters in Florida (see Maiolo et al. 1992). In the mid-1980s I worked closely with clammers, clam buyers, scientists, and state agency bureaucrats in an experimental "co-managed" resource rehabilitation, which reinforced lessons about how to deal with risk, uncertainty, and ignorance, including the value of designing interventions to improve learning (McCay 1988). Acheson's work on lobstering and lobster territoriality also led him to direct anthropological involvement in fisheries management policy, in collaboration with an economist and a biologist, providing academic arguments and design suggestions for major changes in policy within the state of Maine (Acheson and Steneck 1997). Finally, anthropologists have contributed to the workings of organizations such as the International Union for the Conservation of Nature and the International Whaling Commission. One contribution is to substantiate the importance of small-scale coastal fishing communities (McGoodwin 1990). Another is to inform assumptions about and characterization of aboriginal and small-scale coastal whaling, as well as "subsistence" harvesting, in international marine mammal policy (Freeman 1993; Kalland 1993).

Conclusion: On Environmental Anthropology

This review of maritime anthropology is not complete, but it should serve to introduce some of the major directions taken, particularly the work directly relevant to environmental studies. In conclusion, let me note how difficult it is to delimit environmental anthropology. Environmental anthropology concerns both causes and consequences of patterns and changes in natural environments, and those causes and consequences can be found at many levels and in many kinds of phenomena. For example, the causes of change in marine environments can include the so-called "driving forces" of large-scale environmental change, such as population growth and migration, economic forces of industrial capitalism, and the evolution and diffusion of a hungry consumer culture—as well as regional and global climate change, itself affected by some of the same anthropogenic "drivers."

Causes can include regional sociodemographic trends, such as the movement of people to coastal areas, with consequent competition for scarce waterfront space and increased pollution of coastal waters, or changes in the level and pattern of demand for seafoods in general or particular species or sizes of species. They could include more specific phenomena, such as the demand for exotic and endangered species arising from ideas about aphrodisiacs as well as newfound demand for "natural" remedies and "nutraceuticals." The causes of environmental change may also involve very particular events, such as the use of a heavy dredge that demolishes a nursery ground for a certain species of fish (Ames 1997) or, at a larger scale, a devastating accident such as the oil spilled from the mammoth tanker *Exxon Valdez* in Alaska in 1989. Moreover, both causes and consequences can be shaped by the politics of identity, ethnicity, class, race, and gender, in particular places or industries.

Once we have chosen a research question, the answers or explanations are matters for empirical determination rather than prejudged categories. This is in contrast to the "question-begging" practice of insisting that certain factors are important in advance of inquiry. To my mind, "environmental anthropology" refers to the anthropological study of environmental change rather than to any particular set of methods or theories or any particular notion of what should or should not be included in the analysis. The point, then, is that we need to keep our minds and research plans open to a wide range of potential explanations once we have identified the questions for study.

In a marine fisheries context, environmental anthropologists might try to explain why one coral reef is severely damaged and another is not or the reasons for the decline (or increase) in abundance of a particular species or population of fish, shellfish, or marine mammals. This may lead to questions about why particular actions were taken, decision-making structures and knowledge bases for making decisions, and reasons for compliance or resistance to regulations. Although it makes sense to include an examination of the question of access, as in the examples given above from fisheries research, one must be careful not to limit the research to that question, because open or restricted access may be beside the explanatory point in a given case. A good example is in the recent Newfoundland cod crisis, where the reason for collapse of northern cod in the late 1980s had nothing to do with the rights of inshore

fishermen to fish for cod but rather seems to have been the result of a confluence of environmental change, scientific error, bureaucratic rigidity, and politics (Finlayson and McCay 1998). An applied environmental anthropologist
might also be asked to determine which communities or social groups or individuals are affected by changes in the marine environment or the regulations used to protect that environment, the nature and causes of their vulnerability to such changes, and how they respond to them.

Those questions in turn may lead us in many different directions. Explanations could be found in the specifics of local families or fishing crews and the
intentions and opportunity structures of the people in them, in local structures of authority and institutions that affect access, or in the demands and interests of fish buyers or banks. They may be found in the presence, or absence,
and details of sea tenure institutions, cooperatives, and government agencies.
The answers may require examining governmental taxation policy or changing ideas about what is good or "modern" in life. They might include demographic changes or changes in the price of fuel. Our accounts may lead us to
examine legal traditions and institutions as well as politics. Religious beliefs, ethnic affiliation, psychocultural orientations, labor unions, kinship
connections—it all depends. Finally, as "environmental" anthropologists we
must keep an eye to the natural history of the cases we study and ask, "What
is happening to those fishes and shellfish, those dugongs and turtles, those
mangroves and eelgrass beds, and the people dependent on them, and why?"

References

Acheson, James M. 1981. "Anthropology of Fishing." *Annual Review of Anthropology*
    10: 275–316.
———. 1988. *The Lobster Gangs of Maine.* Hanover, N.H.: University Press of New Eng-
    land.
———, and Robert S. Steneck. 1997. "The Role of Management in the Renewal of the
    Maine Lobster Industry." In Gísli Pálsson and Guðrún Pétursdóttir, eds. *Social Im-
    plications of Quota Systems in Fisheries.* Proceedings of a seminar held in the West-
    man Islands, Iceland, May 9–16, 1996. Copenhagen: Nordic Council of Ministers.
Acheson, James M., and James Wilson. 1996. "Order Out of Chaos: The Case for Para-
    metric Fisheries Management." *American Anthropologist* 98(3): 579–94.
Amarosi, Thomas, P. Buckland, A. Dugmore, J. H. Ingimundarson, and T. H. McGov-
    ern. 1997. "Raiding the Landscape: Human Impact in the Scandinavian North At-
    lantic." *Human Ecology* 25(3): 491–518.
Ames, Edward P. 1997. *Cod and Haddock Spawning Grounds in the Gulf of Maine.* Port-
    land, Maine: Island Institute.
Ames, Kenneth M. 1994. "The Northwest Coast: Complex Hunter-Gatherers, Ecology,
    and Social Evolution." *Annual Review of Anthropology* 23: 209–302.
Andersen, Raoul, ed. 1979. *North Atlantic Maritime Cultures.* The Hague: Mouton.
Andersen, Raoul, and Geoffrey Stiles. 1973. "Resource Management and Spatial Com-
    petition in Newfoundland Fishing: An Exploratory Essay." In Peter H. Fricke, ed.,

Seafarer and Community: Towards a Social Understanding of Seafaring, 44–66. London: Croom Helm.

Andersen, Raoul, and C. Wadel, eds. 1972. *North Atlantic Fishermen: Anthropological Essays on Modern Fishing*. St. Johns: Institute of Social and Economic Research, Memorial University of Newfoundland.

Apostle, Richard, Gene Barrett, Petter Holm, Svein Jentoft, Leigh Mazany, Bonnie McCay, and Knut Mikalsen. 1998. *Community, State, and Market in North Atlantic Fisheries: Challenges to Modernity in the Fisheries*. Toronto: University of Toronto Press.

Binkley, Marian. 1994. *Voices from the Offshore: Narratives of Risk and Danger in the Nova Scotia Deep Sea Fishery*. St. John's, Newfoundland: ISER Books.

———. 1995. *Risk, Dangers, and Rewards in the Nova Scotia Offshore Fishery*. Toronto: University of Toronto Press.

Brox, Ottar. 1969. *Newfoundland Fishermen in the Age of Industry: A Sociology of Economic Dualism*. St. John's: Institute of Social and Economic Research, Memorial University of Newfoundland.

Casteel, Richard W., and George I. Quimby, eds. 1975. *Maritime Adaptations of the Pacific*. The Hague: Mouton.

Castilla, J. C., and M. Fernandez. 1998. "Small-Scale Benthic Fisheries in Chile: on Co-Management and Sustainable Use of Benthic Invertebrates." *Ecological Applications* 8(1), Supplement: S125–S132.

Cole, Sally. 1991. *Women of the Praia: Work and Lives in a Portuguese Coastal Community*. Princeton, N.J.: Princeton University Press.

Cordell, John, ed. 1989. *A Sea of Small Boats*. Cultural Survival Report 26. Cambridge, Mass.: Cultural Survival, Inc.

Davis, Dona L., and Jane Nadel-Klein. 1992. "Gender, Culture and the Sea: Contemporary Theoretical Perspectives." *Society & Natural Resources* 5(2): 135–47.

Diegues, Antonio Carlos Sant'Ana, ed. 1992. *Tradition and Social Change in the Coastal Communities of Brazil: A Reader of Maritime Anthropology*. Sao Paulo: University of Sao Paulo.

Finlayson, Alan Christopher. 1994. *Fishing for Truth: A Sociological Analysis of Northern Cod Stock Assessments from 1977–1990*. St. John's: Institute of Social and Economic Research, Memorial University of Newfoundland.

———, and Bonnie J. McCay. 1998. "Crossing the Threshold of Ecosystem Resilience: The Commercial Extinction of Northern Cod." In Carl Folke and Fikret Berkes, eds., *Linking Social and Ecological Systems: Institutional Learning for Resilience*, 311–37. Cambridge UK: Cambridge University Press.

Firth, Raymond. 1966. *Malay Fishermen: Their Peasant Economy*. London: Routledge & Kegan Paul.

Fitzhugh, William, ed. 1973. *Prehistoric Maritime Adaptations of the Circumpolar Zone*. The Hague: Mouton.

Freeman, Milton M. R. 1993. "The International Whaling Commission, Small-Type Whaling and Coming to Terms with Subsistence." *Human Organization* 52(3): 243–51.

Fricke, Peter H., ed. 1980. *Seafarer and Community: Towards a Social Understanding of Seafaring*. London: Croom-Helm.

Garrity-Blake, Barbara J. 1994. *The Fish Factory: Work and Meaning for Black and White Fishermen of the American Menhaden Industry*. Knoxville: University of Tennessee Press.

Griffith, David, Manuel Valdes Pizzini, and Jeffrey C. Johnson. 1992. "Injury and Therapy: Proletarianization in Puerto Rico's Fisheries." *American Ethnologist* 19(1): 53–74.

Hamilton, Lawrence, and Oddmund Otterstad. 1998. "Demographic Change and Fisheries Dependence in the Northern Atlantic." *Human Ecology Review* 5(1): 16–22.

Jentoft, Svein. 1993. *Dangling Lines: The Fisheries Crisis and the Future of Coastal Communities: The Norwegian Experience.* St. John's: Institute of Social and Economic Research. Memorial University of Newfoundland.

Johannes, Robert E. 1977. "Traditional Law of the Sea in Micronesia." *Micronesia* 13: 121–27.

Kalland, Arne. 1993. "Management by Totemization: Whale Symbolism and the Anti-Whaling Campaign." *Arctic* 46(2): 124–33.

Lieber, Michael D. 1994. *More Than a Living: Fishing and the Social Order on a Polynesian Atoll.* Boulder, Colo.: Westview.

McCay, Bonnie J. 1978. "Systems Ecology, People Ecology, and the Anthropology of Fishing Communities." *Human Ecology* 6(4): 397–422.

———. 1980. "A Fishermen's Cooperative, Limited: Indigenous Resource Management in a Complex Society." *Anthropological Quarterly* 53: 29–38.

———. 1981. "Development Issues in Fisheries as Agrarian Systems." *Culture & Agriculture* 11: 1–8.

———. 1988. "Muddling through the Clam Beds: Cooperative Management of New Jersey's Hard Clam Spawner Sanctuaries." *Journal of Shellfish Research* 79(2): 327–40.

———. 1998. *Oyster Wars and the Public Trust: Property, Law and Ecology in New Jersey History.* Tucson: University of Arizona Press.

———. 2000. "Sea Changes in Fisheries Policy: Contributions from Anthropology." In E. Paul Durrenberger and Thomas D. King, eds., *State and Community in Fisheries Management.* Westport, Conn.: Greenwood.

McCay, Bonnie J. and James M. Acheson, eds. 1987. *The Question of the Commons: The Culture and Ecology of Communal Resources.* Tucson: University of Arizona Press.

McCay, Bonnie J., and Carolyn F. Creed. 1990. "Social Structure and Debates on Fisheries Management in the Mid-Atlantic Surf Clam Fishery." *Ocean & Shoreline Management* 13: 199–229.

———. 1999. *Fish or Cut Bait: A Guide to the Federal Management System.* 2nd ed. Fort Hancock, N.J.: New Jersey Marine Sciences Consortium.

McCay, Bonnie J., and Svein Jentoft. 1996. "From the Bottom Up: Participatory Issues in Fisheries Management." *Society and Natural Resources* 9(3): 237–50.

———. 1998. "Market or Community Failure? Critical Perspectives on Common Property Research." *Human Organization* 57(1): 21–29.

McEvoy, Arthur F. 1986. *The Fisherman's Problem: Ecology and Law in the California Fisheries, 1850–1980.* Cambridge: Cambridge University Press.

McGoodwin, James R. 1990. *Crisis in the World's Fisheries.* Stanford, Calif.: Stanford University Press.

McGovern, Thomas H. 1990. "The Archaeology of the Norse North Atlantic." *Annual Review of Anthropology* 19: 331–51.

McKean, Margaret A. 1992. "Success on the Commons: A Comparative Examination of Institutions for Common Property Resource Management." *Journal of Theoretical Politics* 4(3): 247–81.

Maiolo, John R., Jeffrey Johnson, and David Griffith. 1992. "Applications of Social Science Theory to Fisheries Management: Three Examples." *Society & Natural Resources* 5(4): 391–407.

Maiolo, John R., and Michael K. Orbach, eds. 1982. *Modernization and Marine Fisheries Policy.* Ann Arbor, Mich.: Ann Arbor Science.

Malinowski, Bronislaw. 1935. *Coral Gardens and Their Magic.* New York: American.

———. 1948. *Magic, Science and Religion.* New York: Doubleday.

———. 1984. *Argonauts of the Western Pacific.* Prospect Heights, Ill.: Waveland Press.

Marcus, Joyce. 1987. "Prehistoric Fishermen in the Kingdom of Huarco." *American Scientist* 75: 393–401.

Matthews, David Ralph. 1993. *Controlling Common Property: Regulating Canada's East Coast Fishery.* Toronto: University of Toronto Press.

———, and John Phyne. 1988. "Regulating the Newfoundland Inshore Fishery: Traditional Values versus State Control in the Regulation of a Common Property Resource." *Revue d'études canadiennes* 23 (1&2): 158–76.

Matthews, Elizabeth, ed. 1995. *Fishing for Answers: Women and Fisheries in the Pacific Islands.* Suva, Fiji: Women and Fisheries Network.

Nadel-Klein, Jane, and Dona Davis, eds. 1988. *To Work and to Weep: Women in Fishing Economies.* St. John's: Institute of Social and Economic Research, Memorial University of Newfoundland.

Norr, James L., and Kathleen F. Norr. 1992. "Women's Status in Peasant-Level Fishing." *Society and Natural Resources* 5: 149–63.

Orbach, Michael K. 1977. *Hunters, Seamen, and Entrepreneurs: The Tuna Seinermen of San Diego.* Berkeley: University of California Press.

Ostrom, Elinor. 1990. *Governing the Commons: The Evolution of Institutions for Collective Action.* New York: Cambridge University Press.

Paine, Robert. 1957. *Coast Lapp Society,* Vol. I. Tromsö, Norway: Tromsö Museum.

Palmer, Craig, and Peter Sinclair. 1997. *When the Fish Are Gone: Ecological Disaster and Fishers of Northwest Newfoundland.* Halifax, Nova Scotia: Fernwood.

Pálsson, Gísli. 1991. *Coastal Economies, Cultural Accounts: Human Ecology and Icelandic Discourse.* Manchester: Manchester University Press.

Pinkerton, Evelyn, ed. 1989. *Cooperative Management of Local Fisheries: New Directions for Improved Management and Community Development.* Vancouver: University of British Columbia Press.

Pinkerton, Evelyn, and Martin Weinstein. 1995. *Fisheries That Work: Sustainability through Community-Based Management.* Vancouver, B.C.: David Suzuki Foundation.

Poggie, John J., and Carl Gersuny. 1974. "A Fishermen's Co-operative: Open System Theory Applied." *Maritime Study Management* 1: 215–22.

Pollnac, Richard B., and Susan Jacke Littlefield. 1983. "Sociocultural Aspects of Fisheries Management." *Ocean Development and International Law Journal* 12(3–4): 209–45.

Pringle, Heather. 1997. "Death in Norse Greenland." *Science* 275 (14 Feb.): 924–26.

Robben, Antonius C. G. M. 1989. *Sons of the Sea Goddess: Economic Practice and Discursive Conflict in Brazil.* New York: Columbia University Press.

Ruddle, Kenneth. 1989. "Solving the Common-Property Dilemma: Village Fisheries Rights in Japanese Coastal Waters." In F. Berkes, ed., *Common Property Resources,* 168–98. London: Belhaven Press.

————, and T. Akimichi, eds. 1984. "Maritime Institutions in the Western Pacific." In K. Ruddle and T. Akimichi, eds., *Senri Ethnological Studies 17*. Osaka: National Museum of Ethnology.

Ruddle, Kenneth, and Robert E. Johannes, eds. 1985. *The Traditional Knowledge and Management of Coastal Systems in Asia and the Pacific*. Jakarta: Regional Office for Science and Technology for Southeast Asia, UNESCO.

Smith, M. Estellie. 1982. "Fisheries Management: Intended Results and Unintended Consequences." In John R. Maiolo and Michael K. Orbach, eds., *Modernization and Marine Fisheries Policy*, 57–93. Ann Arbor, Mich.: Ann Arbor Science.

————. 1988. "Fisheries Risk in the Modern Context." *Maritime Anthropological Studies (MAST)* 1(1): 29–48.

————. 1990. "Chaos in Fisheries Management." *Maritime Anthropological Studies (MAST)* 3(2): 1–13.

————, ed. 1977. *Those Who Live from the Sea: A Study in Maritime Anthropology*. St. Paul, Minn.: West.

Suttles, Wayne. 1987. *Coast Salish Essays*. Seattle: University of Washington Press.

Vayda, Andrew P., and Bonnie J. McCay. 1978. "New Directions in Ecology and Ecological Anthropology [adapted version]." In V. Reynolds and N. Blurton-Jones, eds., *Human Behaviour and Adaptation*, 33–51. London: Taylor & Francis.

Vayda, Andrew P., and Bradley Walters. 1999. "Against Political Ecology." *Human Ecology* 27(1): 167–79.

Vayda, Andrew P., Bonnie J. McCay, and Cristina Eghenter. 1991. "Concepts of Process in Social Science Explanations." *Philosophy of the Social Sciences* 21(3): 318–31.

Wilson, James A., and Peter Kleban. 1992. "Practical Implications of Chaos in Fisheries: Ecologically Adapted Management." *Maritime Anthropological Studies (MAST)* 1(1): 66–78.

Zulaika, Joseba. 1981. *Terranova: The Ethos and Luck of Deep-Sea Fishermen*. Philadelphia: Institute for the Study of Human Issues.

13

The Discourse of Environmental Partnerships

Eric C. Poncelet

As a discipline, anthropology has long been interested in how human beings and cultures influence, and are influenced by, their natural environments. During the past century, much of this interest centered on the study of subsistence patterns by which human populations manage to survive in their varied environments. These analyses highlighted the diverse hunting and gathering methods of food foraging groups as well as the distinctive horticultural, pastoral, and intensive agricultural strategies of food-producing populations.

Anthropological Approaches to Human–Environment Relations

Starting in the 1950s and 1960s, anthropology began adopting a more systems-based approach to the study of human–environment relations.[1] The focus shifted away from subsistence practices as cultural features and toward the relationship of human activities to macroscale, homeostatically oriented ecosystems. Some of these studies looked at energy and material flows, comparing the efficiency of different subsistence techniques and tracing the progression of energy through human populations (e.g., Lee 1969; Winterhalder and Smith 1981). Others concentrated on adaptive patterns, emphasizing how social and cognitive structures function to keep humans in balance with their ecosystems in the face of short- and long-term environmental change (e.g., Rappaport 1968, 1979).[2]

In the latter part of the twentieth century, the focus shifted again, this time away from how humans exist in equilibrium with their environments and toward how humans have been actively disrupting any such assumed stability.

Anthropologists increasingly began directing their attention toward cases of environmental degradation and resource overexploitation; the social, political, and economic dynamics that incite these outcomes; the disproportionate ways in which different populations are implicated and affected; and the conflicts that have arisen in response.

The Evolving Environmental Domain

Today, anthropological engagements with the environment are focusing on a new set of human–environment relations. Four general features differentiate these relations from past formulations. The first concerns the growing range and scale of environmental challenges now facing human populations. Some of these problems, such as those of waste disposal, deforestation, and desertification, have long histories. Others, such as the quandaries of acid rain deposition, ozone depletion, and human-induced climate change, are altogether new. What characterizes all of these environmental dilemmas, however, is their increasing capacity to transcend traditional political and social boundaries.

A second distinguishing characteristic of the current environmental domain, especially in the developed West, concerns a shift in what Weale (1992) calls the "politics of pollution." Prior to the 1980s, societal responses to issues of environmental degradation came primarily via the enactment of laws and the institution of regulatory agencies. Since the mid-1980s, however, this strategy of control by administrative rule has been augmented by a new policy approach. In particular, governments have begun making efforts to better integrate environmental policy into other policy arenas. This has led to the diversification of actors in the policy domain as well as to an increase in attention paid toward economic and social concerns in the search for solutions to environmental problems. The former guiding objective of *pollution control* has been supplanted by the new overarching goal of *sustainable development.*

A third attribute of contemporary human–environment relations concerns a shift in the nature of environmental conflict. Since the rise of the conservation movement in the West a century ago, environmental conflict has been dominated by disputes among private interests over the quality of a population's immediate physical environment (Glasbergen 1995). Commonly, these disputes pitted proponents of economic growth and development against individuals or groups suffering the environmental deterioration induced by such activities. In many of these instances, economic developers simply denied any environmental wrongdoing. Today, better substantiated evidence of negative environmental impacts, along with a political climate in which it is becoming more and more untenable to take a position *against* the environment, is making it increasingly difficult for economic actors to flat out disavow the environmental damage that they effectuate. The environmental conflicts that predominate are therefore less focused on the verity of environmental problems and more concerned with how to interpret or define them (Hajer 1995). Given the new prevailing goal of sustainable development, today's environmental conflicts are increasingly centered around how best to resolve acknowledged environmental problems without adversely impacting economic growth (Glasbergen 1995).

A final feature characterizing today's environmental domain has been a shift in the loci for environmental action. Whereas human impact on the environment was much more direct in the past, it is now becoming increasingly mediated by institutions, especially with regard to preservation efforts (Brosius 1999a; Escobar 1995). Governmental regulatory agencies, while not new to many countries, are one such type of institution currently playing an increasingly important role in initiating and enforcing environmental protection. A second area of increased institutional activity comes from the business sector. While industrial production has been the cause of many environmental problems in the past, a growing number of companies are now taking proactive actions to safeguard the environments that they affect. The not-for-profit sector constitutes a third realm of increased institutional activity. More and more people are choosing to take environmental action via participation in or support for the burgeoning number of environmental nongovernmental organizations (NGOs) now existing or emerging throughout the globe. Of particular interest to this chapter, individual organizations from all three of the governmental, business, and NGO sectors are now beginning to come together in a collective, cooperative fashion to resolve environmental problems of common concern. We see this taking place locally in attempts to resolve environmental conflicts through the processes of environmental dispute resolution and mediation. We also see this occurring internationally in the form of such global scale multisectorial initiatives as the United Nations Conference on Environment and Development and the Convention on Biological Diversity.

This shift in the loci of environmental problem solving from the individual to the institution is significant because of the role that institutions play in defining and delimiting the possibilities for action. As institutions inscribe particular discourses and practices, they enable certain approaches for dealing with environmental problems while simultaneously precluding others (Brosius 1999b).

Multistakeholder Environmental Partnerships

This chapter examines multistakeholder environmental partnerships as an example of a cooperation-based mediating institution increasingly being used to address environmental concerns in the industrialized West. Its objective is to improve current understandings of how such partnerships work and to raise questions regarding their implications for society's diverse stakeholders by exploring the role that *discourse* plays in these institutions.

We begin by defining what is meant by *multistakeholder environmental partnership*. Each word in this phrase describes a critical element. The term *stakeholder* indicates that the individuals and groups participating in these initiatives are acknowledged to be affected by the environmental problem of focus and therefore deemed to have the right to contribute their perspectives, knowledge, and experience to the production of solutions. The prefix *multi* reveals that these partnerships are not intrasectorial or bilateral initiatives but involve representatives from all three of the governmental, business, and environmental NGO sectors. The term *environment* differentiates these types of partnerships from similar collaboratives arising within the domains of health care, education, and urban renewal. Finally, the term *partnership* signifies that participation is voluntary and collaborative. Interaction proceeds from a desire to reach consensus, a commitment to trust, and a willingness to act in consideration of and respect for alternative perspectives and interests. Participants define project goals in common, share in the processes of decision making and implementation, and assume collective responsibility for actions taken.

Between the years 1994 and 1998, I conducted research with four such partnerships in the European Union (EU) and the United States. These included an EU–level partnership aimed at promoting sustainable development in Europe, a regional level partnership directed toward ameliorating the water quality of a river running through the Walloon region of Belgium, a local-level partnership focused on preserving biodiversity in a Belgian commune, and a national-level initiative concentrated on improving natural resource management in the United States. This chapter draws upon data from the last of these.

A U.S.–Based Case Study

The U.S.-based environmental partnership, which I have entitled the Collaboration for Improved Management of Natural Resources, or CIMNR,[3] was initiated in the early 1990s by several representatives from business who were interested in coming up with innovative alternatives to what they perceived as overly expensive and inefficient conventions for regulating industrial pollution. These actors were also convinced that this could best be achieved via collaboration among a wide variety of interests, including members of government and the environmental community. These initiators solicited the assistance of a neutral administrating body before going on to convene a three-year multistakeholder partnership to address these issues. After the success of this first project, the group turned its attention in 1997 from pollution to natural resources. Over the next two years, approximately forty participants met quarterly for intervals of two to three days to explore how the current management of natural resources in the United States might be made more sustainable. Composing this partnership were representatives from the resource intensive industrial sectors of mining, forestry, petroleum, and energy production; regulatory agencies and legislative bodies from the state and federal levels; and regional, national, and international-level environmental NGOs. Participation was by invitation only and coordinated by the administrating body. Funding for the initiative came by way of donations from the major corporate participants and in the form of grants from several philanthropic foundations and the U.S. Environmental Protection Agency.

Theoretical Perspective and Project Goals

Two main theoretical perspectives guide my study of multistakeholder environmental partnerships. The first is practice theory as elucidated by Bourdieu (1977, 1990). To date, analyses of environmental partnerships have come primarily from the domains of management, planning, and policy studies. These inquiries—many of which are directed toward objectively modeling partnership structures, operations, and decision-making processes[4]—have been marked by a tendency to reduce action within cooperative processes to the rational pursuit of instrumental interest (Habermas 1984; Schwarz and Thompson 1990; Woodhill and Röling 1998). A practice-based approach, on the other hand, encourages us to focus on what people are actually saying and doing in partnership settings. In particular, it invites us to examine how actors draw upon historically derived cultural knowledge in contexts marked by the interaction of participants of varying experience, knowledge, political power, and economic means. Rather than viewing collaborative processes as a product of conflicting material interests, my goal here was to explain partnership practices as the direct consequence of interacting and, at times, colliding meaning systems.

To accomplish this, I directed my analytical attention toward what I call the *sociohistoric differences* at play in these partnerships. This refers to the different ways of understanding, talking, and acting that the diverse stakeholders bring with them to these collaborative processes. I attempted to discern these sociohistoric differences by focusing on the varying cultural models (Quinn and Holland 1987) that participants utilize to make sense of the environmental issues of concern and by highlighting the discourses via which these ideas and assumptions are expressed.

The second perspective guiding my approach comes from cultural production theory as expounded by Johnson (1987) and Willis (1977, 1981). This theory reminds us to treat these sociohistoric traits not as predetermined or fixed but as in continual formation and reformation as they butt up against one another in the process of collaboration. This theory also leads us to recognize that the production, reproduction, and reformulation of these sociohistoric differences is influenced by the non-neutrality of these settings, as certain discursive logics, just as the individuals who promote them, tend to carry more weight and authority than others (Bakhtin 1981; Bourdieu 1982; Foucault 1970).

In addition to demonstrating the effect of sociohistoric factors on the practice and products of multistakeholder environmental partnerships, a second goal was to discern from this analysis potential benefits and drawbacks of this type of collaborative approach and to critically comment on the implications of environmental partnerships for the future of environmental problem solving. My interests here go beyond simply evaluating their effectiveness as decision-making tools. I am also concerned with the broader ramifications that the promotion of environmental partnerships has for the different stakeholders in society.

Methodological Approach

My method for examining the case study environmental partnerships was ethnographic. In order to gain information on the types of practices common to the partnerships, I observed and participated in all types of partnership gatherings. These included meetings in which decisions were formally made as well as meals, receptions, and other functions in which participants interacted in a more informal manner. My data on the sociohistoric differences came largely from semistructured interviews as well as from written texts produced by the partnerships themselves. The interviews were strategically selected so as to adequately represent the business, governmental, and NGO sectors; the variation in size of the participating organizations; and differing levels of support for the project. The interviews were open-ended and designed to elicit naturally occurring speech. Topics of discussion included personal and organizational information, environmental partnerships in general, and the case study partnership in particular.

The Privileged Discourse of Ecological Modernization

This chapter revolves around the discovery of the existence of a single "privileged" discourse in all of the environmental partnerships studied. By this, I mean that one discourse in particular was generally viewed as "more appropriate and efficacious than others" by the partnership participants (Wertsch 1991: 124). This was the discourse of *ecological modernization.*

Ecological modernization—as a distinct though by no means complete or totally coherent set of ideas, concepts, assumptions, and categorizations giving meaning to the world—is marked by several major characteristics (Hajer 1995: 24–30).[5] First, it approaches environmental issues from an economistic perspective. It seeks to define environmental actions in terms of costs and benefits, thus rendering environmental change calculable. Second, ecological modernization promotes the interdependence and integration of economic development and long-term environmental preservation. It rejects any assumed fundamental opposition between economic growth and environmental protection and portrays them instead in positive sum, "win-win" terms. The concepts of *sustainable development* and *pollution prevention pays* are the quintessential expressions of this logic. Third, ecological modernization favors anticipatory and preventative approaches to environmental action. It does so in lieu of more traditional reactive and curative strategies of environmental management. Fourth, ecological modernization places the blame for many of today's environmental problems on the prevailing structures of modern industrial society. For instance, it denounces the environmental inefficiency of profit-maximizing capitalist practices. Of importance, however, ecological modernization also looks to these very same political, economic, and social institutions and processes for solutions to these problems. It places special emphasis on the roles of science and technology in this regard. Finally, ecological modernization advocates collective, cooperative approaches to environmental management. It presumes that no problem would remain unresolved if only society's diverse interests would all work together toward finding a solution.

Evidence of Ecological Modernization

Numerous examples from the interviews, partnership publications, and meeting discussions illustrate the use of the discourse of ecological modernization in the CIMNR partnership. The discourse appears, for instance, in the economistic treatment of the environment. This was particularly prevalent among business sector participants who often spoke of the environment as a means toward economic advantage. Along these lines, one businessman described the most important environmental goal of his company to be that of

> integrating environmental considerations into business planning so that when strategic business plans are made, environmental considerations are brought in up front into them with the idea that you can actually use environmental performance or excellence as a competitive factor.

The ideology of ecological modernization is also apparent in remarks presuming a positive sum relationship between economic prosperity and environmental protection. A representative from a national-level environmental NGO explained that for him, participating in the CIMNR partnership, has

> reinforced my general sense that there are better ways to do things. There are win-wins out there, but you've got to find them, and you have to work to get them. . . . I do believe in the multiple benefits, win-win logic. I do think that it's important to get the economic gains in addition to the environmental gains. I do see them coupled, because I think it builds the strength.

Other examples further demonstrate the presence of the discourse of ecological modernization in this partnership. The discourse is evident in statements indicating the preference for anticipatory, proactive approaches to environmental action. In the CIMNR final report, the partnership asserted:

> We believe that, wherever possible, environmental impacts should be prevented before they arise. For this reason, we recommend that prevention be considered the first course of action and be informed by an integrated systems approach.

Ecological modernization's emphasis on improving rather than replacing prevailing economic and political structures is evident as well. This is apparent in the possible solutions that the partnership considered in its attempt to improve current natural resource management practices. An environmental NGO representative described the partnership's objective as that of

> coming up with specific proposals for tax changes, and maybe institutional changes, trade policy changes, [and] fiscal policy changes to better insure that desirable environmental behavior [is] compatible with the private sector's built-in behavioral incentives to act in ways that [are] rewarded economically.

Finally, the belief that environmental protection can best be achieved via cooperative action on the part of society's diverse interests is demonstrated by the numerous comments made regarding the important role to be played by multistakeholder partnerships in these efforts. Along these lines, a representative from the governmental sector declared:

> I passionately believe that these [issues of natural resource management] are big issues and have to be dealt with by a broader public from a positive perspective—that if we are to advance as a society, and if we are to be in any way sustainable into the next millennium, we've got to think in different ways. We've got to develop new norms and new values. We've got to have an ethical construct to guide our behaviors. We've got to advance future interests in preference to current interests. . . . Collaborative ventures play a major role because they bring people together. I honestly do not understand how [these changes] can happen without some sort of organizing arena in which these [issues can play out]. They don't play out in the general body politic. They don't play out in the economic arena. Nowhere do these issues arise other than in a disciplined, organized collaborative.

Ecological Modernization as the Privileged Discourse

Just because participants employed the discourse of ecological modernization, however, does not prove its privileged status. To demonstrate this, I will show how in instances of conflict between competing discursive logics, participants were able to find common ground in the discourse of ecological modernization. Two examples serve to illustrate.

Conflict over the Role of "Stewardship" in Natural Resource Management

A first instance of the privileging of ecological modernization concerns a recurring debate that centered around the utility of the concept of "stewardship" as a means for improving natural resource management in the United States. One particular manifestation of this conflict grew out of an argument between two individuals: Darcelle, an environmental manager from a large corporation in the energy sector, and Kirk, a representative of an international-level environmental organization. Darcelle initiated the dynamic when she stated that if her corporation does good stewardship, it should be able to receive some competitive advantage in return. Her point was that given the current regulatory and economic incentive systems, her company is all too often penalized for attempting to be a "good steward." Kirk was visibly disturbed by this statement and asked Darcelle what kind of compensation her firm wanted. Was it just public recognition? Darcelle responded that it was broader than that. She wants Wall Street to value her corporation accordingly. Kirk responded somewhat derisively that this was purely an economic motivation.

The meeting facilitator, sensing dissension, stepped in at this juncture and pointed out that Kirk and Darcelle have different understandings of stewardship. Per the facilitator, Kirk sees stewardship as an ethic—as something people do voluntarily because of its intrinsic value. The idea of receiving economic compensation for doing the right thing goes against this ethic. Darcelle, on the other hand, sees stewardship more along the lines of a practice. She has no problem reconciling profit-driven behavior and stewardship so long as the behavior accomplishes the natural resource conservation goals of stewardship.

Shortly after this interlude Darcelle picked up the discussion again, arguing that people need to be more creative in their attempts to promote stewardship. She described how her organization, in collaboration with a prominent environmental group, developed an energy efficiency program that had the end effect of decreasing resource consumption while at the same time earning a profit for her company. At this point, Ken, a representative from a federal regulatory agency, objected to Darcelle's position, stating that the CIMNR partnership's goal is not to defend corporate bottom lines but to protect the environment. Another environmental NGO member, Cathy, seconded Ken, declaring that she too opposed Darcelle's definition of stewardship. Echoing Kirk's position, Cathy contended that stewardship ultimately originates out of "enlightened" rather than "material" self-interest and proceeds in the form of short-term sacrifices for long-term gain.

Eric, a representative of the environmental NGO that had worked with Darcelle's company on the energy efficiency project, came to Darcelle's defense here, cautioning against Ken and Cathy's line of reasoning. He stressed that the group needed to break through this "trade-off paradigm." Instead of asking for environmental benefits in exchange for economic sacrifice, the participants should be asking themselves, "How can we achieve better stewardship of resources *and* have it be profitable?" Kirk and Cathy continued to resist this line of reasoning, however, replying that the energy efficiency project was not about stewardship but about perverse incentives and regulatory barriers. Kirk, in particular, was still irked by the idea that corporations will only "do the right thing" if they are compensated financially for doing so.

Darcelle reentered the debate at this point. Picking up from Eric's comments, she replied that for her, being a good steward means that the impacts of her company on nature are not "negative" but "sustainable." She also felt that society should value such actions by her company, and not only economically. Shortly thereafter, Mark, an influential representative from state government, closed the discussion by stating that in the context of sustainability, stewardship includes not only resources but human beings and livelihoods. It is therefore hard to eliminate the economic component even if people want to do so.

The following day, representatives from both sides of the conflict gathered together in a working group that was assigned the goal of producing a common understanding of stewardship. At the end of their meeting, they concluded to the plenary that stewardship needs to be understood as being influenced not only by individual and group moral responsibilities but by economic and environmental policies as well. They recommended that stewardship be understood as both an "ethic" and a "practice," because only in this way may it be prioritized to achieve "win–win" success factors.

In interpreting this conflict, I suggest that we view the discussion as an interaction between two competing discourses. On one side were representatives from the environmental community (Kirk and Cathy) and a federal regulatory agency (Ken), who were speaking from a position most closely associated with what Dryzek (1997) has termed the discourse of "green romanticism." On the other side of the debate were representatives from business (Darcelle), an environmental NGO (Eric), and state government (Mark), who were espousing ideas subsumed under the discourse of ecological modernization.

Green romanticism is one of a number of environmental discourses founded upon the assumption that limits exist to the amount of environmental degradation that can be sustained by the planet. Like many of these, it also arises out of a critique of Enlightenment values and assumptions. In particular, it decries the anthropocentric arrogance, instrumental reason, and materialism upon which Western industrialized economies are based. Finally, green romanticism promotes as the key to resolving current environmental problems the cultivation of more empathetic and less manipulative approaches to nature.

In the above-described conflict, the discourse of green romanticism was most evident in the objections made to the profit-oriented nearsightedness of the business sector and in the assertion that stewardship arises not from short-term economic interests but from short-term sacrifices made for the purpose of achieving long-term environmental well-being. What transpired in the interchange, however, was that when these provocative, green romanticist challenges were issued, they elicited and were ultimately undermined by responses from the position of ecological modernization. The most powerful of these ecological modernization ideas was the condemnation of the assumed economic–environmental trade-off paradigm upon which the green romanticist objections were based. The promoters of ecological modernization made this argument by championing the concept of "sustainability" as the true goal of stewardship and by calling for actions that, rather than merely penalizing business, encourage the development of solutions to natural resource problems having both environmental and economic benefits.

The privileging of ecological modernization is demonstrated by the fact that the entire partnership was able to achieve consensus around the ecological modernization view of stewardship. In their final recommendations to the plenary, the bipartisan working group resolved the conflict by redefining stewardship as both an "ethic" influenced by environmental values and morals *and* a "practice" driven by economic and political constraints. This definition integrated the economy and the environment into a new "win-win" conceptualization of the term.

Conflict between the Mitigation and Prevention Working Groups

A second example illustrating the privileging of ecological modernization concerns another conflict that spanned many of the CIMNR meetings. The controversy here was over how best to accomplish the partnership's general goal of improving natural resource management in the United States. Two alternative ways of approaching this were proposed, and the partnership decided to split itself into two separate though not exclusive working groups to better address them. The first working group directed its attention toward the limitations of the existing regulatory regime. In particular, this group sought to envision ways by which natural resource management rules might be reformulated to make the regulatory process more efficient and cost-effective. The group was comprised primarily of representatives of large firms already embroiled in litigation on a host of mitigation issues. Also present were several environmentalists generally opposed to any relaxation of existing regulatory standards and a couple of federal regulators responsible for writing and implementing such rules. This group named itself the "mitigation group" and focused its work on the relationship between federal mitigation laws and big business.

The other working group started out by looking at some of the land and water conservation issues currently facing different geographical regions of the United States. Although its overall goal, like that of the mitigation group, was to improve the tools that exist for making natural resource management decisions, this group assumed a much broader focus. The participants were interested in examining decision making at the level of the individual as well as at the level of the large firm. They also hoped to address economic and cultural, as well as political and legal, barriers to effective natural resource management. A major concern here was to come up with innovative ways for reforming existing economic practices and institutions—such as in the areas of tax, trade, and fiscal policy—that promote destructive environmental behaviors. This working group was composed of a broad mix of representatives from the industrial, agricultural, and land development segments of the business sector; an assortment of large and small environmental NGOs; and a range of state and federal governmental officials. They began by calling themselves the "land and water group."

Although participants were free to move from one working group to the other, and several actors actively did so, what was interesting about this bifurcation was the level of animosity that rapidly developed between the two groups. The land and water group considered the mitigation group to be much too narrowly focused in its approach to natural resource management, while the mitigation group deemed the land and water group to be rather unfocused and indeed unrealistic in its aims given the time and expertise constraints of the partnership. The mitigation group also considered its counterpart to be too top-down oriented in its desire to search for large-scale changes. A power dynamic also existed between the two groups. In a manner revelatory of its self-perceived minority status in the partnership, the mitigation group began referring to itself as the "rebel group."

At the meetings that followed, the mitigation group continued to work on improving the use of mitigation as a means of protecting natural resource systems. The land and water group, on the other hand, redefined its focus, and it did so in counterposition to the mitigation group. The land and water group came to the conclusion that what they were really interested in was "prevention"—that is, in the changes that need to be instituted so as to avoid having to mitigate in the first place. They defined such preventative actions in terms of "stewardship" and officially renamed themselves the "path to excellence for enterprise stewardship of natural resources working group." Most participants simply referred to it as the "prevention working group."

The tension between these two working groups remained for another meeting or two. During this time, several participants expressed concern over whether or not the two working groups would be able to reconcile their differences and reunite. The resolution of this conflict was instigated by certain members of the prevention group who began promoting the concept of "stewardship" as a unifying concept for the two working groups and indeed as the key path by which to attain the CIMNR partnership's overall goal of sustainable natural resource systems. Although some members of the mitigation group initially resisted this maneuver, the entire partnership eventually came to consensus around this idea. In the CIMNR final report, the partnership presented prevention and mitigation as "action agendas that apply the stewardship approach to the task of reconciling economic development and natural resource management," though it also recommended that "prevention be considered as the first course of action." The partnership defined the "stewardship path" as

> built upon explicit recognition that the current set of environmental laws and regulations is necessary but not sufficient to achieve sustainable natural systems. We recognize that our existing rules and regulations will continue to provide enforceable safeguards to protect the environment. But, to be successful, any stewardship path must go beyond basic compliance with existing laws by encouraging innovation and cooperation among the public and private sectors, individuals and communities. We believe these efforts have considerable untapped potential to realize a stewardship path to sustainability—a path that will draw on a common cooperative approach to secure healthy natural systems.

As with the first case example, we may again broadly interpret this conflict in terms of an interaction between two competing discourses. The mitigation working group spoke for the most part from the perspective of what Dryzek (1997) calls "administrative rationality," while the prevention group adopted the discursive logic of ecological modernization. Administrative rationality is a problem-solving–oriented discourse stressing the rational management of public interests. It privileges scientific knowledge, technical expertise, professional administration, and bureaucratic structures in the resolution of environmental problems. In the United States, this approach is embodied in the existing regulatory regime and in such institutions as the Environmental Protection Agency and the Department of the Interior. This discourse also has elements of what Harvey (1996) refers to as the "standard view of environmental management." It is characterized by a reactive, curative, and after-the-event approach to environmental problems, which treats environmental problems as something that you simply deal with once they arise. The mitigation working group expressed this logic via their emphasis on the regulatory dimension of natural resource management, in their attempts to improve rather than obviate existing regulations governing mitigation practices, in their focus on the technical aspects of mitigation, and in their willingness to address natural resource issues after they have already become problematic.

The prevention working group, on the other hand, operated much more clearly from the perspective of ecological modernization. This was evident in their emphasis on prevention as the first line of environmental defense and in their desire to modify some of the economic constraints driving natural resource use so that economic and environmental factors work with rather than against one another. This was also apparent in their advancement of "stewardship" as the primary means by which to improve the current management of natural resource systems. Stewardship, again, is a distinctively ecologically modernistic concept, as evidenced by its preventative orientation; its promotion of uncoerced, collective, and cooperative action over legalistic mandates; and its intention to produce substantial environmental improvements without challenging conventional economic and political structures.

Several factors reveal the privileged status of the discourse of ecological modernization in this conflict. First, the mitigation working group clearly signified its self-perceived subordinate position by referring to itself as the "rebel group." Secondly, in the CIMNR final report, the partnership identified mitigation as a secondary natural resource management strategy behind that of prevention. Finally, and most importantly, the two working groups were able to come to consensus around the ecologically modernistic idea of "stewardship" as the key to sustaining healthier natural resource systems.

Implications for Stakeholders

The presence of a discourse hierarchy in the multistakeholder environmental partnerships studied has important implications for the individuals or organizations participating or considering participation in these types of collaborative initiatives.[6] Most importantly, this characteristic advantages partnership participants who utilize the privileged discourse over those who do not. In particular, those who promote the privileged discourse acquire prestige by having it be accepted by others, and those who choose to adopt it gain legitimacy simply by doing so. This makes it possible for actors who traditionally have been weakly positioned in the environmental domain to assume positions of status and authority in these settings. It also serves to discredit those actors who refuse to adopt this dominant practice.

The fact that the privileged discourse in the partnerships studied was that of ecological modernization has particular ramifications for the different types of organizations, as mediating institutions, participating in these proceedings. It is evident from the above data that no one sector has a monopoly on the use of this discourse.[7] Representatives of the business, governmental, and environmental NGO sectors all employ the discourse of ecological modernization and are consequently all subject to the benefits of doing so. What I argue in this section, however, is that certain sectors and certain stakeholders within these sectors derive more benefit than others. I also contend that these benefits entail their own risks.

The Business Sector

Of the three major sectors, the business sector appears to benefit the most from the prominence of the discourse of ecological modernization in environmental partnerships. The main reason is that ecological modernization nicely accommodates the growth-oriented priorities of market capitalism. In particular, ecological modernization favors only those environmental problem-solving approaches that attend equally to economic needs. In addition, ecological modernization promotes the quantification of potential solutions in terms of financial costs and benefits and the pursuit of proactive, preventative measures that circumvent inefficient regulatory restrictions. These strategies and techniques are already part of the expertise that many corporations bring with them to environmental partnerships, and this will allow such corporations to take leadership roles in these settings.

Where the prominence of ecological modernization in environmental partnerships is most problematic for the business sector is among those companies that traditionally have acted reactively and unilaterally when dealing with environmental issues. Such companies will appear as laggards in multistakeholder settings, and their prestige and authority will suffer accordingly. Another potential obstacle for all business participants concerns the reluctance of partnerships privileging ecological modernization to critically examine the impact of prevailing economic structures, such as those of market capitalism, on current environmental dilemmas. While this tendency toward reproducing the status quo will no doubt appeal to many business participants, it will also expose them to charges of "greenwashing" contending that corporate participation in multistakeholder partnerships is little more than business-as-usual with a slick green veneer (Rowell 1996).

The Governmental Sector

Within the governmental sector, environmental partnerships privileging the discourse of ecological modernization present the greatest advantages to those governmental institutions and representatives promoting either collaborative approaches to environmental problem solving or the devolution of the state. These types of partnerships constitute a step toward smaller government, as they share the costs and responsibilities of environmental protection with both the corporate and not-for-profit sectors. These partnerships also allow governmental officials to assume a new function in their service to the public. They permit public authorities to take on the more positive role of "facilitator" of both economic growth and environmental protection rather than the more traditional and negatively perceived roles of "controller" of economic production or "commander" of the public good.

Problems arise, however, for governmental representatives who believe in the preeminence of existing regulatory regimes and are less willing to relinquish control over the corporate sector or to share decision-making power with the people whom they are supposed to be representing. These types of public authorities will command less prestige in these settings.

The NGO Sector

Within the environmental community, environmental partnerships privileging the discourse of ecological modernization present the greatest opportunities to those more "moderate" environmental groups already espousing this ideology. For these organizations, ecological modernization provides a basis of common understanding and values from which they may engage the governmental and business sectors in the pursuit of their environmental causes.

Such partnerships are most troublesome for the "radical" wing of the environmental movement. These are the organizations that typically advocate radical green ideas and pursue conflict-based modes of environmental action. Several potential hazards stand out here. First, ecological modernization's advancement of collaborative environmental problem solving serves to delegitimize the oppositional approaches of such radical groups. In the CIMNR case, we may argue that the promotion of improved individual and corporate stewardship as *the* key path by which to protect natural resource systems constitutes a threat to the viability of other paths, such as those of protest-derived political and economic reform. Secondly, ecological modernization is notable for its capacity to appropriate some of the elements of radical environmentalism, such as the recognition of capitalism's deleterious relationship with the environment, while at the same time stripping these elements of their radical content (Harvey 1996). This is dangerous for radical environmental groups that participate in partnerships dominated by ecological modernization thinking because it causes these groups to appear complicit with the reproduction of prevailing societal power structures. This, in turn, may diminish the credibility that these organizations have in the eyes of their own constituents. Finally, the promotion by ecological modernization of such terms as *sustainable development* or the CIMNR version of "stewardship" is problematic for radical groups, as this shifts priority away from the concept of *environment* as an autonomous subject meriting serious attention and action in its own right. In the pursuit of sustainable development or the CIMNR partnership's "stewardship," the environment can no longer be examined outside of its economic context. This constitutes a threat to the legitimacy of those radical green discourses that promote ecocentrism or the intrinsic value of nature in a manner independent of economics.

Implications for Anthropology

In the continuing evolution of human–environment relations, multistakeholder environmental partnerships constitute a relatively new and increasingly important manner by which people are attempting to deal with their natural environments. Individuals and organizations alike are utilizing these partnerships to resolve existing environmental problems as well as to minimize the environmental impacts of future economic development decisions.

The discipline of anthropology has much to offer current understandings of these institutions. As illustrated in this chapter, anthropology provides a methodology and a useful theoretical orientation for examining how these partnerships work as well as a means for evaluating their value as an environmental decision-making tool. Participant-observation is ideally suited for revealing what people actually say and do in partnership settings, and anthropology's traditional interest in the sociohistoric dimension of social processes is helpful in highlighting the effect that interacting meaning systems have on the actions induced. In the analysis presented here, this approach encouraged us to conceptualize environmental partnerships as arenas in which decidedly unequal ideas come up against one another in struggles for legitimacy and dominance. This led to the finding that ideas subsumed under one discourse in particular, that of ecological modernization, tended to prevail over others in the partnerships studied.

In its ongoing efforts to advise public policy, it is critical that anthropology make such findings available to social actors looking to initiate or participate in such collaborative endeavors. Like most institutions, multistakeholder environmental partnerships are not neutral. Those partnerships that privilege the discourse of ecological modernization will benefit certain stakeholders more than others, and this will ultimately delimit the types of actions that these partnerships may induce. Anthropology has the capacity, and the responsibility, to help explicate what these limitations will be.

Notes

1. See Ellen (1982) for a history of anthropological approaches to the environment.

2. See Moran (1990) for an exposition on the use of the ecosystems concept in anthropology.

3. As is typical of much ethnographic research, I use pseudonyms for the organizations and individuals discussed.

4. For example, see Long and Arnold (1995); Selin and Chavez (1995); Venter and Breen (1998).

5. See also Christoff (1996) and Dryzek (1997) for further discussion on ecological modernization.

6. For a discussion of the broader implications of environmental partnerships for the future of environmental action, see Poncelet (2001).

7. The evidence presented demonstrates that participants from all sectors utilize competing discourses as well. In fact, just because a participant utilizes one discourse in one particular circumstance does not preclude that participant from utilizing another discourse in another context.

References

Bakhtin, Mikhail M. 1981. *The Dialogic Imagination: Four Essays by M. M. Bakhtin.* Edited by Michael Holquist, translated by Caryl Emerson and Michael Holquist. Austin: University of Texas Press.

Bourdieu, Pierre. 1977. *Outline of a Theory of Practice.* Cambridge, UK: Cambridge University Press.

————. 1982. "The Economics of Linguistic Exchanges." *Social Science Information* 16: 645–68.

————. 1990. *The Logic of Practice.* Stanford, Calif.: Stanford University Press.

Brosius. J. Peter. 1999a. "Green Dots, Pink Hearts: Displacing Politics from the Malaysian Rain Forest." *American Anthropologist* 191(1): 36–57.

————. 1999b. "Analyses and Interventions: Anthropological Engagements with Environmentalism." *Current Anthropology* 40: 277–309.

Christoff, Peter. 1996. "Ecological Modernisation, Ecological Modernities." *Environmental Politics* 5(3): 476–500.

Dryzek, John S. 1997. *The Politics of the Earth: Environmental Discourses.* Oxford: Oxford University Press.

Ellen, Roy. 1982. *Environment, Subsistence and System: The Ecology of Small-Scale Formations.* Cambridge: Cambridge University Press.

Escobar, Arturo. 1995. *Encountering Development: The Making and Unmaking of the Third World.* Princeton, N.J.: Princeton University Press.

Foucault, Michel. 1970. "The Discourse on Language." Appendix to *The Archaeology of Knowledge.* New York: Pantheon.

Glasbergen, Pieter. 1995. "Environmental Dispute Resolution as a Management Issue: Towards New Forms of Decision Making." In P. Glasbergen, ed., *Managing Environmental Disputes: Network Management as an Alternative,* 1–18. Dordrecht, The Netherlands: Kluwer Academic Publishers.

Habermas, Jürgen. 1984. *The Theory of Communicative Action: Reason and the Rationalization of Society (Volume 1).* Translated by Thomas McCarthy. Boston: Beacon.

Hajer, M. 1995. *The Politics of Environmental Discourse: Ecological Modernization and the Policy Process.* Oxford: Clarendon.

Harvey, D. 1996. *Justice, Nature and the Geography of Difference.* Cambridge, Mass.: Blackwell.

Johnson, R. 1987. "What Is Cultural Studies Anyway?" *Social Text: Theory/Culture/Ideology* 16: 38–80.

Lee, Richard B. 1969. "!Kung Bushman Subsistence: An Input-Output Analysis." In D. Damas, ed., *Contributions to Anthropology: Ecological Essays.* National Museums of Canada Bulletin 3 94, 230, Anthropological Series 86. Ottawa: Queen's Printers for Canada.

Long, Frederick J., and Matthew B. Arnold. 1995. *The Power of Environmental Partnerships.* Fort Worth, Tex.: Harcourt Brace.

Moran, Emilio, ed. 1990. *The Ecosystem Concept in Anthropology: From Concept to Practice.* Ann Arbor: University of Michigan Press.

Poncelet, Eric C. 2001. *Partnering for the Environment: Multistakeholder Collaboration in a Changing World.* Lanham, Md.: Rowman & Littlefield.

Quinn, Naomi, and Dorothy Holland. 1987. "Culture and Cognition." In D. Holland and N. Quinn, eds., *Cultural Models in Language and Thought,* 3–40. Cambridge, UK: Cambridge University Press.

Rappaport, R. A. 1968. *Pigs for the Ancestors: Ritual in the Ecology of a New Guinea People.* New Haven, Conn.: Yale University Press.

————. 1979. *Ecology, Meaning, and Religion.* Richmond, Calif.: North Atlantic Books.

Rowell, Andrew. 1996. *Green Backlash: Global Subversion of the Environmental Movement.* London: Routledge.

Schwarz, Michiel, and Michael Thompson. 1990. *Divided We Stand: Redefining Politics, Technology and Social Choice.* Philadelphia: University of Pennsylvania Press.

Selin, Steve, and Deborah Chavez. 1995. "Developing a Collaborative Model for Environmental Planning and Management." *Environmental Management* 19(2): 189–95.

Venter, Andrew K., and Charles M. Breen. 1998. "Partnership Forum Framework: Participative Framework for Protected Area Outreach." *Environmental Management* 22(6): 803–15.

Weale, Albert. 1992. *The New Politics of Pollution.* Manchester: Manchester University Press.

Wertsch, James V. 1991. *Voices of the Mind: A Sociocultural Approach to Mediated Action.* Cambridge, Mass.: Harvard University Press.

Willis, Paul. 1977. *Learning to Labor: How Working Class Kids Get Working Class Jobs.* New York: Columbia University Press.

———. 1981. "Cultural Production Is Different from Cultural Reproduction Is Different from Social Reproduction Is Different from Reproduction." *Interchange* 12(2–3): 48–67.

Winterhalder, Bruce, and E. A. Smith, eds. 1981. *Hunter-Gatherer Foraging Strategies: Ethnographic and Archaeological Analyses.* Chicago: University of Chicago Press.

Woodhill, James, and Niels G. Röling. 1998. "The Second Wing of the Eagle: The Human Dimension in Learning Our Way to More Sustainable Futures." In N. Röling and M. Wagemakers, eds., *Facilitating Sustainable Agriculture: Participatory Learning and Adaptive Management in Times of Environmental Uncertainty,* 46–72. Cambridge, UK: Cambridge University Press.

Index

Oregon, 203–22
organismic analogy, 75

Pacific Northwest: environmental
    change in, 203–22; linguistic and
    biological diversity connections in,
    30; maritime cultures in, 254–55
Paine, Robert, 257
paleo-decisions, 85
paleo-meanings, 84–86
Papua New Guinea, 26, 35, 188
partnerships: definition of, 276;
    environmental, 273–91; formation of,
    15
past, 72–73
Pawley, Andrew, 35
Peluso, Nancy, 8, 16
Penan people, 8, 150–76; and state,
    154–55
Perin, Constance, 234–36
perturbation, 92
Peru, 31, 126–27
Peters, Pauline, 8–9
Piaroa people, 41
Pi-Sunyer, Oriol, 124
place: of ethnographic inquiry, 152–54,
    162–66; in historical ecology, 206;
    sacred, 191–93; in Sarawak campaign,
    154–60. *See also* space
place-naming, 31–32
plasticity, 115
policy. *See* environmental policy
political agency, and environmental
    discourse, 151, 164
political ecology, 4, 7–9, 113–31; of
    human biology, 117–28
political economy: culture and, 244–45;
    and public policy, 240–42; and urban
    land in United States, 223–53
political risk, in environmental justice,
    139–40
pollution: cultural models on, 61–62;
    politics of, 274; in urban areas,
    120–21
Poncelet, Eric C., 273–91
population approach, 116
postmodernism, 105n2; definition of,
    91; and environmental science,

99–102; influences on, 101; and
    interdisciplinary studies, 104
poverty, biology of, 125–28
present, 72–73; ethnographic, 162–63
preservation, of indigenous cultures, 154
prevention, versus mitigation, 283–86
privatization, participatory, 262–64
processes: definition of, 76; ecological,
    76
projects, 3–4
property rights, 228–31; maritime, 259;
    views of, 241
property taxes, 232–33, 237
psychosocial stress, and adaptation, 115
public policy. *See* environmental policy
Pyne, Stephen, 78

racism, environmental, 133
rain forests, 94, 157–58
Rajan, Ravi, 13
ranching, in State of Jefferson, 212–14
Rangan, Haripriya, 8
Rappaport, Roy A. "Skip," x, 56, 101, 188
Reagan administration, 133
realtors, 234
Redman, Charles, 86
regionalists, new, 227
Reichel-Dolmatoff, Gerardo, 189
relationships, and folk taxonomies, 35,
    60
religion: anthropology and, 177–200;
    biodiversity loss and, 40; and
    environmental archaeology, 83; and
    resource management systems, 56,
    58, 189; significance of, 178–79
Reno, Ronald, 82–83
resistance: as adaptation, 127; by Penan
    people, 156–58; to spiritual ecology,
    188
resource management, 203;
    anthropologists and, 134;
    community-based, 259; conflicts in,
    281–85; cooperative, 259–60, 266;
    ecosystem management, 205, 218; by
    indigenous societies, 56–59, 189–90,
    208–9; sustainable, 66, 159–60
restoration, of environments, 86, 203
Rio Summit, 3, 150

About the Contributors

J. Peter Brosius is associate professor of anthropology at the University of Georgia and president of the Anthropology and Environment Section of the American Anthropological Association. His research has focused on the international campaign against logging in the East Malaysian state of Sarawak, on the island of Borneo. He is the author of *After Duwagan: Deforestation, Succession, and Adaptation in Upland Luzon, Philippines* (1990) and numerous articles on conservation, social justice, and human ecology.

Carole L. Crumley is professor of anthropology at the University of North Carolina at Chapel Hill and a member of the executive board of the Carolina Environmental Program. A founding member of the AAA Anthropology and Environment (A&E) Section, she was secretary of the American Anthropological Association (1997–2000) and A&E president (1997–99). She studies the historical and political ecology of landscapes in Burgundy, France.

Michael R. Dove is professor of social ecology and anthropology and chair of the Council for Southeast Asian Studies at Yale University. His research focuses on the impact of local versus extra-local factors on biodiversity; the history of market linkages in the tropical forest; theoretical aspects of sustainable development; the study of developmental and environmental institutions, discourses, and movements; and the sociology of resource-related sciences.

Don D. Fowler is the Mamie Kleberg Professor of Anthropology and Historic Preservation at the University of Nevada, Reno and a past president of the Society for American Archaeology. His research interests are the prehistoric archaeology of Western North America and the history of anthropology.

Donald L. Hardesty is professor of anthropology at the University of Nevada, Reno. He is a historical archaeologist who specializes in the late historic colonization of the American West, a past president of the Society for Historical Archaeology, and current (2000–1) president of the Register of Professional Archaeologists. His research interests include the social and environmental impacts of mining and other industrial technologies in the American West.

Alice E. Ingerson is associate director and senior fellow at the Institute for Cultural Landscape Studies of the Arnold Arboretum of Harvard University. She has done research in Ireland, on the politics of language choice and poetry, and in Portugal, on political theater and on land ownership and labor history under the Salazar dictatorship. She has worked as an editor, writer, teacher, and researcher with the Forest History Society (affiliated with Duke University) and the Lincoln Institute of Land Policy. Her current research focuses on connecting history and science to community and place, particularly for landscapes in New England.

Barbara Rose Johnston is senior research fellow at the Center for Political Ecology. Her research interests involve the intersection between environmental quality and social justice. Recent projects include documenting the human environmental impacts of nuclear testing and reviewing the history and legal standing for reparations and the right to remedy in dam development projects.

Willett Kempton is associate professor in the College of Marine Studies, University of Delaware, and senior policy scientist at the University's Center for Energy and Environmental Policy. Kempton conducts research on cultural models of environmental issues, ranging from global climate change and energy efficiency to *Pfiesteria piscida*. Currently, he is also carrying out an ethnographic study of local environmental groups in order to understand the relationship between environmental identity and environmental action.

Thomas L. Leatherman is professor of anthropology at the University of South Carolina, Columbia. He has conducted research in the political ecology of diet, nutrition, and health in the Andes, Mexico, and coastal South Carolina. His recent research focuses on dietary commoditization and the penetration of junk foods in Mayan communities of the Yucatan.

Luisa E. Maffi holds a B.A. in linguistics (University of Rome) and a Ph.D. in anthropology (University of California at Berkeley). She is co-founder and president of the international NGO Terralingua: Partnerships for Linguistic and Biological Diversity, as well as a research collaborator at the Smithsonian Institution's National Museum of Natural History in Washington, D.C. Her research interests are in linguistic and cognitive anthropology; ethnobiology; and the relationships between linguistic, cultural, and biological diversity.

Bonnie J. McCay is professor of anthropology and ecology in the Department of Human Ecology, Cook College, Rutgers, New Brunswick, N.J. Her research interests include interactions of humans with their natural environments, with a special focus on fisheries and situations of common rather than private property.

Eric C. Poncelet, is a visiting scholar in the Department of Anthropology, University of North Carolina. His current research interests are directed toward processes of multistakeholder collaboration and partnership in the environmental arena with an areal focus on the European Union and the United States.

Leslie E. Sponsel is a professor and director of the Ecological Anthropology Program at the University of Hawaii. His teaching and research interests include cultural, historical, radical, and spiritual ecology as well as anthropological aspects of war and peace studies, human rights, and advocacy. From 1974 to 1981 he made several field trips to the Amazon in Venezuela where he worked with Yanomami (Sanema subgroup), Curripaco, and Ye'kuana. Since 1986, he has been working with Thai colleagues in southern Thailand on aspects of Buddhist ecology and sacred places in relation to biodiversity conservation. Sponsel serves on the advisory board of the Forum on Religion and Ecology at Harvard University. Among numerous publications, Sponsel has edited various books, including *Indigenous Peoples and the Future of Amazonia: An Ecological Anthropology of an Endangered World* (1995); *Tropical Deforestation: The Human Dimension* (1996 with T. N. Headland and R. C. Bailey); *Endangered Peoples of Southeast and East Asia* (2000); and *Sanctuaries of Culture and Nature: Sacred Places and Biodiversity Conservation* (forthcoming).

R. Brooke Thomas is professor of anthropology at the University of Massachusetts, Amherst. His research interests are in high-altitude human adaptation and ecology. Since the 1960s he has conducted research on biocultural adaptations of the high Andean Quechua and on the impact of mass tourism on the lowland Maya of the Yucatan Peninsula, Mexico.

Anna Lowenhaupt Tsing is professor of anthropology at the University of California, Santa Cruz. She is author of *In the Realm of the Diamond Queen: Marginality in an Out-of-the-Way Place* (1993) and editor of *Uncertain Terms: Negotiating Gender in American Culture* (with F. Ginsburg, 1990). Her current research focuses on environmental dilemmas in and beyond Indonesia. Her study considers both social protest and financial capital in the reformation of rainforest landscapes.

Kathryn R. Winthrop has been an archaeologist in the public and private sectors for over two decades, and is currently the Bureau of Land Management liaison to the Army Environmental Center. Her areas of interest include historical ecology, relations between anthropology/archaeology and the federal government, and Pacific Northwest prehistory.